GARDENS OF HELL

GARDENS OF HELL

Battles of the Gallipoli Campaign

PATRICK GARIEPY

Potomac Books

AN IMPRINT OF THE UNIVERSITY OF NEBRASKA PRESS

Images are from the author's collection, unless otherwise stated.

Library of Congress Cataloging-in-Publication Data
Gariepy, Patrick.
Gardens of Hell: battles of the Gallipoli Campaign / Patrick Gariepy.
pages cm
Includes bibliographical references and index.
ISBN 978-1-61234-683-0 (hardcover: alk. paper)—ISBN 978-1-61234-684-7 (PDF) 1. World War,
1914–1918—Campaigns—Turkey—Gallipoli Peninsula. 2. Gallipoli Peninsula (Turkey)—
History, Military—20th century. I. Title.
D568.3.G37 2014
940.4'26—dc23   2013050490

Set in Sabon by Renni Johnson.

To my Muse, whose physical and emotional beauty
is unmatched in the universe.
Without her, this work would not have been possible.
Thank you, my wife.

————

And to 42,000 British and Dominion troops who died
at Gallipoli fighting a campaign that could not have been won,
in a place most had never heard of, against an enemy who
would rather have been their friend.

CONTENTS

List of Illustrations . . ix

Acknowledgments . . xi

Introduction: The Road to Gallipoli . . 1

1. "A Day Which I Shall Not Forget": The Battle Is Joined . . 9

2. "The Results Were Disastrous": Forcing the Dardanelles . . 17

3. "Death on the Eve of Battle": The Preparations . . 27

4. "My God It's All Horrible":
The Landings of April 25, 1915—Anzac . . 36

5. "This Place Was Littered with Dead from the Boats":
The Landings of April 25, 1915—Helles . . 59

6. "Had We Gone Forward We Should Have Been Wiped Out":
The Battles of April—Helles . . 107

7. "They Died like Gallant Officers and Gentlemen":
The May Battles . . 131

8. "A Lot of Our Poor Fellows Were Drowned":
The War at Sea . . 155

9. "We Had the Great Experience to Have a Glimpse of Hell":
The June Battles . . 187

10. "There Was No One Left to Fire":
Battles of August and the Final Offensives . . 224

11. "Not *Actually* All the King's Men":
The Battles of July 12 and August 12 . . 248

12. "And All Suffered Severely": The Great Storm,
November 27–28, 1915 . . 269

13. "We Have Lost the Game": Evacuation . . 281

Notes . . 301
Bibliography . . 311
Index . . 357

ILLUSTRATIONS

Following page 154

1. Lt. Andrew Bulman

2. Lt. James B. Innes

3. Pvt. William E. C. Campion

4. Pvt. James Rigby

5. W Beach

6. Gully Beach

7. John Geo. Everett

8. Lt. Leslie J. Water

9. Dvr. Alfred Cecil Hickson

10. Infantry

11. Turkish soldier

12. Turkish airplane

13. Cottonera Hospital, Malta

14. Cottonera Hospital, Malta

15. Turkish War Memorial at Gallipoli

16. Twelve Tree Copse Cemetery

ACKNOWLEDGMENTS

———

Before *Gardens of Hell* was a book, it was a research project. My late husband wanted to record the name, rank, and any personal information he could find for every man at the Gallipoli campaign. He posted queries in magazines, went on the radio and television in some areas, joined historical associations, and traveled to Turkey and England for this information. In the course of his search for stories of the men, he found people who shared his love of the subject, people who would give information about family members who had been there, and people who helped him with his research.

This is a small acknowledgment of these people. Pat was proud to share your stories, and he was proud of the number of friends that he met in the course of this journey. For all of you who gave of your family history, your time, your expertise, and for many of you, your friendship, thank you. This book would not be possible without you.

Karlann Greenwood Gariepy

Marguerita Adam, Peggy Alexander, Jeannine Alkins, Mary Amato, Richard Wallace Annand (vc), Glenys Archibald, David Aspinall, Kathryn Atkin, Ron Austin, Andy Bagent, Keith Bailcy, Peter Bamford, Anton Bantock, Frank Barnes, Graeme Barron, Jean Barry, Hazel Basford, Margaret Beadman, Sue Beckwith and Martin Beevis, Alex Bell, Richard G. Bell, Debbie Bennett, G. A. Bird, Peter Bird, Susie Bissell, Joe Bissett, Mark Blaydes, Beryl and Stuart Blythe, Richard Bourne, Raewyn Bowsher, Steve Brett, Tim Bridges (Worcestershire Yeomanry Cavalry Museum), Roger Broady, J. M. Brown, Richard Brown, Robert Browning, Steve Brumpton, Brenda Buckeridge, Donald J. Burke, Rod Cairns, Ian Campbell, Alison Carpenter, Carolyn Carr, Lyn Carseldine, Harry Carson, Paul Cesnavicius, Molly Charles, Steve Chambers, Beryl Chappell, Donald Charles, Carol Charlwood, Clare Church, Roy Claffey, Kylie Clifford, Elisabeth Coleman, Laura Flynn Colegrave, Carol Collins, Bernie Conlen, Brendan Cook, Tim Cooper, Yvonne Cooper, Linda Corbett, Sharon Cornwall, Lucinda Coultas, Elizabeth Craig, Graham Crofts, John Crowe (MLIA), William Cruikshanks, Alistair Cuthbert, Sharon Daff, Marie Dallman, Kevan Darby, George Davidson, Harry Davies, Jim Davies, James S. Deane, Peter Dearsley, Ronald Devlin, Diane Dick, Wendy Dolton, Deborah Donner, Charles Dorian, Stephen Doyle, Joe Duggan, Glenda Eaves, Godfrey Eden, Martin Edwards, Vivian Edwards, Susan Eldridge, Richard Entwistle, Ed Erickson, Russell Evans, Garen Ewing, Alison Faulkner, Kari Fay, Nick Fear, John Ferguson, Jean Field (Manchester Regiment), Alexander Findlater (Royal Dublin Fusiliers), Terence George FitzGibbon, Eric Flack (Highland Light Infantry), Diana Flatman, Rod Fletcher, Jørgen Flintholm, Richard Flory, Mai Fogarty, Stan Foote, Geoff Foster, John K. Fowlie, Bronwyn Fraley, Meredith Francoise, Rita Garbett, Patricia Gascoigne, Ian Gill, Robert and Gloria Glatz, Daphne Glen, Lillian Glugover, Celia Goodman, John G. Gordon, Jeanne Goulding, Susanna Greenwood, Harry Griffett, Derek Griffis, John Patrick Griffiths, Franklin Grigg, Russell Gurney, Dawn Hadfield, Claudine Hall, Sheila Halliwell, Cdr. Ian Hamilton (RN), Rob Hamilton, Alan Hancox, Mrs. Ray Harding, Ted Harris, John Hartley, David Hatchard, Geoff Heckles, Dorcas Hendershott, G. I. Henderson, Tony Hennessey, Michael Hernon,

Andrew Hesketh, Eileen Higgs, Carol Hill, Lt. Col. T.J.B. Hill, Mark Hone, Barbara Horrocks, Marguerite Innes Short Holmes, Barbara Holt, Ian Hook, Diana Horvitz, James Houlker, Earl Howard, J. E. Hughes, John H. Humsby, Ruth Hunt, Dawn Hurst, Campbell and Joan Ingram, Sharmaine Jarvis, Steven John, Gordon Johnson, Noel Johnson, Grant Jones, Harry Jones, Ken Kelsall, Marilyn Kenny, Scott King, Margaret Kirkman, David Kirton, R. G. Kitchenn, Joyce Kolze, Jack Lamphier, Ann Langdale, Marion Langston, David Lee, Tammie Lee, Mary Leitch, Edward Lever, Peter Levin, Peter Liddle, Michael Lions, Gillie Lomax, Arthur Gratton Long, Tony Lund, Margo Lurvey, Ken Lyall, Alison McCall, Terry McCartney, Tia McCombes, Jim McConnachie, Alisa McCullough, Jean MacDonald, Liam McFaul, David McGrath, Marilyn McHaffie, Judi Machin, Maggie McKay, Steve McLachlan, Terry Macleod, Iain A. Macmillan, Ian Charles McNay, Graham Maddocks, Mary Madigan, Howard Mallinson, Audrey Malloy, Alan Markland, Bernadette Marks, Tom Marsh, Kathy Martin, Barbara Mason, Tom Mather, John W. Maunder, Clive Mellor, Alistair G. Mills, June Millson, Margaret Modinos, Brian Monaghan, Murial Monk, Peter Moore, Philip Morris, Mike Morrison, Lynette Morrissey, Terry Moss, Reg Moule, Harry Mount, Stephanie Moxham, John Mulhall, Grant Napier, Joe Napier, Col. W.G.A. Napier (re), Mike Nash, Aaron Nelson, Michael Noon, Sheila Norton, Peter Oldham, Dr. Jack Oliver, Joseph O'Raw, Alan Osborne and Carol Cox, James F. O'Sullivan, Liz Outlaw, Joyce Owen-Reece, Steve Palmer, Anne Park, Brandon Park, David Park, Bob Parker, Mervyn Parry, Ted Parry, Mary Pavezka, Graham Perham, M. Pettigrew, Derek Pheasant, Tony Pope, Casper Pottle, Colin Powney, Tony Prentice, Gordon Price, Donald Charles, Phillip Radford, Dick Rayner, Fred Redpath, John Reilly, Angela Richardson, Gavin Richardson, Matthew Richardson, Hatty Rickards, Sue Rickhuss, Kate Rimmer, Margaret Roach, Ann-Marie Roberts, Hilda A. Roberts, John Roberts, Derek Robertson, Violet Robertson, Michael Robson, John Rodgers, E.C.A. Rogers, Peter Roots, George Ross, David Row, Graeme Rowe,

Sheila Rowlands, Lyn Russo, Frank Scott, Keith L. Scott, Ralph Seccombe, Derek Sharpe, Donald Sharwood Spence, Jenny Shaw, Dr. Allan Skertchly, Katherine Slay, Judith Sloan, George R. Smail, Eddie Smith, Gordon Smith, Mike Smith, Norman Smith, Pat Smith, Vicki Smith, Jul Snelders, Peter Sore, Ted Sparrow, Peter Spearink, Donald Sharwood Spence, David Snook, Linda Vesey Sokalofsky, John Steane, Frank Stevens, Frances Stewart, Margaret Stansfield, Ken F. Stewart, Peter Stewart, Sarah Stickland, Bob Stinchcombe, Dallas Stott, Margaret H. Strand, Jennie Stringer, Penny Sudhurst, Terry Sullivan, Bill Sutton of Marton, Sir Rodney Sweetnam, Lieutenant Greg Swinden, Ken Switzer, Jessie Taylor Szmidt, Bronwyn Tarrier, Ruth Taylor, Tony Testa, Myra Thomas, Aileen Thompson, Carol Thompson, Bill Thompson, Robert Thompson, Nick Thornicroft, Richard Thornton, Derek Tilney, Bernadette Tither, Christine Tomkowicz, Jon Toohey, Sue Tout, Doreen Travis, Beverley Tracey, Helen Tracy, Rydal, Kenneth Tromans, Irene Trumper, Bob Turnbull, John Turpie, Liz Turpin, Jim Type, Dr. David Upton, Anthony Vaughan, Shea Vowles, John Wainwright, John Wakeling, Roy Walkden, Peter Walker, Wendy Walker, Jean Wallwork, Ivan Walter, Joyce Ward, Mark Ward, David McM. R. Warnes, George Watt, John Watts, Sarah Wearne, David Webb, Laura Webb, Joanne Webber, Judith Romney Wegner, Pat Weller, James Wellings, Steve Western, Richard Westland, Jeannine Whiffen, Clo White, Mary Aileen White, Stella Whitelaw, Doreen Muriel Smith Whitting, Brian Wickham, Harry Willey, Darren Williams, Hugh Williams, Arthur Ashley Willis, John D. Wills, Martin Wills, Don Wilson, Lorraine Wilson, Klaus Wolf, Grantley Woods, Kathleen Woodward, Ethel Wooldridge, and Julia Young.

GARDENS OF HELL

Introduction

The Road to Gallipoli

Personally I think Churchill ought to be shot.
—Lt. F. A. Yeo, No. 4 Squadron, Royal Naval Air Service Armoured
Car Detachment, Dardanelles, May 20, 1915

World War I was a war of alliances that began decades before, out of fears that the great nations of Europe would begin attacking one another. It was sparked by the assassination of the Austrian archduke Franz Ferdinand and his wife in Sarajevo. The gunshot that felled this one man has come to be called the "shot heard 'round the world."

The war was fought in Europe, Africa, Asia, and the Middle East as well as the world's oceans and in the air. But how did a conflict that was fought primarily in western and eastern Europe spread to Turkey—the Ottoman Empire—a country that wished to remain neutral? Quite simply, two of the conflict's greatest protagonists, Great Britain and Germany, pushed Turkey into it.

Much has been written about the war and the events leading up to it. The facts important to this story are that two alliances faced off against each other. The Central Powers, Germany and the Austro-Hungarian Empire, were later joined by Turkey and Bulgaria and were the aggressors. Against it was the Triple Entente made up of

Great Britain and its Dominions (Australia, Canada, India, New-foundland, New Zealand, and South Africa), France, and Russia. Later, as their partners against the Central Powers increased in number, the group of nations were referred to as the Allies. They battled Germany on the eastern and western fronts; the Austro-Hungarian Empire in the Balkans and Italy; and the Turks at Gallipoli, in the Balkans, and across the Middle East. When Bulgaria joined the Central Powers in October 1915, fighting took place in Salonika, in northeastern Greece.

On August 2, 1914, two days before Great Britain and Germany declared war, the Ottoman Empire secretly signed a pact with Germany. This guaranteed that Turkey would aid Germany in the event it had to go to war against Russia on the side of Austria-Hungary and that Germany would come to Turkey's aid if it was militarily threatened by Russia. This was important for Germany because Russia's only warmwater ports were on the Black Sea, which was reached from the Aegean via the Dardanelles Straits and the Sea of Marmara. The straits would have to be blocked so the Russians could not be supplied by its allies through these ports. But for the time being the Turks were maintaining their neutrality and refused to sign declarations of war.

That changed on November 6, when Great Britain and France declared war on Turkey. The reasons for the declaration were many, and it may be argued that Turkey was pushed into the war by both Germany and Great Britain. Turkey, which feared Russian aggression, was unprepared to meet such an attack, either militarily or logistically. Germany could provide military expertise, arms, and equipment and was aggressive in its efforts to show the Ottomans what it was capable of. The alliance began in 1913, after Turkey requested Germany's assistance in rebuilding and modernizing its army following its defeat in the Balkan Wars of 1912–13. Germany's efforts were amplified after the outbreak of war in 1914. If Turkey could keep the Russians occupied, the tsar's army would be less of a threat to Germany and Austria-Hungary on the eastern front.

In an effort to bring the Ottoman army into line with those of the Entente, German general Otto Liman von Sanders was given command of the Turkish First Army in August 1914. He was not a popular man. He was stern and self-centered, with no concern for the lives of the men under his control—especially if they were Turks. They did not trust him because he was more concerned with pushing Germany's aims than Turkey's. In March 1915 he was given command of the Turkish Fifth Army, which defended the Gallipoli Peninsula. In his memoirs he stated that he was responsible for planning and carrying out the improvement of Turkey's defenses. In fact, the Turks did most of the planning and all of the work, while von Sanders was primarily responsible for organizing the manpower to do so. As was his way, he would take credit for much that he was not responsible for during the Gallipoli Campaign.

Great Britain inadvertently drove Turkey into the arms of the enemy. Immediately after the outbreak of war, the British government confiscated two battleships purchased by Turkey that were nearing completion in English shipyards. The Turks paid for these ships by public subscription, and with their confiscation, anti-British feeling in the country soared. Britain made no apology for the confiscation but did promise to remunerate Turkey at a later date. It needed the ships for the Royal Navy, and that was that.

On August 10, 1914, the German battle cruiser SMS *Goeben* and the light cruiser SMS *Breslau* arrived at the mouth of the Dardanelles. During the voyage they were tailed by a British naval squadron. Upon arrival the Germans requested permission to enter. International law prohibited warships from moving through the straits, but permission was granted. Germany gave the two vessels to Turkey as replacements for the confiscated battleships. On August 15 control of the Ottoman navy was turned over to German rear admiral Wilhelm Souchon, who had arrived on the *Goeben*. Turkey claimed to have purchased the two ships, but Great Britain knew otherwise. In retaliation the British squadron that had followed the German vessels blockaded the entrance to the Dardanelles. When the squadron refused to allow a Turkish torpedo boat to exit the straits on September 27, the Turks closed the Dardanelles to Allied merchant shipping. This was a real blow to Great Britain and France. They desperately needed a warmwater port through which they could supply Russia with arms and through which Russia could send its grain westward.

Germany was eager for the Turks to declare war on the side of the Central Powers, and on October 27 Souchon led the Ottoman navy into the Black Sea to attack the Russians. On October 29 the Turks bombarded the port cities of Odessa and Sevastopol, sinking two Russian ships. On October 31 Turkey declared war on the Triple Entente, and on November 5 Britain declared war on Turkey.

On November 3, under orders from First Lord of the Admiralty Winston Churchill, British ships bombarded the Turkish village of Kum Kale, on the Asiatic side of the Dardanelles, and Fort Sedd-el-Bahr, on the European side. The bombardments were partially successful, but the primary result was that they spurred the Turks into action. The Turks immediately began building up their defenses—forts and trenches at strategic locations, heavy artillery in those forts, mobile howitzers, searchlights, and naval minefields—along both sides of the straits. The minefields were placed in lines at intervals across the Dardanelles.

The howitzers were particularly threatening for two reasons. First, they were mobile. This made them difficult to hit, especially by ships that were themselves moving. Second, they fired in a high trajectory. Instead of shooting directly at the sides of the ships, they could drop their shells onto the wooden decks, then explode inside the compartments below.

The decision to "force" the Dardanelles—to eliminate the Turkish defenses along both sides of the Dardanelles Straits, thus allowing the Royal Navy and the French navy to sail unhindered into the Sea of Marmara—was not immediate. Churchill proposed the idea after Britain declared war on Turkey. At the time it was considered unfeasible because of the demand it would place on the Royal Navy, which was already fully occupied against the Germans closer to home and as far away as the Pacific Ocean. As the Turks, with the help of German advisors, strengthened their defenses along the straits, the plan was considered even less practical. Nevertheless, Churchill persisted, and by the end of December 1914 people were beginning to listen to his convincing, though misleading, arguments. The war on the western front was going nowhere because the German defenses were so strong, and movement by either side had virtually ceased. The fighting had devolved into trench warfare, and the British realized that if progress was going to be made, it would have to be made elsewhere. They realized that a blow would have to be struck against the Germans on some other front, one that would help Russia so it could keep up the pressure from the eastern front.

On January 2, 1915, a message was received in London from Russia reporting a Turkish invasion of the Caucasus. The message also requested that Britain attack the Turks in an effort to draw their attention away from Russia. What the British did not know was that by the time the message arrived in London, the Russians had already decimated the Turkish force. Sympathetic to the plight of Britain's ally, Field Marshal Lord Horatio Kitchener, secretary of state for war, and Churchill both determined that a "demonstration" should be made in the Dardanelles to lure the Turks away from Russia. The navy would be given the job due to a lack of troops, and Kitchener told Churchill that he only envisioned a small operation. He had neither the troops nor the munitions to spare for anything larger. Kitchener's intention was to bluff the Turks into thinking that they were going to attack the Dardanelles, but Churchill had something bigger in mind. He wanted to force the Dardanelles using only the Royal Navy; troops would only be required after Constantinople had surrendered. It was a ridiculous notion. Even if the navy could force the straits, troops would obviously have to eliminate the defenses on land so the ships could be resupplied and the men occupying Constantinople could be reinforced. Studies made before the war by the army and navy had determined that both troops and ships would be required, and Churchill knew it. In fact, in 1911 he had written that it would be impossible to force the Dardanelles with ships alone. But Churchill was driven by a desire for success, and Constantinople would be a colorful feather in his cap. To be fair, however, he was not the only one who liked the idea. It is perhaps more accurate to say that he was the most enthusiastic supporter and certainly its prime motivator. He did, in fact, mislead the prime minister, Herbert Asquith, and his War Council into thinking that such an endeavor would be successful. In doing so, he muted the objections of the officers serving under him at the Admiralty.

Winston Churchill was an egocentric and ambitious man who began his adult life as a soldier. A graduate of the British army's elite military college, Sandhurst, he saw action in South Africa during the Boer War. Later, he devoted his life to politics and writing. He was by no means a brilliant soldier, but he was enthusiastic. As a politician, he threw body and soul into his work and had a bullheaded devotion to whichever political cause he was committed to at the moment, earning him few friends in the process. He did not care about maintaining allegiances to either of the political parties, Liberal or Conservative, both of which he was allied to at different times during his career. Nevertheless, in August 1911 Asquith appointed him head of the Admiralty, a position that Churchill coveted. He believed that war in Europe was imminent, that Britain was unprepared, and that the Royal Navy was the branch of service that was most capable of winning such a war. In 1911 the Admiralty was in need of reform. With Churchill's reputation for drive and his interest in military and naval affairs, the prime minister felt he was the perfect choice. He would regret his decision. Even though Churchill desperately wanted control of the navy, he had never served in that service and did not understand the intricacies of naval operations. He saw it as a massive gun, to be used defensively or offensively—but he did not know how to load, aim, or fire it.

Churchill asked Vice Adm. Sackville Carden, the commander of the Royal Navy squadron blockading the Dardanelles (the Eastern Mediterranean Squadron), to present a plan to force the straits. He received it on January 11 and presented the plan to the War Council two days later. It consisted of seven phases:

1. Destruction of the defenses at the entrance to the Dardanelles, consisting of four forts referred to as the Outer Forts, or Outer Defenses.

2. Sweeping the minefields from the area between the Outer Forts and the Narrows and knocking out the forts and mobile guns guarding them.

3. Destruction of the defenses at the Narrows.

4. Sweeping the minefield beyond the Narrows.

5. Destruction of the forts beyond the Narrows.

6. Sailing the British and French fleets into the Sea of Marmara.

7. Operating in the Sea of Marmara and patrolling the Dardanelles.

Carden was a cautious, experienced man with more than thirty years of service behind him. He thought it might be possible to eliminate the Turkish defenses with ships alone, but he was not certain. In fact, he felt that ground forces would be needed to deal opposition ashore. Churchill, having no idea of the difficulties involved, did not convey Carden's concerns to the War Council. True, he wrote in 1911 that such an undertaking would not be possible without troops, but something had changed since then. In October 1914 the Germans had laid siege to the forts defending the Belgian city of Antwerp, and they had successfully reduced them with heavy artillery. This action impressed Churchill, and he thought it would be possible to do the same thing to the Turkish forts with his heavily armed battleships. But he failed to consider several important points, such as the fact that the Belgians were not firing into the backs of the Germans. In the Dardanelles the ships would be fired on from two sides—the European and Asiatic sides of Turkey through which the straits flowed. Also, the Germans had used howitzers in Belgium, which dropped shells on top of the guns inside the forts without having to go through their walls first. Ships' guns fired in a flat trajectory, meaning that they shot *at* the target. When firing from the extreme ranges, the ships would have trouble getting their shells to fall on the guns behind the walls of the forts. In most cases they would first have to shoot *through* the walls. The mobile guns would not only be hard to hit but would be difficult to find in the first place.

Churchill did consider the mines, although he did not realize that there were no minesweepers with which to locate and destroy them. But he was a persuasive man—so persuasive, in fact, that he could simply out-argue the chief naval officer under him, the first sea lord and admiral of the fleet, Lord John Fisher, without the admiral being able to fight back. Fisher sat silent in the meetings with the War Council, feeling that he should not contradict his boss in front of others. He knew Churchill was wrong, as did the Admiralty officers who were not in attendance at the meetings, but he felt powerless to act. They all knew that at that stage of the war Britain did not have the men, ships, or munitions to fight on two fronts.

With little discussion, however, and believing the operation would be a limited one, the War Council accepted the plan, and on January 15 Carden was told to begin preparations. The Dardanelles Campaign was about to begin.

I

"A Day Which I Shall Not Forget"
The Battle Is Joined

Vice Admiral Carden received orders to begin his campaign against the defenses guarding the Dardanelles Straits on February 5, 1915. Churchill ordered two battalions of the Royal Marine Light Infantry—the Chatham and Plymouth Battalions—to join Carden's fleet on February 6 for service ashore. The plan was for them to land and demolish any guns in the Turkish forts that the battleships could not.

An Admiralty memorandum was issued on February 15 that stressed the need for ground troops if the Royal Navy was unsuccessful. Thus, Kitchener agreed to make the army's Twenty-Ninth Division available. This was the army's only regular division not yet engaged on the western front, and his decision was a controversial one. Field Marshal Sir John French, commander in chief of the British army in France and Flanders (the British Expeditionary Force [BEF]), had been promised the division as a reinforcement, and he argued strenuously for it. His argument went unheeded, but he persisted, and on February 19 Kitchener reversed his decision. At the same meeting he suggested that the First Australian Division and the New Zealand Infantry Brigade should be sent to support the fleet instead.

On February 18 Churchill ordered the Royal Naval Division (RND) to the Aegean, and the French government dispatched a division of

French and Colonial troops—to be called the Corps Expéditionaire d'Orient (CEO)—to assist. The divisions sailed for the Greek island of Lemnos, fifty miles from Gallipoli. There, what would become known as the Mediterranean Expeditionary Force (MEF) established its forward base at Mudros, which has a natural harbor capable of handling a large number of ships. Two days later troops from the Australian and New Zealand Army Corps (ANZAC) that were training in Egypt were also ordered to Mudros. It was a surprise for them because they thought they were going to fight in France. Kitchener had no faith in the ability of either the RND or the "Anzacs," as the Australians and New Zealanders were called. In fact, when Prime Minister Asquith asked him if he felt it would be wiser to use these colonial troops to support the navy instead of the Twenty-Ninth Division, he replied, "Quite good enough if a cruise in the Sea of Marmora was all that was contemplated."[1] The coming campaign would prove that his lack of faith was unwarranted. The Anzacs and naval infantrymen would be every bit as capable as the professional soldiers of the Twenty-Ninth.

The Royal Naval Division was an anomaly. It was Churchill's brainchild. As first lord of the Admiralty, he found himself with more marines and reservist sailors than he had ships on which they could serve. So, he decided to turn them into infantrymen. The division consisted of twelve infantry battalions: four of Royal Marines and eight of men from the Royal Naval Volunteer Reserve, strengthened by stokers already serving in the navy and veterans recalled from the Royal Naval Reserve, who would serve as the battalions' noncommissioned officers. The Royal Marine battalions were named after their home stations—Chatham, Deal, Plymouth, and Portsmouth. The RN battalions were named after admirals of the Napoleonic Wars—Anson, Benbow, Collingwood, Drake, Hawke, Hood, Howe, and Nelson. The battalions were supported by units of the Royal Marines—cyclists, medics, and engineers—but had no artillery directly assigned to them. Few of the men had seen action, and most of the sailors, having enlisted after the outbreak of war, had never even been to sea. Many had never even seen it. The division first saw action during the siege of Antwerp in October 1914, but far more men were captured by the Germans than were killed in combat. In fact, roughly half of the men in the division were taken prisoner and interned for the duration of the war. Those who made it out of Antwerp returned to England, and the division was hastily strengthened with new recruits.

Kitchener had another change of heart on March 10. He decided to send the Twenty-Ninth Division to the Aegean after all. He stressed, however, that it was not to be used as an invading force. It was only to be used for garrisoning the Turkish forts subdued by the navy. He also stated that the division was only "on loan" and had to be returned if called for.

Field Marshal Lord Horatio Kitchener was a man of extensive military experience. The son of a stern army officer, he was educated privately in Switzerland and was first commissioned as an officer in the Royal Engineers. He served as a volunteer with the French army during the Franco-Prussian War of 1870–71. From 1874 to 1882 he carried out intelligence work for the British government, and in 1882 he was posted to Egypt, where he commanded an Egyptian cavalry regiment. In 1898 he commanded the British troops that crushed the Sudanese at the Battle of Omdurman. For his services in the campaign, he was created Baron Kitchener. During the final eighteen months of the Second Boer War (1899–1902), he campaigned against Boer guerrillas by herding their families into concentration camps and establishing a line of blockhouses to isolate and ultimately defeat the enemy. He was a brilliant military planner, but he did not shine where Gallipoli was concerned. His halfhearted support of the campaign produced confusion and delay, and he vastly underestimated the enemy. He knew that the Turks had been involved in three wars since the beginning of the twentieth century and had lost them all. He knew that their army was neither industrious nor resourceful. He knew that the Turkish infrastructure did not lend itself to the rapid dispatch of men or supplies: roads and railroads were terribly inadequate. In short, he did not feel that the Turkish army could stand up to the drive and might of the British army. If it did not collapse before the naval onslaught, it would certainly give up if confronted by the army. He was to be proven very, very wrong.

The first phase of the assault on the Dardanelles began on February 19, when the Royal Navy attacked the so-called Outer Defenses—the four forts located at the entrance to the straits. In that attack damage was inflicted on the forts themselves, but none of the guns inside were hit. When the Turkish gunners answered the ships' fire, they caused no casualties.

Bad weather prevented the resumption of the attack until February 25. On that date the RN managed to knock out the guns in Forts Kum Kale and Sedd-el-Bahr, but it did so at a cost. During the exchange of fire, the battleship HMS *Agamemnon* was hit by a shell from No. 1 Fort at Cape Helles, and the British suffered their first combat fatalities of the campaign. Chief Petty Officer A. W. Young was working in *Agamemnon*'s signals center at the time. He recorded: "Ship hit 7 times by fort No. 1 gun is 9.45"–weight of shell roughly 400 lb. Had three killed and seven wounded unfortunately. Was at dressing station, cannot say I enjoyed the experience but got used to it in time. Things went very well. Went aft and found our show in a fine old mess where shell had gone through ships side. Managed to secure several bits of shell etc. We hear that day's work was quite successful . . . No other ship had casualties and we were quite unfortunate over ours. In evening we were ordered to Tenedos to repair damage and transfer wounded to Hospital ship *Soudan*."[2]

Ordinary Seaman William Mason died within minutes of being struck in the neck and chest by a shell fragment. Leading Seaman George Small was hit in the forehead by a shell splinter and lingered for three hours before breathing his last. Petty Officer Bertie Worthington also took three hours to die. Their loss must have been a horrifying eye-opener to their shipmates, few if any of whom had seen men injured in battle. Young, with several years of service behind him, betrayed little emotion throughout his diary, though he certainly felt the loss. His tone was the rule, not the exception, in such accounts. Indeed, the ability to mask one's emotions is required by every combatant if he is to continue fighting. To let down one's emotional guard is to reduce or eliminate completely one's ability to fight. But seventeen-year-old midshipman Henry Denham, also on *Agamemnon*, gave a glimpse of his feelings in his description of the men's funeral the following day:

> At 1.30 p.m. we weighed [anchor] and proceeded to sea in order to bury our three dead; a very appropriate place—beautiful, clear, blue water. At 2.20 we started the burial service, the three bodies were borne on stretchers sewn up in their own hammocks and covered over with ensigns. They were committed to the deep in turn by sliding them down a gangplank into the sea whereupon they sank immediately. After this the rifle party under P.O. [Petty Officer] Warren fired three rounds after which there was the Last Post. On the whole it was very impressive even though it is wartime. One cannot realize disasters, or people getting killed, even though they aren't one's closest friends.

Among the wounded was sixteen-year-old Boy 1st Class Walter Mockett. His loss was felt particularly among his fellow crewmen. On March 5 Chief Petty Officer Young recorded: "We heard today of death in 'Soudan' of Boy Mockett, poor kid he was only 16 and ought to have been at home with mother. He had some rotten wounds though, 7, it wasn't unexpected from the first." Denham recorded: "Signal from *Soudan* stated that boy Mockett has died of his wounds; he was only fifteen [*sic*] a day before he got wounded and he seemed so cheery when I saw him in bed on board the hospital ship *Soudan* a few days ago. Tetanus had set in, ending the boy's life."[3]

On February 26 the Royal Navy began its assault on the Intermediate Defenses—those located farther up the straits. The ships concentrated on the guns in and around two main forts—Dardanos on the Asiatic side and Messudieh on the European side. The operation accomplished little because of opposition from mobile howitzers and field batteries, which the ships could not see to fire on. Also that day, naval demolition parties covered by marines landed to finish off the guns in the Outer Forts. Parties from HMS *Vengeance* landed at Kum Kale on the Asiatic side of the straits, and those from *Irresistible* landed on the European side to deal with Sedd-el-Bahr. *Vengeance*'s marines suffered a single, particularly horrifying fatality:

> They landed at [Fort] No. 6 and got into scattered formation immediately. "A" Company was left in Kum Kale while the remainder proceeded up to No. 4. They were fired on by Turks in the windmills at Yeni Shehr which were soon brought down by us and the *Dublin*. It was a fine sight to see the windmills crumple up and fall down. When the party got to No. 4 Fort they smashed up a searchlight and several wires connecting mines but did not blow up the guns. On the way back they were cut off by some Turks in a cemetery. We had some difficulty in finding the point of aim owing to the wrong bearing being passed up. The captain got furious and came and trained the gun himself. He cursed me and told me I ought to have turned Mr. —out. It was rather a difficult position. The Turks were driven off and our Marines got back to their boats. I did not expect half of them to come back. Only one was killed and three wounded. The one killed I am afraid was mutilated—the Turks venting their whole wrath on him. His head was smashed in, four bullet holes in his face, one in his wrist, one in [the] shoulder and one in the knee—this was an explosive bullet and had blown his knee cap off. Both his legs were broken and a bayonet wound [was] in his abdomen.[4]

Word of the landings was passed to the other ships. Chief Petty Officer Young on *Agamemnon* learned of them on March 2, 1915: "1 Sergt of Marines got detached and was wounded others went to his assistance but before they could reach him a polite Turk came out of a house and bashed his head in with the butt end of his rifle."[5] One wonders if the accounts of Turnbull's mutilation made the British fearful of the Turks or if it produced a feeling of hatred. If Young was aware of it, the event obviously bothered men

"A Day Which I Shall Not Forget"

enough that it was recounted among ships. It is likely that this incident contributed to a general feeling that the Turks took no prisoners. Experience later dispelled this belief, but the men who landed on April 25 did so thinking that their foe did not "play by the rules." The man killed, Sgt. Ernest Turnbull, had been a marine since the age of seventeen. Unfortunately, the tasks for which the marines were sent ashore were only partially successful. Demolition parties were landed again at Sedd-el-Bahr on February 27 and at Kum Kale on March 1. No fatalities were suffered in either operation, but neither was the destruction complete. Further landings were required.

Bad weather postponed those operations until March 4. The decision to wait was tragic, though inevitable, and the British would pay dearly for it. The earlier landings had enlightened the defenders to the intentions of the British. The Turks expected further landings at both forts, and they planned a hot reception for the unwanted visitors.

Early that morning two companies from the Plymouth Battalion landed at the two forts. Naval demolition parties were with them, and each group brought along four machine guns. The force detailed to assault Kum Kale, No. 3 Company, landed first. It was tasked with blowing up the guns, then moving through the adjoining village of that name. The men were to push on to the village of Yeni Shehr, so that any approaching Turks would be prevented from reaching the fort long enough for the demolition parties to complete their task. This proved to be a tall order for the 120 marines and the 23-man demolition party and one that they could not fulfill. Turkish resistance was much stronger than expected, and the men were forced to retire to their boats under cover of the warships. Twenty marines were killed, and two died later of their wounds. Three of the men assumed to have been killed were in fact missing. A group of volunteers sailed up and down the coast around Kum Kale for two hours hoping they might turn up, but they did not. The three had become detached from the main force at some point and had been captured or killed. Either way, the Turnbull incident was a good indicator that these men, if they had been captured, were not likely to be spared. They were never heard from again, and in July 1916 the Admiralty ruled that they must have been killed in action.

No. 4 Company, which landed at Sedd-el-Bahr later in the morning, fared no better. It, too, was driven back to its boats under heavy fire, though with fewer casualties. It lost three men killed in action. On March 4, 1915, Pvt. James Thompson of the Plymouths, who did not take part in the landings, noted in his diary: "No. 3 and 4 Companies effected a landing and proceeded into action leaving ship [the transport *Braemar Castle*] at 8 a.m. Left Imbros about 8.30 a.m. sailing into the mouth of Dardanelles. Continued to circle round all day watching bombardment. In the evening ship was shelled by Turkish forts. Shells coming close but doing no damage. No. 3 Coy. [Company] did not come onboard but No. 4 Coy. came onboard about 5 p.m. bringing three dead Marines including Sergeant Minns and 1 dead Turk."[6]

The eight men killed in the two actions were buried at sea. They included Color Sgt. Alfred Barnett, who sustained a gunshot wound to the head at Sedd-el-Bahr and died later that night, and Sgt. Arthur Minns. He was killed by a bullet that had first passed through Pvt. Horace Longridge while they were in a whaler off Kum Kale (Longridge survived).

The day's operations were a failure, but the forts guarding the entrance to the Dardanelles were effectively put out of action. Phase 2—the sweeping of the minefields between the Outer Forts and the Narrows and the destruction of the Intermediate Defenses—could begin.

"A Day Which I Shall Not Forget"

2

"The Results Were Disastrous"

Forcing the Dardanelles

With the destruction of the Outer Forts, the next phase of Carden's plan could begin. The minesweepers were to proceed up the Dardanelles and begin plowing a safe passage through for the warships. Their success was crucial because with the mines in place, the Allied navies would not be able to force the straits and proceed on to Constantinople.

The minesweepers were actually North Sea fishing trawlers, twenty-one in number, from Grimsby in Lincolnshire and Lowestoft in Suffolk. They were unarmed and equipped with inadequate sweeping gear. Additionally, they moved only marginally faster than the currents against which they sailed. Their top speed was five knots; the opposing current was two to four. They operated by sailing up the straits, swinging out their sweeps, and drifting backward, hoping to snare mines while under the protection of the warships. Royal Navy sailors in picketboats would destroy the mines with small cannons when they were pulled to the surface. It was a bold plan to say the least.

Minesweeping began on February 25, at the entrance to the straits. No mines were found. On the night of March 1 the trawlers swept as far as Kephez Point but were driven off without loss by Turkish guns supported by searchlights. They tried again on the night of March 6–7, again without success and without suffering casualties. But on the night of March 8, the fishermen ran into trouble. While sweeping a channel to within three thousand yards of Yeni Kale, the *Okino* from Grimsby struck a mine and sank. The skipper and four crewmen were rescued, but ten other men were lost. Among the missing was the boat's naval petty officer, Petty Officer 2nd Class Alfred Wright.[1] The youngest member of the crew was fifteen-year-old Signal Boy Charles Beer. There appears to have been an official shroud of secrecy concerning this incident, which would have been of great interest in Grimsby. No mention of it was made in either of the two local newspapers.

The *Okino* was a boat with a slightly infamous history. It was one of five fishing trawlers owned by the firm H. L. Taylor that had all been given five-letter Japanese names beginning and ending with the letter O. After the outbreak of war such vessels, along with their skippers and crews, were pressed into service with the Royal Naval Reserve Trawler Section. Popular history tells us that they were willing participants in the war effort, but actual history tells us something different. While many were amenable to "doing their bit" for king and country, a memorandum written to the admiral commanding the coast guard and reserves in November 1914 makes it clear that not all of them wanted to serve. The memo stated that it was common for the fishermen to go absent without leave, disobey orders, or be apprehended by the authorities in a state of drunkenness in a conscious effort to be discharged from the service.

Skipper Richard Hogben of the *Okino* was one of those so accused. On January 22, 1915, the captain in charge of the Lowestoft Naval Base recommended him for discharge from the service because:

1. He did leave his ship and remain absent without leave.

2. On the 21st of January he was in a hopeless state of intoxication at noon, when he should have been taking his ship to sea.[2]

The recommendation resulted in a flurry of communications because the case revealed that there was no punishment on the books for civilians pressed into service as skippers of their own vessels who committed serious infractions. A "suitable" punishment was not determined until the beginning of 1916. The Admiralty decided that the most severe penalty it would impose for crimes by skippers would be a fine of up to thirty days' pay. One wonders if Hogben was sober the night it went down. The official report of the sinking does not say one way or the other.

The trawlers suffered again on the night of March 10–11. After spotting the vessels with their searchlights, the Turks scored hits on two with their guns. Another, *Manx Hero*, was sunk by a mine that it had just located and blown up. Nobody was killed that night, but the strain on the crews was coming to a head. When they came under fire the next night, they retreated. As a result, each trawler's crew was supplemented with three Royal Navy sailors. All were volunteers.

After this episode Carden sent a message to Churchill stating: "Sweeping operations last night not satisfactory, owing to heavy fire. No casualties." On March 13 Churchill demonstrated his displeasure with a response that began: "I do not understand why minesweeping should be interfered with by fire which causes no casualties. Two or three hundred casualties would be a moderate price to pay for sweeping up as far as the Narrows."[3] He also went on to state that the Turkish forts were known to be short of ammunition. They were not.

After receiving Churchill's message, Carden's second-in-command, Vice Adm. John de Robeck, organized a meeting with his officers to devise a plan for knocking out the Narrows defenses. They felt that doing so would allow the minesweepers to complete their tasks, yet they were not enthusiastic about the plan. They knew what the Turks were capable of, and they knew that Churchill did not. The attack would begin on the morning of March 18, and in the meantime operations to reduce the defenses would continue. But Carden would not lead it. The stress of command took its toll, and on March 16 he was replaced by de Robeck. Carden was sent to a hospital on Malta and did not see further active service.

The Narrows, as it is termed, is the point at which the passage through the Dardanelles Straits is narrowest, a mere thirteen hundred meters. It is marked by the town of Chanak (now Çanakkale) on the Asiatic side and Fort Kilid Bahr on the European side. At that point the warships had to contend with several strings of mines, concentrations of forts, and mobile howitzers on both sides. It was a death trap, and the Royal Navy knew it. Still, the defenses had to be overcome if Constantinople was to be taken.

With the assistance of the Royal Navy sailors and the French, the trawlers cleared a path past the Intermediate Defenses to within eight thousand yards of the Narrows forts. This would allow the ships to move close enough to the forts to fire effectively. It also gave them the room they needed to maneuver in Eren Keui Bay.

On the night of March 13–14 the trawlers suffered again. Two of them, the *Fentonian* from Grimsby and the *Star of the Empire* from Lowestoft, collided and were fired on. The *Star of the Empire* lost one man, who died of his wounds later that night. The *Fentonian* lost two.

The Royal Navy suffered far worse that night when the cruiser *Amethyst*, which was covering the minesweepers near Kephez Point, was hit. After the trawlers came under fire, the *Amethyst* exposed itself to the Turkish gunners in an effort to draw their fire. It was hit by several shells, one of which exploded in the stokers' bathroom and another on the mess deck. The carnage was horrific: "We had been ordered to go below and write letters home as well as getting some refreshment. Later at action stations all was going well, with the picket boats pulling the mines away with grappling irons, and suddenly we were the centre of searchlight glare and all hell broke loose. My gun received a direct hit and all but two of us were wounded. In the forepart of the ship, shells killed many men in their hammocks. A watch of stokers all together in the bathroom were wiped out and the upper deck looked like a ploughed field."[4] The number of dead on *Amethyst* was twenty-eight, sixteen of whom were in the stokers' bathroom. The remainder were killed by the shell that hit the mess deck, causing about sixty casualties in all.

"The Results Were Disastrous"

The attack on the Narrows began on March 18. That morning three lines of warships proceeded up the straits into Eren Keui Bay. The plan was for Line A, made up of British battleships, to advance and attack the forts around Chanak and Kilid Bahr from a range of fourteen thousand yards. When Turkish gunfire had diminished to the point that it was safe to advance and fire from a shorter distance, Line B, made up of French battleships, would pass through Line A and attack the forts from a range of eight thousand yards. Line C was to guard the flanks and provide relief for Line B, which would be well within range of the guns in the forts. Two hours after the assault began, destroyers equipped to hunt for mines were to move up and begin sweeping down the straits from the Narrows. The plan seemed a sound one, but the Turks had an unpleasant surprise in store.

The HMS *Agamemnon* led Line A into action, preceded by three minesweeping destroyers. Picketboats with three-pounders (guns firing shells with projectiles weighing three pounds) were to destroy mines that were dragged to the surface. The *Agamemnon* began taking hits as it approached the Intermediate forts, although no serious damage was done. Just after 11:30 a.m. it arrived on station and began firing at Fort No. 13. The other ships in Line A were also hit but not seriously, and the Turkish gunners were not putting up much of a fight. Thus, thinking that Line A's ships had put many of the Ottoman guns out of action, and indeed the Intermediate forts appeared to have been silenced, de Robeck ordered Line B to advance through Line A to begin its assault. As it did so, the Turks opened fire with a vengeance, causing serious damage.

Despite the damage inflicted by the attacking ships, the Turks were more than capable of inflicting their own. The *Agamemnon* was hit twelve times within twenty-five minutes. At 12:20 p.m. the British battleship *Inflexible*, also in Line A, suffered hits on its foretop control station that knocked out its wireless just as the French were passing through the line. A single shrapnel shell killed three men, mortally wounded two officers, and wounded another four. Most of the casualties occurred in the underwater fore torpedo flat and were not recovered until March 25. There it appeared that seventeen-year-old Boy 1st Class Edwin Kemp was nearest the blast. All that was found of the lad was an arm and the back of his skull. For days afterward pieces of skin and bone were being picked up.

The *Inflexible*'s commander, Capt. Richard Phillimore, kept his vessel in action against Fort No. 16 (Hamidieh II) to support the French as they were advancing. Yet French rear admiral Guépratte signaled from his flagship, the battleship *Gaulois*, that he should move out of range of the Turkish guns. It was a wise suggestion. The fire on the *Inflexible*'s forebridge was so serious that it was spreading to the foretop. Having already silenced the battery he was firing at, he moved his vessel out of the British line to prevent his wounded from being burned to death.

At 1:45 p.m. de Robeck felt that the Turkish fire had diminished enough that the minesweeping destroyers could be sent forward. He also ordered Line C to advance because the French ships, which had advanced to within nine thousand yards of the Narrows forts and were the closest to them, were suffering severe damage. The *Gaulois* was so badly damaged that Guépratte ordered the British light cruiser *Dublin* forward to stand by in case it had to be abandoned. The *Dublin*'s commander, Capt. John Kelly, offered to take the French ship in tow, but its captain declined.

A shell that exploded on the quarterdeck of the *Gaulois* only damaged the superstructure but caused a few casualties in the aft 305 mm gun turret. Another shell struck beneath the armor plate. It opened a large hole that sent water rushing into the fore compartments: "Despite his ship's poor condition, Captain Biard did not hesitate to take *Gaulois* back into a possible minefield to rescue a few survivors. He later continued out of the Straits. With her fore compartments flooded, the safety of *Gaulois* relied upon the strength of a bulkhead. Captain Biard had the choice either to go aground on the nearby Turkish coast or to proceed at slow speed out of the Straits, hoping that the bulkhead would hold up. He chose the second option, protected from the enemy's firing by *Charlemagne* which took position between *Gaulois* and the land. On the bridge, he remained very calm, taking great care in maneuvering his ship

"The Results Were Disastrous"

which was already heavy by the bows. And perhaps to stay in good form, just in case, he required his steward to bring him his no. 1 jacket . . . and a glass of port!"[5]

Despite the heavy damage to the Allied ships, it seemed possible that the Narrows forts might be overcome. At about two o'clock that afternoon, however, the attackers received a nasty shock. The French battleship *Bouvet*, advancing along the Asiatic coast, hit a mine and sank within just two minutes. The blast caused its magazine to explode. Out of a crew of 667 men, only 66 were saved: "The French battle-squadron, which had steamed close towards the Narrows, was withdrawing at about 2 p.m. when *Bouvet* suddenly heeled over and quickly started to sink; she disappeared by the stern in about 1½–2 minutes. When she apparently hit the bottom, she remained stationary for a few seconds and then she disappeared altogether. *Gaulois* and *Suffren* then came over at full speed to pick up survivors, also destroyers and some picket-boats; they only picked up about 64, of which our boat got four. *Bouvet* had evidently had a shot in her magazine."[6]

At the time nobody knew that the ship had struck a mine. The area had been cleared days before the attack, but now the destroyers were finding them. The Allies did not know that a single Turkish vessel, the *Nousret*, had laid a string of twenty mines in Eren Keui Bay, parallel to the Asiatic coast, where they had seen British ships maneuvering days earlier. The Turks had calculated that an attack would be made on the Narrows forts from that spot and that enemy warships would have to maneuver right where the *Nousret* had laid its deadly eggs.

The second ship to strike a mine was the *Inflexible*. Its crew had extinguished the fires, and it was back in action again: "I noticed the *Inflexible* was blowing her siren. She was struck at 4:14 p.m. and left in a sinking condition but the inrush of water was stopped and she was anchored in shallow water off Tenedos."[7] The *Inflexible* remained afloat and turned to head back to Tenedos. Yet the damage was so severe—the ship was flooding quickly, and its bulkheads were badly strained—that its captain worried that his ship might go down. He had all of his wounded evacuated into the ship's cutter, but the damaged vessel made it safely to Tenedos.

Unfortunately, the mines had not finished taking their toll. At 4:15 p.m. the battleship *Irresistible* ran into one, then was hit by several Turkish shells after being immobilized by the blast. A number of casualties occurred while the crew was standing on deck, preparing to evacuate their stricken vessel:

> A shell—I think it must have been a 14-inch—hit us somewhere forward. Fair and square it caught us, for the whole ship shook, actually reeled over a little . . . then, a tremendous shock was felt. Half a dozen of our crew were thrown violently over and when order had been regained there was the old *Irresistible* heeling over to port at an angle of fully 45 degrees and our gun pointing in the air like an AA [antiaircraft] gun . . . orders came along to clear the casemate, everybody on deck . . . in a very short time all the ship's company, with the exception of the gun's crew still firing, fell in on the afterdeck. Not a sign of panic . . . Our ship had now righted itself . . . we could see a destroyer speeding towards us, a welcome sight . . . The Turks must have realized how helpless we were, for instantly scores of guns turned upon us . . . At the very moment when the last batch of men were preparing to leave the quarter deck a shell landed amongst them. What followed was too horrible to describe . . . where before stood a dozen men, nothing remained but a few mangled scraps.[8]

When the *Wear* arrived at de Robeck's flagship with *Irresistible*'s survivors at 4:50 p.m., the admiral learned for the first time that mines were the source of his ships' troubles. He had wrongly assumed that floating mines were the culprits, and five o'clock a general recall was sounded. He also ordered the battleship *Ocean* to take the *Irresistible* in tow. The ship's commander, Capt. Arthur Hayes-Sadler, refused, however, on the grounds that he could not take his vessel so close to the Asiatic shore. The *Ocean* was under a strong crossfire from the Turkish guns. Instead, he withdrew his ship in an effort to escape the shells, but at 6:05 p.m. it, too, struck

"The Results Were Disastrous"

a mine. Casualties were light, and the crew was taken off by destroyers. It was abandoned at 7:30 p.m.: "We were hit several times with 14 in shells and during the bombardment the *Irresistible* got mined. When we got near to her a 14 in. shell struck the foreturret 12 in guns of *Irresistible* and they rolled over into the water. A moment or two after our ship, the *Ocean*, struck a mine and our engines were put out of action, so we were stuck there helpless, with shells coming over pretty thick. We got the order to abandon ship. Three or four Destroyers came alongside and took us all off except one stoker who was below and could not get out."[9]

The Turks' tally for March 18 was a mighty one. Out of a force of sixteen capital ships (fifteen battleships and a battlecruiser) in action that day, three were sunk. Three were so badly damaged that they had to be sent to Malta for repairs. The French battleship *Suffren* was one of them, and the *Gaulois* had to be beached on Rabbit Island so that it could be repaired to the point that it could sail to Malta.

The *Inflexible* was the third ship sent to Malta, but only after it was beached at Tenedos for emergency repairs. The *Irresistible* and the *Ocean* were kept afloat until they could be abandoned, with the intention of being recovered during the night. Both sank before they could they could be towed back to Tenedos.

In terms of casualties the Turks lost twenty-six killed and fifty-three wounded. On the Allied side the *Bouvet* lost by far the most men. British fatalities were miniscule by comparison. It is a testament to the tenacity of the damage control crews that so few lives were lost.

The British and French lost the day. Despite his intention to continue the assault on March 19, de Robeck did not. He realized that the attack could not continue without ground troops, which would be required in large numbers. Small landing parties simply did not work. Long-range fire by ships' guns could not deal with smaller, better-hidden targets or mobile weapons. He also realized that even if his ships could make it to Constantinople, the support ships would suffer greatly from guns and mines and would not be able to keep his warships supplied.

Thus, plans were drawn up for a ground attack. Gen. Sir Ian Hamilton, commander in chief of the Mediterranean Expeditionary Force, arrived on March 17. The following day he toured prospective landing beaches, which allowed him and his staff to begin planning almost immediately. He chose two landing areas: Helles, at the tip of the Gallipoli Peninsula; and the beach north of Gaba Tepe, twelve miles north of Helles. The more northern site was referred to as "Z Beach" by the planners but would later be called "Anzac," after the Australian and New Zealand troops who would be the first to land there. The Twenty-Ninth Division would land on five beaches at Helles—S, V, W, X, and Y—and would be tasked with moving six miles inland to capture a hill called Achi Baba on the first day. The first group of Australians to land at Anzac would move five miles inland and east to a hill called "971" (Koja Chemen Tepe to the Turks). A second wave of Australians and New Zealanders would move through them and onto a hill called "Mal Tepe." At the same time, the Royal Naval Division would make a diversionary landing at Bulair along the Gulf of Saros. Part of the French force would land at Kum Kale on the Asiatic side, in an effort to keep the Turkish guns there from firing into the backs of the British at V Beach. The rest of the French would float about in their transports, to give the Turks the impression that they were going to land elsewhere on the Asiatic side. As soon as the British were established on land—it was hoped within forty-eight hours—the French would join them at Helles.

The landings were scheduled for April 23. The two-day preparations—boarding the troops and moving them to their prospective debarkation areas—were set to begin two days earlier. But once again the weather had the final say, and the landings were pushed back forty-eight hours. The new date would be April 25, 1915. The Dardanelles Campaign had ended, and the Gallipoli Campaign was about to begin.

"The Results Were Disastrous"

3

"Death on the Eve of Battle"

The Preparations

The plan of attack for April 25 was ambitious. Its success hinged on two points—surprise and rapidity of movement. From the beginning it was doomed to failure, and many British and Australian staff officers knew it. But Hamilton would not hear their protestations.

The naval assaults and small landings totally eliminated the element of surprise. *Enseigne de vaisseaux* L. Lucas, who served on the battleship *Gaulois* in 1915, wrote: "In our opinion, the sole result of these shows along the coasts was to alert the Turks, urging them to reinforce the defence and supply ammunition to the forts. All these maneuvers seemed so ridiculous to us that we thought they were just ingenious devices to delude the enemy while a major operation was being prepared somewhere else."[1]

The decision not to continue the naval assault after March 18 gave the Turks the opportunity to entrench deeper and to fortify the points at which they could reasonably expect the Allies to land. Egyptian newspapers reported the arrival of specific units from Great Britain and its dominions, making the jobs of enemy spies even easier. So did British officers, who were sent to purchase locally the vessels needed to convey troops, animals, and supplies to shore. To top it all off, troops practicing amphibious landings and the arrival of transports at Lemnos made it obvious to even the casual observer that an invasion was coming and soon. The only things the Turks did not know were exactly when and where it would take place. This was Hamilton's only trump card.

On March 12, 1915, Gen. Sir Ian Hamilton, then commander of Britain's home defenses, was called into Kitchener's officer and abruptly notified that he had been chosen to command the military expedition to the Dardanelles, to be called the "Mediterranean Expeditionary Force" (MEF). Hamilton knew nothing about Turkey or the Turks, but he was a qualified soldier with decades of experience behind him—some of it on Kitchener's staff—and he accepted the post without question. During the meeting he was given very little information about either the enemy or his goals. Essentially, he was told that he would command the Australian and New Zealand troops then serving in Egypt, the Royal Naval Division (RND), the French Corps Expéditionnaire d'Orient, and the Twenty-Ninth Division. It was also made clear that the Twenty-Ninth was only on loan and had to be returned to Kitchener for use elsewhere—meaning France—as soon as circumstances allowed Hamilton to do so. Kitchener also remarked that he hoped a military landing would not be necessary, and he told Hamilton that he could not take his own chief of staff, Maj. Gen. Gerald Ellison, with whom he had worked for many years. Instead, he would take Maj. Gen. Walter Braithwaite. Hamilton had worked with him in the past and liked him but could not understand why he was not allowed to take Ellison. He seemed to hold Kitchener in awe, and he knew better than to challenge the field marshal. In the meeting Braithwaite requested a contingent of airplanes from the Royal Flying Corps. But Kitchener, demonstrating the contempt with which he would treat future requests for resources at Gallipoli, turned on him and responded, "Not one!" He also made it clear that Hamilton was to make any requests through him and not through the commander in chief of the Imperial General Staff, Sir James Wolfe Murray, which would have been the proper channel. Hamilton also resolved not to go behind Kitchener's back to make requests

"Death on the Eve of Battle"

for naval support through Churchill, whom he knew would satisfy any requests he made.

The following day Kitchener briefed Hamilton and Braithwaite. He imparted little information about the enemy and informed Hamilton that he would be left to his own devices after arriving in the Aegean. Kitchener also reiterated that his troops were only to be used in the event that the Royal Navy failed to overcome the Turkish defenses. If he needed to land his troops, he could only do so once his entire force was assembled. He could not, for example, land the RND and the Anzacs before the Twenty-Ninth Division had arrived. He was also told that if he did land his men, he could only do so on the European side. If that happened, they were to "burn their boats." That is, they were to carry on until they eliminated Turkish opposition, so the navy could sail up to Constantinople.

With that he and Braithwaite were packed off across Europe and over to Lemnos. They took with them a hastily created staff. Hamilton did not know any of these men, some of whom had no previous military experience. They departed the day after meeting with Kitchener and took the only intelligence documents he had to give them: a handbook on the Turkish army published in 1912, some inaccurate maps, and two small guidebooks to Turkey. Hamilton was not given, and would never see, the up-to-date intelligence reports held by the War Office. Also, he was not told that Lemnos had an acute fresh water shortage and no harbor facilities to allow cargo to be loaded and off-loaded. He could only take his general staff with him because the others—his Quartermaster General and Adjutant General staffs—had not yet been appointed. The Quartermaster General staff, referred to as the "Q staff," was responsible for all supplies, and the Adjutant General staff, referred to as "A staff," was responsible for all personnel issues, including reinforcements and medical arrangements (evacuation and treatment of casualties).

In 1915 Hamilton was one of the most experienced generals serving in the British army. He first saw action in Afghanistan in 1872 and was twice recommended for the Victoria Cross, Britain's highest gallantry decoration. Both times, during the First and Second

Boer Wars, the recommendations were turned down for administrative reasons. At the Battle of Majuba Hill during the First Boer War on February 26, 1881, he suffered a gunshot wound from a Boer sniper that permanently crippled his left arm. Later in the war he served as chief of staff to General Kitchener, commander in chief of the British forces in South Africa. In 1902 he was knighted, and on August 4, 1914, he was appointed commander of the Central (Striking) Force in Britain (Britain's home defenses).

It may be argued that the Gallipoli campaign was doomed to failure in March. It was then that Kitchener informed Braithwaite (who told Hamilton while they were en route to the Aegean) that the Twenty-Ninth Division would not be allowed to take with it a draft of 10 percent reinforcements, which the divisions sent to France had been allowed. That was crucial because of the distance between Great Britain and Gallipoli, and because casualties sustained early in the campaign would be higher than expected. Australia and New Zealand sent a constant supply of reinforcements to Egypt from the start. The British did not receive any until May.

The first troops reached Lemnos in March. They belonged to the Third Brigade, Australian Imperial Force (AIF). The remaining Anzac infantry and support troops then training in Egypt would join them in April, after more transport became available. These men, who had arrived in Egypt as early as November 1914 and as late as February 1915, had been training for months in the desert around Cairo and were anxious to get into combat. They assumed from the beginning that they would be sent to France to fight the Germans. Few of them knew anything about Turkey or why they might be called to fight there. Pvt. Willie Smylie of the Tenth Battalion, AIF, wrote to his mother in Belfast from Egypt that he hoped to meet his two brothers, then serving with the British army, when his battalion arrived in France. He never would. The twenty-two-year-old Irishman, who had immigrated to Australia in 1912 in search of work, was killed at Gallipoli on April 25.

Conditions on Lemnos were primitive, the weather chilly, and the Australians only had enough tents to house one of the brigade's

"Death on the Eve of Battle"

four battalions. So, the four battalion commanders spun coins to see which one would get the tents. The commanding officer of the Ninth Battalion, Lt. Col. Harry Lee, VD (Volunteer Decoration), was the winner. That night his men slept ashore, and the other three battalions continued living on their transports. They remained on the boats for another six weeks, but the winners were less fortunate than they might have imagined. The first night, before the tents were erected, the men slept in the open. There was a driving rain, and the temperature was low. Conditions began taking their toll almost immediately. The first of the Australians, Pvt. Alexander Jones of the Ninth Battalion, contracted pneumonia and died at Mudros on March 10.

The main body of the Royal Naval Division arrived next, on March 12. As a result of poor planning, it departed the island two weeks later for Port Said in Egypt. Bad weather and lack of water and other facilities were among the problems it encountered. The primary reason for the division's departure, however, was that it had left England so quickly that its equipment had been loaded in the transports incorrectly. There were no harbor facilities at Mudros that would enable the ships to be emptied and reloaded so the troops could disembark at Gallipoli with the equipment and supplies in the order they needed them. Fortunately, the Twenty-Ninth Division, which faced the same problem, had already been directed to Egypt. Its holds reorganized, the RND began departing Egypt again on April 5 and returned to Mudros on April 11 and 12. It moved to the nearby island of Skyros on the seventeenth and remained there until it sailed for Gallipoli seven days later. Men were dying in training accidents while still in Egypt, but they perished chiefly from illnesses such as dysentery, typhoid, heatstroke, even venereal disease. One incident resulted in a number of deaths while the troops were en route to Lemnos.

At ten fifteen on the morning of April 16, 1915, the transport *Manitou* was confronted by the Turkish torpedo boat *Dhair Hissar* off Skyros. It was carrying the Royal Field Artillery's 147th Brigade and the Transport Section of the Second Battalion, the South

Wales Borderers, from Alexandria to Lemnos. When it approached, the Ottoman ship was flying a Greek naval ensign,[2] but the crew replaced it with a Turkish ensign as it reached the *Manitou*. The vessel's commanding officer, reported by one witness to have had a German accent, gave the transport's captain three minutes to evacuate his ship before he torpedoed it. Somebody on the *Manitou*—apparently not the captain—requested ten minutes, and ten were granted. With no guns to defend itself, the order to abandon ship was given, and lifeboats were launched. As No. 8 boat was being lowered, the davits broke, and the craft flipped over. It crashed into the one below, killing some of the occupants in the lower boat. Men jumped into the sea, and a number were drowned, some after being hit in the head by objects thrown into the water to act as floats. *Manitou*'s log noted, "We lost 3 boats and lots of Deck Fittings."

When ten minutes had elapsed, the *Dhair Hissar* fired three small torpedoes, all of which missed because the boats were too close. The men in the water were rescued, but the majority never left the ship and continued the journey to Lemnos. One of the Borderers and forty-six artillerymen died in the incident. Seven of *Manitou*'s crewmen also lost their lives. All of the men were officially noted as having drowned.

The *Dhair Hissar* fled shortly after launching its torpedoes. It was pursued by the British destroyers *Jed*, *Kennet*, and *Wear* before being driven ashore at Chios by the British cruiser HMS *Minerva*. Trumpeter Dudley Lissenburg of the 147th Brigade wrote of the chaos that reigned on the *Manitou* that day:

> All the guns, machine guns and ammunition were stored in the hold and we were totally unprepared for what was happening. I don't know how long we were in fact given but certainly I did not move. I saw the first torpedo plop into the sea and begin its journey directly under me as the gunboat was only twenty or thirty yards away. Nothing happened. We raced to look over the starboard side and there it was skimming away with its bow well out of the water like a speedboat. I hurried to the orderly

room and asked the R.S.M. [regimental sergeant major] what I was to do. I expected to have to sound "Stand- to" but was told that the order was every man for himself, scuttle away and find a boat. I was going below to get my lifebelt when at the stairs I was astonished to see the panic-stricken crush of men trying to get up, fighting against those trying to get down [to get their life-belts]. There was chaos on the boat deck too. We had never had boat drill nor been allotted to a particular boat. Lt. Beckett was however using his formidable figure to secure calm as he grasped the muzzle end of a rifle and threatened anyone who rushed at the particular boat he was supervising. I removed my boots and puttees, got into an overcrowded boat which, badly handled by our men, capsized as it was lowered and we were all thrown into the water. Fortunately I was a good swimmer and got away from the side of the ship. The crew of the Turkish gunboat were laughing at us. Our ginger-haired doctor organized us into providing help for the non-swimmers, as did the steward, who had already survived the *Titanic* disaster. We were quite a while in the water before a warship, the *Prince George*, approached us and lowered her lifeboats to pick us up.[3]

One of the ships that sped to the rescue was the transport *Royal George*, which was traveling from Lemnos to Skyros with men of the Royal Naval Division. Its captain, F. J. Thompson, gave an account of the incident and his ship's rescue operations:

At 10.35 a.m. receive S.O.S. signal from S.S. *Manitou* about 18 miles away to the southward, saying he had been torpedoed. We head for scene at all possible speed and fill fore-peak tank (for purpose of ramming). At 11 a.m. pass H.M.S. *Osiris* flying signal "Enemy in sight." Consult with commodore and decide to turn ship away from danger as we do not know if it is submarine or torpedo and dare not risk 1,200 men.

Later we see small craft steaming away from *Manitou* followed by two destroyers, so I turn ship 16 points again and head for *Manitou*, *Somali* following my lead but *Osiris* goes right on as fast as possible to the northward. We arrive on scene at noon and lower all boats but one—and pick up men from wreckage. I maneuver ship alongside one waterlogged lifeboat and raft and picked up over 20 men that way. *Manitou* still floats and appears not to have been hit.

We rescue 102 men, 98 soldiers and 4 crew. I had previously given orders to doctors and chief stewards and we had hot drinks and blankets awaiting them—five poor fellows died after being rescued and one later on . . . Two British destroyers (*Kennet* and *Jedd*) chased the T.B. and forced her ashore on Psara Island. Her crew were interned by Greeks; the T.B. was wrecked by our men. At 5.30 p.m. I hold funeral service for five soldiers, then proceed into Trebuki Harbour.[4]

According to survivors, no lifeboat drill was conducted prior to the incident. Oddly, the ship's captain recorded in his log on April 17, "All boats lowered, troops and crew exercised in rowing." In light of the recollections of survivors and the fact that the soldiers obviously had no experience in lowering the boats, the veracity of this statement must be questioned. Reportedly, some of the officers retired to the saloon for a drink, men looted the officers' cabins, and the transport section's horses and mules were released from their stalls. It was an instance in which responsibility for the deaths could be laid squarely at the feet of the ship's and army officers, who showed a complete lack of leadership. The 147th Brigade suffered more fatalities in this incident than it would at Gallipoli.

It is noteworthy that all of the deaths occurring in the MEF on Lemnos at this stage were Australians and New Zealanders; no British servicemen perished. Every one of the seven deaths was the result of pneumonia; there were no deaths related directly to training. Overwork, insufficient amounts of poor food, and a shortage of water were the chief culprits, all serving to reduce the men's resistance to infection. All of those who died—five Australians and two New Zealanders—were infantrymen. When the weather permitted, their days were spent practicing amphibious landings and

"Death on the Eve of Battle"

route marching up and down steep hills. When it rained, the men were confined to their cramped and stuffy transports, where sanitation was poor. The Australians in the Ninth Battalion had the benefit of fresh air, but nighttime temperatures at Lemnos are cold in early spring. Three of the seven men who died belonged to that unit.

Still, the vast majority of those training at Lemnos were in good physical condition; they were just hungry, bored, and eager to get moving. By the time they left for Gallipoli on April 23, everyone knew his destination. What so many of them did not know, and would never live to know, was exactly what they were supposed to do once they arrived.

The Turks used their time wisely and creatively. Under the guidance of their German advisors, the infantrymen were drilled in marching, which built their stamina and taught individuals to act as part of a group. They also practiced their marksmanship. At night, when they could not be seen by marauding British and French warships, they dug trenches and laid wire, lots of wire. Their stocks of engineering supplies such as barbed wire were so low that they supplemented what they had with rusty wire taken from the fences of deserted farms around Sedd-el-Bahr. The farmers did not need it because all civilians and livestock had been evacuated. The Turks laid it under the waterline where they expected landings to take place—W and V Beaches. The British had shown their hand with the March landings and by the attention they paid to those areas with their ships' guns. Because those beaches were at the tip of the peninsula, the point of entry to the Dardanelles, they were obvious targets for an invasion. The Turks knew that as well as the British did, and they would be ready.

4

"My God It's All Horrible"

The Landings of April 25, 1915—Anzac

The weather would be the clearest in days, crystal clear. If only the planning and intelligence regarding the Turks had been so good. As it was, there would be major confusion about the landing at Z Beach (Anzac), where the Australian and New Zealand troops came ashore. The assaulting troops thought they would be landed a mile south of the spot at which they ultimately were. But evidence suggests that a single Royal Navy midshipman commanding one of the twelve tows made a conscious decision to deviate from his course. He did so in order to avoid heavy Turkish fire from Gaba Tepe, and the other eleven tows moved with him. After the war Australians and New Zealanders came to believe that unexpectedly strong currents—which did not occur that morning— had caused the sailors to land the tows in the wrong place, ultimately resulting in many unnecessary deaths. In fact, it was later discovered that Gaba Tepe was heavily defended by machine guns and artillery. Lt. Gen. Sir William Birdwood, commanding officer of the Australian and New Zealand Army Corps, thought the "mistake" was fortuitous. If the Australians had been put ashore at their original landing place, they would likely have been pushed back into the sea. Capt. Dixon Hearder, machine gun officer of the Eleventh Battalion, Australian Imperial Force (AIF), put it this way: "Later we examined through glasses the place we should have landed at if the Navy had not made a most fortunate mistake. It was a mass of barbed wire entanglements, even under the water. So although our plans were a good deal upset by the spectacle of a huge cliff instead of a gradual rise, the saving in men must have been considerable; in fact it is quite possible we would have been cut to pieces on landing."[1]

Despite the lack of enemy intelligence, Hamilton, Birdwood, and their staffs knew one thing for sure: there would be a lot of Turks. On April 25, 1915, the Mediterranean Expeditionary Force mustered a mere sixty thousand men, not all of them combat troops (twenty thousand French troops would join them later) against thirty-four thousand Turks on the peninsula and an estimated thirty thousand in reserve nearby. The invaders were too few in number to achieve success. Military doctrine at the time recommended a ratio of attacker to defender of three to one. Nevertheless, the invasion would occur. The Turks, after all, were badly trained and fought without enthusiasm. Surely they would retreat or surrender. Surely they did not.

The artillery was woefully inadequate. Due to continuing shortages of guns and shells on the western front, where the war raged most fiercely, Gallipoli got the tail end of what was available. That would not be nearly enough. On paper the numbers were pathetic: only 118 guns out of the 300 that the three divisions should have had, and that included the Forty-Second (East Lancashire) Division, which would not land until May. In addition, the few shells allotted to the British and Dominion artillery—mostly shrapnel—were meant for killing men, not destroying the wire, trenches, or fortifications that protected them. Shrapnel is virtually useless unless fired at infantry attacking over open ground.

When Hamilton was touring possible invasion beaches on March 18, he realized that the task before him would not be easy. He could not see all of the Turkish defenses through his binoculars, but he could see enough of them. The aerial observers had seen far more than he could. Turkish trenches were in evidence at all of the prospective landing places, and the morning sun glinted off the barbed wire that could entangle a soldier until a bullet ended his life. He could not see the machine guns or artillery, but he knew they were there.

The landings would not surprise the Turks. Hamilton and de Robeck knew that. Had a landing taken place when the navy first began its assault, the British might have been able to overrun the stunned defenders. But not now. Now the Turks were simply waiting, and they knew they did not have long to wait. Their spies told them that. The actions of the Royal Navy told them that. And one of their reconnaissance airplanes, which flew daily over the troops marshaling and practicing amphibious landings at Lemnos, told them that. The British could not even defend themselves against that tiny menace. The only aircraft available, heavy seaplanes of the Royal Naval Air Service, could not fly high enough to engage the marauding Turkish craft.

Hamilton and de Robeck knew that the only hope of overcoming the defenders was to land before dawn, when most of the Turks would be asleep and those on sentry duty would not be able to see an approaching invasion force. They knew that it would be nearly impossible to surprise the defenders, but they were going to try.

Helles, at the tip of the Gallipoli Peninsula, was chosen because it was imperative that the British troops move inland and along the coast, toward the Narrows Forts. They could then eliminate the defenses along the European side of the Dardanelles Straits as they went. The ground there is generally flatter—though it is broken by a number of gullies—than it is in the Anzac sector. But Helles was well defended. The Turks knew that they had to take every precaution possible because of its strategic value. They did, and Hamilton knew this. He also knew that if his troops were going to eliminate the peninsula's defenses, he had to put men ashore there.

Hamilton also chose the area just north of Gaba Tepe, about twelve miles north of Helles. He and his staff hoped the Australians and New Zealanders detailed to land there would be able to move inland quickly. They were to take the lower crests and southern spurs of Hill 971 and, most important, Mal Tepe. This hill, located southeast of Hill 971, is roughly a mile and a half northwest of the

"My God It's All Horrible"

town of Maidos. The town was a major marshaling area for Turkish troops and had a small harbor at which they could land men and munitions. The only road from Maidos south to the Helles sector ran along the bottom of the hill. Cutting the road off was thus a priority for the Anzacs. By taking and blocking this route, they not only could prevent Turkish reinforcements from moving south to Helles; they could also prevent those troops already there from retreating to fight another day.

The gentle calm that ushered in April 25, 1915, proved a marked contrast to the hell that would be unleashed on the Anzacs that morning. Despite poor weather conditions the previous few days, that Sunday dawned calm and warm. The sea was like a sheet of glass, and the currents were light. Three battalions of the AIF's Third Brigade formed the Anzac covering force that fateful morning: the Ninth, Tenth, and Eleventh Battalions. They had been conveyed in transports from Lemnos to a rendezvous point off the island of Imbros. There the men were transferred to the battleships and destroyers that would move them closer to shore. The first wave traveled aboard three battleships: half the Ninth Battalion in the *Queen*, half the Tenth in the *Prince of Wales*, and half the Eleventh in the *London*. The other halves of the three battalions, constituting the second wave, were carried in destroyers that followed. They would land as soon after the first wave as possible, their rowboats pulled to shore by the steamboats that had towed the first wave. Rifles were not to be loaded, and only bayonets were to be used. In an effort to maintain the element of surprise for as long as possible and also not give away their positions with muzzle flashes, rifles were not to be fired until after daylight. Then the main body would follow. After the battleships had disgorged their human cargoes into boats and released them two and a half miles out to sea, the destroyers carrying the second wave would move through them and release their boats one hundred yards from shore. The men of the first wave were to drop their packs, form up on the beach, then move forward as quickly as possible, followed by the second. The main body was to begin landing an hour after the first wave, and the entire First Australian Division was to be ashore by nine o'clock. Then the men of the New Zealand and Australian Division could begin landing. When the two brigades forming the main body landed, they were to move through the covering force and on to Mal Tepe and Hill 971. They never would.

At six o'clock on the evening of the twenty-fourth, the men transferring to the destroyers were told to get as much rest as possible over the next five hours. At eleven they were awoken and moved to the battleships. Below in the destroyers, two British sailors served them cocoa.

The men of the first wave were awoken at midnight and were also served cocoa. An hour later the battleships stopped, the moon high above them, and waited for it to drop. Until it did, they risked being seen by Turkish sentries if they moved any closer. Yet they were far enough out to sea that they could safely begin loading the twelve tows—two on either side of each battleship—that would carry the wave to shore. Each of the three rowboats that made up a tow carried four sailors to help with the rowing and a coxswain to steer with the tiller (once the steamboats released them near shore). The steamboats were each commanded by a midshipman. These men—boys—had been in their first year of classes at the Royal Naval College in Dartmouth when war broke out and were pulled out of school to serve on active warships. Most were only fifteen or sixteen years old. British war correspondent Ellis Ashmead-Bartlett, who accompanied the Anzacs, described them as "lieutenants in khaki, midshipmen not yet out of their teens, in old white duck suits dyed khaki, and carrying revolvers and water bottles almost as big as themselves."[2]

The single exception was Midshipman John Metcalf of the battleship HMS *Triumph*, who was nineteen years old. He had joined the Merchant Navy in 1910 and was appointed midshipman in the Royal Naval Reserve on July 1, 1914. The lead tow, which was on the extreme right of the group, was commanded by Lt. Victor Making of the *Queen*. He commanded the steamboat leading Tow 1, and Metcalf commanded the tow to his immediate left, Tow 2.[3] The last tow, 12, was commanded by Cdr. Charles Dix, who was in overall command of the group. During the run-in to shore, the tows were supposed to maintain a distance of 150 yards between one another, for a total distance of 1,650 yards from one end of the force to the other.

As the Australians formed up on deck in the predawn darkness, they were given a tot of rum. They then moved silently down the rope ladders into the waiting rowboats, each ten meters long and able to seat thirty-six men. It was a miracle that nobody was hurt because the soldiers were each carrying eighty pounds of equipment and were extremely excited. By 2:35 a.m. the boats were packed with their human cargoes. When the moon descended at three o'clock, the battleships moved forward, and a half-hour later they stopped and released the boats. The invaders assumed that they would catch the enemy off guard. What they did not realize was that an hour earlier, before the moon disappeared, Turkish sentries had spotted the armada.

No one in the boats spoke during the hour-long journey. Each sat alone with his thoughts, wondering if he would be one of the unlucky ones. They sat shivering, unable to move because they were packed in so tightly, their teeth chattering in the early-morning cold. They had been ordered to roll up their sleeves so the light skin of their arms would make them more visible in the predawn darkness. The planners also hoped that doing so would differentiate friend from foe.

The morning was dark, too dark. That boded well for a surprise landing, but it did not help the midshipmen maintain the required distance between boats. In an age without radar or global positioning systems, the boys had to rely on their eyes. All they could see, however, were the gray wakes created by the steamboats moving next to them. In order to see them, they had to be closer to one another than 150 yards. In fact, visibility only extended to 50 yards, which was the distance they were ultimately able to maintain. The darkness caused another problem. Because the midshipmen had no way of knowing where they were in relation to the other tows, some of those carrying the Ninth and Tenth Battalions moved out of order and in between each other. The two battalions became inextricably mixed.

The plan dictated that the troops would be landed in a specific order—the Ninth Battalion on the right (south), about one mile north of Gaba Tepe; then the Tenth in the center, "four cables (800 yards) north" of the Ninth; and the Eleventh on the left, four cables north of the Tenth. They were to land between Ari Burnu and the beach north of Gaba Tepe. The battalions were to advance on a front as wide as possible and as far inland as the so-called Third Ridge. The Eleventh Battalion would advance northward as far as Battleship Hill, and the Ninth and Tenth would occupy the smaller hills and knolls to the south. The Twelfth Battalion, also part of the Third Brigade, would be held in reserve but would land with the second wave. The main body would then land and advance through the line established by the two waves of the covering force, to the area around Mal Tepe.

The land behind the beach in the intended landing area has a gentle slope. The planners assumed that the men would scramble off the beach and move swiftly inland. Metcalf, however, in the second tow from the right, was rightly afraid that the Turks at Gaba Tepe would rake his boats with machine gun fire. He thus made the decision to deviate from his course and move two points to port (north, or to his left). The tows on his left saw him moving closer, and they shifted their course accordingly. Lieutenant Making in Tow 1 (on Metcalf's right) followed. Dix tried unsuccessfully to get the other boats to correct their courses and had to steer to port in order to move away from the tows approaching on his right. He was a qualified signaling officer, but that morning the only communication device at his disposal was his voice. The midshipmen did not hear him.

Just before four thirty, as dawn started to break, the men in the boats could make out Gallipoli's silhouette against the brightening sky. At about that time there was a fatal occurrence. Each of the steamboats had a funnel that carried its engine's exhaust skyward. The sailors had been told to ensure that no sparks escaped, but in reality there was nothing they could do to prevent that from happening. As the tows were nearing shore the funnel of a boat on the left shot sparks three feet into the air, for nearly a half-minute. A Turkish sentry saw this lightshow and fired a signal flare. The

"My God It's All Horrible"

Australians were spotted and began to feel bullets whip past. The alert Turks, who had lost sight of the battleships when the moon went down, saw the boats approaching and were ready for them.

Metcalf's tow was leading the way. As his steamboat approached the shallows, he gave the order to release the hawser connecting his boat to the rowboats. He then turned to port and headed to the destroyers carrying the second wave. The men in his boats were lucky. They hit the beach just before the Turks opened fire, and a few of them were able to get out and drop their packs before the bullets started to fly. But not everyone. One of the unfortunate ones was Pvt. Edgar Spilsbury of the Ninth Battalion. More than a year later his friend Pvt. Robert Macpherson told a representative of the British Red Cross from his hospital bed in France: "He was killed at the landing on April 25th at Anzac Cove—shot in head and chest. I did not actually see him killed but I saw his body next day. He was buried along with many others in the first cemetery we made at a place called 'Indian Gully.'"

Each of the steamboats was armed with a Maxim machine gun. As he turned, Metcalf wanted to open fire on the Turks he saw silhouetted against the rising sun. He could not. Orders stated that Tow 3 had to fire first. When it did, all hell broke loose. Some of the defenders fell, but men in the boats were also being hit. Some were killed in the boats. Others drowned. "The larger 'launches' and 'pinnaces' grounded in deeper water, whereupon the men tumbled over the bows or the sides, often falling on the slippery stones, so that it was hard to say who was hit and who was not. Most were up to their thighs in water; some, who dropped off near the stern of the larger boats, were immersed to their chests. Others, barely noticed in the rush, slipped into water too deep for them. The heavy kit which a man carried would sink him like a stone. Some were grabbed by a comrade who happened to observe them; one was hung up by his kit on a rowlock until someone noticed him; a few were almost certainly drowned."[4]

Shortly after Metcalf's boats landed, those carrying the Tenth Battalion and the rest of the Ninth came ashore. The Eleventh Battalion landed last, under fire from Turks to the north, and its men appear to have suffered the worst while still in their boats: "In the tows of the 11th Battalion, which were to the north of the point and had still 200 yards of water to cross before they touched the beach, bullet after bullet was splintering the boats and thudding into their crowded freight. Every now and then a man slid to the bottom of the boat with a sharp moan or low gurgling cry."[5]

The officers realized at once that they were in the wrong place. The Eleventh Battalion landed two to three hundred yards north of Ari Burnu. The Ninth and Tenth landed on the tip and south of the promontory. All were supposed to have landed to its south.

As soon as the boats grounded, some men removed the wounded and laid them in the sand about ten yards inland, under cover of the bank. Others immediately sought shelter behind the bank. There they removed their packs and checked their rifles. Their instructions stated that they should form up after dropping their packs, then move off across the gently sloping ground toward their objectives in battalion order. But there was no gently sloping ground, the beach was far too narrow, and the Turks were taking a mighty toll. A handful of men—probably scouts of the Tenth or Eleventh Battalions—suddenly rose up and climbed the sides of Ari Burnu. The southern face of Ari Burnu was so steep that men had to grasp the roots of the gorse plants that dot the promontory for support. Although the north side where the Eleventh landed was not so steep, they were being harassed by a Turkish machine gun five hundred yards to the north. Not everyone got off the beaches.

Many men, despite orders *not* to load or fire their rifles before daylight, did so anyway. Some shot at the Turks on the plateau above. Capt. Graham Butler, the Ninth Battalion's medical officer, ordered the men to cease fire, but it was too late. In their excitement they hit one of their own men, Sgt. Herbert Fowles of A Company: "He was accidentally shot in the back by one of his own men. His last words were: 'It is hard luck being hit by one of our own men.' There was no suspicion of any foul play."[6]

The Australians found themselves confronted by steep, scrub-covered hills. Ari Burnu is the knoll of a plateau that the Anzacs

"My God It's All Horrible"

named "Plugge's (pronounced *Plug-ee's*) Plateau," after the commander of the New Zealanders' Auckland Battalion (the Turkish name was Khain Tepe, or "Cruel Hill"). When it was captured later that morning, he established his headquarters there. Undaunted by the treacherous terrain, the Australians scrambled up, eager to get at the Turks who were firing down on them. The defenders were few—about five hundred infantry soldiers and an artillery battery behind them. The Turks had not expected a landing there, yet there were enough of them to prevent the Australians from forming up and moving in an orderly fashion.

Men found it difficult to move as they reached the plateau. The thick, knee-high scrub that dots the peninsula has rigid, sharp, holly-like thorns. It not only slowed the men down; it also tore their clothing and the wool puttees that they wrapped around their calves for support. The Turks' khaki uniforms blended perfectly with the landscape, and their ammunition, unlike that of the Australians, contained smokeless powder. They were virtually invisible as they lay hidden by the vegetation.

A few Australians were hit as they reached the plateau. Capt. Dick Annear of the Eleventh Battalion was the first Australian officer to die. Capt. Raymond Leane was beside Annear when he was killed: "I seem to have a charmed life. In the landing, Dick Annear and Lieutenant MacDonald with myself, all officers of my company, were storming the heights together. Three Turks jumped up and fired at us, not 20 yards off. Dick was killed, got two of the bullets. MacDonald was wounded. I was missed. Bullets hit the ground all around me, yet none touched me."[7]

Close to Annear was Pvt. Thomas Batt: "Within a few minutes, as other men reached the plateau, the Turkish fire from its farther side began to slacken. A little to the left of Leane two of the enemy jumped up from the trench and fired down at the approaching men. Batt—batman to Lieutenant Morgan of the 11th—fell wounded."[8] Batt survived and was evacuated to one of the ships waiting to transport the wounded to Egypt. Like so many others who were wounded that day, he died at sea. He was buried without ceremony, his body simply dumped overboard.

By the time the first wave was fighting its way off the beach, the second was on its way. The men landed in daylight, and the boats were able to maintain their required distance and order. But unlike the first wave, the Turks could clearly see the second coming, and they watched the destroyers approach with the tows by their sides. Even before they climbed into their boats, the Turks were firing on unsuspecting invaders. One of their victims was recorded by Captain Hearder, commanding officer of the Eleventh Battalion's machine gun section: "One man only had been hit up to date, when a thing happened which made me feel pretty rotten all over. I noticed a boy standing more or less appalled at the din, so I walked up to him and said 'Come on, lad, no one is being hit.' He pulled himself together and went on in front of me to the stern of the *Destroyer*, where there was [a] boatroom. I followed right behind for about 30 feet. In this position the bullets were coming from behind us and the *Destroyer* was bows on to the shore. I stepped aside to pass him when I saw he was all right and just as I did so and got level with him he just said 'Oh!' and pitched forward on the deck. I did feel bad about it."[9] Unfortunately, the name of the fallen Australian has been lost to history.

Many men of the second wave were wounded and killed in their boats. Sgt. Robert Hamilton of C Company, Ninth Battalion, recalled an incident for the British Red Cross Society: "Scott and informant were in the same boat at the Anzac landing. Informant was seated just behind Scott. The boat was a small one of the rowing type. Scott was shot dead in the boat, about 50 yards from the shore. Two other men were shot also. The three bodies were left in the boat when the remaining men leapt ashore. Informant thinks the boat drifted down the shore as the current ran in that direction and a number of discarded boats were carried away."

The second wave's boats began grounding at 4:40 a.m. By that time the beaches were being raked by Turkish fire. Still, the men advanced off the strand with some cohesion and managed to overtake their comrades in the first wave. At about five o'clock the

"My God It's All Horrible"

companies forming the first wave of the Ninth and Tenth Battalions formed up and moved toward their original objective, Third Ridge, to the southeast of Plugge's. The Turks backed off as the Australians advanced. As they did so, they lay down in the scrub and fired at their pursuers. The attackers chased them individually and in small groups, but many advanced too far and were never seen again. Pvt. William Walsh of the Ninth was one of them. His case illustrates the Turkish penchant for collecting the aluminum identity discs worn by British and Dominion troops: "Walsh was in the charge up from the beach with informant on the day of the landing. He was missing at the first roll-call. About a week later a Turkish prisoner was captured and Walsh's disc was found on him. Informant saw Major Salisbury (O/C [officer in command] A Co) in regard to Walsh. Major Salisbury informed informant that the Turks took no prisoners on the day of the landing. Informant concluded Walsh was dead. He was a fine, big fellow, about 41 years of age. His wife does nursing work in Brisbane."[10]

Referred to as "dead meat tickets" by some Australians, identity discs were the only reliable means of identification that would survive both fire and water. The soldiers were supposed to write their names in indelible ink on the cloth tags sewn on the inside skirts of their tunics, but the garments were not always worn, especially in hot weather. Paybooks were carried but were often left in a man's tunic pocket or haversack. Only one disc was issued per man, and when it was gone, a man's identity could often not be determined. Thus, many of the men who died at Gallipoli were never identified because their tags had been taken as souvenirs by the enemy or were lost. In some cases the tag, along with a man's clothing, was blown away by a shell's concussion. At least one such soldier died in hospital in Alexandria, Egypt, and he never was identified.

The first wave companies of the Ninth and Tenth Battalions eliminated the Turkish resistance on Plugge's. They moved forward but not in unison with the second wave, as planned. The Eleventh Battalion on the left was for the most part unable to advance. The Turks, who were several hundred yards away, were firing at them from the northwest. They were preventing the unit from reaching Battleship Hill. When the commanding officer of the Third Brigade, Col. Ewen Sinclair-Maclagan, DSO, landed at five o'clock that morning, he found his troops in total disarray.

The main body should have begun landing at five thirty, an hour after the first wave. The steamboats that should have returned to tow the boats to shore, however, did not follow the plan. Some of their crews, eager to have a go at the Turks, picked up the rifles of the casualties and charged into the fray. Some boats, against orders, conveyed wounded men back to the ships. In either case they were late.

As the minutes ticked by, more Australians were hit while waiting on the destroyers that conveyed them from their transports close in to shore. Turkish guns at Gaba Tepe fired at them from the southwest, and machine guns located at Fisherman's Hut—a small stone structure—hit them from the northwest. Before long the destroyers' decks were awash in blood, their funnels holed by bullets.

The transport *Galeka* carried the Sixth and Seventh Battalions. Its captain, Bernard Burt, was in no mood to see the carnage on his vessel continue. With the infantrymen drawn up on the main deck, ready to climb into the boats that had not yet arrived, he had two courses of action open to him. He could move his ship out of range of the Turkish guns, or he could stay and land the troops with his lifeboats. He chose to land his troops.

The men of the Second Brigade, to which the two battalions belonged, had orders to land to the left of the Third. They assumed that the sailors manning the steamboats would deliver them to the correct spot. But because they did not arrive at the appointed time and casualties on the *Galeka* were mounting, Lt. Col. Harold "Pompey" Elliott, commanding officer of the Seventh Battalion, decided that his troops had to make a start. He chose three platoons of B Company and ordered them to steer their boats to the left of the Third Brigade. At five o'clock the 140-man force, under the command of Maj. Alfred Jackson and Capt. Herbert Layh, climbed into four boats and began rowing the six hundred yards to shore. They did not know, however, that the Third Brigade had landed

"My God It's All Horrible"

in the wrong place. They steered their craft toward the left of the muzzle flashes coming from shore and to the left of the Red Cross flag marking the location of the Third Field Ambulance (which had landed with the second wave). They were sailing straight into hell.

Moving silently but for the splashing of their oars, the men rowed to shore. Their battalion's orders stated that they were to cover the Anzac flank to the south of Fisherman's Hut, and they were not too far off the course that would have taken them there. But that would have been to the right of the spot for which they were steering. Because the Third Brigade was fighting in the Second Brigade's appointed spot, the men of the Eleventh aimed instead for the hut—and the machine guns that were emplaced around it:

> Approaching the shore, the men in the boats caught the sound of rifle firing. Away on their right were other boats, bringing troops of their battalion to land, and over these they could see shrapnel bursting. Jackson's own boats were not advancing into shrapnel but into rifle fire. They saw it cutting up the water ahead. There appeared to be two machine-guns and many rifles at work. After what seemed an endless time in approaching it, they gradually rowed into the field of fire. In the boat with Captain Layh were Lieutenant Heighway and part of his platoon. Five out of six of their rowers were shot, but others took the oars, and the boat did not stop. Layh was in the bows trying to cheer the men, Heighway at the tiller. The boat was scraping on the shingle when Heighway slid forward, wounded. The boat grounded, and Layh threw himself into the water beside it, he was shot through the hip. He turned to see if the men had landed, and was again shot through the leg. With the survivors he scrambled towards the little grass-tufted sand hummocks which here fringed the beach, and lay low behind them . . .

Of the 140 souls in the boats, there were left Major Jackson, Captain Layh, Lieutenant Scanlan, and about thirty-five unhurt or lightly-wounded men. The rest lay in the boats or on the beach dead, dying or grievously wounded.[11]

This small group of men suffered the largest number of casualties of any battalion that morning. Among them was twenty-year-old Pvt. Archibald Alexander, a tobacco stripper from Carlton, Victoria. He is officially recorded as having been killed on April 26, but a report by Cpl. Joseph Carlile of the Seventh Battalion indicates otherwise: "Casualty, together with 50 other men of the company, got into a boat from the transport 'Galeka.' They proceeded to row towards the shore and when within 20 yards of the shore most of the crew were wounded, including casualty. Informant actually saw casualty shot and the boat sink 10 yards from shore. There were several saved, but casualty was not pulled out of the water, and he undoubtedly drowned."[12]

These boats developed an infamous reputation. The following day stretcher-bearers tried to recover the casualties, but several were hit by fire from Fisherman's Hut. For days afterward, efforts to bring them in met with the same result. Some of the dead lay tangled in the boats, some on the beach where they had been shot as they tried to escape to safety. For days the boats moved about in the surf with their motionless cargo. Eventually, the dead were brought in but not without further losses: "There are about twenty dead men lying on the beach near the boats, where they were shot. We thought there were some wounded men still in the boats, so two Australian stretcher-bearers went along to investigate. They were immediately fired on by snipers, and both were wounded. Two New Zealand stretcher-bearers went out to their rescue, and one of these was shot. More volunteers eventually went out, and eventually all were brought in under heavy fire."[13]

The remaining soldiers of the Second Brigade, along with those of the First, landed in their proper order. But instead of moving to the left of the Third Brigade as their orders stated, they were sent to the right, where somebody realized that there were no Australians. The Turks continued to retire, and the attackers charged after them. The Turks stopped at Third Ridge, later called "Gun Ridge." The Australians who made it that far would never advance beyond it. They ended up withdrawing under fire to Second Ridge, where they established three posts only a few yards from the Turks'

"My God It's All Horrible"

front line. These three positions, called (from left to right, or north to south) "Quinn's Post," "Courtney's Post," and "Steele's Post," formed the Anzac front line. They were surrounded by Turks on three sides. Located less than a thousand yards inland, the front formed by these positions had no reserve line behind it and had to be held at all costs. If they fell, Anzac would fall. They never did.

By the time most of the main body landed, the battle had shifted inland. The Turks were still firing on the boats but were mainly concentrating on the Australians who had fought their way inland. By then the strand was clogged with casualties, fresh troops, and supplies. It was too narrow and crowded for the arriving troops to organize themselves so they could move off in search of their objectives as cohesive units. Instead, the arriving battalions were split up as soon as they arrived, and groups were dispatched almost immediately to wherever they were needed. Confusion reigned, and many men, sent ahead to support a group here or fill a gap there, simply disappeared. Turkish reinforcements arrived throughout the day and launched several counterattacks, some of them successful. The Anzacs were so hard-pressed that Birdwood thought he might have to evacuate his troops. He and his staff were so fearful that they would be pushed back into the sea that he allowed only one artillery piece to land. But Adm. Cecil Thursby, commander of the British fleet, said no. He argued that nobody knew where most of the troops were and that it would take two days to gather them all. And there was a another problem: the transports, which had been ordered to remain off Anzac for forty-eight hours in the event that an evacuation was warranted, were jam-packed with the hundreds of wounded that Hamilton's staff had vastly underestimated. No, an evacuation could not take place. Hamilton concurred. The Anzacs must hold, and hold they did.

When the Australians and, later in the morning, the New Zealanders moved up to Plugge's Plateau, they quickly cleared the Turks. They then advanced to the gullies and ridges beyond it. That is where their trouble began, in places with names like Shrapnel Gully, the Nek, Baby 700, Walker's Ridge, and 400 Plateau. The Turks put up relatively little resistance as they retreated from Plugge's, but nature was a difficult enemy. After days of rain leading up to April 25, the gullies that crisscross the peninsula were sheets of mud, and the steep sides of the numerous ravines were covered in scrub that stood higher than the soldiers trying to move through it. The thorns of the scrub—arbutus, ilex, and wild rose—are needle sharp. In order to climb out of the gullies, the men, none of whom wore gloves, had to grab the piercing foliage so they could pull their way up. Hands and clothing were torn, and men were lost to one another. Units became fragmented, and men found themselves alone. If they were lucky, they were within sight of a comrade or two on either side. As the day wore on, the heat became almost unbearable. Men who began the day soaked to the skin and covered in sand now found themselves bathed in sweat that made cuts and scratches burn like fire. And they could not move. To do so would mean certain death.

Before the landings, the Turks had placed range markers and cleared fire lanes so they could shoot accurately at the invaders. If an Anzac fired his weapon, the Turks responded with a fury. Some risked being detected and lived to fight another day. Many were not so lucky:

> The air was torn by a hail of bullets. The bushes around flicked and shed small branches and punctured leaves. The bushes in front bent before the blast of our rifles, others striking in front deluged us with hard-driven pebbles. The flail of doom hung over us. It became useless and fatal to try to shoot. We lay flat against the sunbaked earth. But strangely, for a little time, no one was hit. A sharp smacking noise came from the left. I looked cautiously down the line. "Lizzie" Crowther gleefully showed me his cap. A black round hole showed the back of it. "Not born to be shot," he said. A rash statement to make in the face of fate . . .
>
> Darky Stewart [Pvt. Gordon Stewart] called from the right. "My rifle's done in corp, sling me that bloke's." "Blood from backsight to butt-plate," I said, and was greatly relieved when he said "Never mind, then." From Lieut. Byrne came the message, "Strip the dead and wounded for ammunition." Shuddering afresh, I

"My God It's All Horrible"

did so on my side. Alf. doing the same on the other. Alec Gilpin fell in the last advance. We did not hear Byrne's voice again. All later orders came from Charlie Hunt. There came the smack of another bullet on the left, followed by no outcry. Cautiously, I lifted my head and looked past the dead reinforcement. Good old Alf. Crowther was gone West. "Darkie," I called. "Alf. got his issue." He cursed furiously and started firing. A bullet smacked and his firing stopped. On either side of me were the dead, four or five aside. But I knew the worst was yet to be.[14]

Pvt. Alfred Crowther was listed as missing, and his bones lay there still, hidden somewhere in the scrub.

Lt. Albert Byrne of the Tenth Battalion was mortally wounded:

About 4 p.m. there was a slight lull in the firing. Then I heard a pitiful cry of "Water! water!" I asked the Captain who was next to me at the time, "Who is it?" He said, "Lieut. Byrne" (my platoon commander); "will you go and give him a drink?" He was lying out in the open, so I had to crawl to him. I reached him in safety, and quenched his thirst. There was a clump of bushes on the left of us, about twenty yards away, and if we could reach it we might be there in comparative safety. As he was shot in both legs and in the left side, I had no alternative but to carry him. I raised him as gently as I could and got under him, then staggered to my feet, and had gone half-way then "thud," and down I went on top of my unfortunate officer. I felt a stinging in my thigh, and it was not until I endeavoured to get up and have another try that I realized I had got a bullet and could not use my leg. After lying still for a few minutes (during which the Lieutenant gave another cry, indicating that he had received another bullet) I decided that to stay there was certain death, and started to crawl to the bushes, as I could do no more for Byrne.[15]

Byrne died on the beach the next day while waiting to be evacuated. Shortly before the beloved officer was wounded, one of his men, Pvt. Albert McConnachy, wrote:

Tough men of Broken Hill were in our lot. Big Bill Montgomery, Darky Stewart, Alf Crowther, and Chris Christopherson. Little Lieut. Byrne was striding up and down, as proud as punch. The sun was warm, the sky was blue, and there was no sound of war, but larks were singing. Everyone was now digging except Peter McConnachy, swarthy and contented, who still sat smoking. "Dig in, Peter," I urged, "they'll counter attack."

"Dig in be—," he said. "I'll finish my fag first."

He didn't finish his fag. He died in the roaring blast that suddenly swept across the valley to us.

Peter (the name given to Bert by his tent mates) was first shot through the head and would not fall back—possibly he would have been alright had he done so. The lad was too game, stayed on and got another hit, this time in the stomach below the heart and lungs.

I crawled over to try to talk to Lieut. Byrne when Peter heard and recognized my voice and called out "Is that you Tom?" I answered "Yes Peter. What can I do for you?" "Where are the Stretcher bearers?" he said. I said they will be here in a few minutes—this I said to comfort him (he was dying) well knowing at the time that they (the Stretcher bearers) could not get up to us for hours.

A little later on I crept back to them again. Lieut. Byrne was still suffering terribly and did not die until some time next day. Peter was dead. He could not have lived long. I took his small Khaki handkerchief from his tunic pocket, wiped the blood off his face, had a last look at a good game pal, then covered the face up with the handkerchief and with a heavy heart crawled back to the lines again.

The four New Zealand infantry battalions—Auckland, Canterbury, Otago, and Wellington—that landed later in the day were sent off the beach as soon as they arrived, to whatever part of the line required them. The battalions were quickly split into small groups and did not fight as cohesive units for almost a week. They, too, suffered

"My God It's All Horrible"

in the dense scrub. Pvt. W. H. Rhodes, of the Auckland Battalion, wrote in a letter: "The first day, Sunday, was awful. I cannot describe it to you . . . Our major is wounded, our captain shot through the lungs, and Lieutenants Allen (killed) and Baddeley (missing). The last named is supposed to be wounded in the bush somewhere."[16]

Englishman 2nd Lt. Harold Allen and Lt. Herman Baddeley were members of the Sixteenth (Waikato) Company of the Auckland Battalion. Both were in their early twenties when they were killed in the fighting on the hill known as Baby 700 (it was about seven hundred feet high and was nearer to the beach than Big 700, or Battleship Hill, which was about the same height). The battalion was sent there to support the Eleventh and Twelfth Battalions, parties of which were driven off with the New Zealanders before the end of the day. The hill remained in Turkish hands, and Baddeley's body was never found. Allen's was recovered during the armistice of May 24, when the Turks buried him and several other Anzacs killed and left behind on April 25.

April 25 would come to be called "Anzac Day" in Australia and New Zealand. It would remain a day of horror in the minds of those fated to survive it.

Reporting the First Casualties

The confusion that marked April 25 proved troublesome when it came to determining just who had been killed that day. Many men were listed as "missing." In some cases battalions could not make a roll call until May 2. Often nobody was sure who was killed when or where. In such cases the Australians and New Zealanders would, as a rule, note a man's death as "April 25–28" or "April 25–May 2." In several cases the date of the roll call was recorded as the date of death. This was the case with Pvt. George Larter. He was listed as missing and his death officially recorded as May 2, 1915, the date on which his the Eleventh Battalion was first able to assess its losses. He had actually died of wounds on April 26.

Casualty lists were compiled and telegraphed back to the Third Echelon Headquarters in Cairo. From there clerks telegraphed the information back to Australia, England, or New Zealand, and telegrams were sent to the next of kin. This procedure did not happen right away. It would be weeks in the cases of officers—sometimes months in the cases of other ranks—before names could be sent. The people at home, who had been reading about the invasion and casualties for some time, were naturally concerned about their men. The newspapers carried official explanations for the delay in reporting the names, sanitizing them to protect the sensitivities of the public. It was not explained, for example, that so many men could be unaccounted for or that the forces had been caught completely off guard by the heavy losses. It was simply stated that lists would be published soon and families would be notified as quickly as possible.

The word *missing* was horrifying. It was worse for those who received word that their father, son, or husband was "wounded and missing." In an age without rapid communication, they could only wait and hope. In some cases they learned that a man had turned up in hospital or returned safely to his unit. Perhaps he was a prisoner. For others there was nothing. Some men would not be officially listed as killed until mid-1916, when courts of inquiry held in Egypt and France met to settle outstanding cases. If a man was not reported to be a prisoner of war in Turkey, he was officially listed as having been killed. Sometimes word was received from a mate, writing either to a casualty's family or to his own: "I suppose you will have heard about poor Wilfred Dove. Poor chap. He was killed the same day that we landed. He did not last long after he was shot. If you see any of his family, especially his mother, you can tell them for me that he did not suffer much pain."[17] Pvt. Wilfred Dove of the Second (South Canterbury) Company was officially listed as having gone missing between April 25 and May 1, 1915. He was in fact killed on April 25.

When a man was listed as missing, his next of kin could initiate an inquiry through the British Red Cross Society. Volunteers from that organization visited hospitals in Egypt and elsewhere, questioning the patients. The reports were compiled and copies sent to the family. In some cases a number of reports were gathered about

"My God It's All Horrible"

the same man. In others there was nothing. Often reports contradicted one another. Cases of men with the same name serving in the same battalion compounded the problem.

One such report concerns Sgt. Edwin Ault of the Seventh Battalion, AIF. His death was anything but quick and painless, as the stories told to the families commonly suggested: "Informant was with Sgt Ault on the 25th April. At first they were together but during the charge they became separated and, upon making enquiries afterwards, Informant was told that Ault had been shot in the face and that he then picked up an axe and dashed after the Turks with an axe in his hand. That was the last that was seen of him. It is believed that he went mad, and it is assumed that he was killed."[18] Sergeant Ault was married, with three young children. His widow was not notified of his death until June 9.

Published accounts of the Anzac landings almost all describe the Anzacs charging without fear and the wounded lying quietly, often "cheerfully," waiting calmly to be collected. The reality was quite different:

> The day is ever memorable & the person who sits quietly at home imagining the Red Cross doing his work miles behind the firing lines is a sadly mistaken person. Our poor lads left their bodies mingled with the dead & dying on the first line of fire, where our boys suffered mostly in remote parts, hill tops etc. Where wounded mostly lay & had to be gathered from Turks hidden in secluded spots found our stretcher parties easy marks & with shrapnel overhead our work was far from bright. My own personal feelings are still vivid & my first wild rush in company with comrades [illegible] fallen comrades, attending wounded at the double, whilst hail & lead fall almost incessantly will ever remain imprinted on my memory. I was horribly disturbed the first day while undergoing my baptism of fire & was hourly expecting my call, but thank the Heavens it wasn't my turn. Place yourself a young, healthy person, full of life, thrust among carnage & ruin—picture your thoughts—our guns gave me fearful

frights each explosion—Big Lizzie [the battleship *Queen Eliza-beth*] especially, with her 15 inch guns causing a terrific recoil & explosion. I thought, as I sat crouched on a hilltop dodging shrapnel & her shells flying low over our heads. Death's Gully [Shrapnel Gully] was awful on Sunday & we greatly feared land mines above all things. The carnage here was terrific & here our 3rd [Field Ambulance] lost practically a whole section.[19]

It goes without saying that the men who fought in the Great War were brave. Any man who charges into gunfire can be called brave, as can any man who withstands it under cover without running away. But with that bravery on April 25 went a carelessness that resulted in too many deaths. A number of Australians charged after Turks who might have been taken down with a well-aimed shot, and many were never seen again: "One huge bush man hopped into his middle in water & without waiting to fire at the foe made a dash at a fat Turk with his bayonet. The Turk, who looked an easy capture, wheeled and made off over a steep hill towards his comrades. Our big fellow, now thoroughly aroused, went after him but without avail. The ponderous Turk managed to keep a good two inches between himself & the knife notwithstanding the efforts of our boy to string him on the end. The relative positions were kept until they both disappeared out of sight over the crest into the enemies [*sic*] lines."[20]

It is possible that some of these men would not have acted so recklessly if they and their officers had been briefed about their units' goals. Instead, the only instruction most were given was to advance inland as far as possible. The Anzacs who landed with the main body were better organized, and it would seem that fewer of them acted as rashly as some of those in the first and second waves. Still, whether a man charged into the murk of battle and disappeared or whether he was killed fighting a well-coordinated action is immaterial. The end result was the same. Friends and families were left to mourn the loss of men who had died too young, fighting an enemy who wanted to remain neutral, in a place that most had never heard of.

"My God It's All Horrible"

5

"This Place Was Littered with Dead from the Boats"

The Landings of April 25, 1915—Helles

The landings at Helles were planned on a smaller scale than those at Anzac, but their combined objective was no less grand. The ultimate goal was the capture of a six hundred-foot-high hill called Achi Baba, north of the village of Krithia. As at Anzac, a covering force was to secure the ground ahead of the main landing areas, and the main body would advance through it to secure the hill.

The plan called for a covering force consisting of the British army's Eighty-Sixth Brigade to land at the three beaches in the center of the landing area: V on the tip of the peninsula, W along the western edge, and X to the north of that. Two battalions and one company of the Eighty-Seventh Brigade, along with one battalion of Royal Marine Light Infantry (RMLI), were to capture Y (two miles north of X) and S Beaches (northeast of V). The Eighty-Eighth Brigade would then land at V Beach. With the covering force, it would advance north until its flanks linked up with the troops at Y Beach on its left and S Beach on its right. When this was accomplished, the other two battalions of the Eighty-Seventh Brigade would land at X Beach. After linking up with the two battalions from Y and S, they would move through the Eighty-Eighth Brigade to capture Achi Baba. The division's only reserve was two infantry battalions that would land behind the covering force at X. In an effort to fool the Turks into thinking that a landing was also occurring on the other side of the peninsula, part of the Royal Naval Division (RND) would make a diversionary landing there, at a place called Bulair. The French would land at Kum Kale on the Asiatic side, both as a diversion and to keep Turkish troops there from reinforcing their troops on the peninsula. They also wanted to keep the mobile guns and the guns collectively referred to as "Asiatic Annie" from firing into the backs of the British landing at V Beach.

According to the plan, the landings would begin at five in the morning, and the area surrounding the beaches would be secured by eight. By noon the British would arrive at Krithia, and by evening Achi Baba would be theirs. This low hill, with its commanding view of the area, was important because as long as the Turks held it, they would be able to look down on the invaders and guide their artillery onto them.

This plan incorporated some major deficiencies. First, it allowed only for success; no consideration was given to the possibility of a delay at any of the beaches or that any of the landings might fail. Second, the planners did not believe that the Turks could mount a serious, coordinated defense. They did.

Y Beach

The first landing was at Y Beach, along the western edge of the peninsula. It occurred at 4:45 a.m. There was no artillery preparation because the British knew that their only hope of success was to surprise the defenders. Artillery would only alert them. But once ashore, that was precisely their goal. The three main beaches were known to be heavily defended, and the planners felt that if they could draw the Turks away from there, those landings would be successful.

This landing was such a surprise that there was not a single Turk there to oppose it. The reason was simple: Y Beach was hardly a beach at all. It was a thin strip of sand overlooked by a two-hundred-foot-cliff, the top of which could only be reached by scaling the steep sides of the gully that runs through it.

"Littered with Dead"

The troops chosen for the job were the First Battalion, the King's Own Scottish Borderers (KOSB); A Company of the Second Battalion, the South Wales Borderers (SWB); and the Plymouth Battalion. The first two battalions were composed of regular soldiers, many of whom had been in the army for years. The First KOSB was in India on the outbreak of war, and the Second SWB was the only British infantry unit to see combat in China, fighting alongside the Japanese against the Germans at Tsingtao in 1914. Many of the marines had enlisted in 1914 and had only had a few months of training. Initially, the plan called for the Plymouths to lead the assault, but their commanding officer, Lt. Col. Godfrey Matthews, asked that the army spearhead it instead. He pointed out that despite their recent experience in the Dardanelles landings, his men had little combat training and were not as good at handling the landing boats as the soldiers were.

His advice was heeded by Maj. Gen. Aylmer Hunter-Weston, commanding officer of the Twenty-Ninth Division and of the operations in the Helles sector. The KOSB would therefore land first, followed by the marines, and the SWB would land alongside the Scots. The other three companies of the SWB would land at the other end of the invasion area—at S Beach. There were not enough boats for the entire battalion to land at S, which was why the battalion was split. Even though the soldiers were going to land first, Matthews was placed in overall command because the commander of the First KOSB, Lt. Col. Archibald Koe, was ill at the time of the divisional briefing on April 21. This was to prove a crucial mistake because Koe was not told that Matthews was in command, and he landed believing that he was. Also, the instructions given to Matthews were vague, and he did not ask for clarification. He was told to advance inland with his troops and cut off any Turks that were withdrawing from the area; to act as a diversion for Turks so their attention would be drawn away from the three main beaches; to capture a gun that was thought to be in the area; and to make contact with the troops landing at X. Matthews appears not to have asked whether communication with the troops at X was to be accomplished by extending his line of troops to that beach or whether he should communicate with them via heliograph, a signaling device that reflected sunlight off a moveable mirror. He did not ask, and he should have.

The troops departed Lemnos early on the evening of April 24. The First KOSB and A Company of the Second SWB traveled in the transport *Southland*, before transshipping to the cruisers *Amethyst* and *Sapphire*. The Plymouths sailed on the transport *Braemar Castle*, then transferred into trawlers. Then they were transferred into rowboats, which carried thirty men each and the sailors that manned them.

The soldiers transferred to trawlers that pulled a total of twenty cutters alongside. The trawlers, manned by fishermen, stopped one hundred yards from shore and shifted their human cargo into the cutters. At 4:45 a.m., as the sun was beginning its ascent, the boats landed in perfect order. Most accounts state that no opposition was met, but one of the marines had a different recollection: "The boats grounded some 50 yds. from shore, and we jumped out into the water and waded ashore. A very difficult task, as the water was over our waist, and we had a desent [*sic*] weight to carry. A few snipers made their presence known from the top of the cliffs, but were soon shelled off before causing any casualties."[1]

When the marines landed at 5:15 a.m., the first soldiers, two scouts of the KOSB, ascended the heights of the cliff above. They were the first men to die in the Helles landings: "The KOSB's scouts (two of them) were killed by a shell from our own ship, who took them for Turks. This happened several times, for a shell from a ship pitched into a section killing and wounding six. We were in an awkward fix, for we were being wiped out by our own men, terrible to think of, and very disheartening."[2]

When the surviving scouts returned and reported that there were no enemy troops in the vicinity, the troops climbed the bluff two hundred yards above the beach via the nullah (Turkish for "ravine" or "gully") that would later be called Y Ravine. They carried food, ammunition, and the shiny, square kerosene tins used for transporting water from Egypt. Because they were expected to link up with the troops landing at X Beach, then move quickly inland, no picks

"Littered with Dead"

or shovels for digging trenches had been issued. This would prove to be a fatal mistake.

A and B Companies of the KOSB reached the top of the bluff first. They then separated and reconnoitered in the territory they expected to advance into later that day. B Company came across a wide, deep nullah on its right—later called Gully Ravine—which ran down to a place the British would name Gully Beach. It was there that the Turks had expected a landing because the beach is wide and the gully provides a wide route up which an invader could quickly move inland. The Scots were surprised to find such a wide depression. According to their maps, it was located much farther inland.

Behind the advancing Scots, C and D Companies, along with the men of the Second SWB, formed a defensive position at the top of the bluff. Because they had no digging implements, they scraped a shallow trench with their small spades. They stacked their packs in front of it for protection. A proper trench it was not, and the packs, filled mostly with cloth items, would do little to stop a bullet.

Meanwhile, half the Plymouth Battalion, which landed last, scouted inland for the Turkish gun thought to be in the area. The other half carried supplies up from the beach. By 6:40 a.m. all were ashore, and Gen. Sir Ian Hamilton was ecstatic: "Opposite Krithia came another great moment. We have made good the landing—sure—it is a fact. I have to repeat the word to myself several times, 'fact,' 'fact,' 'fact,' so as to be sure I am awake and standing here looking at live men through a long telescope. The thing seems unreal; as though I were in a dream, instead of on a battleship. To see words working themselves out upon the ground; to watch thoughts move over the ground as fighting men . . . !"[3]

Farther south, at X, W, and V Beaches, the troops were being held up by stiff resistance. It was so intense at V that Hamilton decided not to land the main body behind the covering force. Instead, he chose to land them at Y, where they could get ashore safely. As was his way, he chose courtesy over common sense. Rather than ordering Hunter-Weston to land the other troops at Y, he merely *suggested* that he do so. He reasoned that Hunter-Weston, as commander of the Twenty-Ninth Division, should make the decisions. And even though Hamilton was overall commander of the operation, he did not think it right to interfere. Maj. Gen. Walter Braithwaite, who had already counseled him badly, agreed. Hamilton described the process:

> When we saw our covering party fairly hung up under the fire from the Castle [Sedd-el-Bahr] and its outworks, it became a question of issuing fresh orders to the main body who had not yet been committed to that attack. There was no use throwing them ashore to increase the number of targets on the beach. Roger Keyes started the notion that these troops might be diverted to "Y" where they could land unopposed and whence they might be able to help their advance guard at "V" more effectively than by direct reinforcement if they threatened to cut the Turkish line of retreat from Sedd-el-Bahr. Braithwaite was rather dubious from the orthodox General Staff point of view as to whether it was sound for GHQ to barge into Hunter-Weston's plans, seeing he was executive Commander of the whole of this southern invasion. But to me the idea seemed simple common sense. If it did not suit Hunter-Weston's book, he had only to say so. Certainly Hunter-Weston was in closer touch with all these landings than we were; it was not for me to force his hands: there was no question of that: so at 9.15 I wirelessed as follows:
>
> "GOC in C. to GOC *Euryalus*."
>
> "Would you like to get some more men ashore on 'Y' beach? If so, trawlers are available."

Hunter-Weston did not respond. He was so preoccupied by the fighting on the three main beaches that Hamilton had to prod him further. When he finally did respond, at eleven o'clock, it was simply to say, "Admiral Wemyss and Principal Naval Transport Officer state that to interfere with present arrangements and try to land men at 'Y' Beach would delay disembarkation."[4] Rather than press the point further, Hamilton left the matter alone.

Although there were no Turkish troops at Y when the British landed, that soon changed. Small parties were encountered shortly after seven, and before noon the enemy was shelling the British position above the beach. At one o'clock a large party of Turkish infantry, along with machine guns and field artillery, was on its way. The troops scouting in front were recalled, and the men were put to work improving their meager defenses. At 2:30 p.m. the Turks began the first of series of small attacks: "All went well until about 4 p.m. in the afternoon when the enemy scouts and snipers got busy, and it became necessary not to expose ourselves unnecessarily as they had already picked several off. The first casualty being Pte. McGuirk shot through the head, he died shortly after being hit."[5] Three of Plymouth's companies were on the right of the line; the SWB were on their left; the KOSB were on the Welshmen's left; and Plymouth's fourth company was on the extreme left, next to the Scots.

When the main Turkish force arrived at about five o'clock, it launched a full-scale assault. British warships fired on the attackers and turned them back:

> Shortly after the snipers made their appearance the order was passed along the line: a large body of Troops advancing over the skyline. This message was followed by another: A larger body of Troops advancing over the skyline. As our platoon had taken up a position about 10 yds from the top of the cliff it was not possible to see them advancing for some time after; they were about 800 to 900 yds away, advancing in massed formation, shouting and waving their rifles above their heads. As soon as they came within a reasonable distance we opened fire upon them. They still rushed on, until the two Cruisers who were supporting us, the H.M.S. *Goliath* and *Dublin*, each fired a Broadside, which completely scattered them.[6]

Unfortunately for the marines, the ships' guns hit them as well: "The ships hit the cliff above us, blowing one man's eye out and smashing up another one."[7]

Night was drawing near, and the British soon learned that the Turks had no fear of fighting at night. Both sides knew that the warships would not fire without being able to see their targets. The

British knew what was coming, and each man took as much ammunition from the wooden ammo crates as he could carry. At seven thirty the enemy launched another assault. The Turks attacked the right of the line from Gully Ravine, but the assault seemed weak. They were attempting to split the force and to isolate the marines and Scots on the left. This would give them a better chance of beating the entire force:

> Shortly after it grew dark, they made their first charge. As we expected, they came up to within 10 yds of our trench, but by keeping up a rapid fire we held them back. They retired for a short time, but there was a regular hail of bullets hitting the parapet of the trench and almost blinding us with dirt. The dirt was also getting into the mechanisms of our rifles, which added to the difficulty of keeping up rapid fire. Shortly after they retired, their bombers got to work and came within a few yards of our trenches. They were shot down, however, but it was very difficult to see more than fifteen yds away from our position, for apart from being dark, and the ground scrubby, it was a dark background. They then made another attack in their usual close formation, but it was no trouble to hit them. We simply mowed them down, although we could not actually see the effect of our fire. The fact that they never got into our trench told that they were having a lot of casualties.[8]

The Turks launched four assaults that night with cries of "Allah, Allah!" None were successful. In several places they broke through the Scots' lines, and hand-to-hand combat ensued, but each time they were driven off. The war diary of the First KOSB noted that during the night a brazen German officer "walked up to our trench and said 'You English surrender, we ten to one.' He was there upon hit on the head with a spade [entrenching tool] by a man improving his trench."[9] When they did reach the British line, they were easily driven off. But the Turks were not the only ones to die that night. All along the line they managed to take a mighty toll on the invaders.

"Littered with Dead"

A heavy rain fell during the night. Still, the Turks attacked, and with the onset of daylight, the carnage continued. They were not the only ones inflicting casualties on the invaders. At 5:30 a.m. Lieutenant Colonel Koe visually signaled the warships for assistance, and fifteen minutes later the *Goliath* came to the infantry's assistance. Unfortunately, the first two rounds landed among the marines, killing several. The Turks were undaunted by the shelling and attacked again almost immediately. They broke through the British lines on the right and in the center, and men began running for their lives. The marines and Scots on the left held, however, and officers on the right organized a counterattack. They forced the Turks out of their lines and drove them back for good. No more attacks were launched against the British above Y Beach.

Matthews knew that he could not hold out without more men and ammunition, and his requests for both had gone unheeded. He therefore ordered his men to leave their positions and move south to link up with the troops at X Beach. A KOSB officer pointed out the difficulty of moving their wounded, however, and the fact that there were an unknown number of Turks between them and X. Matthews continued to send requests for help, but he received no answer, so he took the only action he felt he had open to him. He ordered his troops to evacuate Y. What could have been a victory turned into a rout.

Hamilton observed the troops on the beach before they took to their boats. Yet instead of taking matters into his own hands, he complained about Hunter-Weston's inaction:

Sometime about 9 a.m. [April 26], we picked up a wireless from O.C. [officer commanding] "Y" Beach which caused us some uneasiness. "We are holding the ridge," it said, "till the wounded are embarked." Why "till"? So I told the Admiral that as Birdwood seemed fairly comfortable, I thought we ought to lose no time getting back to Sedd-el-Bahr, taking "Y" Beach on our way. At once we steamed South and hove to off "Y" Beach at 9.30 a.m. There the *Sapphire*, *Dublin* and *Goliath* were lying close inshore and we could see a trickle of our men coming down the steep cliff and parties being ferried off to the *Goliath*: the wounded, no doubt, but we did not see a single soul going *up* the cliff whereas there were many loose groups hanging about on the beach. I disliked and mistrusted the looks of these aimless dawdlers by the sea. There was no fighting; a rifle shot now and then from the crests where we saw our fellows clearly. The little crowd and the boats on the beach were right under them and no one paid any attention or seemed to be in a hurry. Our naval and military signallers were at sixes and sevens. The *Goliath* wouldn't answer; the *Dublin* said the force was coming off, and we could not get into touch with the soldiers at all. At about a quarter to ten the *Sapphire* asked us to fire over the cliffs into the country some hundreds of yards further in, and so the *Queen E.* gave Krithia and the South of it a taste of her metal. Not much use as the high crests hid the intervening hinterland from view, even from the crow's nests. A couple of shrapnel were also fired at the crestline of the cliff about half a mile further North where there appeared to be some snipers. But the trickling down the cliffs continued. No one liked the look of things ashore. Our chaps can hardly be making off in this deliberate way without orders; and yet, if they are making off "by order," Hunter-Weston ought to have consulted me first as Birdwood consulted me in the case of the Australians and New Zealanders last night. My inclination was to take a hand myself in this affair but the Staff are clear against interference when I have no knowledge of the facts—and I suppose they are right.[10]

Among the 296 casualties suffered by the First KOSB was the commanding officer, Lt. Col. Archibald Koe. He was mortally wounded around the time of the counterattack on the morning of April 26, his fiftieth birthday: "Next morning [April 26] when we reached Colonel Koe he was being held up by two other men. The Colonel was coughing blood and was quite unable to speak. He had a dreadful stomach wound. Distressed and overcome, Colonel Matthews, without a word to the others, laid his hand gently on his shoulder and said, 'My poor fellow,' and then he hurried back to our own battalion."[11]

Koe died on the hospital ship *Guildford Castle* and was buried at sea the following day. Capt. Ted Marrow of the same battalion left a widow and one child to mourn his loss. On April 28 Maj. John Gillam, an Army Service Corps officer attached to the Twenty-Ninth Division at W Beach, wrote of his friend: "On shore I find the KOSB's arriving from 'Y' Beach, where they have had a rough handling. 'Y' Beach appears to have been evacuated. I find a lot of officers I know have gone, including Koe, the Colonel, a very fine type of man. He really should never have come out, for he was in indifferent health. He was shot in the arm, which had to be amputated, and he died shortly afterwards."

Hamilton's final entry about Y Beach reads: "At 4.50 we were opposite Krithia passing 'Y' Beach. The whole of the troops, plus wounded, plus gear, have vanished. Only the petrol tins they took up for water right and left of their pathway up the cliff; huge diamonds in the evening sun. The enemy let us slip off without [a] shot fired. The last boatload got aboard the *Goliath* at 4 p.m., but they had forgotten some of their kit, so Bluejackets [sailors] rowed ashore as they might to Southsea pier and brought it off for them—and again no shot fired!"[12]

S Beach

The smallest of the landings was also the most successful. The goal was to secure the right flank of the main landing area. S Beach involved the other three companies of the Second South Wales Borderers—B, C, and D. In addition, there were twenty-one medics from the Royal Army Medical Corps and thirty sappers from the 1/2nd London Field Company (TF) of the Royal Engineers. A detachment of twenty-four sailors from the battleship HMS *Cornwallis* towed the boatloads of troops to shore, unloaded supplies, and evacuated the wounded. Men of the ship's RMLI contingent were detailed to land and take a Turkish trench on the Borderers' left flank, near the beach.

The plan called for *Cornwallis* to transfer the troops into four trawlers at five in the morning. Then the men would move into rowboats for the final run in to shore. Unlike most of the troops who landed that day, the Borderers had received no amphibious landing training. So, each vessel carried a coxswain and bowman to guide the boats while the soldiers rowed. Upon landing, D Company was to charge up the steep headland on the eastern end of Morto Bay known as De Tott's Battery. Because the hill was steep and they were expected to move quickly, they would land in shirtsleeve order (without their wool tunics) and without their packs. The "battery" was actually the stone remains of an eighteenth-century artillery position designed by the French engineer Baron de Tott. In April 1915 it was held by only a handful of infantrymen, who were using it as an observation post. The other two companies were to land on the eastern end of the bay, charge up the wooded, gently sloping hill, and take the trenches at the top. The area was garrisoned by a platoon of Turks from the 2/26th Infantry Regiment who were supported by a few field guns located inland. The engineers would follow the attacking riflemen and consolidate the captured positions, repairing damage caused during the assaults and preparing the trenches for any attacks that might come from inland.

The soldiers transferred to *Cornwallis* at midnight on April 24–25, then were treated to a hot meal. They were then told to get as much rest as possible over the next couple of hours. Few could. Reveille was sounded at 3:30 a.m., and the men donned their equipment. None had been allowed to remove their uniforms, not even their boots, for their brief period of restless slumber. One hour later they were ready to go.

At 5:00 a.m. the four trawlers arrived on schedule, each pulling six rowboats, three on either side. Each of the rowboats carried thirty-four soldiers and two sailors. After the men climbed down into the trawlers on rope ladders slung over the *Cornwallis*'s sides, the boats began slowly putt-putting their way toward Morto Bay. Although the sea was calm, the voyage was eventful. As the trawlers worked their way against the currents, which moved faster than their engines were capable of going, the Turks sighted them and opened fire with their field guns, hitting one of the vessels amidships but causing no casualties. The *Cornwallis* and other ships fired back, forcing the Turkish artillerymen to keep their heads down. Because they could only fire intermittently for fear of drawing a response from the British naval guns, they had to fire quickly and without being able to aim properly. Turkish riflemen crouched in their trenches and held their fire—for the time being.

According to plan, the trawlers were to make straight for the bay so the men could land around dawn. But the surrounding sea was choked with warships and minesweeping trawlers, so the boats had to contend with both congestion and currents. It was not until seven o'clock, well after sunup and four hundred yards from shore, that the *Cornwallis* signaled the trawlers to transfer the men into the rowboats. The trawlers had gone as far as they could go without grounding.

The riflemen clambered into the rowboats as the sailors worked to keep their craft steady. Once loaded, the boats shoved off. According to orders from the commanding officer of the Second swb, Lt. Col. Hugh Casson, the men sat absolutely still and quiet, each in his assigned spot. The rowers each had a backup, assigned to take his place in case he was hit as the boats made their way to shore.

As the boats neared land, Turkish infantrymen opened fire. Their iron bullets sent up little spouts of water as they hit the otherwise calm sea. Others found their targets in the Welshmen, but none hit the sailors. As the boats grounded, the riflemen jumped into the surf, some up to their necks in the deeper-than-expected water. A few— carrying equipment, rifles, and ammunition weighing eighty-eight pounds—slid down to a watery grave. While some pulled wounded comrades through the surf to shore, others charged immediately uphill toward the enemy trenches.

D Company was the first to land and charged up the hill behind the company commander, Maj. Edward Margesson. Because the trench above was constructed behind the crest of the hill, the defenders were unable to see the Welshmen, and they were unable to fire at the Turks. Naval shells exploding around De Tott's Battery, however, hurled rocks at the Welshmen and caused some injuries. Just below the crest, they regrouped before moving to the top of the hill. There they found partially destroyed stonewalls around the position, ranging in height from two to twelve feet. Men moved in two directions and quickly overtook the defending Turks. Some were shot as they did so, including Margesson. After taking the trench, the Borderers quickly consolidated the position and began firing on the defenders in the trench opposite. The Turks fired down on the men of B and C Companies as they charged up the gently sloping, wooded hill to take the trenches above them: "We all managed to get ashore at last in about half an hour and got in under cover, some keeping up the fire, then we had to pull ourselves together and were told to get ready by the officers to charge. We charged across the open and we had no difficulty in taking [the] trench that was in front of us. We captured or killed the Turks that occupied the trench and got to our objective with in [sic] an hour of our landing on the beach."[13]

Behind the Welshmen were some of the sailors whose job it was to pull in the boats. They had landed with rifles, and a few, dressed in white cotton uniforms, charged after the soldiers. Only one young seaman was hit but not fatally. Total losses for the SWB were fourteen men killed, among them Lt. Robert Behrens and Major Margesson. He died an hour after being hit in the chest by a Turkish bullet. These two men epitomized the losses suffered by the British army in the early part of the war. The Twenty-Ninth was the only Regular Army division not already committed to battle on the western front, and many of the army's professional officers had already been killed or maimed. Margesson and Behrens were both graduates of the Royal Military College at Sandhurst, and the army could ill afford to lose such valuable men so early in the campaign. No marines or sailors were lost, nor were any of the engineers or medics who landed with the Borderers.

Behrens did not die immediately either. Mortally wounded, he was conveyed back to the *Cornwallis* in a rowboat. He died later

"Littered with Dead"

that day and was buried at sea. Margesson was buried on the evening of April 25, three yards away from one of De Tott's walls. As would happen to so many of the graves left by the invading forces when they evacuated Gallipoli, his could not be located by the Imperial (later Commonwealth) War Graves Commission. Thus, he is today commemorated on the Helles Memorial.

The assault on S Beach was over by 8:30 a.m., and despite their fears, the Borderers were not attacked in their newly won positions. They were, however, harassed by snipers, who caused a few casualties, but the Turks did not attempt to recapture the position. The Welshmen turned it over to the French on April 27.

Months later Casson visited the site of his victory but as a brigadier general in command of the 152nd Brigade of the Fifty-Second (Lowland) Division. On September 22, 1915, Maj. Joseph Vassal, the medical officer of the French Fifty-Sixth Colonial Regiment, wrote to his wife: "A few days ago I conducted the British Brigade-General H. G. Casson, 152nd Brigade, around my Eski Hissarlick dressing station and the former position of De Tott's Battery. The General wished to revisit this corner of Gallipoli, which he conquered on April 25, and see the graves of the soldiers who have been killed at his side . . . He was touched with the care that had been given by the French to the English graves. Overlooking the incomparable panorama of the Straits are the graves of Major C. E. Margresson [sic] and his orderly. He told me what had happened on April 25 and how the Major was killed. I am going to have a stone placed on his grave and write to his widow."[14]

V Beach

While the assault on S Beach was a rapid success, V Beach was just the opposite. The defenders nearly drove the invaders back into the sea, and the Royal Navy did little to help the vulnerable infantry.

V Beach is a natural amphitheater. A cliff is on the right of the beach, high ground lies in front, and, perched on a rise to the right, is Fort Sedd-el-Bahr. The enemy covered the beach from this higher ground. The British knew it was heavily defended and that their only hope of success was to get a large number of men ashore quickly following a naval bombardment. For that reason Cdr. Edward Unwin, commanding officer of the communications yacht *Hussar*, made a novel suggestion. He proposed converting the collier *River Clyde* into a kind of Trojan horse in which troops could be moved quickly to shore. The idea was an ingenious one and would provide the necessary means for conveying a large number of men to the largest of the three main beaches. They could reinforce the first wave of a covering force, which would land before them from tows. According to Unwin's plan, two large sally ports would be cut into either side of the ship, aft of the port and starboard bows. From these openings gangways lowered with ropes would provide the soldiers with their means of egress. Because the collier would ground a short distance from shore, a steam hopper called the *Argyll* would provide a bridge from the *Clyde* to the beach. This vessel was towed alongside the collier, and its momentum, once released, was meant to carry it to shore. As it glided forward, its crew of six Greeks, under the direction of Midshipman George Drewry and Seaman George Samson, would steer it in front of the *Clyde*. Once there, the gangways would be dropped, and the twenty-one hundred soldiers inside would rush across the *Argyll* and onto the beach. In the event Unwin's calculations were off, he arranged for the *Argyll* to tow three modified rowboats to make up for any gap between ship and shore. He seemed to have thought of everything.

Among the units that landed at V Beach was the First Battalion, the Royal Dublin Fusiliers. Half of the men of W Company were detailed to land at the Camber, a piece of dead ground below Seddel-Bahr Village, directly across the peninsula to the east. Their goal was to capture the village. At V Beach proper the first wave consisted of three companies of the First Dublins, along with fifty men of the Royal Naval Division's Anson Battalion. These two groups would land first, from five tows pulled toward shore by the mine-sweeper *Clacton*. Each tow consisted of four rowboats pulled by a steam pinnace, each rowboat manned by a midshipman and six sailors from the battleship *Cornwallis*. After this group landed,

"Littered with Dead"

the *Clyde* would be grounded and its troops landed. The soldiers would be covered by eight Maxim machine guns operated by men of No. 3 Squadron of the Royal Naval Air Service's Armoured Car Division, who were stationed around the collier's bridge. On board were the other half of W Company and the entire First Battalion, Royal Munster Fusiliers. The Dublins, along with Z Company of the Munsters, were to help the Dublins who landed at the Camber take Sedd-el-Bahr Village. They would then move on to take Hill 114, which stands behind the village and had a small fort and barracks on top. These men would exit the *Clyde* from the starboard (right) side, which would face the village. X Company of the First Munsters would exit from the port side. They were to take Fort No. 1, which stood atop the cliffs to the left of the beach and had been destroyed in the earlier naval bombardments. The Munsters' other two companies, W and Y, were to remain in reserve. Also in reserve were two companies of the Second Battalion, the Hampshire Regiment and the 1/1st West Riding Field Company of the Royal Engineers. No. 13 Platoon of the Anson Battalion was to carry stores to shore once a successful landing had been made. Medical treatment would be provided by men of the Royal Army Medical Corps's Eighty-Ninth (1/1st Highland) Field Ambulance.

The troops destined for V Beach began their journey to Gallipoli on the afternoon of April 23, when they moved to Tenedos. They were tense and displayed none of the joviality that some of the others felt as they departed for their meeting with destiny: "We left [Mudros] at 5.30 p.m. on April 23rd for the great adventure . . . A perfect evening, as we steamed stealthily out on H.M. [*sic*], H.M.T. 'CALEDONIA,' an incident memorable for its solemnity and one might say grandeur. Men-of-war, transports and ships of every sort 'Dressed Ships.' All the crews cheering us on our way, and those with bands playing us a farewell . . . What struck me most forcibly was the demeanour of our own men, from whom, not a sound, and this from the light-hearted, devil may care men from the South of Ireland. Even they were filled with a sense of something impending which was quite beyond their ken."[15]

The next day the Dublins and Ansons who would land in the open boats transferred to the *Clacton*, and those who would land on the *Clyde* boarded it. Early on the morning of the twenty-fifth the Ansons and Dublins were awoken and given a hot meal, then they climbed down the rope ladders and into the rowboats tied to the sides of the pinnaces. The sailors from the *Cornwallis* were already onboard, having spent a cold night sleeping in their boats. The men on the *Clyde* were also awoken and given a cup of hot cocoa before the vessels sailed for Gallipoli.

The rowboats were supposed to land first, following an hour-long bombardment by the battleship *Albion*. The pinnaces towing the rowboats met with the same problem as those that landed at S Beach: a stronger-than-expected current. They did not arrive until after 6:30 a.m., so the *Albion* continued firing on the area behind the beach. And there was another problem. At 6:10 a.m. the *Clyde*, which should have grounded after the tows had landed, found itself far ahead of them. Unwin thus decided to circle the *Argyll* in an effort to follow the original plan. In doing so, the khaki-painted vessel lost some of the momentum necessary to propel it forward to form the bridge. The collier grounded at 6:22 a.m. without so much as a jolt, eight minutes before the rowboats arrived. But it grounded much farther out than Unwin had planned—one hundred yards—and the *Argyll* beached fifteen yards away, too far to be of any use. The men onboard waited anxiously for the first wave to land.

The pinnaces cast off their boats fifty yards from shore, and the starboard tow headed for the Camber. As the remaining tows neared shore, *Albion* shifted its fire farther inland to avoid hitting the infantrymen. It ceased firing before they landed. The Turks, who had deserted their positions when the bombardment began, filed back to their trenches, unseen, and held their fire until they saw the boats cast off. Most of their positions did not appear on British maps and were so well concealed that *Albion*'s observers missed them.[16] The two forts, which had been partially destroyed in the March bombardments, provided excellent cover for some of the defenders. The thick barbed wire—there were three strong belts in front of the trenches—was also visible. Yet *Albion* was stationed too far out to sea—approximately 1,450 yards—to be able to target the defenses accurately. When it did fire, its gunners were further hampered by the smoke and debris thrown up by the explosions. They were firing blind but managed to knock out two of the Turks' four pom-poms.[17] Unfortunately, the barbed wire was largely untouched, and the Ottomans were anything but demoralized by the bombardment. The damage was slight, and the invaders would pay for it with their lives.

When the pinnaces released their boats, all hell broke loose: "At this moment the Turks, whom everyone had thought were dazed and routed by the preceding naval bombardment, opened fire with everything they had, the range was short—something like one hundred yards frontally and up to three hundred yards on the flanks—for the cove where the landing was taking place was roughly bow shaped and quite small."[18] The Turks opened fire on the boats and took an awful toll. The heavily equipped soldiers, packed tightly into the narrow wooden craft, slumped forward and back as they were hit, making it difficult for the sailors to row. Some were burned as their boats caught fire. Craft were holed and began to sink. Others drifted aimlessly, the men inside all dead or wounded. One of those hit as his boat moved toward shore was the First Dublin's second-in-command, Maj. Edwyn Fetherstonaugh. The commanding officer, Lt. Col. Richard Rooth, was killed instantly as the boat he was in hit the beach.

In some cases the men leaped out of their boats as they neared land. Many either slipped or failed to gain a footing and went under. They sank like stones in the three-foot-deep water under the weight of their equipment. Some jumped out of the boats as they grounded and hid behind them in the shallows. One of those was Stoker 1st Class William Medhurst. When the boat he commanded grounded, he yelled, "Jump out, lads, and pull her in!" All but one of the other sailors in his boat had been killed and all but three of the Dublins. Medhurst leaped out one side and the other sailor out the other. Both took cover, the seaman with two of the soldiers. As the tide pushed the boat's stern, Medhurst was exposed to the Turks' fire and was killed. He left a wife, already a widow with three children. Eighty years later the only memory their daughter had of her daddy was seeing him off at the train station at the outbreak of war. Of the soldiers it was estimated that more than half of the seven hundred men were killed or wounded in their boats. The surf was literally red with blood, and bodies and boats moved aimlessly with the tide: "As the RIVER CLYDE came inshore a very heavy fire from rifles, machine guns & pom poms was directed at her & also on the boats' tows that ran in alongside soon after. This fire was so accurate that those in the boats were practically wiped out & very few got ashore. Wounded men jumped from the boats & took cover on the far side but were all eventually shot down & drowned."[19]

Among the casualties was Father William Finn, Catholic chaplain to the First Dublins. The morning before the landing he heard his men's confessions, said Mass, and gave Holy Communion while their transport was anchored off Tenedos. On April 25, before the Dublins destined to land in the first wave departed, he asked Rooth for permission to join him so that he could minister to the casualties. Rooth reluctantly agreed, and a place was found for the padre in his boat. It was a fatal request. The brave chaplain was wounded in the right arm just after jumping out of the boat, but he continued on to the beach. After making it to land, he began ministering to the wounded but had to hold his injured arm with his left hand in order to give absolution. He was suffering great pain. While blessing a dying Dublin, he was hit in the head by a piece of shrapnel and killed. He had joined the army the previous November from his tiny parish in Market Weighton, Yorkshire, and his were brave actions for a man who was not a career soldier. Days later, when the fighting was over, he was buried. A simple cross was made from the slats of an ammunition crate with the inscription "To the memory of Father Finn" and placed over his grave.

Finn was popular with the other chaplains. In 1916 his friend the Rev. Oswin Creighton, the Eighty-Sixth Brigade's Church of England chaplain, wrote:

"Littered with Dead"

I have . . . heard that Father Finn asked to be allowed to land with his men, and had been put into one of the first boats, and was shot either getting off the boat or immediately after getting ashore. The men never forgot him and were never tired of speaking of him. I think they felt his death almost more than anything that happened in that terrible landing off the *River Clyde*. I am told they kept his helmet for a very long time after and carried it with them wherever they went. It seemed to me that Father Finn was an instance of the extraordinary hold a chaplain, and perhaps especially an R.C. [Roman Catholic], can have on the affections of his men if he absolutely becomes one of them and shares their danger.

At a chaplains' meeting held some weeks later, two, a Presbyterian and an R.C., undertook to see that Father Finn's grave was properly tended. He was buried close to the sea on "V" beach, and a road had been made over the place. I think they managed to get the grave marked off with a little fence.[20]

The survivors made for a five-foot-high sandy bank, a few yards from the water's edge, that ran for several yards along the beach. At about that time the *River Clyde* lowered its gangways, and the Royal Navy Air Service (RNAS) machine gunners opened fire against targets they could not see. Drewry and Samson on the *Argyll* began dragging the lighters towed by their vessel toward the bow of the *Clyde*. The collier had beached to the left of a rock spit. So, Unwin ordered one of the pinnaces to maneuver the boats into position next to the spit to form a bridge. When the pinnace backed off for fear of grounding, Unwin and Able Seaman William Williams dived in to finish the job. Drewry, who had made it to shore, removed his belt, revolver, and tunic and waded out to help. Together Unwin and Williams pulled on a rope to steady the lead lighter. After forming a precarious bridge with two of the boats, a ship's cutter, and some planks, Unwin called for the disembarkation to begin: "Within five minutes of the 'CLYDE' beaching 'Z' Coy. [Company] got away on the Starboard side. The gangway on the Port side jammed, and delayed X Company for a few seconds, and out we went, the men cheering wildly, and dashed ashore with Z Company."[21]

As the Munsters stepped onto the gangways, they were met with a hail of fire from the ruined forts on their flanks and the trenches in front. Those who were hit fell into the sea or in heaps on the lighters. Bullets also entered the ship through the portals, ricocheting off the steel plates. Some of those hit on the gangways fell backward, knocking the heavily laden men behind them into the sea to drown in the shallow water below: "I sent out my first 2 companies, X under Capt GEDDES & Z under Capt HENDERSON, X on the port side & Z on the starboard. Z got away a little before X. They were to go out by platoons so that there should be no crowding on the lighters. These companies were very gallantly led by their officers. The fire directed on the exits from the vessel being very accurate & men were hit before they left the vessel."[22]

Capt. Eric Henderson was hit twice on the gangway. Geddes made it to the beach unscathed, but the forty-eight men behind him were felled by machine gun fire. The few who survived made their way to shore to join the Dublins. Together they huddled in a mass under the burning sun, without food and only the tepid water in their quart-sized water bottles to slake their thirst: "We all made, Dublins and all, for a sheltered ledge on the shore which gave us cover. Here we shook ourselves out, and tried to appreciate the situation, rather a sorry one. I estimated that I had lost about 70 percent of my company, 2/Lieuts. Watts and Perkins were wounded and my CQM Sgt. [company quartermaster sergeant] killed. Henderson was wounded. He died from his wounds later. Lieut. Pollard killed, and 2 Lieuts. Lee and Lane wounded, all of Z. Company. Capt. Wilson, the Adjutant, and Major Monck-Mason were wounded on the Clyde itself."[23]

The plight of those unfortunate Irishmen was watched by men on the transports that were waiting to come ashore. The sight was a distressing one, even from a distance of a thousand or more yards. At 8:30 a.m. on that terrible day, Maj. John Gillam, destined to land at W Beach that afternoon, noted in his diary: "It is quite clear now, and I can just see through my glasses the little khaki figures on shore

"Littered with Dead"

at 'W' Beach and on the top of the cliff, while at 'V' Beach, where the *River Clyde* is lying beached, all seems hell and confusion. Some fool near me says, 'Look, they are bathing at "V" Beach.' I get my glasses on to it and see about a hundred khaki figures crouching behind a sand dune close to the water's edge. On a hopper [*Argyll*] which somehow or other has been moored in between the *River Clyde* and the shore I see khaki figures lying, many apparently dead. I also see the horrible sight of some little white boats drifting, with motionless khaki freight, helplessly out to sea on the strong current that is coming down the Straights [*sic*]."

After an hour of maintaining the floating bridge, a shell exploded, and Williams was hit by a piece of shrapnel. He released his grip on the rope, and Unwin was no longer able to steady the lead boat. It began to drift. He dropped the line in an attempt to save Williams, who died in his arms. Later Unwin would have to be pulled out of the water, the fifty-one-year-old mariner totally exhausted from his exertions. Both men, along with Midshipman Drewry, were awarded the Victoria Cross for their actions that day. For the time being no more troops would leave the collier. It was not until 8:00 a.m., after Drewry and a few others managed to form a bridge between the lighters and the stranded hopper, that men were able to begin landing again. Maj. Charles Jarrett led half of Y Company of the Munsters out of the *Clyde* and across the new bridge. So many of his men were hit, however, that he sent one of his officers, Lt. Guy Nightingale, from the beach back to the collier to request that Tizard cease the operation. He agreed, and no more troops were sent ashore.

Inside the *River Clyde* those who had so far been spared the hell of almost certain death on the gangways were not safe either. Despite the navy's best efforts to silence the guns on the Asiatic side, they failed to hit at least one:

Three shells hit the ship, and then one of the battleships put the gun out of action. The first shell went in the boiler room without killing or wounding anyone; the second hit the ship aft, crashed through No. 4 hold, came through the upper deck, then on the main deck, port side, and took off the legs of two soldiers. They died after about twenty minutes. I was only two yards away from these dear men. The hold was packed with troops as thickly as ever you could stow men together, and the terrible sights and the cries of the wounded will never be forgotten by those who are alive to tell the tale. I often think it was good that one like myself was there, as I did not lose my nerve under fire, and helped to prevent the men from being panic-stricken. I now went down to my men, who were in No. 4 lower hold, and I addressed them, and told them to keep cool, to try and keep their heads as I did . . .

While I was talking to the platoon another shell came in and killed three of them. This was the second shell I had seen explode within a few minutes; it was rather bad, especially for young lads like these, but I knew I was there to show them an example and take care of them. I have often wondered since what would have happened had that gun not been put out of action when it was; they had the correct range.[24]

Although no more troops landed from the *River Clyde* that morning, casualties continued to occur. The Dublins who landed at the Camber had done so unopposed, but they were nearly wiped out when they moved into Sedd-el-Bahr Village. The survivors were forced to retreat. With all of their officers gone, most were evacuated by a boat from the *Queen Elizabeth*. A party of fourteen unwounded survivors linked up with Captain Geddes and two men approaching from the left, but they found that the ruined Fort Sedd-el-Bahr was heavily defended by riflemen and machine guns. They did not attempt to attack. Instead, they moved back to the little bit of cover afforded by the sandy bank on the beach.

At 10:00 a.m. the gun firing on the *Clyde* was silenced. It was then possible to evacuate wounded off the ship's stern and for reinforcements to board. At that hour the second wave also started to come ashore. It was composed of men of the Fourth Battalion, the Worcestershire Regiment, and the other two companies of the Second Hampshires. With them was the commanding officer of the Eightieth-Eighth Brigade, Brig. Gen. Henry Napier, and his brigade major, Maj. John Costeker, Distinguished Service Order (DSO). They traveled in the same boats used by the Dublins three hours earlier, and the awfulness of their journey was clearly evident: "The four boats had already been used that morning. From them some of the Dublin Fusiliers had landed. The boats were much damaged by fire, and blood mixed with sea water ran over the boots of the troops as they sat packed in the laden boats."[25]

The boats were towed toward the *Clyde* by a steam launch, which steered toward the starboard side of the collier and the bridge of lighters. As they approached the shore, bullets pierced the sea around them. Men were hit, but not so many as in the first wave. As they neared the lighters, they could see the heaps of dead and dying Munsters piled on them, the mounds of flesh being repeatedly riddled as the Turks fired at the gangways and sally ports. Lt. Col. Herbert Carrington Smith, the commanding officer of the Second Hampshires, called down from the bridge of the *River Clyde* for the pinnace to take the boats over to the port bow. There they were tied to the lighter nearest the collier. The boats carrying the Hampshires tied up on the starboard side, and the men made it to cover behind the sandbank with only fifteen hit out of fifty.

Arriving at the makeshift bridge, Napier, Costeker, and the Worcesters climbed out of their boats and onto one of the lighters. But they encountered a problem. The lighter nearest the shore had drifted with the current, and the bridge was broken. They were stopped short of landing, and as they stood in the open, wondering what to do next, the Turks took advantage of the inviting targets. The Englishmen could only lie flat and hope to avoid the hail of bullets. Many were hit, including Napier and Costeker. They had gone first into the *River Clyde*, then returned and tried to cross to shore via the *Argyll*: "I saw General Napier killed. He went down the gangway just in front of me followed by his Brigade Major Costello [*sic*]. He was hit in the stomach on the barge between our ship and the beach. He lay for half an hour on the barge and then tried to get some water to drink but the moment he moved the Turks began firing at him again and whether he was hit again or not I do not know, but he died very soon afterwards, and when I went ashore the second time, I turned him over and he was quite dead. Costello was killed at the same time."[26] So many of the Worcesters were hit that the remainder of the battalion was diverted to W Beach. Those who were not killed trying to land on V were led into the *Clyde* by their senior surviving officer, Maj. H. A. Carr.

Although the Hampshires suffered only a few casualties and those on the *River Clyde* were relatively safe, they did suffer two fatalities that day, most notably Carrington Smith. He was hit by a Turkish bullet at about 3:00 p.m. as he stood on the bridge: "Colonel Carrington Smith, who took over command of the Brigade when General Napier was killed, was looking round the corner of the shelter of the bridge through glasses [binoculars] at the Turkish position on shore when he was caught by a bullet clean in the forehead and died instantly."[27]

The landing at V Beach was ultimately successful, but the loss in men was staggering. What had begun as a creative endeavor turned into a rescue operation by late morning. Men from the *Clyde* worked to recover the wounded under fire, and more were killed. Sub-Lt. Arthur Tisdall, a platoon commander in the Anson Battalion, led some of his men and RNAS machine gunners into the water to bring in the wounded. Tisdall survived the day and was awarded the Victoria Cross for his bravery. He would be killed on May 6, however, when he exposed his head over the top of a trench. He never knew that he had won Britain's highest gallantry decoration.

Darkness allowed those still on the *Clyde* to join the men already ashore, still sheltering behind the sandy bank. It also allowed the wounded to be evacuated. Many would die in the overcrowded, understaffed hell of the hospital ships. First, they were moved to the holds of the *Clyde*, then evacuated off the stern of the ship. The night was an awful one. Men continued to fall to Turkish bullets, and they had almost nothing to eat or drink. To make matters worse, it rained.

"Littered with Dead"

The men of the Twenty-Ninth Division hailed from all over the United Kingdom. They were missed not only by their families and friends but also by the municipalities in which they had been trained and housed. Places such as Coventry and Nuneaton, where the Munsters and Dublins had respectively trained, were particularly hard hit by the V Beach massacre. The colorful career soldiers were popular with the locals and were mourned for years afterward. One story, which appeared in Coventry's *Evening Telegraph* of March 7, 1985, epitomizes the feeling of loss that was felt:

Mrs. Procter has unearthed photographs of that time [when the First Royal Munsters were billeted in Earlsdon, Coventry, before departing for Gallipoli] because this year is the 70th anniversary of the disastrous Gallipoli landings of the First World War.

Two of the soldiers became friendly with her parents, who gave them hospitality. They had come in tropical kit straight from Egypt, and found Coventry cold and bleak.

Mrs. Procter, who still has a photograph of the two men, Martin O'Malley and his friend (whose name she cannot recall) and remembers the day they were issued with new boots, when Martin regarded them and said quietly: "I expect they are for my grave."

Shortly afterwards, the soldiers, who had become part of the Earlsdon scene, having been made welcome by the people with whom they were billeted, marched away.

Everyone waited for news of the Fusiliers, and then came the tragedy of the landings.

Yes, their friend Martin was killed and among his effects was found a photograph of 10-year old Elsie on her cycle.

It was returned to the family with a covering letter and her father had the letter and photograph framed.

Mrs. Procter concludes: "Rather a sad little story serving to illustrate the horror and futility of war."

Pvt. Martin O'Malley of the First Battalion, the Royal Munster Fusiliers, was from Limerick and was eighteen years old. He was one of those who landed with Major Jarrett and was likely buried in the mass grave filled in by men of the Anson Battalion. After the war his was one of many thousands whose graves could not be identified.

Due to the threat of Turkish snipers and because the men fit for action were needed for the fighting inland, it was not possible to collect the dead for burial until April 28: "I remember that on Wednesday, April 28th, I and a party of men picked up all the dead on the beach and from the water; we placed in one large grave two hundred and thirteen gallant men who gave their lives for their country."[28]

Maj. John Gillam visited V Beach two days after the landings and arrived there as the Ansons' burial party was at work:

We dip down to "V" Beach, a much deeper and wider beach than "W," and walk towards the sea. Then I see a sight which I shall never forget all my life. About two hundred bodies are laid out for burial, consisting of soldiers and sailors. I repeat, never has the army been so dovetailed together. They lie in all postures, their faces blackened, swollen, and distorted by the sun. The bodies of seven officers lie in a row in front by themselves. I cannot think what a fine company they would make if by a miracle an Unseen Hand could restore them to life by a touch. The rank of major and the red tabs on one of the bodies arrests my eye, and the form of the officer seems familiar. Colonel Gostling, of the 88th Field Ambulance, is standing near me, and he goes over to the form, bends down and gently removes a khaki handkerchief covering the face. I then see that it is Major Costeker, our late Brigade Major. In his breast pocket is a cigarette-case and a few letters; one is in his wife's handwriting. I had worked in his office for two months in England, and was looking forward to working with him in Gallipoli.

It was cruel luck that he was not even permitted to land, for I learn that he was hit in the heart shortly after Napier was laid low. His last words were, "Oh Lord! I am done for now." I notice also that a bullet has torn the toe of his left boot away; probably this happened after he was dead.

I hear that General Napier was hit whilst in the pinnace, on his way to the *River Clyde*, by a machine gun bullet in the stomach. Just before he died he said to Sinclair-Thomson, our Staff Officer, "Get on the *Clyde* and tell Carrington Smith to take over." A little while later he apologized for groaning. Good heavens! I can't realize it, for it was such a short while ago that we were all such a merry party at the "Warwick Arms," Warwick.[29]

The *River Clyde* remained at V Beach until long after that fateful April day. Later it was towed off and repaired and went on to sail again after the war. The valiant ship's life ended in 1966, when it was sold for scrap. It was an unfitting end for one of the heroes of the campaign.

W Beach

W Beach, like V, is a kind of natural amphitheater. The 350-yard-wide strand, flanked by cliffs on either side, is fronted by high sandy ground that is split by a gully. The beach is 15 to 40 yards wide. The British intended to use it for landing men, transport animals, guns, and stores as well as evacuating casualties. It is an area naturally suited to defense, and the Turks knew that a major landing would occur there. As with V Beach, the British assumed that the Turks would not put up much of a fight and that the defenses could be easily overcome. They were wrong. So were the Turks, who assumed that their defenses were impregnable.

The goals of the W Beach landing were fairly straightforward. The Lancashire Fusiliers were to secure the beach and the ground in front, then link up with the troops landing at X on the left and V on the right. All would then move inland in an unbroken line to take Krithia and Achi Baba. First, they would have to take Hill 114 on the left of the beach and Hill 138 on the right. These hills were so called because of their elevation in feet above sea level.

The Turks defended W Beach with only one infantry company (roughly 250 men). This was a relatively small area, with little room for a large number of men, which the Turks knew would cause suffering for the troops when the inevitable naval barrage began. Their defenses consisted largely of strong belts of barbed wire covered by riflemen and machine guns. A string of rusty fence wire, gathered from the deserted farms around Sedd-el-Bahr, was laid under the waterline. Crude mines, constructed from torpedo warheads, were planted on shore and under water near the surf's edge. It was a formidable defense, and the wire would form the greater part of it, more than the Turks expected. Their wire was much thicker than that used by the British, and the small wire cutters used by the invaders had difficulty cutting through it: "The barbed wire used by the Turks in Gallipoli, German no doubt, was of a kind we had not seen before. Its centre wire was enormously thick, and at the closest intervals strong sharp barbs of unusual strength were well twisted on the main strand. The formidable spikes were capable of dealing serious wounds, and as compared with the barbed wire used at home it was as a rope to cotton."[30]

The covering force for W Beach was the First Battalion of the Lancashire Fusiliers, another of the Twenty-Ninth Division's veteran Regular Army battalions. Three companies—A, B, and C—departed Tenedos on the *Euryalus* on the afternoon of April 24. This was also the ship on which Hunter-Weston and his staff were traveling. D departed on the *Implacable*. The plan called for A and B Companies, along with the battalion's machine gun section, to capture Hill 138 on the right of the beach. C Company was to take the trenches facing the beach, on either side of the gully, then move on to Hill 114 to the left. There they would assist the Second Battalion, the Royal Fusiliers—which would land at X Beach to the northwest—in its assault on the hill. The latter, also on the *Implacable*, would be in their own tows, trailing alongside the battleship when it let loose the tows carrying D Company. After taking Hill 138, A and B Companies were to link up with the troops assaulting V Beach. D Company, which would land on the left of these three companies, was to be the reserve. Fifty men of the Ansons would unload stores and ammunition. Unlike the beaches on either side of W, no reserve units were to land behind the Fusiliers. The staff believed

"Littered with Dead"

that resistance at W would be quickly overcome and that the battalions landing at X and V would wipe out any Turkish reinforcements that approached W.

The battleships *Euryalus*, *Swiftsure*, and *Albion* began bombarding the known Turkish positions before daylight. As soon as the barrage began, the Turks retreated to dugouts out of the line of fire. The gunners hoped to obliterate the wire that Hamilton had seen while assessing the landing area. They did not.

At three in the morning the Fusiliers were awoken, given breakfast, then transferred into their boats. They would travel to the beach in eight tows, each consisting of a steam pinnace pulling four rowboats. They began their fateful journey an hour later, while the barrage was taking place. The current was stronger than expected, and it took an hour and a half for the boats to make the journey. As the sun rose, the gunners found it difficult to see what they were shooting at. A mist had blown in and was mixing with the smoke of the bursting shells. To make matters worse, the rising sun was casting a shadow over the beach. The gunners ceased firing for a time before resuming the bombardment. When the pinnaces released the rowboats fifty yards from shore, the ships ceased fire. And the Turks moved back into their trenches.

As the boats neared land, they could see the glint of wire on shore and the disruption of the surf caused by the strands just under the water's surface. The Turks opened fire, hitting the Fusiliers from three sides: "We never got a shot fired at us till the oars were tossed around and then they started in earnest. The first bullet that struck the mate brought up loud jeers from our men, but poor devils they little thought what they were in for. Brockbank the runner was in my boat, he has a charmed life as he left his rifle on board and ran back for it and never got touched. C. S. Wilson was about the first man I saw hit, he got out first from the boat next me and was hit in the stomach once. I didn't need Kipling's words to stop me from looking twice at him. Gus was hit through the head above his eyes. I hope he won't lose his eyesight. Meakins was hit—his arm badly shattered, I am afraid he will have lost it. Kealy had his arm broken."[31]

D Company landed on the left and was protected by the cliffs of Tekke Burnu. Until then they were at the mercy of the Turks. When their boats were close to shore, the Englishmen leaped out and into four feet of water. Some were hit as they disembarked, including Capt. Tom Maunsell, a native of Nova Scotia whose brother had been killed in France two months earlier. Several slipped and drowned under the weight of their packs, while others were shot in the water. Some tripped over the submerged wire. Mines exploded under water. Only two of the boats actually made it to shore with their men. The survivors moved quickly through the surf and sought protection on the beach. There they lay in their waterlogged uniforms, their rifles fouled by sand and seawater. The officers' compasses, watches, and binoculars were useless after being submerged. Those with wire cutters worked like the devil to cut through the thick strands with their inferior tools, twisting and turning in a vain effort to snap them. Some resorted to standing up and pulling out the iron stanchions that held the wire in place. Most of those who did were killed or wounded. Many were hit after being stopped behind the steel barriers: "I got up to my waist in water, tripped over a rock and went under, got up and made for the shore and lay down by the barbed wire. There was a man there before me shouting for wire-cutters. I got mine out but could not make the slightest impression. The front of the wire by now was a thick mass of men, the majority of whom never moved again."[32]

Turkish riflemen took careful aim and hit many of the brave men toiling to cut through. Capt. Richard Willis, commanding officer of C Company, wrote:

We toiled through the water towards the sandy beach, but here another trap awaited us, for the Turks had cunningly concealed a trip wire just below the surface of the water, and on the beach itself were a number of land mines, and a deep belt of rusty wire extended across the landing place. Machine guns, hidden in caves at the end of the amphitheatre of cliffs, enfiladed this. Our wretched men were ordered to wait behind this wire for the

"Littered with Dead"

wire cutters to cut a pathway through. They were shot in helpless batches while they waited, and could not even use their rifles in retaliation, since the sand and the sea had clogged their action. One Turkish sniper in particular took a heavy toll at very close range until I forced open the bolt of a rifle with the heel of my boot and closed his career with the first shot, but the heap of empty cartridges round him testified to the damage he had done.

Eventually, the Fusiliers pulled out their bore brushes and oilers and cleaned their rifles so they could return fire. By 7:15 a.m. Turkish fire began to diminish, and the attackers broke through the wire. This move enabled them to establish a defensive line, so the only risk to those still on the beach was the odd stray bullet. Then they filed through the gaps in the wire and began their climb up Hill 138 to attack the Turks in the redoubt on top. As they did so, a shell fired by one of the battleships landed among the Englishmen, killing several and driving the rest back down to the beach. They thought they had hit a landmine. Before long they tried again but ran into wire covered by riflemen entrenched behind it. Among the casualties was Lt. Alwyne Porter. His loss made a great impact on one of his fellow lieutenants, Ainslie Talbot. The young officer was killed by a bomb that was lobbed at him as he ascended the hill: "By jove it was pretty hot that Sunday morning. I can hardly write about it yet. Poor old Porter was killed by a hand grenade I think climbing up the cliff on my right. I am awfully sick he got knocked over . . . Porter was a good pal of mine. I often used to try to get him to write to you. He was also a very good shot and a topping sportsman and companion. I must say I simply can't believe that any of the regiment are dead yet."[33]

D Company landed on the left with Brig. Gen. Steuart Hare, their brigade's (Eighty-Sixth) commanding officer. He had seen the beating the other three companies were taking and directed the boats to land under Tekke Burnu. Accompanying him was his brigade major, Thomas Frankland. The men grounded their boats and climbed to the top of the cliff, where they occupied a disused trench. Frankland spied a group of Turks in a nearby trench and took action: "We saw the men being collected in large numbers to the left, and after a time these were led up the cliffs . . . The Turks spotted this and some came charging forward to drive our men into the sea. To keep the men cool, the Brigade Major, 86th Brigade, Frankland, seized a man's rifle and set an example by bowling over two leading Turks."[34] The others ran off, and the Fusiliers occupied their trench.

As soon as this group of Turks was sent packing, Hare, Frankland, and a group of signalers moved to the right, to try to make contact with the Second Royal Fusiliers. Before they had gone two hundred yards, they were fired on by Turks on Hill 114. Hare was severely wounded and had to be evacuated. Frankland managed to contact Lt. Col. Henry Newenham, in command of the Second Royal Fusiliers, to tell him that he was now leading the Eighty-Sixth Brigade, but the colonel could do nothing until his men took the hill. The brigade was thus left without a commander and with nobody to coordinate the operations of the various units. It was up to the individual commanders to act on their own initiative, so C and D Companies advanced toward Hill 114 in an effort to join up with the Royal Fusiliers. They did so at 11:00 a.m., and the hill was taken.

At seven thirty that evening Frankland moved south along the beach to a ruined lighthouse. He intended to establish brigade headquarters there and to organize an attack on Hill 138. By that time the tows carrying the Ansons and the support troops had arrived. The Ansons were sent up Hill 138 to support the Lancashire Fusiliers. By that time the survivors of B Company were attacking the hill, and Frankland went up to the cliff above the lighthouse with the fifty survivors of A Company to prepare for an attack. They were fired on from a hill called Guezji Baba, about three hundred yards north of Hill 138, which was not on their maps. Thinking that this was Hill 138—and without any working compasses—Frankland and his men attacked *that* hill (the commanding officer of B Company, Capt. H. Shaw, mistook Guezji Baba for Hill 114, which was northeast of V Beach). This miscalculation split the force that should have attacked the actual 138. Both attacks floundered as the Fusil-

"Littered with Dead"

iers were once again confronted with barbed wire. Frankland was killed at 8:30 a.m., as he was scouting toward V Beach. His older brother, Capt. Robert Frankland of the 1/8th Lancashire Fusiliers, would arrive later in the campaign and be killed at the Battle of Krithia Vineyard on August 7. The Rev. Oswin Creighton wrote of the gallant major: "Major Frankland was quite one of the finest officers who came out with the Division. He had been out in France since the beginning of the war, and when he returned to take over duty as Brigade-Major of the 86th Brigade he was very much over-strained and suffering from sleeplessness. However, he threw himself into his work with indefatigable zeal, and was always at the service of anyone who came to him. The voyage out considerably rested him, and it was with a fiery enthusiasm that he went off to the landing. The Brigade Staff landed on 'W' beach . . . I afterwards saw his grave just at the top of the steep cliff by the lighthouse."[35]

The Lancashire Fusiliers, who were supposed have taken their objectives without support, were instead reinforced. At 8:30 a.m. the main body scheduled for the V Beach landings, joined them. Hunter-Weston diverted them there because of the difficulty of landing troops at V. The first to land were two companies of the First Battalion, the Essex Regiment: "On the morning of 25th April we were on big boats standing out at sea. We had our breakfast at 3 o'clock in the morning and it was Irish stew and that was the last time I saw a piece of bread. Anyway, we had to climb down these ropes, the Lancashire Fusiliers went first and we followed them and what we had to do was to climb down the side of ships on ropes and there were so many rowing boats. I think there were six rowing boats in each tow and there would be about eight of our fellows in the boats. Then we had a little power boat that took us nearer Lundy [sic] beach at Gallipoli, then we had to paddle with our hands. We got so many killed I ended up with only two in my boat before we were under the cliff edge and all you could see on our left were dead Lancashire Fusiliers."[36]

The rest of the battalion landed at ten o'clock that morning. One company was sent to defend the high ground on the south side of the gully, which took pressure off the Fusiliers attacking toward

Hill 114. The other joined in the assault on Hill 138. Halfway up the hill, they ran into wire and suffered casualties as they worked to cut their way through.

At noon the other three companies of the Fourth Worcesters, along with the remainder of the Second Hampshires, Col. Owen Wolley-Dod, the general staff officer, grade 1, of the Twenty-Ninth Division, landed at twelve thirty and took charge. He ordered the battleships *Euryalus* and *Swiftsure* to fire on the redoubt atop Hill 138. They fired for twenty minutes, but the results were negligible, and it was again left to the riflemen to continue the assault:

> The redoubt was protected by a thick belt of high barbed wire, a formidable obstacle, hardly damaged by the fire of the ships, and under close fire from the redoubt. The only instruments available were the hand wire-cutters carried by the troops. Volunteers were called for and many came forward. Led by Captain A.D.H. Ray and Captain J. O. Nelson the volunteers crept forward through the grass and set to work.
>
> As they clipped away at the wire, bullets came from the redoubt and struck all around them. Undeterred, the wire cutters crawled forward under the fence and continued their work. Many turned on their backs and thus cut away at the wire above them. The wire was hot and one after another those brave men were killed or wounded. But lanes were gradually cut through the wire, and at about 2 p.m. the whole line, Essex and Worcestershire, advanced. The redoubt was rushed and the advance was stopped by uncut barbed wire and by sharp fire of rifles and machine-guns from a second redoubt on another hillock, three hundred yards beyond.[37]

The other hill was Guezji Baba. When the Englishmen were stopped by this additional barrier, Capt. Archibald Ray was mortally wounded. He died after nightfall on the beach. When word was sent back that he had been hit, X Company of Fourth Worcesters was sent into the fray and began hacking away at the seemingly endless wire: "Private A. Mountain led forward the wire cutters. Crawling through long grass into the entanglement he crept beneath the wire. The watchers in rear saw his arm rise out of the grass and his wire cutters snap at the wire above him. Each time his hand went up, a shower of bullets struck round him and sprayed into the dead ground beyond. Presently he was hit; his hand fell. Other volunteers crawled forward to take his place."[38]

Pvt. Arthur Mountain was killed, but before long the Worcesters overcame the wire. They charged the Turks with fixed bayonet, and the defenders took flight. Then the Fusiliers, with some of the Worcesters who had been held up near the ruined lighthouse, moved east toward V Beach. They ran into wire *again* and were hit by heavy defensive fire from Fort No. 1 (which overlooked V). They were stopped in their tracks and could go no farther. Nor could the Worcesters, who had taken the redoubt on Guezji Baba. They, too, were stopped by heavy fire coming from trenches located farther down the hill.

At 4:35 p.m. Wolley-Dod ordered W Company of the Fourth Worcesters, which had been held in reserve, to turn the parapets and start burying the dead.[39] The fallen were a grim-looking lot: water- and sand-sodden lumps of wool covered in dried blood, some unrecognizable as human beings. Nothing could prepare the burial party for what lay ahead. There was no adrenaline to steel them, as there was in battle. There was only shock at what they saw and touched, a feeling that was exacerbated when they recognized the face of a friend.

At five o'clock Wolley-Dod received a message informing him that the men trapped at V needed help. He sent an order to Lt. Col. Douglas Cayley, commanding officer of the Fourth Worcesters, to attack toward Fort No. 1. He did not know that the Worcesters, along with the Lancashire Fusiliers from the lighthouse, were already on their way. But because no progress was being made and darkness was approaching, Wolley-Dod called a halt to the day's efforts. He sent orders to the groups on either side of W Beach to dig in for the night.

The assault on W Beach was a success. But the cost in men had been high—too high. The number of men killed in the Worcesters, Hampshires, and Ansons cannot be broken out from those killed at V Beach because the battalions also suffered casualties there. Of the sailors from the HMS *Euryalus* who landed the Lancashire Fusiliers, sixty-three out of the eighty involved were killed or wounded. Among them was Able Seaman Jack Everett from London. A career sailor mobilized from the Reserve on the outbreak of war, he was married in January 1915 while his ship was coaling in Harwich, Essex. He was hit in the head by a bullet while rowing a boatload full of wounded to a waiting ship and was taken to the transport *Mercian*. He died that night and was buried at sea, sewn into a hammock weighted down with an iron bar.

The First Lancashire Fusiliers landed at W Beach with approximately 950 men. Of that number, 5 officers and 153 other ranks were killed in action. Among them was Acting Cpl. Edgar Appleton of Brighton, Sussex:

> Our losses in the landing were terrible, and most of the casualties were being caused by the enemy in a trench right on the beach, so as soon as we could get ashore, as many men as could possibly be collected at that point were called upon to take this trench at the point of the bayonet. Amongst others was Corpl. Appleton (Darkie we always called him), and his section whom he was leading. The party charged up the hill only to be brought up near the top by a terrific rifle and machine-gun fire. However, they got on the move again, and about 15 yards from the Turkish trench Corpl. Appleton was struck by a hand grenade, which killed him instantly. His chief injuries were in the head. Darkie's Platoon Officer and Sergt. were killed on the beach, and Section Commanders were left to their own discretion. He never flinched, and was gallantly leading his section when he was killed.[40]

The First Essex reported the loss of three officers killed and three wounded, with fifteen other ranks killed and eighty-seven wounded. None of the supporting medics were wounded nor the engineers who built the exits off the beach.

The W Beach landing was so intense that six members of the First Lancashire Fusiliers were awarded the Victoria Cross (VC).

"Littered with Dead"

No other vc's were awarded for W. There would be hard feelings about that decision in years to come, but that does not minimize the gallantry shown by the recipients. One of the awards was posthumous, and two of the remaining five recipients were killed later in the campaign. On May 19, 1915, W Beach was officially renamed "Lancashire Landing" in honor of the men who stormed that fatal shore on the morning of April 25, 1915.

X Beach

Four tows carrying two companies of the Second Battalion, the Royal Fusiliers, were released from the *Implacable* at the same time it released the boats with the Lancashire Fusiliers bound for W Beach. These men, bound for X Beach on the northwest side of the Gallipoli Peninsula, were to land simultaneously with those landing at Y to the north. The Second Royal Fusiliers were part of the Eighty-Sixth Brigade. The battalion's two remaining companies were transported in two minesweepers and were later conveyed to the beach in the same boats that the *Implacable* was then towing. This covering force was to be followed by the First Battalion, the Border Regiment, and the First Battalion, the Royal Inniskilling Fusiliers, which were part of the Eighty-Seventh Brigade. As at V and W Beaches, fifty men of the Anson Battalion were also to be landed to unload food and ammunition.

X Beach is a narrow, sandy beach about two hundred yards long. At its edge is a cliff rising to about one hundred feet. At the time there were no paths leading up to the cliff, and its location prevented it from being shelled from the Asiatic side. The Turks did not expect a landing there. As such, they dug only a few trenches and did not use any of their precious barbed wire. Only twelve riflemen were there to greet the invaders, but reinforcements were located a short distance to the north, in Gully Ravine.

The boats carrying the Fusiliers were each crewed by one midshipman and two sailors. Each tow consisted of six rowboats towed by a steam pinnace. The *Implacable*'s captain was a daring sort named Hughes Campbell Lockyer. He and his gunnery officer, Lt.

John Scott, had developed a plan to overpower any defensive fire the Turks might throw at the soldiers. Instead of keeping his ship 1,000 yards offshore, as his orders dictated, he would steam in to 450 yards—the closest he could get without stranding his vessel— and fire pointblank with everything his ship had.

As the *Implacable* was about to release the tows, the Turkish riflemen opened fire, and the battleship responded with a massive barrage. Lockyer had no idea that the enemy force was so small, and his gunners struck the cliff with a vengeance. The boats thus moved toward land with the ship's guns firing overhead, and the astonished Turks could do nothing but run. When they were one hundred yards from shore, the pinnaces released the boats, and the men rowed for all they were worth. Thanks to Lockyer's initiative, the Fusiliers landed with no casualties and were able to trek up to the cliff unhindered. His actions that day would earn him a knighthood. After the infantrymen landed, he shifted his fire to the ground behind X, but after some of his guns' rounds landed too far off target—near the troops landing at V Beach—he was ordered to withdraw his vessel.

The plan of attack for X was a simple one. After securing the beach and the cliff above it, the Royal Fusiliers were to take Hill 114 on the right (with the help of D Company of the First Lancashire Fusiliers) and establish a defensive line just inland and to the northeast of the beach. There they would also link up with the troops landing at Y. The main body—the Borders and the Inniskillings— were the reserve for the entire Twenty-Ninth Division. They were not to be used unless absolutely necessary.

At 6:30 a.m. the first two Fusilier companies (W and X), along with the battalion's headquarters and machine gun section, were on top of the cliff. By that time the other two companies, Y and Z, were climbing out of the boats. So far, it was a perfect operation.

Problems began shortly after the commanding officer of the Second Royal Fusiliers, Lt. Col. Henry Newenham, divided his battalion and sent the four companies inland toward their objectives. He sent X Company to the left (northeast) and led W Company and part of Z Company against Hill 114. Y Company remained on the beach, where it unloaded boats and waited in reserve. The Ansons cut a path from the beach up to the cliff.

Several hours later, at about eleven o'clock, Hill 114 was captured. The Turks had heavily entrenched the hill and laid primitive landmines. It took more than three hours of fighting, sometimes with bayonets, to take the trenches. Newenham was slightly wounded but remained on duty. An unknown number of Turks were killed, and others managed to escape, but the British took sixty prisoners. One unusual casualty was Fleet Surgeon Adrian Forrester on the *Implacable*. Men on the vessel, which had moved farther out to sea, watched the attack on the hill and cheered when they saw that it was captured. Forrester, who was standing on deck, was hit by a stray bullet and killed instantly.

After taking the hill, Newenham reorganized his men, and they moved against the trenches on the reverse (northeast) side of the hill. There, too, they met heavy opposition but took their objective. Rather than move too far ahead of X Company, Newenham's companies stayed where they were and held what was then the right of the British line at X Beach.

X Company, on the left, met no opposition for the first three hundred yards, but then its luck ran out. When the *Implacable*'s guns sent the small Turkish garrison packing, they ran toward the companies waiting at Gully Beach. One of them was sent to meet X Company, under Capt. Frank Leslie. His company took the first line of trenches, but all hell broke loose when they moved on to the second line at about nine that morning. At the time the commanding officer of the Eighty-Seventh Brigade, Brig. Gen. William Marshall, was atop the cliff with Maj. William Daniell, commanding officer of Y Company, surveying the situation. Part of Y, which was still working on the beach, was called up to reinforce Leslie's men, but the Turks were putting up strong resistance. Their casualties mounting, the British in the center started to fall back. It was the weakest part of the line because the bulk of their strength was concentrated on their flanks. Part of Z Company and the remainder of Y were thrown into the fray, but Leslie's company lost so many men that they had to fall back under cover from Z Company's rifles. Their casualties were staggering, and Leslie was among the dead: "Captain Frank Leslie, who commanded my Company, passed peacefully away on April 25th. His gallantry and coolness under very heavy fire saved many lives. He ordered me to leave him and take some men back to another position, to cover his retirement, and soon after I left him he was shot in the head. He suffered no pain. He was buried where he so gallantly fell."[41]

By the time Marshall sent reinforcements up to help Leslie's men, the First Borders had landed and were waiting anxiously on the beach. They could hear the heavy firing above them and were ready to get into the fight. Marshall ordered them up to the cliff at once in case he needed to send them forward.

Once there, the Borders did not have long to wait. They could see the fighting going on in the distance and had difficulty standing still. At 10:30 a.m. Newenham contacted Marshall by field telephone and asked for reinforcements. The Turks were pressing him, and he did not have enough men left to hold his position. Marshall ordered one of the Borders' companies and two of their machine guns forward to help the beleaguered Fusiliers on the northeast side of Hill 114.

At about that time Marshall saw men from Leslie's company running toward him, with the Turks in hot pursuit. The Border Regiment's captain, George Harrison, yelled to the men of C and part of D Companies, "Fix bayonets, charge!" The infantrymen quickly withdrew their bayonets from their leather scabbards and fixed them under the muzzles of their rifles. With a cheer the excited riflemen took off running after the Turks, who were by then only four hundred yards from the edge of the cliff. They ran six hundred yards, sending the astonished Turks running in the opposite direction. But they did not all turn tail. Some, along with those in their trenches, met the charging Borders with a hail of fire. Rather than chase the Turks any farther, the Borders halted and dug in.

Just before the Fusiliers bolted, Marshall called Maj. Charles Vaughan, DSO, the second-in-command of the Borders, up from

"Littered with Dead"

the beach to observe the situation with him. As the Borders were preparing to charge, the Turks fired a volley that hit some of the riflemen as well as Marshall and Vaughan. Marshall was slightly injured and remained at his post, but Vaughan was killed instantly.

The Borders halted their advance at about one in the afternoon, and the men of the First Royal Inniskilling Fusiliers, who had landed about four hours earlier, were waiting on the beach. Interestingly, their commanding officer told them that if a man was hit, he should try to empty his ammunition pouches "as he fell" so that those coming up behind him could stop and grab this valuable commodity. One man, Sgt. William Smalls, is known to have done so and survived to tell about it.

Marshall had two options. He could extend his line north to link up with the men at Y Beach and south to assist at W, or he could stop and dig in. He chose to stop because a heliograph signal from Y had informed him that the troops there were (at the time) unopposed. The only thing he knew about W was that the troops there were still trying to fight their way up Hill 138 and Guezji Baba. Because the Borders and Inniskillings were the Twenty-Ninth Division's only reserve troops, Marshall decided to stay put and wait for orders from Hunter-Weston. He organized his men into an eight hundred–yard–long arc, with the Borders on the left, the Inniskillings in the center, and the Royal Fusiliers on the right, along the edge of Hill 114.

X Beach was a success. It was later called "Implacable Landing" in honor of the ship that supported the landings there.

Kum Kale

The French landed at Kum Kale, on the Asiatic side of the straits, on the morning of April 25. Heavy currents delayed the landing until 9:00 a.m. The village was in total ruin following the attacks in March, and the Turks had no defenses in the immediate area. Three infantry battalions were located nearby, however, and were quickly dispatched against the invaders. The French landed the Six-ième Régiment, Colonial Mixte (Sixth Mixed Colonial Regiment).

This unit consisted of one French Colonial and two Senegalese battalions, the second group armed with rifles and *coupe-coupes*. These were short, wide-bladed machetes with which the black Africans reaped a terrible harvest of death and mutilation. Many of the native French were recruited in Lyon after the outbreak of war and were going into action for the first time. The Senegalese had already seen action in Morocco and at Ypres on the western front. When winter came in 1914, they were moved into garrisons in Nice and Mentone because they were not used to the harsh European winters. The regiment's commanding officer, Lt. Col. Charles Noguès, had also fought against natives on the Ivory Coast.

The French also landed a battery of rapid-firing 75 mm guns along with engineers, signalers, and a machine gun company from the Fourth Regiment of Chasseurs d'Afrique. Medical staff consisted of twenty-one surgeons, a chemist, and two administrative officers, supported by stretcher-bearers and orderlies. The ships that carried them into battle—the *Savoie*, *Vinh Long*, and *Ceylon*—were all converted to treat wounded as soon as the troops departed for shore. They also brought barbed wire but had neglected to bring the stanchions on which to erect it. So, after the first battle they strung it on the corpses of Turkish soldiers who had fallen in front of their positions.

Maj. Joseph Vassal was the Sixth Mixed Colonial Regiment's surgeon and the senior medical officer for the landing. He watched the action unfold from the auxiliary cruiser *Savoie*:

> In disembarking, the first boat had an officer killed and the whole crew pulverized. The two engineer officers were killed. One young lieutenant was hung, no doubt tortured . . .
>
> In another battalion Blanchard was wounded, Braun is wounded, the Colonel is wounded by the bursting of a shell just as he was leaving the Château d'Europe. Among the circle round the Colonel a lieutenant was cut in two, three men were pulverized, two lost their legs, and his orderly had the whole of his rump carried away.[42]

"Littered with Dead"

Vassal was shocked at the state of the wounded as boatload after boatload arrived for treatment. The first came shortly after eleven o'clock, and they kept coming into the night:

> The convoys of wounded follow each other rapidly. From twilight of the 25th till the first rays of dawn the next day we are leaning over wounded in an atmosphere of blood, of groans, and of indescribable horrors . . .
>
> [They] are mounted on the deck from the bottom of the boats, and form a long line of stretchers. We are able to put six wounded at a time on the big tables of the children's playroom of the *Savoie*.
>
> Sometimes not even a single groan is heard; the silence is impressive. Our fellows are admirable.
>
> The wounds of the night are, nevertheless, frightful. A sergeant-major comes back to us only to die. His chest was crushed by shrapnel; and for a moment we saw his heart, almost bare, still beating. There is a Senegalese with his head torn, a foot missing, and three fingers of a hand gone. Another black, waiting his turn on a chair, is asked "Beaucoup malade?" "Non, il y en a un peu!" The doctor looks. Both legs have been torn off by a shell.
>
> In the middle of the night I was called from the operating room on deck. It was to see a friend who had just been brought back wounded. He said he was cold, then swooned. He is going to die, his wound has bled profusely. But at last, after our united efforts, he regained consciousness.[43]

The assault was supported by the one Russian vessel to take part in the campaign, the light cruiser *Askold*. Known to the British as the "Packet of Woodbines," because its five funnels resembled an open pack of cigarettes, the vessel provided boats and men to land troops from the transport *Vinh Long*. In the process the Russians suffered their only casualties of the campaign: "The first boats return to the *Savoie*. In one I see, as it comes alongside, a wounded man who is being brought to us. It is a Russian sailor who has been hit by several bullets. He lies unconscious at the bottom of the boat; his clothes are covered with blood. One bullet has gone through his arm, a second right through the abdomen, a third has broken one of his legs. Nothing to be done for him; and he died at 12 o'clock without regaining consciousness."[44] Several of the ship's crew were also lost when a 240 mm shell from one of the Turkish forts hit its forward gun turret.

As soon as the first boats neared shore that morning, they came under fire from machine guns, rifles, and artillery. Once ashore, the invaders shot Turks down in great numbers. The Turks were excellent marksmen, however, and their gunners were more than capable of defending themselves.

The French quickly took Fort Kum Kale, then moved on to the deserted village. The Turks were laying in wait for them within the cemetery just outside and opened fire as the French advanced. Second Lt. Joseph Bonavita fell at the head of his troops, cane in hand, after making it out of the fort.

The French were reinforced during the night and planned an attack for six o'clock following morning. It never took place. Instead, Turks came out of the cemetery and surrendered, carrying their weapons in one hand and waving white handkerchiefs in the other. About seventy of them emerged and dropped their weapons. The French stopped firing and led their prisoners into the enclosure fashioned from bodies and barbed wire.

Some of the Turks continued firing, even after their officers ordered them to stop. More also appeared and followed the surrendering riflemen but would not give up their weapons. Confusion grew as the French interpreters tried to make them understand that they must drop their rifles. In the meantime a French officer and an Arabic interpreter went into the Turkish lines to negotiate the surrender.

While this was going on, Turks sneaked into the village's unoccupied buildings. They fired on the French, and a small group captured a French machine gun section. They opened up on the invaders with the captured weapons, killing and wounding many. The position was quickly silenced by one of the French 75's, but not before two more officers were mortally wounded. Turks scattered to the nearby buildings. Men of the First Regiment du Génie (engineers) helped the French riflemen break into the enemy-held houses. The

"Littered with Dead"

riflemen's commanding officer, Capt. Henri-Jule Ferrero, was killed in the process. Another of the regiment's officers, Lieutenant Lefort, was dragged into a building by a group of Turks and was never seen again: "During the recapture of the village a captain and eight men were taken prisoners. This officer, who was a German, spoke French quite well. He was asked what had become of Lieutenant Lefort. It was generally believed that he had been tortured and hung."[45]

In retaliation Noguès ordered that a captured German advisor to be tied to a stake. He offered him his life in return for information about Lefort, but he offered none. He and other prisoners were then turned over to their captives for execution: "The Colonials, who had suffered much in this new affair of the village, and who believed their adversaries were acting in bad faith, excitedly surrounded the prisoners. Already shining blades were flashing from their scabbards. Some of the Senegalese stamped with their feet and gesticulated furiously. Stray shots were let fly."[46] But Noguès pacified the bloodthirsty Africans, and the prisoners' lives were spared.

At two that afternoon the French persuaded the Turks to surrender, following a torrent of rounds from the *Savoie* and the 75's. Hundreds dropped their weapons and left the cemetery, waving their handkerchiefs. The battle was over. But the Turkish battery on In Tepe fired a few parting shots, one of which wounded Noguès. Many were killed and wounded, and one officer, Lieutenant Weingling, "went insane."

The landing at Kum Kale was a success. It prevented the Turks from sending reinforcements to the European side—they would not do so until April 29—and prevented them from moving their mobile guns into the open to harass the men landing at V Beach. The French troops' orders called for them to evacuate the position within twenty-four hours because it was not possible to maintain forces on both sides of the straits. By the time they departed to take over V Beach in the early morning hours of April 27, they had killed or wounded 1,730 Turks and captured another 500. The attackers suffered 778 casualties in the short time they were ashore, however, and there were no reserves to fill their depleted ranks.

Overall the Helles operation was a success. But barely so. Casualties were higher than anyone on the General Staff had expected. This was due to sheer ignorance and a lack of imagination on their part. Because Kitchener had denied the Twenty-Ninth Division the customary 10 percent reinforcements, there was nobody there yet to replace the battalions' casualties. The exhausted soldiers had no option but to hold the line and keep fighting, with little food or water and no sleep. Exhaustion would dog them for the entire campaign. The men were starting down a long road of debility caused by fighting, exhaustion, stress, depression, poor diet, and abysmal sanitary conditions. But the Turks also lost heavily, with some units suffering 50 percent casualties. Had Kitchener the common sense to send those reinforcements, the situation might have been capitalized on. As it was, all the British could do was lick their wounds.

The diversionary landing at Bulair was a farce. It did not fool the Turks into diverting reinforcements away from the actual landing areas. Some of the RND troops simply got into boats, headed toward shore as darkness was beginning to fall, then headed back when it was too dark for the Turks to see that the event was a ploy. In an effort to prevent unnecessary casualties (none occurred), an officer of the Hood Battalion, Lt. Cdr. Bernard Freyberg, swam more than a mile to shore, armed only with a revolver and flares in a waterproof canvas bag slung around his neck. His plan was to ignite the flares on shore after dark in an effort to draw the Turks' attention, then to fight off any he encountered with his revolver before swimming out to a waiting ship's cutter. But he failed see any Turks and was able to walk some distance inland to one of their trenches. There he found only dummies guarding the coast. He swam back to the cutter and for his efforts was awarded the Distinguished Service Order. The following year he would win the Victoria Cross for gallantry in France.

6

―――

"Had We Gone Forward We Should Have Been Wiped Out"

The Battles of April—Helles

Darkness at Helles did not bring with it the much-feared Turkish counterattacks. The exception was Y Beach. At S, W, and X the troops all experienced a sleepless, cold, wet night with little food or water while digging in and doing their best to keep alert. Incessant small arms fire from both sides broke the night's silence, allowing only a few the luxury of sleep after their digging was done.

The situation was different at V Beach, where the troops could not advance because of ongoing Turkish fire. Darkness, however, allowed those still on the *River Clyde* to land. Casualties were removed from the beach to the dressing station established on the *Clyde* by the Eighty-Ninth Field Ambulance. The dead were left lying where they fell.

One of the men who would help break the deadlock was Lt. Col. Charles Doughty-Wylie, an intelligence officer on Hamilton's staff who had arrived at V Beach on the *Clyde*. The forty-six-year-old officer, wounded in the Boer War and with extensive service in Asia and the Near East, had served in Constantinople as director of the Red Cross units there during the Balkan War of 1912–13. He loved Turkey and its people and did not relish the thought of taking up arms against them.

Another was Capt. Garth Walford, the brigade major of the Twenty-Ninth Divisional Artillery. Hunter-Weston dispatched to the *River Clyde* after dark on April 25 to organize an assault on Hill 141. He was one of those who underestimated the fighting ability of the Turks. Like so many of the highly educated officers who landed at Gallipoli on April 25, he saw the assault as a modern-day crusade in which Christian would triumph over Infidel. He and Doughty-Wylie, neither of whom was expected to lead troops into battle, only to organize them, were instrumental in breaking the deadlock at V. Both would pay for their bravery with their lives.

An attack on Hill 141 required that the troops on the beach first clear Fort Sedd-el-Bahr on their right, then the village behind it. Both areas were filled with Turks, who sheltered in the rubble and fired on the invaders with virtual impunity from small arms fire. True, the warships were taking their toll on the defenders, but their ammunition was in short supply, and they had to husband their high-explosive rounds for the eventual assault up the straits. Their shrapnel shells were devastatingly effective against flesh and bone when they exploded above ground, out in the open. But they, too, were in short supply.

It was impossible to advance during the night. Although the Turks in the trenches immediately facing the beach withdrew after dark, snipers remained, and the defenders were still in the fort, the village, and atop Hill 141. The Dublins and Munsters had lost almost all of their officers and were at the ends of their tethers: "We had at this period a number of cases where men's nerves cracked, the result of what they had been through, and we had to get them out of the line."[1]

The troops experienced terrible emotional and physical stress, were wet through after a night spent in the rain, and most had been without sleep for two days. Men they had lived and worked with for years were suddenly gone. Some lay under the warm, gentle surf of the Aegean, their lifeless eyes staring skyward toward the heaven they now occupied. Others lay nearby in the sand, some missing heads or limbs. Many were so badly disfigured by the converging

"Had We Gone Forward"

fire of the Turkish machine guns that they hardly appeared human. If there is a hell, surely V Beach must have been it.

Before dawn plans were drawn up for an attack. First, the battleship *Albion* would bombard the fort for thirty minutes, until 5:30 a.m. Maj. Arthur Beckwith, the senior surviving officer of the Second Hampshires, which had landed during the night from the *River Clyde*, would lead the assault on the fort and village. On the left a party led by Lt. Col. Weir Williams, a staff officer, would lead an attack that would meet up with Beckwith's group to assault Hill 141.

The attack on the left faltered from the start due to a Turkish machine gun fire, but the *Albion* quickly took care of that. None of the Irishmen were hit by the harassing machine gun, but they took cover and did not immediately advance. Williams moved toward W Beach on the left to see if any progress might be made to link up with the troops there. He felt that further progress at V was impossible.

At five thirty Beckwith led his troops—a mixture of Dublins, Munsters, and Hampshires—against the fort and captured it in short order. But as the troops exited through the postern gate into the village, they were hit with a murderous fire and stopped. They had not known that a short Turkish trench was covering the gate.

Seeing this, Walford left the *River Clyde* to assist Beckwith's men. He ran to the front of the group and, with Capt. Alfred Addison of the Hampshires, led the men out of the gate and into the village. There they were confronted by a new kind of hell as unseen Turks attacked them from the burned-out shells of the buildings. The attackers dropped left and right but fought the Turks like the devil himself with bullets and bayonets, even fists. They exacted a heavy toll on the defenders and eventually secured the village. But lives were lost, among them Addison's: "Addison, of the Hants, is gone; he met his end in the village of Sedd-el-Bahr. He was leading his men, firing right and left with his revolver. He met a Turk coming round the corner of a street; he pulled the trigger of his revolver, nothing happened. He opened it, found it empty, threw it to the ground with a curse, went for the Turk with his fist, but was met by a well-aimed bomb, which exploded in his face, killing him instantly."[2]

Walford was killed by a Turkish bullet while trying to lead another group through the gate. Before he was killed, he signaled the *Clyde* that he was getting no support from the left side of the village. Hearing this, Doughty-Wylie and Capt. George Stoney, V Beach's military landing officer, left the collier to organize help. Stoney moved to the center, where the barbed wire stood untouched, and Doughty-Wylie went to the right, toward the village. Unarmed and carrying only his cane, he was unfazed by the bullets whizzing past and striking the masonry of the fort around him. Even after a bullet knocked his cap off, he continued toward the village, never pausing to duck for cover. At one point he picked up a rifle with a fixed bayonet and led an assault through the village. He soon dropped the weapon in favor of his cane and moved around, encouraging the men. After about three hours, they took the village. Then, after requesting the *Albion* to shell the redoubt on Hill 141, he led the charge up the hill. It was the last act of a valiant man: "We went through the fort, through Sedd el Bahr village and we took Hill 141. And after we took the hill we dug in a bit of a trench and laid down there and Colonel Doughty Wylie was with us. He went all through the village. I'll never forget him because he had one puttee on and all he had was a walking stick. I didn't see a revolver and he came all through the village with us and, he was stood up—I was laid down here with the company—and he was stood up alongside me, and his orderly and they were shouting to him to get down. 'Get down, sir, you'll get hit,' because there was sniping. And he wouldn't and an explosive bullet hit him right there, below the eye, blew all the side of his face out. And his orderly got killed."[3] Also killed was Maj. Cecil Grimshaw, the adjutant of the First Dublins who took over command of the battalion after Lt. Col. Rooth was killed. He had survived captivity with Winston Churchill during the Boer War.

By three in the afternoon the hill was taken, and V Beach was secured. Doughty-Wylie was laid to rest where he fell and remains there still. After the war, when the Imperial War Graves Commission was moving the isolated graves at Gallipoli into newly established

"Had We Gone Forward"

cemeteries, the Turks granted him the unique honor of remaining where he had breathed his last. He and Walford were awarded posthumous Victoria Crosses, and Hill 141 was renamed "Doughty-Wylie Hill." The following day the French arrived from Kum Kale and took over the sector comprising V and S Beaches.

V Beach was not secured by the victors of Sedd-el-Bahr and Hill 141 alone. On their left Stoney collected a number of men, many of them Munsters, and a party of fifty was given the job of clearing the barbed wire under fire. They succeeded, chiefly due to the initiative of 6'6" tall Irishman Cpl. Billy Cosgrove, who hailed from a tiny village in County Cork. The so-called Giant of Cork, finding that he could not cut through the thick wire with his cutters, tossed the useless tool aside and stood up through a hail of Turkish bullets. Wrapping his arms around one of the stanchions that secured the wire, he yanked it out of the ground, then called on others to follow suit. They did, and some were killed or wounded in the process. Among them was the group's leader, company sergeant Maj. Alfred Bennett. He was killed instantly by a bullet in the head as he struggled with one of the posts.

Once the wire was breached, the Irishmen charged seven hundred yards to the enemy's trench, killing and wounding everyone they encountered. Cosgrove was wounded by bullets from a Turkish machine gun as he charged ahead. The gallant Irishman was awarded the Victoria Cross. He retired from the army in 1934 but died in hospital two years later, one of his brothers by his side, as a result of the wounds he had suffered on April 26, 1915. He never married and died poor. A quiet, unassuming man, he did not like to speak of his exploits on April 26.

The troops that landed on April 25 were too battered and exhausted to do much of anything. Hunter-Weston understood that an immediate advance was out of the question, even though he knew from his patrols' reports that the Turks, with the exception of snipers, had pulled back. They, too, were licking their wounds and awaiting reinforcements. For the British there was also the problem of artillery, which was desperately needed to support an assault and harass the Turks. But guns were in short supply, and the horses needed to move them were not delivered on time. There were also too few shells for the guns and almost no high-explosive rounds, which were required for destroying trenches and barbed wire. The majority of those that were delivered were shrapnel. This problem would dog the British throughout the campaign. Priority was given to units fighting on the western front, and even they were not receiving what they needed.

Another problem was food and water. Water was delivered in shiny, square kerosene tins that were filled in Egypt. They were not rinsed before being filled and had to be delivered to the front by mule. But for the first couple of days there were no mules. Thus, for the first crucial days after landing, the troops manning the front lines were not only exhausted; they were thirsty and half-starved as well. They could not have mounted a serious attack if they wanted to.

Nevertheless, Hunter-Weston knew that he had to make a move. After learning that the Turks had backed off, his intention was to attack on April 27. But circumstances were against him. The French, who had only begun disembarking the night before, were not yet established. His resources were also perilously short. In terms of men he had only received two more battalions, and those that had landed on April 25 received no reinforcements at all. Nevertheless, he would attack. He *had* to attack before the Turks could bring up reinforcements.

On April 27 Hunter-Weston's staff drew up plans for an attack the following day, but brigade commanders did not receive them until the early hours of April 28. The battalion commanders received them just before dawn, and the attack was to commence at eight in the morning. The infantrymen, some of their units depleted by more than 50 percent, had no idea of what they were supposed to do.

The goal of the assault was to reach a point at which a line could be established for an attack on Achi Baba. In order to accomplish it, the British line would make a sweeping move to the right, like the second hand on a watch, and would pivot from the French positions on the right at S Beach. The new line would run from Hill 236, a

"Had We Gone Forward"

quarter-mile northeast of S Beach on the right, to the mouth of Gully Ravine on the left, and forward of Krithia in the center. The French Colonials would attack from their sector on the right, the British Eighty-Eighth Brigade would attack in the center, and the Eighty-Seventh Brigade would attack on the left, astride Gully Ravine.

The day opened sunny and warm, a light breeze playing through the cypress and olive trees and the colorful wild iris that grew up through the grass. The British artillery disturbed the morning with its opening bombardment, beginning as planned at eight o'clock. Shortly afterward, the infantry began its assault. At first the riflemen made good progress and were only harassed by the odd sniper. But as they moved deeper into enemy territory, the attackers began falling in greater numbers. Over the last two days the Ottomans had received substantial reinforcements, and they continued to arrive during the attack. The defenders had used the lull in fighting to dig more trenches and emplace their machine guns in well-concealed positions. They had also cut trees into odd shapes and measured the distance from their guns so they could gauge the range of the attackers as they passed them.

As would happen so often at Gallipoli, the French Colonials retreated after meeting major resistance from a gully called the "Kereves Dere." Their white officers, conspicuous among the black Senegalese troops and wearing distinctive white sun helmets, were obvious targets for the Turks. The normally brave Africans, much feared by the Turks for their fighting prowess and their horrible *coupe-coupes*, tended to break and run when their European officers fell, Leaving the British's right flank vulnerable to Turkish attack. The British troops began suffering heavier casualties as a result. Maj. A. J. Welsh, of the First King's Own Scottish Borderers (KOSB, Eighty-Seventh Brigade), recorded his disgust at the retreating French: "During the advance we passed on our L. [left] a battalion of the R.N.D., who were retiring to the beach for dinners,[4] and on the R. [right] some French Colonials, who were lucky not to be shot by being mistaken for advancing Turks, retired through us, also rearward bound."[5]

On the left the Eighty-Seventh Brigade was meeting heavy resistance. While battalions such as the First KOSB advanced in good order despite heavy casualties, some men broke and ran. At least one, a member of the Second South Wales Borderers, was shot in the back and killed by one of his own men when he did. A group of the First Borders retreated after a large body of Turks charged it. The Ottomans leaped up and surprised the Englishmen. Fortunately for them, observers on the battleship *Queen Elizabeth*, from which Hamilton and his staff were watching the incident through binoculars, saw what was happening. The ship's gunners opened fire with one of its massive fifteen-inch guns, exploding a single shrapnel shell over the Turks. Thirteen *thousand* shrapnel balls rained down on the attackers, killing almost all of them:

> The Turks were no longer in mass but extended in several lines, less than a pace between each man. Before this resolute attack our men, who were much weaker, began to fall back. One Turkish Company, about a hundred strong, was making an ugly push within rifle shot of our ship. Its flank rested on the very edge of the cliff, and the men worked forward like German Infantry in a regular line, making a rush of about fifty yards with sloped arms and lying down and firing. They all had their bayonets fixed. Through a glass every move, every signal, could be seen. From where we were our guns exactly enfiladed them. Again they rose and at a heavy sling trot came on with their rifles at the slope; their bayonets glittering and their Officer ten yards ahead of them waving his sword. Some one said they were cheering. Crash! and the Q.E. let fly a shrapnel; range 1,200 yards; a lovely shot; we followed it through the air with our eyes. Range and fuse— perfect. The huge projectile exploded fifty yards from the right of the Turkish line, and vomited its contents of 10,000 [*sic*] bullets clean across the stretch whereupon the Turkish Company was making its last effort. When the smoke and dust cleared away nothing stirred on the whole of that piece of ground. We looked for a long time, nothing stirred.[6]

The explosion of that single round slowed the Turkish advance in that part of the line.

The unexpectedly strong Turkish resistance required that Hunter-Weston throw all of his reserves into the battle. Once again, the battalions suffered heavy casualties, especially the Dublins and Munsters. As a result, they were temporarily combined into a composite battalion the following day. They would be officially referred to as the "Dubsters" until May 19, when much-needed reinforcements and some of those wounded in the first three days of the campaign arrived to fill out the two battalions.

By the end of the day the French were right back where they had started, and the British had advanced only a short distance. The infantry was simply not up to the task. Artillery support, with the exception of the naval guns, was so feeble that many men did not even know they had any. Only twenty-eight guns were ashore when the battle began. The artillerymen had few animals to tow their weapons far enough forward to be of much use, so the gunners did their best to manhandle them. Despite their best efforts, they had very little ammunition. Thus, the First Battle of Krithia failed because of a lack of reinforcements, a lack of artillery, exhaustion, and heavy Turkish resistance.

The state of the British on April 28 is reflected in the regimental history of the King's Own Scottish Borderers: "It was a curious day—the 28th. The 29th Division were dog tired and one-third under strength. The artillery support was incomplete. The country was unreconnoitred. Units were somewhat mixed. No one was in his expected place. General Marshall was not with his brigade but was O.C. [officer commanding] British troops. For part of the day he was minus a staff. The brigades were commanded by battalion commanders, as Brig.-Gen. Napier was dead and Brig.-Gen. Hare had been wounded at the landing. Hardly a battalion had its original C.O. [commanding officer] to lead it. And yet the most competent judges are of the opinion that, with just a little more drive in the shape of reserves, Krithia and Achi Baba might have been ours."[7] Still, the front was advanced in places. The new line was called the

"Eski Line" (after Eski Hissarlik, which was located to the south of its southeasternmost point). After further British advances, it became a reserve line that the Turks never crossed.

Diary accounts of the battle are scarce. One of them, written by a stretcher-bearer, is typical of those recorded: "Out all day bringing in the wounded. Shelled all afternoon with shrapnel, nearly all of them wasted. We had to retire & advance time after time. In fact it was a very hard day to all. Finished up with a drenching. Awful night."[8]

The casualty count for the First Battle of Krithia is officially recorded as 2,000 British killed and wounded out of about 8,500 committed. The French reported losing 1,001 out of about 5,000. It would be days before all of the wounded could be accounted for. On April 29 Staff Sgt. James Hall of Y Battery, Royal Horse Artillery, noted in his diary: "Wounded infantry crawling back with terrible wounds. Helped some behind the guns, bandaged them and gave them water. Poor devils had to get back 4 miles to the temporary shore hospital."

The Turks reported 2,378 killed and wounded. Total British casualties for the day are questionable, as are most of the daily casualty counts for Gallipoli. Unlike the Australians and New Zealanders, who recorded a range of dates when they were not sure when a man was killed, the British insisted on a precise date. All too often, the date recorded was wrong (it was worse for Indian army units). While most were accurately recorded, the British would sometimes note the date on which a man was determined to have been killed as his actual date of death. Some men killed on April 25 are listed as having died on April 30 or May 2 because that was when their battalions drew up their casualty lists. With regard to the First Battle of Krithia, physical and mental exhaustion was a factor. The men had not been well fed for several days, making it difficult to compile accurate lists. They were tired, their heads filled with the fog of battle, and they were physically weak. Officers, who were responsible for compiling the lists, suffered the same problems as their men but had the added difficulty of maintaining their mental

"Had We Gone Forward"

faculties so they could lead their troops. It was no easy task. Some, especially the older ones, were not up to it.

Anzac

At Anzac the Australians and New Zealanders spent their first night evacuating wounded, establishing their base on the beach, and doing their utmost to keep the Turks at bay. There were still major gaps in their lines, and nobody was sure who was where in the dark. The Turks were in the same position. They were also disorganized and had suffered heavy casualties, and most of them were new to the area. Many of the Turks were often just as lost as the Australian and New Zealand Army Corps (ANZAC) troops were.

While the staff on the beach feared that an evacuation would be necessary, those fighting in the front lines were under no such illusion. They *would* hold the enemy back, and they *would* advance. With no knowledge that an evacuation was being contemplated, they spent the cold, wet night digging in with their entrenching tools and whatever digging implements could be scrounged from the beach. Stragglers, of which there were hundreds, were sent to places where there was a gap in the line or units were short of men. These men had become separated from their battalions for various reasons. Some Australians returned to the beach as the fighting died down so they could tell their stories to later arrivals. Food and water were carried to the front lines, and wooden crates of ammunition were lugged forward to replenish depleted stocks.

During the night many of the infantrymen worked hard on their trenches and rifle pits because they feared the Turks would launch a major attack the following morning. They did not. They were still badly disorganized, and with the coming of daylight, the British ships fired on anything that moved in and behind their lines. The Turks were not silent, however. Their artillery harried the Anzacs, and snipers took their toll. Rifle and machine gun fire continued throughout the night. Many Anzacs, especially Australians, suffered because they expected to advance when daylight came, and they saw no use in expending what little energy they had on digging in. No one will ever know how many died as a result of their foolishness, but the number was great.

The Anzacs spent April 26 deepening their trenches and trying to fill the gaps in their line. For the most part they were successful, but there were exceptions. The Turks still had control over the head of Monash Valley, from their vantage point on Baby 700, and this was a source of considerable danger for the invaders. This valley provided their only means of travel to the all-important Second Ridge, and many men lost their lives trying to reach and depart the three important defensive posts—Quinn's, Courtney's, and Steele's Posts—which faced the Turkish line there. Of the three, Quinn's Post was, and would remain, the most crucial point in the line and the most heavily defended. The ANZAC and Turkish fronts were only a few yards apart at that point, and the Turks worked especially hard to kick the Anzacs out of their precarious foothold. Unfortunately for the men who would garrison Quinn's, they were open to Turkish small arms fire from three sides. The bones of some of the hundreds who fell there are still to be found in the scrub covering the steep slope running from the back of the post down the valley below. I have seen them.

The day was quiet in the sector, at least in terms of major assaults. Turks still probed forward, and both sides fired on one another. The Anzacs used it as a day for reorganizing their battalions and bringing in the remainder of the Australian Fourth Brigade, which had been prevented from landing the day before because the boats were conveying wounded men to the ships. There was one major exception to the day's activities.

On April 26 the Second Australian Brigade held the line from Bolton's Ridge, running northeast and onto 400 Plateau. On its left were the First and Third Australian Brigades, which were inter-mixed from the previous day's fighting. Their line extended as far as Quinn's. At that point the line bent back toward the beach, across Monash Gully to the center of Russell's Top and down Walker's Ridge toward the sea. New Zealanders were on Walker's Ridge and were mixed in among the Australians, and both were fighting in iso-lated groups throughout the sector, either lost or cut off.

On the right the part of the line held by the Second Australian Brigade was just a jumble of rifle pits and groups of men in gullies, waiting for the order to attack. They were among those who saw no point in digging in. But to be fair, they had few picks or shovels, Turkish fire was too heavy for most of them to risk standing up, and it was difficult to reach the men in that part of the line to pass along orders. They suffered an unknown number of casualties, including 2nd Lt. Thomas Evans, the commanding officer of the Third Battalion's machine gun section:

It devolved on him to stop the firing of a machine gun of another battn. which was firing too close to our troops, and the ground was swept by a heavy rifle and machine gun fire. However, he safely returned, to my great relief. Later, whilst I was temporarily at another part of the firing line, the same gun again became dangerous, and a message reached your son to that effect from Major Brown, of my battn. Lieut. Evans again went over, and when returning stopped to succour a wounded man who had been left in the open. Having bound up the man's wound, he tried to carry him back to safety, but was hit repeatedly. Though badly wounded he still tried to save his man to the admiration of all those who saw his gallant conduct. An attempt was made by my men to rescue them, but your son was riddled with bullets and died a hero. I may mention that I recommended your son for the V.C. on account of his distinguished valour in the field, and his name is one of three in my battn. who were specially mentioned in Sir Ian Hamilton's Despatches.[9]

Shortly after noon on April 26, the commander of the First Australian Division, Maj. Gen. William Bridges, toured the front line to learn about the situation in that area. He wanted to see if there was a gap between the Second and Third Brigades, as he had been told, and was not at all pleased with what he found. Seeing the poor state of his men's positions, he ordered them to straighten their line and dig in. Specifically, he wanted the men of the Sixth and Seventh Battalions, on McKay's Hill, to move forward until they were in line with the Tenth Battalion on their left and the Fourth Battalion on their right. The men of the Tenth and Fourth Battalions were to move forward slightly to conform to the new line. The Fifth Battalion, under Maj. Richard Saker, also moved forward, Bridges having bluntly criticized the state of his men's poorly dug trench.

Thus, following the general's orders as best they understood them, the men of the various battalions moved forward at about three o'clock. But they did not know how far they were supposed to go or exactly what they were supposed to do. As a result, and because organized communications were nil, most of the officers led their men forward thinking that they were actually making the anticipated advance. Battalions not ordered to join in the move did so anyway, thinking that an advance was being made and not wanting to be left out. As they advanced, they were caught in the open by the waiting Turks. Australians fell left and right, hit by bullets and artillery rounds fired from Chunuk Bair and Scrubby Knoll to the northeast and Gun Ridge to the southeast. Two hours later the Ninth and Fifteenth Battalions were also in the fight, the Fifteenth losing heavily (the Ninth suffered no fatalities). During the night the Turks had managed to move reinforcements into the area, and they hit the Australians hard. Bridges, who had not ordered the men to attack, did not even know that they had done so until after the fact.

The losses suffered in that movement were heavy, and the Australians had little to show for their efforts. The Turks took a particularly high toll on the officers. One of those lost was the Fourth Battalion's commanding officer, Lt. Col. Astley Onslow Thompson. He was hit while returning to his original position on 400 Plateau: "Colonel Onslow Thompson and others who were with him, their line having gone and no instructions having been received, decided to return to the Australian lines. They endeavoured to reach them, not by direct retirement, but by moving forward diagonally to their left. As they did so, the Turks opened fire. Onslow Thompson was killed. Lieutenant Massie picked up his body and carried it toward the trenches, but the fire proved too severe. The Colonel's body remained in front of the line until it was found by the 3rd Battalion

"Had We Gone Forward"

when digging a forward sap on May 11."[10] Unlike many of those killed during the advance, the colonel's body was buried but hastily: "The grave of Colonel Onslow Thompson was found against one of our trenches. Like a fine soldier, he was killed and buried under the Hill, [by] a Bullet of the enemy. So shallow is the grave that his boots are seen protruding from the soil around."[11]

This incident is unusual for another reason, not simply because the assault was not ordered and without structure. Several of the men listed as missing in action on April 26 are noted in missing in action reports as having been killed on April 25. There do not appear to be any reliable reports of men listed as missing on the twenty-sixth. Many of the dead were erroneously reported as having been seen in hospitals in Egypt and England.

Another drama unfolded the following day at Walker's Ridge and Russell's Top, on the extreme left of the Anzac line. It was on April 27 that Ottoman lieutenant colonel Mustafa Kemal, the commanding officer of the Nineteenth Division, launched his counterattack all along the Anzac line. Kemal, who would later be known as Kemal Atatürk, the father of modern Turkey, was a brave and capable soldier. On April 25 he declined to wait for orders to move his division into the line and personally led one of its infantry regiments, the Fifty-Seventh, into the fight.

On April 27 the Fifty-Seventh Regiment fought bravely again, although Kemal did not personally lead it. Opposing these troops was the Second Battalion, Australian Imperial Force (AIF), under Lt. Col. George Braund, VD. The forty-nine-year-old Englishman, who was a member of Australia's parliament, had raised and trained the battalion and was, like most of his men, in action for the first time. He was unpopular with his men. They considered him to be a strict disciplinarian and thought his professional background, managing director of a storekeeping firm, impeded his ability to lead blue-collar workers into battle. His men did not know that his beginnings in Australia had been just as humble as some of theirs, working in the linen department of the firm that he would later direct. Braund was awarded the Victorian Decoration for his service as an officer in the Citizen Forces, and his men made fun of the initials VD that followed his name. Add to that the fact that he had a shrill voice and was partially deaf, and you have an officer in whom most men had no confidence. That was all about to change.

Kemal's attack was launched against the length of the Anzac line, but for a variety of reasons it came off only piecemeal. A lack of communications played a significant part in the failure, as did the fact that the newly arrived Turkish reinforcements were just as lost in the new territory as the Anzacs had been when they landed. Some of the men had not been fed properly; one regiment's hot meal arrived just as it was leaving for the front line. The Anzacs, by now familiar with their surroundings, put up extremely heavy resistance, and the Turkish attacks simply fell apart.

The exception was that of the Fifty-Seventh Infantry Regiment. It attacked the Anzacs holding Walker's Ridge and, rising above it to the west, Russell's Top. Two companies of New Zealand's Canterbury Battalion were on the left, on Walker's Ridge. On their right was Braund's Second Battalion. Some of the New Zealanders who had been beaten off Baby 700 on April 25 were on Russell's Top. One company of the Thirteenth Battalion, AIF, was on their right. On the Thirteenth's right was a gap across the head of Monash Gully, then the Sixteenth Battalion, AIF, which was defending Pope's Hill. All of the men were operating with little water, under constant pressure from Turkish snipers, and with little or no sleep. Braund's men had not slept since before the landing.

The Second Battalion, and the units on its left and right, had been harried by Turkish snipers and small probing attacks almost constantly since April 25. But on the morning of April 27 sniper fire against Braund's position became heavier. Daylight brought the revelation that during the night Turks had advanced close to his line and dug a trench. Rather than wait for them to attack, he took the lead. At eight o'clock that morning he ordered Capt. George Concanon, commanding officer of C Company, to take the trench using bayonets. It was full of Turks waiting to attack. Concanon and his men took the position, but 84 men were killed or wounded within only fifteen

"Had We Gone Forward"

minutes. A series of back-and-forth attacks left them back where they had started, but Braund's intent had only been to drive out the offending Turks, not to advance. The attack kept the Turks immediately in front of his position at bay, but he lost too many men in the process. Shortly before ten o'clock a group of 140 reinforcements, composed of stragglers from various units, arrived to help. All the while Turkish snipers and machine guns hidden in the thick scrub continued hitting his men. Braund's only recourse, because his men could not see the enemy, was to drive them out of the scrub at the points of his men's bayonets. More men were lost, among them Concanon:

> At about 9 a.m. on Tuesday 27th April I was ordered to reinforce C. Company (Concannon's [*sic*]) as they were being pressed by the Turks. On the way to the position my men were to occupy I met Capt. Concannon who remarked how glad he was to see me still alive and then said, "God has been good to me during the past two days." Later in the morning the Turks advanced through the scrub and came very close to the trenches we had taken from them earlier in the fighting, and which we had occupied ever since. There was no field of fire from their trenches because of the dense scrub in front so we advanced with the bayonet and drove the enemy off. Capt. Concannon was on the left and I was on the right, and as soon as we emerged from the bushes the enemy turned some machine guns, also heavy rifle fire, on us. We gained the position we wanted with considerable loss and the men were ordered to lie down and take advantage of any cover. At this stage I saw Capt. Concannon for the first time since the meeting earlier in the morning before mentioned. He was then walking immediately in rear of the firing line making towards me rallying and encouraging the men. The whole time the enemy's fire was very heavy and sweeping our position. He kept on until within about five feet of me when he fell mortally wounded, dying in about a couple of minutes. L/cpl Bristow of "A" Co. went to his assistance but saw nothing could be done and while rendering assistance received a wound from which he died later.[12]

Concanon was an unlikely man for the brave deeds he had performed. A banker in civil life, he had been forced to end his studies at Cambridge early because of ill health. He would not be the only member of his family to fall victim to Gallipoli. His uncle Maj. Richard Jenkins arrived at Gallipoli with the Twentieth Battalion in September and was killed on December 11.

Down on the beach, the ANZAC staff was oblivious to Kemal's counterattack because it was occurring in such piecemeal fashion. But Braund kept in constant telephone contact. He was fortunate to have had this access, as it allowed him to request supporting fire from the navy. During the day the ANZAC staff decided to allot control over the various portions of the sector. The prominence that became Walker's Ridge was turned over to the New Zealand Infantry Brigade under Brig. Gen. Harold Walker, for whom it was to be named. The day before, he had celebrated his fifty-third birthday on the beach. He arrived on the ridge at 10:30 a.m. and spent a half-hour assessing the situation in which Braund and the New Zealanders found themselves. Realizing that trouble was brewing, he called on the New Zealand Expeditionary Force's Wellington Battalion, under Lt. Col. William Malone, to reinforce the positions. His battalion was in reserve in Howitzer Gully at the time and was eager to get into the fight.

The day was hot, and Malone's men, in their woolen uniforms and full combat gear, panted their way up the steep hillside to the ridge. They were lucky to have had a proper breakfast that morning. But water was always short, and the men, moving fast, did not have the luxury of stopping to quench their thirst. Halfway up they were ordered to drop their packs. Reaching the top before noon, they found that there was not enough room for them and the original defenders to take shelter. As a result, many men were hit. In fact, as the last of the Wellington's arrived, some of the first members of their battalion to have arrived were being carried back down the hill on stretchers.

At 1:30 p.m. the strain caught up with the Anzacs, and the left of their line began falling back. They were quickly rallied and sent back, but Braund knew something had to be done if his force was to keep going. Two days of fighting, with no sleep and little water, was proving to be too much. The military way is to keep men's minds off their problems by keeping them busy, and Braund did just that. He ordered them to fix bayonets. Then he personally led them forward against the Turks, who had not reoccupied the trench they had dug the night before but were lying well hidden in the scrub. The lucky ones ran and were shot in the back by the advancing Anzacs. Those who opted to stay and fight were bayoneted where they lay.

The rush of adrenaline was just what the Anzacs needed. They chased their tormentors until they realized that to go farther under the increasing Turkish fire would mean certain death. Braund ordered his men to dig in, but they eventually had to retreat to the trenches dug after Concanon's advance, just forward of their original position. No reinforcements were available, and it was the only option open to him. He ordered his line to retire by sections at 2:30 p.m.

Kemal's attack there was just beginning as the left of the line was about to pull back. Six lines of Turks appeared and began moving forward from the hill opposite the ANZAC Walker's Ridge and Russell's Top. The men on the left of Braund's advanced line saw what was happening and made a run for the rear. They were stopped by a group of New Zealand Engineers who had just arrived to help dig a trench. They told the retreating riflemen that they were reinforcements, so the men returned to the line. At about that time the Seventeenth (Ruahine) Company of the Wellington Battalion arrived and strengthened the position.

Fortunately for the beleaguered Anzacs, a British battleship saw the lines of advancing Turks and fired three ranging shots. The first fell short, landing in the trenches of the Australian Sixteenth Battalion on Pope's Hill. The second went long. But the third, rumbling over the heads of the defenders, burst right over the Turks. Six more rounds followed, and that was the end of attack. But surviving Turks did not all break and run. Most fell to the ground, took cover behind the scrub, and fired at the Anzacs.

At nine that night the Turks launched another attack, one that introduced the defenders to a hell of a different kind: hand-to-hand combat in the dark. With so little natural light, the assault was particularly frightening because of the various sounds that seemed to be amplified in the darkness. The attackers moved forward with cries of "Allah, Allah!" Their officers, yelling commands, were accompanied by buglers, their instruments pouring out signals indiscernible to the exhausted defenders. Cries of "Stretcher-bearer! Stretcher-bearer!" punctuated the night as Anzacs fell to the unseen enemy. In the dark the medics did their best to aid the injured and to bandage them in what little light nature saw fit to grant them, then moved on toward the next cry for help. When they had it, they dispensed a morphine tablet, a quick bandage, and a word or two of encouragement. Unfortunately for most of the wounded, this would be the only medical treatment they would receive for several days.

Even using bombs, which the Anzacs had not yet encountered, the Turks were unable to overcome the exhausted defenders. These small, round, iron hand grenades, which were ignited with match-lit fuses, were a curiosity to the Australians. They had their first chance to examine them when they were taken from Turkish corpses the following day. During the attack they proved to be harmless because they all fell short of the defenders' trenches. The problem was the Turks' tactics; one man would crawl toward the trench and yell instructions to the bomber behind him, who would then throw his weapon and hope for the best. Apparently, the "best" never occurred, so the blasts served only to provide a momentary burst of light and noise. Nevertheless, Turks did get in among the Anzacs and had to be driven off with bayonets and bullets. The attack ended at ten that night, when the surviving Turks were put to flight by one of the Wellington's machine guns.

The following day the men of the Second Battalion were sent back to the beach to rest. The battalion's losses in its first three days at Gallipoli were staggering: 16 officers and 434 other ranks killed and wounded, out of 31 officers and 937 other ranks who had landed on April 25. Among the Canterbury Battalion's casualties was a South African who had fought against the British during the Boer War: "De Villiers, who fought against us in South Africa, stopped a burst from a machine gun. He had six bullets through his chest and head and was still conscious when taken out."[13] Cpl. Louis De Villiers would linger for more than three years before dying in New Zealand on November 22, 1918, eleven days after the war ended.

Miraculously, only twenty-two men of the Wellington Battalion were killed that day. Malone, their commanding officer, was furious that they had been called forward to reinforce Braund's line in what he saw as senseless attempts to hold the line by simply feeding men into it. In his diary he left a detailed account of the events, and it is clear that he did not think much of the Australians:

> Next morning [April 27], Tuesday, we were sent up another gully in which two howitzers were placed [Howitzer Gully], and then to a place on the beach N. of Divisional H. Qrs. and then told to draw two days' rations and march N. along the beach to where a big ridge came down from the high country surrounding the bay [Walker's Ridge].
>
> Duly away we went. Arrived at the foot of the ridge, found Gen. Walker, and heard a roar for reinforcements coming down the hill. Irresponsible men, Australian privates, passing the word for "Reinforcements at the double"! Gen. Walker told us to send up a Company at once, packs to be left at the bottom.
>
> I enquired what they were to do? Where to go? And what was the position? I was told they would be met at the top and put right. So away they went.
>
> No sooner gone than yells of the same sort from the Australians. Another Company of men ordered to follow the first one. The Companies were (1st) Wellington West Coast, (2nd) Hawke's Bay. Some of the best soldier men in the world. They were being sent to chaos and slaughter—nay murder.
>
> I then brought up the remaining 1½ Companies to about half way, which the Brigadier [Walker] told me to hold in reserve. On doing so more yells for reinforcements.
>
> I took it on myself to stop the yelling and to say that no more reinforcements should go up in that irresponsible way. I went up myself to find out the position.

A long climb up along a ridge. I struck a sort of natural fort along it, entrenched and occupied by about 40 Australians and two machine guns, and one Major—a fat chap. I asked him what he was doing there sending down yells for reinforcements. He said he was passing the yells on. I asked him why he did not go himself and take his men with him. He said he had orders to stay.

I went on, passing a score of Australian wounded, lying all along the track. Finally I got to a Colonel Braund, who said he was in command of the show. I asked for some explanation of the situation and why he had left his own men down on the ridge and called for reinforcements from the New Zealanders. He didn't know and knew nothing. Had no defensive position, no plan, nothing but a murderous notion that the only thing to do was to plunge troops out of the neck of the ridge into the jungle beyond.

The Turks, of whom very few were seen by my officers, were lying down, shooting down all the bits of track that led from the ridge inland, having range marks fixed and dropping our men wholesale.

Majors Young and Cunningham [Wellington Battalion] soon grasped the situation and told who they could to dig in. This was begun but Colonel Braund came along and ordered the Platoon Commanders to go on and plunge into the jungle further and further.

On their protesting he claimed as Senior Officer their obedience to his orders, and so on and on they went and got slaughtered. Lt. Wilson and his machine guns were treated in this way.

Braund had ordered Lt. Edmund Wilson to take two of his machine guns forward. In a senseless waste of life Wilson was killed and two of his sergeants were hit while moving the heavy weapons forward and setting them up. Other members of the two teams were also hit. The remaining gun, manned by a corporal and two privates— one with a shattered hand—was the one that drove the Turks off later that night. Malone continued:

"Had We Gone Forward"

I made Col. Braund send back and take all the Australians forward and to shift his H.Qrs. forward. I then went back to Brigade H.Qrs. to report and was told to bring up my remaining 1½ Companies to the fort.

After getting them up I started to go forward again up the track to get a grip on things but was met by an Australian Colonel tearing down the track yelling "Fix bayonets! The Turks are coming." I whipped back to the fort and put two machine guns in front slope with a line of the best shots of the Ruahine [Company], and sorted the other men out in readiness to hold back the Turks.

I really believed we were in for a solid thing and told the men we would have to stick it out at all costs. I then went forward, and found that the panic, for such it was, had been stopped, thanks mainly to Major Hart [second in command of the Wellington Battalion], who had been sent on by me ahead of a Reserve to get a hang of things and to report to me when I came back.

He, like the good chap he is, steadied the men—in this being helped by Capt. Cox. I sent forward a Platoon of the Ruahine Company to help stiffen up things, and, on order being restored and no Turks appearing, went forward to a spot close to the top of the ridge and established my H.Qrs. . . .

I got an immediate demand from Colonel Braund for more reinforcements, but sent him a firm refusal. He then said as I would not send him up more reinforcements, he would have to retire to his first position. I told him he ought never to have left it . . .

Col. Braund then came to see me and on my asking why he had been doing as he had, said that the truth was he feared that if he didn't go on his men would run away. I said that was no reason to sacrifice aimlessly my men.

I sent and reported to Gen. Walker and asked that the whole of the Australians be withdrawn as soon as possible.

He came back with me to the position. We struck lots of Australians who hadn't moved. I ordered them up and drove them ahead, pelting the leading ones on the track, when they stopped, with stones, and putting my toe into the rear ones.

The Australians moved at six o'clock the following morning. After that Malone wrote:

> It was an enormous relief to see the last of them. I believe they are spasmodically brave and probably the best of them had been killed or wounded. They have been, I venture to think, badly handled and trained. Officers in most cases no good. I am thinking of asking for a Court Martial on Col. Braund. It makes me mad when I think of my grand men being sacrificed by his incapacity and folly. He is, I believe, a brave chap, because he did not keep out of the racket. If he had, it would have been better for us.
>
> I would not have minded losing my men, if only it was a fair go, but to have them thrown away is heartbreaking.

Firsthand accounts of the fighting that day are few. The Second Battalion, which lost so many men, only officially recorded eight fatalities on April 27. Because so many of those lost that day were killed in Braund's charges into the scrub, many of the bodies would not be recovered for burial until days later and in some cases not until the armistice of May 24, 1915. Malone wrote in his diary on April 28: "We are unable to bury many of our killed. The whole of the scrubby slope opposite to us is full of snipers. Dead shots. They pick off even our periscopes, and to go out is sure death. Still at night our men do go out, and we have buried all those lying in the last exposed places." The few who could be recovered were buried in Walker's Ridge Cemetery. The majority are commemorated on the Lone Pine Memorial. Most could not be found or were so badly decomposed when they were that they could not be identified. Such was the state of things at Gallipoli, and so it would be for the entire campaign.

"Had We Gone Forward"

7

"They Died like Gallant Officers and Gentlemen"

The May Battles

With the failure of the First Battle of Krithia, the British and French forces were even further depleted. For the next two days there was a respite in infantry assaults by both sides. Men slightly wounded during the landings also began returning to their units. Although few in number, their return gave both an emotional boost to those who had been fighting what to many was already a losing battle.

The respite proved useful not only for the British and French but for the Turks as well. Having realized that no more attacks were going to be launched on the Asiatic side, they moved reinforcements to the Helles and Anzac sectors. They knew that if the invaders were going to be pushed back into the sea, they would have to be hit again soon, before they moved too far inland. Additionally, they knew that the best way to avoid the devastating power of the British naval guns was to advance their positions close to the enemy, so that both naval and land-based artillery would have difficulty firing without hitting their own troops: "Painful as it was for me, I now had to give orders to abstain from further attacks on the Seddulbar [Helles] front and to remain on the defensive. But not an inch of ground was to be yielded as the enemy was not far from Eltschitepe [Achi Baba] ridge, his next great objective. I ordered the Turkish troops of the first line to entrench themselves as close to the enemy as possible. A distance of a few paces between the hostile lines would inhibit the fire from the ships which would now equally endanger the troops of both sides. This was explained to the leaders and their troops."[1]

At Anzac the Australians and New Zealanders did their best to strengthen their lines against a series of strong Turkish offensives. Always costly for the attackers and usually less so for the defenders, thousands of Turks lost their lives in attacks utilizing a bare minimum of tactics. The results were always the same: a great many lives lost for no ground gained.

The Turks worked hard to drive out the invaders from the moment they landed. They began their counterattacks on April 25 and were somewhat successful that day. Ottoman riflemen and machine gunners drove the Anzacs off Baby 700 and managed to hold that small hill, but that was a unique event. Despite their best efforts, they never did drive Allies back in any sector.

Five days after landing, the Anzacs were all too aware that their positions were in imminent danger of being overrun. Although their immediate front was held by the three adjoining posts on Second Ridge, the Turks still dominated Monash Valley, the thruway that ran along the base of the ridge. The enemy could thus fire into the backs of the defenders and into the left side of the all-important Quinn's Post. Among the many victims of this ongoing harassment was Pvt. Alexander Mackie of the Thirteenth Battalion, Australian Imperial Force: "About 26th [sic] April, at Quinn's Post, Mackie was shot in the back from our rear by a sniper. At this time snipers were scattered everywhere. Mackie lived only about an hour."[2]

On April 30 Generals Birdwood and Godley issued orders to advance the line forward the next day at five in the afternoon. Because the Turks on Baby 700 posed the greatest threat to Monash Valley and the backs of the three posts, the Anzacs' primary goal was to capture that hill and reestablish the left of the Anzac line. They would also assault Dead Man's Ridge and the Bloody Angle, north of Quinn's. For a variety of reasons, however, the date of the attack was postponed until the following day, May 2. First, at three in the afternoon on May 1, the Turks were attacking the Anzac positions (they were driven off), so all available personnel were needed for defense. Second, Godley wanted to attack as close to sundown as possible so that the Royal Navy would have enough light to provide fire support safely. Finally, the scouts needed more time for reconnaissance.

At 6:30 p.m. on May 2, after a short bombardment by ships' guns and land-based artillery, the Anzac infantrymen moved off. It was a bloodbath for the attackers, most of whom were physically and emotionally depleted. The first to fall was likely Lance Sgt. Fred Talbot of the Sixteenth Battalion: "Witness says that Taylor was killed on 2nd May, 1915, at Dead Man's Ridge about 6.45 p.m. quite early in the advance and before they got to the top of the ridge. He was shot through the stomach by a rifle bullet. Witness took his hand and asked him where he was hit, but he could not speak and merely looked at witness and died within two or three minutes in the presence of witness."[3]

As the men topped the ridge, dead and wounded were sent tumbling backward, down the hill they had just climbed: "Merwyn [sic] Gray was a chum of mine and was killed on 2/5/15 between Dead Man's Ridge and Bloody Angle, on the left of Quinn's Post by a machine gun which got them from the left as they went up. I stepped across his body as I was advancing."[4]

Men continued to advance through the night but were finally stopped and dug in. Two New Zealand infantry battalions—Otago and Canterbury—had joined the assault late the previous evening. As the new day dawned, the Turks spotted them in their newly established positions and opened fire. The Otagos, having suffered badly during the night and thinking their position hopeless, broke and ran. The Canterburys then made an orderly retreat, one or two men at a time. Sgt. Walter Leadley of the Canterburys wrote in his diary on May 3, 1915:

We were sent into the firing line at 10 p.m. last night behind Otago. Shortly afterwards Otago and the Australians on our right made an attack on the Turkish position, and attempted to capture the ridge they were occupying. They went over the top cheering and shooting, and for half an hour we could hear them cheering as they charged up the opposite ridge. Otago had about 600 casualties in this action. The remainder reached the top of the ridge, but could not hold it, and had to retire a little way down the slope, where they hung on.

We were sent out to reinforce them, taking picks and shovels with us for the purpose of digging in, but as we left the trench, two Turkish machine guns were trained on us, and scores were killed or wounded. I lost three of my signallers here.

When it was seen that we could not reach Otago without suffering heavy casualties, we were withdrawn.

The assault was a complete failure, and approximately one thousand men were killed or wounded. Pvt. Ellis Silas of the Sixteenth Battalion recorded his memories of the battle in his diary:

At 6 p.m. we march off. Half way to the Hill which we are to take we had a rest for tea, biscuits, bully beef, cheese and jam—I went down to a water hole in a gully; it was very peaceful down there, the sun slanting through the thick foliage; it was difficult to realise that all around us was such Hell. Lieut. Geddes was also there—a man whom I remember, at our concerts, used to sing very charmingly—poor chap, this was his last night in this world. Just as the sun was setting, throwing its rich colour o'er all the landscape, we formed up for the final march off for the attack—it was difficult going, crawling through the gully which skirted the foot of the hill we were to attack. We were to attack at 7 sharp, prior to which our artillery was to support us—our Battalion, No. 6 platoon supported by the 15th Battalion on the right, 13th on the left. Lieut. Geddes looked at his watch—"It is 7 o'clock, Lads," he said, "Come on, lads, at 'em." Up we rushed— God, it was frightful—the screams of the wounded, bursting of the shells, and the ear-splitting crackling of the rifles. In a very few minutes the gully at the foot of the hill was filled with dead

"They Died like Officers and Gentlemen"

and wounded—these poor lumps of clay had once been my comrades, men I worked and smoked and laughed and joked with—oh God, the pity of it. It rained men in this gully; all round could be seen the sparks where the bullets were striking.

The failure of this attack demonstrated to the Anzac leadership the futility of carrying out massive assaults with the meager resources at hand. Thus, with the loss of so many men for a gain of zero territory, Godley ordered that additional large-scale offensive action at Anzac should cease until further notice. Shelling and raids would continue.

The Turkish attack of May 1 was also a failure. Together these two actions taught both sides important lessons. The Turks realized that the Anzac positions, especially Quinn's Post, were strong enough to withstand an all-out assault, though they would make another fateful attempt on the night of May 19–20. The Anzacs learned the same lesson about the Turks on May 3. Both sides used the relative respite following the attacks to deepen and extend their trench lines and to improve their field fortifications and barbed wire defenses. The fighting in the sector devolved into the kind of trench warfare being fought on the western front.

On the night of May 1–2 the Turks launched blistering attacks against the British and French troops in the Helles sector, and they nearly broke through. The first to be hit were the Dubsters, who were holding the part of the front line that crossed Krithia Nullah with only eight officers and seven hundred other ranks, less than the strength of a single battalion. The British part of the line held, though in some areas the pressure was almost too great. In one area the saving grace was a single Territorial Force battalion (akin to the U.S. Army National Guard), which was thrown in at the last minute. Its men's excellent marksmanship turned the Turkish assault, and the day was saved. Sgt. Dennis Moriarty of the First Munsters recorded an entry about the battle that night in his diary: "9 p.m. they started an attack, I am sure I will never forget that night as long as I live. They crept up to our trenches (they were in thousands) and they made the night hideous with yells and shouting Allah, Allah. We could not help mowing them down. Some of them broke through in a part of our line but they never again got back as they were caught between the two lines of trenches . . . Some of the best men in the Regiment [were] killed. When the Turks got to close quarters the devils used 'hand grenades' and you could only recognize our dead by their Identity Discs."

After the deadly attacks Hamilton cabled Kitchener about the Turkish assaults and noted that his forces were holding. He received a response on May 4 stating that he must not give the enemy the chance to bring up more reserves. The British and French must attack at once. This was the instigation for the Second Battle of Krithia.

Birdwood agreed to loan Hamilton the Second Australian Infantry Brigade and the New Zealand Infantry Brigade for the coming battle. He also agreed to send a battery of New Zealand artillery and four batteries of Australian artillery, which were waiting in their transports off Ari Burnu because there were still no suitable places for them to establish themselves at Anzac. The 125th Brigade of the Forty-Second (East Lancashire) Division had also just arrived at Helles from Egypt, as had the Twenty-Ninth Indian Brigade. Four companies of Indian Brigade—two each from the Sixty-Ninth and Eighty-Ninth Punjabis—were relegated to duties on the beach because they were Muslim and the British were not sure that they would fight the Turks with as much vigor as they should. Nevertheless, Hamilton would have a greater force with which to resume his attack. Therefore, instead of aiming merely for the capture of Krithia and a point from which he could launch an attack on Achi Baba, he also aimed for the capture of the hill itself.

The forces arrayed against the Turks were not nearly as massive as they should have been. As before, the Allies were unable to provide the three-to-one ratio of attacker to defender that was considered necessary for success. The British and French were able to muster twenty-five thousand infantry for their assault, and the Turks were holding their lines with twenty thousand. The Turks also had six batteries of field artillery arrayed against a possible attack, with a howitzer battery emplaced on Achi Baba for maximum effect. With their high trajectory they were capable of dropping a shell straight down on their attackers, blowing great holes in the massed formations. Nevertheless, Hamilton felt that because of his larger force, he stood a better chance for success.

The attack would occur in three phases. It would commence at 11:00 a.m. on May 6, when the Turks were awake, fed, and alert. In the first phase the Allied line would advance one mile. In the second the French on the far right would remain in place, while the British in the center and right of the line would swing to the right, like the second hand on a watch. The British would capture Krithia and then stop outside the village, to the east. In the third phase a British infantry brigade would advance through the British line to capture Achi Baba from the south and the west.

May 6 dawned beautifully, though the sky was overcast enough that the meager British aerial reconnaissance was unable to operate. As Capt. Kenneth Gresson of the Canterbury Battalion described the area to be attacked in his diary that day: "The fields of the peninsula for the most part open pasture land with cottages and fig trees dotted about here and there. The whole countryside was a blaze of color as the meadows were thick with wild flowers all in bloom— the red poppy predominating."

For the attacking troops the natural beauty of their surroundings was deceptive. They knew that they had a tough time ahead, in part because they were not sure what they would be up against. As usual, the battalions did not receive their orders until a short time before the assault was launched, and there was no opportunity for the troops to be briefed properly. In fact, the war diary of the First Munsters noted that orders were not received until two hours before the men were supposed to go into action. But by then they were used to the shortcomings of their senior leadership. They knew that the only people they could rely on were themselves. It was no way to fight a war, but they had no choice. They could but soldier on and hope either for success or a "blighty" wound, one just serious enough to get them into a hospital in England.

At 10:30 a.m. the British artillery opened fire, and the Turks, as usual, retreated to their reserve positions. A half-hour later the gunners ceased fire, the Ottomans returned to their trenches, and the British climbed out of theirs. It was a long, frustrating move across the bullet-swept no-man's-land. The entrenched enemy was invisible, and there was no one on whom they might vent their rage with bullet or bayonet. The Turks' trenches were hundreds of yards away and well camouflaged. Their machine guns, located somewhere in or ahead of the trenches, took a massive toll. They were so well hidden and so far away that not even the muzzle flashes were visible, and they could not be located by the sound of their fire. As their comrades fell around them, the attackers felt as though some invisible hand, sweeping their friends away en masse, was at work. It was a terrible ordeal that many felt would end only when their lives were snatched from them: "The Turkish fire was murderous and we lost a lot of men. There were no trenches to be seen but the Turks must have had their machine-guns perfectly sighted. It was terrifying; fewer men rose after each rush but we still charged forward blindly, repeatedly changing direction, but it did not appear to make the slightest difference. The fire was coming from all directions yet we could not see a single Turk or any sign of a trench."[5]

In the center of the line the five battalions of the Eighty-Eighth Infantry Brigade were the first to move off (three battalions formed the main attacking force, with two in reserve behind them), attacking on a strip of land later referred to as "Fir Tree Spur," between Gully Ravine and Krithia Nullah. After advancing several hundred yards under heavy fire, they were stopped by rifle fire and two Turkish machine guns in Fir Tree Wood. Later in the afternoon they attacked again and gained a few more yards of ground. At 4:00 p.m., however, after being stopped again by artillery and the elusive machine guns, the brigade dug in. Despite strong Turkish resistance, the brigade's losses were relatively light: "At 11 am a general advance started. The 88th Brigade on the left, the Naval Brigade in the centre and a Brigade of French troops on the right. Our artillery commenced the bombardment of the hill that was to be taken and

"They Died like Officers and Gentlemen"

such a din I will never forget. Our Brigade were [*sic*] in reserve and when the enemy's artillery started they gave our trenches 'what oh.' They were trying to find our artillery who were well in rear and it just shows the kind of gunners they have got. Our troops gained a mile of ground right along the whole front and fortunately there were very few casualties on our side. They kept peppering all night but we held the ground we had won."[6]

The French, supported on their left by the Second Naval Brigade (which linked the Eighty-Eighth Brigade with the French), were not sure about the role the sailors were to play in the assault, so they did not leave their trenches until 11:40 a.m. The Turks, aware that an attack was inevitable, were ready for them. The Brigade Métropolitaine, which made up the right of the French line (and was at the farthest end of the Allied line on the right), advanced to the mouth of the Kereves Dere before being stopped by heavy fire. On the left of the French line, and linking them to the Second Naval Brigade, were the Senegalese of the Brigade Coloniale. They, too, made good progress but eventually pulled away from the naval infantrymen, causing a break in the line. The sailors, who had advanced farther than the French troops, were thus forced to pull back later in the day in order to maintain contact with the French. The Sixth Mixed Colonial's medical officer visited the battlefield that morning and wrote: "I went to the battlefield. There were soldiers hiding in trenches. One could hardly see them, so great was the disorder around. English guns, French guns, stretcher-bearers with wounded. And it went on and on. One's imagination can suggest nothing like the reality . . . At nightfall my hands were still sticky with blood and antiseptics. I ate half a tin of bully beef, biscuits and an orange, and drank some wine. The wounded continued to come in. There was no rest. We were all tired out and looked like ghosts, dirty, horrid, excited. All the same, when we came together, the same feelings of pity and reprobation united us. Nothing in the world is worse than war."[7]

Among the hundreds of French to fall was the youngest known casualty of the Gallipoli campaign, Désiré Bianco of the Cinquante-

Huitième Régiment d'Iinfanterie Coloniale. At thirteen he was also the youngest French soldier to die in World War I. Not only was he too young to serve; he had no reason to be at Gallipoli. He was Italian.

By the end of the day the British and French had advanced between four and five hundred yards, but they were still short of their goal. They did not reach the main Turkish defensive line. Indeed, the attacking troops were so far away that they could not even see it. Still, the Allies suffered relatively few casualties, and at ten o'clock on the night of May 6, orders were issued by the Twenty-Ninth Division for an attack the following morning.

An artillery bombardment would again precede the infantry assault, but because the stock of ammunition had been reduced to almost nothing a day earlier, it would only last for fifteen minutes. The infantry would go over the top at 10:00 a.m., with the intention of accomplishing the goals of the first and second phases of the previous day's assaults.

The bombardment began at 9:45 a.m. on May 7, but it was so weak and ineffectual that many Turks were not aware that a concerted bombardment was taking place. When the infantry attacked fifteen minutes later, they also were not certain that an all-out assault was taking place. By the end of the day the surviving Allied troops were right back where they had started. Among those lost was 2nd Lit. Humphrey Hoyle of the 1/5th Lancashire Fusiliers. On May 7, his second day in action, he was wounded in the arm and leg during the assault on Gurkha Bluff. Minutes later he was shot in the face and killed. Pvt. Frederick Collinson, a Boer War veteran from Bury, Lancashire, was hit about ten yards in front of the first Turkish trench and died eight days later on a hospital ship. His commanding officer, 2nd Lt. George Horridge, wrote:

> We came to a trench. Then we advanced still further and the amount of rifle fire we were under seemed to get bigger still. I began to lose control of the platoon because I simply couldn't see them in the scrub. All I could do was blow my whistle and

"They Died like Officers and Gentlemen"

we would advance with the line in front of us and I hoped that the n.c.o.'s were doing their job. Eventually we got to one trench behind the front line. Next to me was an old soldier named Collinson. We got out of the trench and we had to go at the double because fire was very heavy. The bullets were hissing round, swish swish swish swish swish. We ran halfway and then got behind a mound. After a minute or so's rest, I said to Collinson, "Look. We've got to go on," and off we set again. I wasn't too bad a runner and I outstripped Collinson and eventually leapt into the front line trench. I'm sorry to say Collinson, in the last ten yards, got hit through the chest or stomach. We got him in, but he died later.

Hamilton and Hunter-Weston felt that they had to continue the push or risk the campaign devolving into one of trench warfare like that being fought on the western front. The forces that had been in action were by now depleted. The survivors were tired, hungry, and on the verge of breakdown. Still, there were fresh bodies to throw into the fight. Australians and New Zealanders were waiting in reserve, and the British 127th Brigade, composed of four Territorial Force battalions of the Manchester Regiment, had arrived on the night of May 6. Thus, behaving like a losing gambler with a fresh stack of chips, Hamilton decided that the attack must continue. It would begin at ten thirty the following morning. As before, a weak barrage would precede the attack, the guns trying in vain to hit targets the gunners could not locate.

According to the plan, the New Zealand Infantry Brigade would capture Krithia. To do so, it would leave its trenches and attack around and through Fir Tree Wood. The New Zealanders called the ground in front of the wood the "Daisy Patch," in reference to the plants that flourished there. They would be protected on their left by the Eighty-Seventh Brigade, which would infiltrate along Gully Ravine and try to silence the machine gun posts there. There would be no attack on their right. What seems to have escaped the planners was the fact that the four New Zealand battalions were mere shadows of the units that had landed on April 25. They had since received reinforcements, but the battalions were still understrength. The new troops had very little marksmanship training. Further, the commander of the New Zealand Infantry Brigade, Col. Francis Johnston, received his orders so late that he was not able to brief his battalion commanders until 10:10, only twenty minutes before the attack was to commence. The only real orders the attacking infantrymen had were to move forward. Facing them were at least nine Turkish battalions supported by machine guns and artillery. The assault was doomed to fail before it even began.

One of those destined for the battle was Pvt. Holger Randrup of the Auckland Battalion. He wrote in his diary that morning: "Beautifully fine morning. Whole battlefield spread out in front in gradually rising ground for about two miles. N.Z., Australian and Indian troops in one line right across the peninsular and in front is the Imperial line plainly visible by the smoke from their breakfast fires." This was the last entry in his diary. Randrup would not live to see another day.

The artillery, what there was, opened on schedule at 10:15 a.m. Apart from holing an already cratered landscape and further obscuring the view of the attackers, it only served to alert the Turks that another attack was coming. The infantry went over the top at ten thirty. On the right the Second South Wales Borderers and First Royal Inniskilling Fusiliers left their trenches, moving scouts and small patrols along Gully Ravine in an effort to locate and silence the Turkish machine guns that would fire into the left flank of the New Zealanders. But instead of finding the machine guns, the machine guns found them. Those who were not killed were forced to retreat.

In the center the New Zealanders climbed out of their trenches and began the long move up to the front line held by the British. It was from there that their attack was to begin. The Wellington Battalion was on the left, the Aucklands in the center, and the Canterburys on the right. The Otago Battalion was in reserve. The first to move were the men of the Canterbury Battalion, who advanced fifty yards before the Turks hit them with shrapnel. They caught the Wellington and Auckland Battalions as they left their trenches. The

"They Died like Officers and Gentlemen"

New Zealanders had eight hundred yards to go before they reached the British front line, held by what was left of the Dubsters: "That first dash—I believe I was the first man out of all our line—not only gave me a thrill of self-importance but probably saved my life, for we had covered 50 yards or more before the hail of fire began. At any rate, the scouts had no casualties, but the other unfortunates, rising to follow our slaughter, were slaughtered."[8]

Moving as fast as they could, carrying their rifles at trail arms (in their right hands, down by their sides), the infantrymen did their best to escape the deadly Turkish fire. But the only defense they had was hope. There was no place for them to take cover. It was a maddening, costly rush to the British trench from which they were to launch their assault. But they did not reach it—the enemy fire was too heavy. The Turkish artillery was joined by machine guns and riflemen, which raked the line like a satanic broom. Hundreds fell. Others, seeing the futility of that rush, tried to escape but were hit in the back. Most simply went to ground, doing their best to scoop a little bit of protection out of the earth with their hands and hoping that the Turks would not notice the movement. Sgt. Walter Leadley, also of the Canterbury's, made it as far as the first Turkish trench:

> I watched the 12th Nelson Company [of the Canterbury Battalion] make an advance over open country called the Daisy Patch. There was absolutely no cover for them. They lost their commanding officer, and several men were casualties. Ray Lawry came up and led the 2nd Company over the same place, with a good dash. He got through safely, setting a fine example of courage to the men. He is a plucky beggar.
>
> Our turn to go across came next, and we went over the top in open order, with the best of luck. At once we were greeted with a terrible fusillade of rifle and machine gun fire, which was deadly. The man on my right had his brains shot out into his face, and the chap on my left was shot through the stomach. Halfway across the patch I tripped over a root and fell down. I lay still two or three minutes until I had recovered my breath. Then the bullets started

plugging up the earth all round me, so I got up again and made for the Turkish trench as hard as I could go. I reached it without being hit, but was almost dropping with weakness. There was no room in the trench for me, so I jumped into a river bed close by and found a safe place . . .

We lost over 200 men in this attack.[9]

Despite the failure of the scouts on their left to locate and silence the Turkish machine guns, the Wellingtons advanced the farthest, about three hundred yards. The Auckland and Canterbury Battalions on their left got two hundred yards before they were stopped. The assault was a complete failure. Among the officers who fell was Capt. Ateo Frandi, a native of Italy serving with of the Wellington Battalion.

At last, 10 o'clock. A nod from Captain Frandi, who is going out from the Company on our left and we are over the parapet and walking steadily forward . . . Again we are over the parapet, in a field of daisies and poppies. Here and there be queer huddled heaps in the sulphur-coloured uniforms of the enemy. The little spurts are getting thicker. I look furtively over to Frandi on the left. He is still walking coolly on. I can't run while he walks. An eternity passes . . . A semi-circle of spurts shows us where a machine-gun has opened on us. "Come on Blackmore," I cry. I can stand it no longer. I was never very fast on the track, but beat Blackmore by 40 yards . . . The attack is late—10.45. Here they come—a steady, even line, ten paces interval. They swarm over the parapet and walk steadily on, non-coms watching and checking. The air above me whistles and sings. Whizz! They are almost blotted from view. The enemy's batteries have opened on them . . . "Poor old Frandi is out!" This, the requiem of one of the bravest men I have ever known, and I have seen some brave ones in the last five weeks.[10]

"Daisy Patch" was an ironic name for a piece of ground that cost so many lives. But it was a fitting name for that precious little bit of earth. Covered with a colorful mixture of daisies and poppies, it is an area that in any other time would rate a moving poem to the gifts of Mother Nature. After May 8, 1915, it would only result in memories of horror and death that the men who were there and their family members back home shuddered to think of.

Hamilton should have seen the khaki-clad lumps of fallen humanity as an indication that his plans had failed, and he should have stopped there. He did not. Instead, he issued orders for another attack at four that afternoon. This time the artillery would fire all of the ammunition it could possibly spare in a fifteen-minute-long bombardment, beginning at five, and the infantry would attack at five thirty. The French would have to attack, too, and the British would use their remaining reserves. The Eighty-Seventh Brigade would attack and try to take the upper portion of Gully Ravine and the lower reaches of Hill 472 on the left; the New Zealanders would again attempt to take Krithia via the Daisy Patch; the Second Australian Brigade would attack through the Composite Naval Brigade and along the Krithia Spur, as far as it could go; and the French would attack the Turkish positions along the Kereves Dere on the right.

Earlier in the day the Australians had received orders to move up so they could support the New Zealanders if necessary. At 11:30 a.m. they marched out of their bivouacs and moved toward Krithia Nullah. There they were out of view of the Turks, but they took the precaution of digging in anyway. Around five o'clock the four battalions received their first reinforcements since leaving Egypt. These raw troops arrived just as the blooded riflemen were preparing their supper, a modest meal of boiled bully beef, biscuits, and jam. Before eating, the newly arrived troops were allotted to their platoons.

At 5:15 p.m. the Allied artillery opened up, and despite the small stocks of ammunition left, the bombardment was the largest carried out by land-based artillery since the campaign had begun. But just as before, it only alerted the Turks that another attack was coming. At five twenty two of the Australian battalions—the Sixth and Seventh—began moving toward the trenches held by the Composite Naval Brigade along Central Spur, but instead they were hit by Turkish shrapnel. Fortunately, the rounds were badly timed and found few targets in the flesh of those brave men. The leading battalions were soon followed by the Fifth and Eighth Battalions. The Australians had been given no time to reconnoiter the ground over which they were attacking, and the men had no idea what to expect. They only knew that they were supposed to advance. So advance they did, frightened but undaunted, their eyes focused on the sailors' position.

Reaching the trench, which the Australians dubbed "Tommy's Trench," the men leaped in for a quick breather. They stayed for about two minutes. The left of the trench was held by the First Lancashire Fusiliers and the right by the Royal Naval Division's Drake Battalion: "They dropped into this for a breather and a rest. Almost immediately the Brigadier came into my view of the parapet and said, 'Don't stop here. The Eighth Battalion will get there before you.' I said, 'We are only stopping for a breather, Sir.' He said, 'Go on. Push on. You need not run. Walk.' I got out of the trench and pushed on at a walk, taking as many men with me as I could get hold of."[11]

What the Australians had not realized, because nobody told them, was that Tommy's Trench was not, in fact, a Turkish trench that had been captured by the British. It was not until they had leaped in that the British informed them that the Turks were still hundreds of yards away. The men were confused by this revelation and were not sure whether or not they were to hold the line with the British or continue on. But they were ordered to continue moving, and as they climbed back into no-man's-land, Turkish bullets tore into their ranks.

One of the most unlikely victims of the assault was Driver Bob Langlands of the Australian Field Artillery's Second Brigade Ammunition Column. He had deserted his unit immediately after landing at Anzac: "Langlands deserted from the Troopship 'Armadale' as she was lying off Anzac on 26th April 1915. He was a sentimental 'bloke,' who had ideas of going out and killing Turks by the dozen. He deserted for this purpose. [I] was afraid he was going to do so, and 'sneaked' his clothes in order to prevent it, but he got away

"They Died like Officers and Gentlemen"

and swam ashore. He had a father or uncle or some such relative in the 7th Btn. It was reported to the section to which [I] belonged that Langlands had joined the 7th Btn. and that he was killed at Cape Helles."[12] Langlands was reportedly allowed to remain with the infantry and was appointed acting corporal. He was killed by a machine bullet in the abdomen and listed as missing after the attack.

The Australians made good progress, despite mounting casualties. But at six in the evening they halted. They had advanced five hundred yards and were finally in sight of the Turkish front line. The survivors started digging in, forming a shallow line that they were determined to hold. As they did so, they continued to fall victim to the accurate Turkish fire. One of those hit was Pvt. William Churchill, who had joined the Sixth Battalion from the Third Reinforcements less than an hour earlier: "Churchill was killed in the charge of May 8th. He fell shot through the chest, just at the end of the charge when B. Coy. was digging itself in. Witness was with him when he was wounded. Churchill lived for about an hour after he had been shot, and witness remained with him till he died."[13]

The French launched their assault just as the Australian advance was ending. Leading the attack were drummers and buglers, the infantrymen advancing behind them in their bright red trousers and dark blue coats. Their determination was finally paying off. They reached the forward Turkish trenches and drove the defenders out. But the attackers were not content with that prize and charged after the survivors, who were scurrying toward the safety of their machine guns. Those guns took a mighty toll, driving the French back to the captured trenches that they had consolidated and made their own. This place, which they named "La Redoubte Bourchet," remained in French hands for the remainder of the campaign.

During the night the Allies used the lull in fighting to firm up their front line and to close the gaps between the different brigades. The New Zealand Infantry Brigade linked up with the Eighty-Seventh Brigade on their left, forming a defensive line that crossed Gully Ravine. On their right the New Zealanders moved their line forward to connect with the Second Australian Infantry Brigade. The

Australians were linked to the Second Naval Brigade on the left of the French line.

The Second Battle of Krithia was a virtual failure that resulted in a loss of sixty-five hundred British and Dominion troops. It was so ineffectual that the Turks hardly mention it in their official history of the campaign. The battle is barely recalled in England, but the losses suffered that day are still remembered in Australia and New Zealand. It epitomized the Gallipoli Campaign in its entirety. Three weeks after the battle, Maj. Joseph Vassal wrote to his wife: "There on the left you can see, along a green meadow, the last traces of the battle of Krithia. It was a terrible thing. Fifty of ours, in grey-blue cloaks, are there, elbow to elbow as if at drill. They are looking towards the enemy, and I see they have their guns pointed in their hands . . . They are all dead there together, asphyxiated by a shell or riddled by machine guns. At first glance one would swear that they are not dead, or that they are just going to get up. But on looking closer one can see opened corpses. The breeze is laden with dreadful odours."[14] Even though the Anzacs intended to fight a purely defensive campaign in their sector, the Turks had no such intention. Their desire to throw the attackers back into the sea was just as strong as it had been on April 25.

On May 5, after their failed attack of May 1–3, General von Sanders ordered Turkish troops at Helles to switch to a defensive role. But after the failure of the Second Battle of Krithia, he decided that an all-out offensive in one of the sectors had to be made. Anzac was chosen for several reasons. First, the proximity of the Turkish and Anzac trenches made a successful surprise attack a real possibility. Second, the Anzacs were so close to the sea that it might actually be possible to push them back to the water's edge, sending the survivors scrambling for their boats. Third, the Helles sector was at the tip of the peninsula and could be hit by ships' guns from three sides. At Anzac the naval gunners could only fire at the Turks from the west.

The attack would occur along a one-and-a-half-mile-wide front under cover of darkness in the early morning hours of May 19. A

"They Died like Officers and Gentlemen"

fresh division, the Second, had arrived from Constantinople on the Sixteenth. With that, the Turkish force at Anzac amounted to approximately 42,000 men. Opposing them were only 17,356 men (just over 12,000 of them infantry). Unlike the Anzacs, most of whom saw action for the first time after landing at Gallipoli, the Turkish Second Division was composed largely of well-disciplined, experienced veterans of the Balkan Wars of 1912–13. And they were ready for a fight.

Essad Pasha, the commander of Turkish troops in the Anzac sector, wanted the assault to take place on the left of the line, specifically at the Nek and the head of Monash Valley, where the defense was weakest. Von Sanders, on the other hand, wanted the Second Division—which was not familiar with the area—to attack the center of the line, where the defense was strongest. Other troops would simultaneously attack the right and left of the line, without artillery or machine gun support. To make matters worse, the other three Turkish divisions were depleted after weeks of heavy fighting. Von Sanders's tactical idiocy would be the death knell for thousands that night.

The Anzacs realized something was up on May 18, when the usual chatter of Turkish rifle and machine gun fire, which had been constant since the landing, began to die down. Even the snipers were quiet: "Considerable excitement prevails today owing to the sudden cessation of the Turkish guns. It certainly feels strange to have absolute silence from this quarter, & various suggestions are offered by the various officers & men at this strange act. Probably it may be a ruse, or exhaustion of ammunition."[15] Then, at 5:00 p.m., the Turks opened their heaviest bombardment so far on the sector, many rounds also hitting the beach: "Work under heavy shell fire. This grew worse about 6.30. Several heavy shells hit within a few yards of this dugout and the neighbouring ones, but did not burst. A little farther off they did explode, or striking the sea, raised tall columns and high fountains of white water. Colonel Chaytor badly wounded in the shoulder. A great loss to us."[16]

Earlier in the day the Royal Naval Air Service sent up an airplane piloted by Lt. G. L. Thompson to spot for the battleship *Canopus*, which was attempting to attack a Turkish cruiser that had been firing on positions at Anzac. Although the *Canopus* was too far away to hit the cruiser, Thompson made a shocking discovery: two valleys behind the Turkish lines were packed with troops. He circled above them, trying unsuccessfully to get the *Canopus* to open fire, before returning to his base at Imbros. After he landed, another plane was sent over to confirm Thompson's report. He not only confirmed the sighting; he also noticed Turkish troops disembarking from four small steamers at Akbashi Liman on the other side of the peninsula. After assessing that report, Birdwood's headquarters was informed by telegraph to expect a night attack. This dispatch was not the only intimation of an attack. On May 19 Capt. Hon. Aubrey Herbert noted in his diary: "A Turkish officer just brought in says that the real attack is to be this afternoon, now at 1.30." Secrecy was not on the side of the Turks that day.

During the war there was a standard time at which men "stood to." All of the troops manning frontline trenches were awoken and ordered to man the fire steps, ready to meet a possible attack. Generally, no assault materialized, and at a given time they were ordered to "stand down." Some men went back to sleep, while those on duty went about their business.

At Anzac the troops had stood to at 3:30 a.m. But on May 19 they were ordered to do so a half-hour earlier. Some units, such as the Auckland Mounted Rifles (AMR), stiffened their men's resolve with rum. The spirit was part of the normal ration issue for British and Dominion troops, especially before going into action. It was a strong brew, issued to units in large clay jugs stamped SRD for "Special Ration Depot." Much of the rum was laid down during the Boer War and was especially strong. Generally, a man's spoon was filled with rum, or just enough was poured into his cup to cover the bottom. But the AMR was overzealous in its issue and filled the cups half full. For many young men, not used to strong spirits, the coming assault was nothing but a blur.

The early order to stand to was a propitious one because the Turks attacked at three twenty. Wearing their woolen greatcoats to fend

"They Died like Officers and Gentlemen"

off the early morning cold, Anzacs all along the line were ready and waiting when the Ottomans moved forward, trumpets blaring and cries of "Allah, Allah" punctuating the atmosphere. Two rounds fired by two unknown individuals raised the alarm, and the Anzacs opened a murderous fire all along the line.

Turkish infantrymen, led by officers waving sabers and buglers indicating the direction of the advance, charged ahead. Some units did not shoot until the attackers were within twenty yards of their trenches. At that range, even in the dark, they could not help but hit somebody, and the Turks were mowed down by the thousands. It was a clear night, and the moon was showing ever so slightly. But it was enough to glint off the tens of thousands of Turkish bayonets, and they marked the targets for the Anzac defenders. Relatively safe themselves, the riflemen stood on the fire steps of their trenches— some got out of their trenches—and fired with impunity at their attackers. Eleven machine guns, all sighted to cover one another, fired into the dark masses, in some cases cutting men nearly in half.

Some of the Turks turned and ran. Most fell dead or wounded. Some tried to escape the wall of lead. Riflemen fired their weapons so fast that the barrels became too hot to touch; oil in the wooden stocks seeped out onto their hands as wood heated up and bolts began to jam. Those who could contain their excitement tried, in the absence of light, to get at the brass oilers in the buttstocks of their rifles. Not many could. Still, they managed to keep firing in spite of their malfunctioning weapons. The noise was deafening, and some men were unable to hear properly for several days after the attack. It was an absolute slaughter: "All through the night (19/5/15) the Turks kept coming up & were mown down, again & again, & considering all we lost comparatively few men from their rifle fire. At times it was necessary to leave the trenches & rush them back otherwise they would have been too close to be healthy but our men worked without orders with the bayonet & it soon told on these mass rushes."[17]

The men of the Auckland Mounted Rifles, on the far left of the line, were in a relatively weak position. Still, they were able to stem the Turkish tide. One troop, under the command of Lt. Cornelius James, was nearly wiped out as it held the Turks back from a trench that was little more than a shallow ditch. In total the regiment lost twenty-three killed that night and about that many wounded.

To the right of the AMR were the Wellington Mounted Rifles: "From midnight a heavy rifle & machine-gun fire opened on us & at dawn all their big guns & all ours also. All the warships started work & the row was deafening. Then attacked heavily on both flanks. The Australians on right hand & A.M.R. on left bore the brunt, & suffered heavy losses. They recon the Turks lost 1,000 on left flank and a lot more on right . . . The Aucklanders lost 20 killed & a lot wounded. One of our machine-gunners, Hastie was killed, and Fritz Mothes wounded by rifle bullet, & Arthur Sanson shot through shoulder by shrapnel bullet."[18]

The experience of the Australians in the center and left of the line was much like that of the New Zealanders. Turks were shot down in droves but caused few casualties themselves. At Courtney's Post, next to Quinn's and held by the Fourteenth Battalion, the situation was different. It was there that the Turks made a notable break-through. The Turks' entry into Courtney's was hardly a monumental event. For all of the thousands of Turkish riflemen involved that night, only about thirty made it in. That could have meant disaster for that portion of the line had it not been for the efforts of Lance Cpl. Albert Jacka.

When the Turks hit Courtney's, grenadiers crept up and threw bombs into the Australian trench, killing two and wounding at least two others. They then climbed down into the undefended bay. Jacka, whose company was in support, was standing in an adjacent bay. After a couple of unsuccessful attacks, he finally charged the group alone, killing two with his bayonet and shooting another seven. The remainder beat a hasty retreat, leaving twenty-six rifles behind. For his gallantry Jacka was awarded Australia's first Victoria Cross of the war. That night his battalion lost eleven men killed and seventy wounded. The battalion's only officer to lose his life was Jacka's commanding officer, Lt. William Hamilton, who was just five days short of his twenty-first birthday. He fell battling the Turks who made it into his company's trench: "It was a terrible night, and the hordes of Turks shouting 'Allah! Allah!' seemed overwhelming; but we stuck it out. About 3 o'clock there was a fierce rush, and seven Turks got into our trenches. A very dear chap named Hamilton, a Duntroon lieutenant, ran up, and was immediately shot through the brain. Crabbe with a few men followed up, and shot and bayonetted the lot, so none got out alive."[19]

Farther to the south, at a protuberance in the Australian line called the "Pimple," the Second Battalion was holding the line. There three Turks from the Forty-Eighth Regiment made it into the frontline trench. Lt. Harold Barton shot and killed one before being killed himself. Capt. Gordon Wallack, the battalion's adjutant and temporary commanding officer, was felled by a sniper when he peered over the top of his trench to view the multitude of Turkish bodies in no-man's-land. The twenty-nine-year-old career soldier had enlisted in the army as a bugler at the age of eleven.

The main attack was beaten back by 5:00 a.m., but smaller attacks continued until eleven in the morning. That afternoon General Headquarters ordered Birdwood to send his troops against the Turks, thinking that they were too badly beaten to offer much resistance, but some of his officers wisely talked him out of it. The GHQ staff, being so far removed from the action, apparently did not consider the fact that the Turks still had their machine guns and artillery and that they would be expecting the Anzacs to take advantage of their misfortune. When one hundred men of the Wellington Battalion began climbing out of their trench to attack the Turkish positions at the Nek, they were greeted with a withering fire that confirmed the fears of the men who had counseled Birdwood.

It was estimated that 3,420 Turks were killed and untold thousands wounded. Some of these men managed to make it back to their own lines, but many died on the field under the hot sun, the fire from both sides making it impossible for the Red Crescent stretcher-bearers to reach them. In some cases the Anzacs pulled wounded men in with grappling irons or used hooks attached to long sticks.

Occasionally, they found that a man was not injured at all. Some tried to cheat fate by playing dead and were unable to make their way back to their own lines. Anzac losses amounted to approximately 160 men. Unlike any other major battle fought at Gallipoli, nearly all of the fallen defenders were able to be recovered for burial, and few were listed as missing. Von Sanders was moved enough by the number of men lost that he took responsibility for his poor planning: "I feel that the attack was an error on my part based on an underestimation of the enemy."[20] He could not bring himself to take full credit, however. He was not willing to admit that the tactic he chose was totally lacking in imagination and that he, not just the Anzacs, was personally responsible for so many deaths.

This assault taught the Anzacs once and for all that their enemy, despite the stories they had heard, were brave fighters. To the Anzacs the fact that the Turks charged to their deaths without apparent thought for their own well-being demonstrated their enemies' devotion to the defense of their country. In actuality the Turks were just as frightened as one could be, charging over unknown ground in darkness punctuated by thousands of muzzle flashes. It was a harrowing experience, but it signaled a turning point for the Anzacs. The Turks were no longer heartless beasts. They were men, like themselves.

1. Lt. Andrew Bulman, 4th Battalion, King's Own Scottish Borderers.

2. Lt. James B. Innes, 4th Battalion, King's Own Scottish Borderers.

3. Pvt. William E. C. Campion, 2nd Battalion, South Wales Borderers.

4. Pvt. James Rigby, 6th Battalion Border Regiment.

5. W Beach.

6. Gully Beach.

7. Able Bodied Seaman John
Geo. Everett, HMS *Euryalus*.

8. Lt. Leslie J. Water, 15th
Battalion, AIF.

9. Dvr. Alfred Cecil Hickson, Army Service Corp.

10. Infantry from the Australian 1st and 2nd Brigades. Wikimedia Commons.

11. Turkish soldier.

12. Turkish airplane.

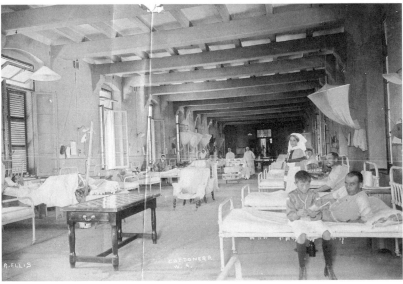

13 and 14. Cottonera Hospital, Malta.

15. Turkish War Memorial at Gallipoli.

16. Twelve Tree Copse Cemetery, a Commonwealth War Graves Commission Cemetery at Gallipoli.

8

"A Lot of Our Poor Fellows Were Drowned"

The War at Sea

The Royal and French navies performed a variety of roles at Gallipoli. Battleships, cruisers, destroyers, and monitors provided fire support. Submarines traveled up the Dardanelles as far as Constantinople, sinking Turkish ships and shelling targets on land. Hospital ships treated casualties off the coast and evacuated them to hospitals as far away as England and France. Transports, in addition to taking men to Gallipoli, evacuated casualties to make up for a lack of hospital ships. Trawlers swept for mines and transported men to and from Imbros and Lemnos. Other vessels served as ammunition, supply, and water carriers. One, the *Manica*, carried an observation balloon used for spotting targets for warships. The *Ark Royal* was a converted merchant ship that operated as the world's first aircraft carrier. French vessels performed the same functions as those of the British, but there were fewer of them. Even the Imperial Japanese and Russian navies contributed one vessel each to the fighting.

After the landings on April 25, Allied vessels could travel to and from Gallipoli virtually unmolested, so long as they did not stray near the Narrows forts. They were still prey to land-based guns on both sides of the straits, but these weapons posed an even greater threat to the unarmored craft that delivered men, animals, and supplies to the beaches. The warships would not remain unmolested by their naval counterparts for long, however. The first victim was the British battleship *Goliath*.

On May 10 the Royal Navy was warned that four or five Turkish destroyers were known to be operating in the Dardanelles and that they might attack under cover of darkness. The intelligence was partially accurate. In the early morning hours of May 13, the Turkish torpedo boat destroyer *Muavenet-i-Miliet* moved northward along the fog-shrouded banks of the peninsula, on the European side, from Chanak toward Helles. The 620-ton craft was commanded by Binbaşi (Lt. Cdr.) Effendi. He was assisted by two German naval officers, Oberleutnant (Lt.) Andreae and Leutnant (Ensign) Sebeling. The operation was under the overall command of another German naval officer, Kapitänleutnant (Lt. Cdr.) Rudolph Firle. Some key ratings were also German. Able to attain a speed of thirty-five knots per hour, the vessel was state-of-the-art.

By steaming slow under cover of darkness and dense fog, and with most of the British sailors asleep in their hammocks, the *Muavenet* avoided the watches posted on the destroyers *Bulldog* and *Beagle*. Some men later reported, however, that they had in fact seen it but believed it was a British destroyer on patrol. The Turkish boat spotted the old battleship in Morto Bay. At the time it was firing in support of the French at the Kereves Dere and was scanning inland with its searchlight. The *Goliath* and another battleship, the *Cornwallis*, had been ordered there to support their ally, whom Hamilton felt was under more pressure than the British fighting in the sector. At 1:15 a.m. the *Goliath*'s watch spotted the destroyer and challenged the intruder three times in Morse code with signal lamps. The *Goliath*'s watch officer also challenged the *Muavenet* by voice and received a reply in good English, likely from one of the German officers. He realized something was amiss, but before the battleship could fire a shot, the *Muavenet* launched two torpedoes. One hit the *Goliath* near the forward turret, and one struck near the forward funnel. As the ship began listing severely, it was hit by a third torpedo near its rear turret. In a cloud of black smoke, the stricken vessel exploded and capsized in about four minutes, trapping hundreds of men below decks. To make matters worse, the jolt from the explosions jammed the locks on the casement doors, which prevented many from escaping.

The *Muavenet-i-Millet* escaped unharmed. For this singular victory Kapitänleutnant Firle was awarded the German Iron Cross First Class, the Austrian Iron Cross, and the Turkish Order of Mejidie. The other officers were awarded the German Iron Cross Second Class, and the sultan of Turkey presented engraved gold watches to each of the men.

The *Goliath* went down with a loss of 570 officers and crew. Only 22 officers and 164 ratings were rescued. This event was the single greatest loss of life suffered by the Royal Navy during the campaign. Many men recorded this astonishing event in their diaries: "I received the signal in the morning watch, the signal send all available boats to rescue survivors. Then stand by to get under weigh. Nobody knew what had happened. Later we heard the whole story. A Turkish destroyer had come all the way down from Chanak through our patrols, turned round, put 3 torpedoes into the *Goliath*, who was at anchor in Morto Bay. The *Goliath* managed to fire one 12-pdr. [twelve-pounder cannon] at the enemy and then she sank in 3 minutes. The destroyer managed to get up again scot free . . . Everybody who could in the *Goliath* jumped overboard. But most of the ship's company, thinking they were being fired at, had cleared below the upper deck. Boats were immediately sent but only 22 officers and 140 men were saved."[1]

In 1916 an anonymous midshipman who survived the sinking described his experience that night. At the time the torpedo hit, he was asleep in his pajamas:

CRASH!-BANG! Cr r rash! I woke with a start, and sitting up in my hammock gazed around to see what had so suddenly roused me. Some of the midshipmen were already standing on the deck in their pyjamas—others, like me, were sitting up half dazed with sleep. A part of ship's boys crowded up the ladder from the gun-room flat, followed by three officers; one of these, a sub-lieutenant R.N.R. [Royal Naval Reserve], called out: "keep calm, and you'll all be saved."

Up to that moment it had never dawned upon me that the ship was sinking, and even then I thought it improbable until I noticed that we were already listing to starboard. Then I got up and walked up the hatch to the quarter-deck. The ship was now heeling about five degrees to starboard, and I climbed up to the port side. It was nearly pitch dark . . .

Gradually a crowd gathered along the port side. "Boat ahoy! Boat ahoy!" they yelled; but, as the ship listed more and more, and there was no sign or sound of any approaching vessel, the men's voices seemed to get a bit hopeless. The Commander was urging on a gang who were trying to get some heavy timber overboard; but, as we listed further and further over, they found it impossible to get it up on the port side and I couldn't get round to starboard, as the capstan and the Captain's hatch and skylight were in the way. At last they gave it up, and going to the side joined their voices to those of the crew, who were trying to attract the attention of any vessel that might be in the vicinity.

Inside, everything which was not secured was sliding about and bringing up against the bulkheads with a series of crashes. Crockery was smashing—boats falling out of their crutches—broken funnel-guys swinging against the funnel casings. She had heeled over to about twenty degrees, then she stopped and remained steady for a few seconds. In the momentary lull the voice of one of our officers rang out steady and clear as at "divisions": "Keep calm, men. Be British!"[2]

The boy jumped overboard and swam to the *Lord Nelson*. As he did so, he could hear the screams of his drowning shipmates behind him.

Among the casualties was the *Goliath*'s commander, Capt. Thomas Shelford, who was on the ship's bridge when it went down. The anonymous midshipman wrote, "There was no news of the Captain. Some days later I heard that his body had been picked up, and

"A Lot of Poor Fellows Drowned"

it was thought that he had been killed by the falling of the pinnace when the ship turned over just before she sank."[3]

Midshipman James Faed, aged fifteen, was sleeping below decks and managed to escape the ship, but he did not survive the ordeal. One of the ship's officers, Sub-Lt. Charles Van der Byl, wrote to inform his family:

> I am sure it will be some comfort to you to hear how much we all loved your son in the *Goliath*, and how much we miss him. I was Sub-Lieutenant of the Mess, and had only been in the ship about two months, but during that time I saw a great deal of him, and got to love him very much. He was the life and soul of the gun-room, and always most cheerful and optimistic. His best friend was Macleod, who was also drowned. They always used to go ashore together and buy curios for you. He really was a charming boy, loved by all who knew him. On the night we were sunk he was sleeping outside my cabin, and I saw him when I turned out. He had got his safety waistcoat on, and was going quietly up the ladder on the quarter-deck. He seemed as cheerful as usual, and perfectly cool. When I got on to deck a few seconds later he was just going over the port side with two other "snotties" [midshipmen]. That was the last I saw of him, and I shall never forget his cheery little face absolutely full of confidence and calm assurance as it could be. He was picked up unconscious by one of the *Euryalus* boats, and died on board, and was buried at sea early the same morning. Poor boy! I hoped and prayed he might have been saved, and we were all miserable when we heard he had gone too. He was an absolute "white man," the best and finest of us all, and everybody respected him for it. It is always the good who die young.[4]

Every British warship carried a complement of Royal Marine Light Infantrymen, whose job it was to assist with boarding operations, the ship's security, and small landings. The *Goliath* lost sixty-nine of its marines that day, among them Frederick Wall from Fleetwood, Lancashire. He left a widow and seven children to grieve for him at his home station, Plymouth. The oldest was nine, the youngest only a year old.

This tragedy was another example of the British taking the abilities of their non-Christian adversaries for granted. Had they known that there were submarines in the area, the *Goliath* and the other battleships would have been protected by the steel torpedo nets with which they were supposed to skirt themselves. These nets, however, were attached to arms that swung out from the sides of the vessels and produced a drag that slowed them down when they moved. They also did not expect submarines. Although they knew Turkish torpedo boats might be operating in the area, they did not take the precautions they should have. Perhaps the *Manitou* incident had lulled the Royal Navy into a false sense of security.

After the *Goliath* went down, all British and French warships were ordered to anchor outside the straits at night, off Cape Helles. But the precaution was a useless one, as they would soon discover. The Turks needed a deterrent to the Allied ships that were shelling them at will, so they asked the Germans for submarines. On April 25, 1915, the German submarine U-21 under Kapitänleutnant Otto Hersing departed Wilhelmshaven on Germany's North Sea coast and set sail for the Aegean. To avoid detection, he guided his vessel northward around Scotland. Hersing was well known for his exploits earlier in the war. While on patrol in the North Sea on September 5, 1914, his vessel sank the light cruiser HMS *Pathfinder* in the Firth of Forth. The ship and 259 members of its 270-man crew disappeared under the sea in only four minutes. The *Pathfinder* had the unlucky distinction of being the first ship sunk by a submarine during the war—and with a single torpedo.

U-21 arrived at the Austro-Hungarian naval base of Cattaro in the Adriatic on May 13, having sailed four thousand miles in eighteen days. After refueling and carrying out repairs, it set sail for the Dardanelles. A week later it arrived on station, and on May 25 it found its first victim. Midshipman Henry Denham on the battleship *Agamemnon*, which was off V Beach that morning, described his ship's encounter with Hersing: "Off Seddul Bahr: at 7.21 a.m. the periscope of a hostile submarine was sighted by one of our destroyers, less than a mile from us, and at 7.30 a.m., a little nearer us, by a trawler. This news was greeted with cheers, loud and prolonged, by everyone in the bathroom. Suddenly at 7.45 the submarine showed her periscope 400 yds off our port quarter between us and *Swiftsure*, three or four times evidently getting in position to loose off, but luckily *Swiftsure* fired a couple of rounds so close that he had to clear out of it and was later observed proceeding N.W. up the coast to Gaba Tepe. Conditions for submarine very bad, flat calm, no wind and clear water."[5]

It was the Grimsby trawler *Minoru*—unarmed and equipped only to sweep for mines—that sounded the alarm by blowing its sirens. The only thing it could do was warn the destroyers, whose job it was to deal with the undersea menace. The British destroyer *Harpy* gave chase. When the sub passed between *Agamemnon* and *Swiftsure*, its pursuer fired and missed.

Hersing's orders stated that he was to operate off Anzac. That was where he headed next, and the British were able to determine from his movements that it must have been his destination. In an effort to spot the marauder from the air, the balloon ship *Manica* launched its observation balloon, and the transports were ordered to head for Imbros or Lemnos.

At 12:25 p.m. the destroyer *Chelmer* sighted the telltale white wake of U-21's periscope and gave chase. At the time the battleship *Triumph* was off Anzac. It had been providing fire support for the ground troops but was taking a break, and several of its crew were sunning themselves on deck. The ship's captain, Maurice Fitzmaurice, knew that a submarine was lurking nearby, and his vessel was prepared. It was moving slowly—about five or six knots—with its torpedo nets out, its watertight doors closed, and its light guns manned.

It is impossible to say which saw the submarine first—the *Chelmer* or the *Triumph*. The *Chelmer* spotted Hersing's periscope five hundred yards off *Triumph*'s starboard beam, but before it could fire a shot, the *Triumph* fired and missed. Then it was Hersing's turn. He did not miss.

When it encountered U-21, the HMS *Vengeance* was on its way to Anzac: "When we arrived at Gaba Tepe S.N.O., N.T.O., Commander Lambart and Captain Ward, R.M.L.I., came on board and the *Canopus* left. She reported a submarine about ten minutes later . . . I was helping in the I.O. when suddenly there was an awful crash and I thought we had been torpedoed. I went on deck to see what was up. It was about 10 p.m. and what I saw was the *Triumph* healing [*sic*] right over and sinking rapidly. She went down in 8 minutes except for her propellers, which remained above water for about half an hour. Lots of destroyers, sweepers, etc., went to the rescue and only about 50 were drowned including the Engineer Commander and an assistant Paymaster R.N.R. [Royal Naval Reserve]."[6]

Midshipman John Metcalf survived the sinking. He recorded details of the ship's loss after a conversation with another surviving officer, Cdr. Wilfrid Egerton, RN:

A torpedo, which must have been fitted with cutters, cut its way through the torpedo netting and exploded on the hull of *Triumph*. The Ship's Company were then ordered to get into the water on to the outside of the torpedo nets in order to avoid being trapped down by the nets if the ship rolled over.

Commander Egerton went down from the Bridge on to the Fo'c'sle Deck and I think Captain Fitzmaurice went down with him (probably still wearing his monocle). It must be remembered that the torpedo nets did not extend forward nor aft of the armoured belt, and so the chance of being trapped by them if one dived from either Fo'c'sle or Quarterdeck did not exist.

One of H.M. Destroyers, having seen the torpedo explode, was coming to *Triumph* to render assistance.

Commander Egerton realized that *Triumph* was about to turn over and shouted "Bugler, sound the charge," but nothing happened. He turned round expecting to see his Bugler and was annoyed that the Bugler was not there. In his agony, for it must be remembered that he was responsible for about a thousand lives, he said "Where's that bloody bugler?" At that moment the Bugler

"A Lot of Poor Fellows Drowned"

jumped through the door from the Shelter Deck dressed only in the lanyard of his bugle. "Sound the charge," the Commander said to him. The Bugler sounded Charge, then threw his bugle as far as he could into the sea, and promptly dived in after it.

Immediately after the torpedo exploded, one of the midshipmen apparently wished to save some personal possession, and went down to the Tiller Flat to retrieve it from his sea-chest. He returned to the Quarterdeck fully dressed, just as the commanding officer of the destroyer put its bows close to *Triumph*'s stern. The midshipman (I think his name was Nunwick) jumped easily on to the destroyer's fo'c'sle. The destroyer then had to drop astern as *Triumph* was beginning to turn over.

Before going to the Dardanelles, *Triumph* was on the China Station, and in 1914 took part in the bombardment of the forts at Tsingtao. It was usual in those days for H.M. Ships to employ a certain number of nationals on board. *Triumph* had a Chinese Messman and some stewards in the Wardroom, which facilitated the purchase of fresh fish and vegetables from Chinese merchants for the Officers' Mess. These Chinese were still employed on board when the Ship arrived in the Mediterranean. Just after the Ship turned turtle the propellers appeared in the air, and one of them was seen to be turning round very slowly, with a Chinese steward clinging to one of the blades.

The steward survived.

Those on land, Turk and Anzac alike, could see the British ships rushing about, but they had no idea what was happening. That all changed when the torpedo struck. Both sides stopped firing, stood up, and watched the spectacle unfolding before them. The Turks cheered. The Anzacs stood in stunned silence:

> Tuesday the 26th [*sic*] broke calm & peaceful & we who were resting kicked off our clothes & turned in for some slumber. About 12 30 pm our attention was directed seaward & there a most pitiful sight rewarded us for our look. Our own ship "HMS Triumph" was in difficulties, having been torpedoed by a German submarine.

All eyes were directed toward the rare sight & our hearts were full of sorrow for the souls aboard. For a few minutes she lay over on her starboard then completed a full tilt & remained thus bottom upwards for quite a while. Then with a swirl & rush all that we observed of a once mighty ship was a few bubbles where the final plunge had been taken. Even as I write I cannot believe that I actually witnessed the sinking of a battleship; it was so unreal & not like one is expected to see—either pictured or described. The actual sinking occupied only ten & [a] half minutes so I don't know how the men fared who were aboard. Rumour said over a hundred lost their lives but as no official roll call has been listed it is impossible to attest any number. The scene in & around the spot today is alive with small craft & destroyers are circling with the hopes of capturing this scourge in our midst. The *Triumph*, before sinking, let [*sic*] her bow guns at some object close by & unofficially it is believed accounted for her assassin.[7]

U-21 launched a single torpedo from a distance of about three hundred yards, which cut through the *Triumph*'s antisubmarine net. Hersing watched the white bubbles of his torpedo's wake as it sped silently toward the battleship's bow. For several seconds after the explosion, *Triumph* was lost to sight as it was shrouded in smoke, falling water, and chunks of coal. As soon as it was visible, *Chelmer* rushed to its aid. In the ten minutes it took for the *Triumph* to capsize, the destroyer took men off the stricken ship via its stern walk. Other boats picked up survivors in the water. A half-hour after capsizing, *Triumph* went under, and the troops on shore resumed their war. Miraculously, out of a crew of five hundred, only seventy-three lost their lives.

One unusual casualty was Stoker Petty Officer William Powell, who was the servant of *Chelmer*'s captain, old Lt. Cdr. Hugh England. After the *Triumph*'s survivors were taken on board, England ordered that they be given spirits to help revive them. Powell took advantage of the situation and drank a hefty amount. Some of his

"A Lot of Poor Fellows Drowned"

shipmates found him drunk and unconscious and put him to bed in his hammock. A short while later he died of alcohol poisoning.

Hamilton, who had relied on the battleships to provide the artillery support that his own guns could not, was flabbergasted when he received news of the *Triumph*'s loss: "This moment, 12.40 p.m. the Captain [of his headquarters ship, the HMS *Arcadian*] has rushed in to say that H.M.S. *Triumph* is sinking! He caught the bad news on his wireless as it flew. Beyond doubt the German submarine. What exactly is about to happen, God knows. The fleet cannot see itself wiped out by degrees; and yet, without the fleet, how are we soldiers to exist? One more awful conundrum sent to us, but the Navy will solve it, for sure."[8]

Hersing, enthralled by the sight of the great ship's death, momentarily forgot about his own boat's safety and continued peering through his periscope. The destroyers noticed it and moved in quickly for the kill. Knowing that the *Triumph* could go down suddenly and take his own vessel to the bottom with it, Hersing took U-21 under the capsized battleship at full speed and retreated to fight another day. That day came less than forty-eight hours later.

On the morning of May 27 the British battleship *Majestic* was anchored off Helles with its nets out and as close to shore as it could safely be. It was ready to fire on the Turks if asked do so. Destroyers protected the transports in the area, and minesweeping trawlers were operating at the entrance to the straits, keeping a lookout for submarines. If they sighted one, they were to blow their sirens and hoist red flags—the signal that a submarine was known to be operating in the area.

After sinking the *Triumph*, Hersing took U-21 to the bottom, where it lay motionless and waited for the patrolling warships to end their search. After twenty-eight hours he surfaced under cover of darkness so he could recharge his depleted batteries and rid the submarine's interior of the usual accumulated odors. He had learned that the Russian light cruiser *Askold* was operating off Helles, so he headed south to find it. Instead, he found the *Majestic*, resting at anchor off W Beach.

At that time the battleship was firing on Turkish positions with its twelve-inch guns. Destroyers and other vessels milled around in an attempt to screen it from submarines. Still, Hersing was able to maneuver his vessel close to his intended prey. He had to, or he ran the risk of expending a valuable torpedo on one of the less valuable screening vessels. The *Majestic* sighted U-21's periscope at 6:45 a.m. only four hundred yards off its port beam. The ship's guns opened fire as soon as the slim black tube was sighted, but it was not quick enough. Hersing had the advantage, and as the *Majestic* loosed off its first round, a torpedo was already passing between the destroyers and transports, headed for the mighty vessel. It struck amidships, passing through the battleship's torpedo net as though it were made of butter. A second torpedo struck almost immediately, and within four minutes the *Majestic* had capsized. No officers were lost, but thirty-two ratings were killed in the explosions or were drowned in the torpedo nets as they tried to struggle to the surface.

Among the troops who witnessed the death of the *Majestic* was Able Seaman Joseph Murray of the Hood Battalion. While many observers watched the spectacle from land or other ships, he had a box office seat:

We arrived on "W" beach before breakfast. Again we were told we could have an hour in the water before commencing work. This is a nice habit we are getting into. For a whole hour we knew exactly what we had to do. We were ordered to parade under the cliffs at 7.30 and see that we were all there on time. We lost no time in getting into the water. It was cool and refreshing.

About a dozen of us swam towards H.M.S. *Majestic* lying close inshore. All the other warships and transports had gone. My intention was to get near enough to scrounge something to eat. The lads afloat had plenty to spare and a stale loaf would be improved by a dip in the sea. I have not seen any bread since coming ashore over a month ago but I think I would recognize a loaf if one is aimed at me.

I was deluding myself that I would reach the ship first. I had

"A Lot of Poor Fellows Drowned"

about a five-yard lead and was swimming strongly when I heard a deep thud and the water seemed to vibrate violently. I got a lovely mouthful and, half choked, struck out frantically. I thought I had struck the wash from a trawler. I had lost sight of the *Majestic* and no wonder, for I had been turned completely round and was swimming away from her. Puzzled for a moment, I suddenly realized that she was heeling over. Her torpedo nets were out and hundreds of men were lining her deck. Many dived, some jumped and others scrambled over on to her side as she slowly heeled over. How amazingly cool everyone seemed to be. Those that jumped took their time; they ambled to a suitable spot and took the plunge, quite unconcernedly so it seemed. In a matter of minutes only the keel was showing above the water like a huge whale. The only visible sign of any urgency was a solitary figure, carrying what appeared to be a small bundle, hurrying along the keel to avoid getting his feet wet as the stern became awash. The bow of the keel remained above the water and there sat the solitary sailor on his bundle.[9]

Although it had capsized, the *Majestic* did not sink. It was lying in such shallow water—nine fathoms—when the torpedoes struck that it was being propped up by its foremast. This left its green-painted bottom showing above the water.

Hersing and his boat would survive the war. He was decorated with Germany's highest military decoration, the Pour le Mérite, and every member of his crew received the Iron Crosses 1st and 2nd Class. His work in the Dardanelles, however, was not finished. On Sunday, July 4, he sighted the French munitions ship the *Carthage* disgorging its deadly cargo into boats to be landed on V Beach. A single torpedo launched by U-21 sent the vessel to the bottom. Fortunately for the French, the loss in life was slight; only six men were killed. Able Seaman Joe Murray witnessed this event too:

A day at the seaside for a change. We have been cutting steps in the cliffs between "W" and "X" Beaches to be used for storing shells. Some French Colonials were being landed by motor boats from a large transport lying quite a distance off shore. We were admiring the fine ship and inwardly wishing we were on board, but changed our minds when she began to sink stern first. In less than three minutes she was perpendicular, with her bows high in the air. She seemed to remain in that position for quite a while before she plunged out of sight beneath the calm surface of the sea. I did not hear any explosion. Only two or three boat-loads from her have landed, unless there have been others which I haven't seen, but I doubt it. I fear many men must have been lost as there would not have been much time to launch many boats. It was all over in a matter of minutes.

I later heard that the ship was called the *Carthage*. Rather an appropriate name, I think.[10]

Some of the survivors were conveyed to V Beach, where they were treated in the French hospital. But luck was still against them. The next day an explosion occurred at an ammunition dump there. Maj. Norman Burge, second-in-command of the RM Cyclist Company, noted in his diary: "We hear it was a large bomb pit & rocket store that blew up in the French lines yesterday. An accident, it was, not a Turkish shell. 2 offrs. & 70 men killed & 200 wounded & the sad part is that they say those same wounded were in the transport which was sunk yesterday evening."

Hersing cast about for another target but found none. In any case, just after firing on the *Carthage*, U-21's hull was damaged by a mine as it was diving to elude the pursuing destroyers. It had to retreat to Constantinople for six weeks of repairs.

With the sinking of the *Majestic*, Hersing had singlehandedly swayed the campaign in the direction of the Turks. The British and French, fearful that enemy submarines would take an even greater toll on their fleets, pulled their warships back to Imbros and Lemnos, which was protected by antisubmarine nets. The admirals felt that hospital ships could still operate safely off Gallipoli because the Turks respected the Red Cross with which they were marked.

The men who relied on the warships' fire felt abandoned. They felt isolated just by being at Gallipoli, but the support of the ships

"A Lot of Poor Fellows Drowned"

was both a physical and an emotional lifeline. Hersing changed all that. Later Joseph Murray wrote: "We now know why the warships and transports have gone. A German submarine is lurking about—in a couple of days we have lost two battleships, H.M.S. *Triumph* off Gaba Tepe and the *Majestic* off Cape Helles, thirteen miles to the south. A few days ago there were ships everywhere; now the *Majestic* has gone, we feel as though the Navy has deserted us."[11]

Battleships and cruisers would visit Gallipoli to provide occasional fire support, but the visits were infrequent and rarely lasted after dark. The only vessels that would provide twenty-four-hour support were the fast-moving destroyers, which shelled Turkish positions at night and used their searchlights to illuminate targets. With the departure of the capital ships, monitors were sent to support the troops on land. Because of their shallow drafts, they were virtually invulnerable to submarines. Tom Carberry, who was serving with the Australian Army Medical Corps, recalled: "After the *Triumph* was torpedoed, our boats left for Imbross [*sic*] Island, which is about 15 miles from Anzac, the reason being most probably, that it was rather dangerous for them in the open where the sub could pick them off without warning. In their place the latest type of monitor appeared on the scene. These boats carry big guns and as they have a draught of only 4 feet, they offer a much smaller target, and the sub has a very small chance of sinking them. These monitors did very good work. The battleships often paid a visit to let the Turk know that they were still taking an interest in the war, and they would let Jacko have a few broadsides to remind him of old times. During these courtesy visits they were always accompanied by the destroyers, in case the submarines should show up."[12]

Another effect of the pullback was an even greater shortage of water at Anzac. Because local wells provided such a small amount, most of the men's supply was transported in barges from Egypt. Without the big ships to provide counter-battery fire, the Turkish guns could shell the barges and other vessels at will. Hospital ships could operate with impunity, but the ambulance carriers and other transports could not. They were also pulled back to the Greek islands. If the naval campaign was going to be won by the Allies, it would have to be won underwater.

The Germans were not the only ones wreaking havoc with their submarines in the Dardanelles. British, French, and Australian submarines also operated, and the Turks suffered losses at sea and on land as a result. Not only did Allied submarines sink Turkish ships; they also shelled targets on land with their deck guns. Occasionally, the British put ships' officers ashore to blow up small installations. Even in their limited numbers and with their meager supplies of torpedoes, they would dictate Turkish naval affairs just as Hersing and his boat impacted the movements of Allied vessels.

The first Allied submarine sent into the Dardanelles was the British vessel B11 under Lt. Norman Holbrook. On December 13, 1914, he traveled up the straits with orders to torpedo any enemy vessel he encountered. After sailing up to Kephez Point on the surface without being spotted, he was forced to dive his boat in order to pass under the five strings of Turkish mines that guarded the straits at the point. When he raised his periscope to ensure that it was safe to surface, he spotted the Turkish battleship *Messudieh*. The outdated warship was stationed there to guard the waterway at the behest of the Germans. Moving his vessel to within eight hundred yards of his unsuspecting victim, Holbrook fired one torpedo. Within ten minutes *Messudieh* capsized and sank, and B11 escaped unharmed after spending a harrowing nine hours under water evading detection. Many of the battleship's crew survived in air pockets and were freed by divers who cut holes in the vessel's hull to release them. It was a miracle that only ten officers and twenty-seven enlisted men were killed. Holbrook was awarded the Victoria Cross for his feat. Both he and his vessel would survive the war.

Unfortunately for the submarines that followed, B11's experience was not the norm, and some were lost. The first was the French boat *Saphir*. After running aground off Nagara Point on January 15, 1915, it was apparently destroyed by Turkish shore batteries, killing fourteen of its twenty-seven-man crew. Next to go was the British submarine E15 under Lt. Cdr. Theodore Brodie. While trying to make his way up the straits early on the morning of April 17, his vessel ran aground near Fort No. 8 due to heavy opposing currents. The stricken submarine was then fired on and disabled by Turkish shore batteries, killing Brodie in the conning tower. Six of his crew were killed by chlorine gas, released when the sub's batteries were exposed to seawater. The survivors were captured, and Turks and Germans swarmed aboard in search of information and technical details. In an effort to prevent it from being repaired and reused against them, the British made several attempts to destroy it. One was made by the submarine B6, under the command of Brodie's brother, but his torpedo missed. Later that night the destroyers *Grampus* and *Scorpion* tried to sink it, but they also failed. Further attempts by B11, seaplanes, and the battleships *Triumph* and *Majestic* were also unsuccessful, though bombs from the seaplanes did prevent a Turkish warship from towing it out to sea. It was not until the night of April 18 that a long picketboat from the *Majestic*, under the command of Lt. Cdr. Eric Robinson, was successful. Carrying two fourteen-inch torpedoes, he took his boat in close and sank E15 before his own boat was sent to the bottom by a Turkish shell. Robinson was rescued and awarded the Victoria Cross for this and other exploits earlier in the campaign. He survived the war and died in 1965.

The next vessel to attempt the journey was also the first Allied submarine to successfully navigate the Dardanelles as far as the Sea of Marmara. It was the Australian boat AE2 under the command of Lt. Cdr. Henry Stoker, an Irish-born Royal Navy officer who had been loaned to the Royal Australian Navy's fledgling submarine service. At two in the morning on April 25, Stoker took AE2 into the Dardanelles, sailing on the surface in order to conserve his batteries.[13] The weather was calm, the sea clear, and no enemy ships were in sight. His orders were to travel up the straits and sink any vessel he found laying mines or carrying troops. In general he was to cause as much trouble as possible. This would not only tie up Turkish naval power in the area; it would also have a huge psychological impact on the populace. AE2 was not sighted until 4:30 a.m., when one of the Turkish shore batteries fired on it. For the first time since entering the straits that morning, he was forced to dive. Traveling at periscope depth—twenty feet below the surface—he continued his journey. But the sea was so calm that his periscope was sighted again two hours later, and Turkish gunners opened fire on him from both sides.

Still, Stoker stuck to his periscope. Focusing directly ahead, he spotted a small cruiser, which he thought was dropping mines. After firing a single torpedo—one of eight the AE2 carried—he dove and hoped for the best. The resulting explosion confirmed that the weapon had hit something, but he was not sure what. The Turks did not report losing any ships that day.

For the next three days he continued his voyage with the Ottoman navy continually dogging him. It seemed as though the Turks were second-guessing Stoker every step of the way, and his boat was fired upon nearly every time it surfaced. Stoker encountered numerous vessels and fired until his torpedoes were gone, but none found their mark. Without a deck gun to engage targets on the surface and its torpedoes expended, Stoker turned the submarine around and headed for home.

At 10:30 a.m. on April 30, tragedy struck just north of Kara Burnu. For some unknown reason, while AE2 was traveling at periscope depth, the vessel suddenly surfaced; nobody knew why. It was sighted and chased by a Turkish torpedo boat that was just a mile away. A gunboat, three miles distant, joined in the chase. Stoker ordered a forward tank filled with water, which caused AE2 to dive suddenly below one hundred feet. A frightening state of affairs, when one considers that the boat's depth gauge only went up to one hundred feet. In an effort to stabilize the vessel, the crew blew the main ballast tank, but the boat again surfaced suddenly and could not be stopped. At ten forty-five and with the torpedo boat still attacking, Stoker ordered all hands—three officers and seventeen ratings—on deck. He then flooded the boat and surrendered his crew to the Turks. Not a single member of AE2's crew was lost during its harrowing voyage, but several would die in captivity.

Other vessels would make the trip after AE2. A number were successful, while others were lost. On September 4 E7 under Lt. Cdr. Archie Cochrane was caught in an antisubmarine net off Nagara while en route to the Sea of Marmara. The next day, the boat still lodged in the net, Kapitänleutnant Heino von Heimburg, commander of the German submarine UB-14, and the boat's cook, Herzig, are said to have borrowed a rowboat. They rowed out alone to the British submarine with a small mine that they lowered by hand with a cable. The explosion broke the net's hold on the submarine, it surfaced, and the Turkish gunboats fired on it. The crewmen threw open the main hatch and exited the boat with their arms in the air, and Herzig and von Heimburg went aboard to take them captive. Cochrane scuttled his vessel, and the crew climbed aboard one of the waiting gunboats, seconds before the sub sank below the surface. At that time von Heimburg's own submarine was undergoing repairs at Chanak. Whether or not the story about him is true is unknown; he refused to verify it. Either way, a mine did explode near E7, and the war ended for its crew. Cochrane, whose boat had wreaked havoc against Turkish shipping and destroyed targets on land with its twelve-pounder deck gun, escaped his captives in 1918.

Submarines of the First World War were anything but spacious, and the tactics they employed were being developed on the spot. Sister Alice Kitchen, serving on the British hospital ship *Gascon*, was given a tour of the HM Submarine E11 while her ship was docked at Malta:

It is a marvelous and complicated mass of machinery inside & yet everything seems to work by the touch of a hand on a wheel or screw & looks so simple. We saw all the torpedoes & the means of firing them was explained to us & looked through the periscope & saw the *Gascon* outside & the people on the wharf quite distinctly & also it was explained to us just how the submarine was sunk under the water (diving). When on business bent, the periscope is never allowed up above the water longer than 3 seconds, which seems very little time in which to take all the bearings sufficient to do their deadly work. They never chase a vessel, only lie in wait for them & when a torpedo is fired into a vessel they just clear out quickly & never show up above water. When you see how little space they have in which to live & sleep on the floor except the Capt. and one other whose bed is a drawer you realize that they could rescue none, not even themselves if anything happened to them. They can stay under water about 40 hrs. without discomfort or fresh supply of air; carry no medical dressings or stores except for burns, never go down more than 20 feet at a time & then only about 60 ft. altogether.[14]

The submarine *Turquoise* was the first French vessel to enter the Sea of Marmara during the campaign. On October 30 it seems to have been hit by fire from Turkish shore batteries (accounts differ) and was captured intact. While searching the vessel, the Turks found papers detailing an intended rendezvous with the British submarine E20 for November 5. Unfortunately for the British, the commander of the *Turquoise* made no effort to destroy his documents. The two subs were supposed to patrol the Bosporus together. The Turks and Germans set a trap and were thus able to capture E20 and its crew.

On November 5, instead of the *Turquoise*, the German submarine UB-14 was waiting for E20 at the rendezvous point off Rodosto in the Sea of Marmara. With a single torpedo, von Heimburg added a British submarine to his list of kills. E20's commanding officer, Lt. Cdr. Clyfford Warren, and nine of his crew were picked up by the German vessel. This was the last submarine lost during the campaign. UB-14's commander, von Heimburg, survived the war and served for a while in the Second World War, before retiring from the Kriegsmarine (German navy) in May 1943. He was captured by the Soviets in March 1945 and died in a prisoner of war camp near Stalingrad the following October.

The Transports

British and French transports operated freely off Gallipoli until the sinking of the battleships in May. The first transport to be sunk during the campaign was also the first to be lost during the war. And it resulted in the greatest loss of life. The *Royal Edward* began life as a civilian vessel. At the outbreak of war it was one of many fast commercial ships requisitioned by the British government to convey the First Canadian Contingent to England. Later it was used to house interned enemy aliens anchored off Southend, Essex. The internees were kept below decks at night.

In 1915 the *Royal Edward* resumed life as a troop transport. On the night of July 30 it set sail from Devonport, Devonshire, with a crew of 220 (most from Bristol, Gloucestershire) under Master Peter Wotton. It carried 32 army officers and 1,350 other ranks. Its destination was Alexandria, then Lemnos, from whence the troops would to be sent to Gallipoli on smaller vessels. Most of the soldiers who sailed on the *Royal Edward*'s final voyage were reinforcements for the Twenty-Ninth Division. It carried fresh units of the Royal Army Medical Corps (RAMC) and the Royal Engineers and small numbers of reinforcements for the other divisions. Some men were returning to the peninsula after recovering from wounds.

Also aboard was the Eighteenth Labour Company of the Army Service Corps. This small unit consisted mostly of married men in their forties who had worked as skilled laborers in civil life. They were supposed to help construct winter quarters and to work on other projects related to the Allied offensives scheduled for August. While in Alexandria on August 9, Trimmer William Bodle deserted (it was his first voyage), and Chief Steward Ernest Glew left "by mutual consent." They were lucky they did. Despite the fear of submarine attacks at this stage of the war, the *Royal Edward*, in kind with the other British transports heading to Gallipoli in 1915, traveled without an escort. This was to prove a fatal error.

The German submarine UB-14 was moved in pieces by train to Pola in the Austro-Hungarian state of Croatia and reassembled in the Adriatic. The vessel was a small one—ninety feet long and ten feet wide—and extremely cramped for the fourteen men who lived and worked inside. UB-14 was on its first voyage. It was designed to be disassembled and transported by rail. On July 16 it sailed for the Aegean, arriving at Bodrum on Turkey's southwest coast on

July 24. There it underwent much-needed repairs, carried out by a maintenance crew that had to travel part of the way by camel.

In August UB-14 departed for Constantinople. The first enemy ship it encountered was a British hospital ship, which its captain (von Heimburg) wisely chose not to attack. The next vessel to cross the sub's path was the *Royal Edward*. At nine twenty on the morning of August 13, less than a mile from the transport, the submarine fired a single torpedo, blowing a hole in the steamer's stern.

The attack caught the British completely off guard, and the men were not ordered to don lifebelts or assemble at their lifeboat stations. In fact, when the explosion occurred, many of the soldiers were undergoing foot inspection on deck, and a large number of them tried to get below to retrieve their lifebelts. This decision was to prove fatal for many. They ran headlong into the men from below rushing toward the lifeboats, and the one group prevented the other from escaping. Due to the severe list that the ship quickly assumed, few of the boats could be lowered, and the men who formed up at their stations were ordered to jump overboard. The *Royal Edward* sank in two and a half minutes, with a loss of 5 sailors and 861 soldiers.

Among the survivors was the ship's surgeon, Dr. Richard Neagle. Days after the sinking he observed:

> I was seated in my Cabin, which is situated on the Promenade Deck on the Starboard Side near the main Companion Way, about 9.15 a.m. on Friday August 13th. I had just finished breakfast and was enjoying a smoke preparatory to going downstairs to the Surgery which is situated about amidships, when suddenly two great tremors ran through the ship, one following immediate on the other, and the second far more violent. Almost at once there was the sound of rifle firing just above my cabin coming from the Boat Deck, and the hooter at the same time gave a long dull blast.
>
> The ship during this period was quivering and it seemed to me like a minor earthquake shock.
>
> I went outside to the Companion Way, crossed it to the Port Side, and ascended the short stair-case leading to the Café and

"A Lot of Poor Fellows Drowned"

the Boat Deck. When I arrived there I took all in at a glance. The ship was sinking at the Stern, water even in this short space of time was pouring in on the aft Well Deck, the small bridge situated just above the Aft Deck being almost submerged even then. Troops and members of the ship's company were going to their various Boat Stations, at the same time most of them were adjusting their lifebelts. The Captain was alone on the Bridge. I immediately hastened down to my Cabin to put my lifebelt on, carefully adjusting and tucking it well under my armpits, which from past experience I knew to be half the battle, and again went upstairs to the Boat Deck. I may say here that I had very little on, just a pair of white duck trousers and a life belt. When I arrived again on the Boat Deck nearly all the Aft End of the "Royal Edward" was under water, it reached almost to the Marconi Room situated at the extreme end of the Boat Deck. The ship also had a slight list to Starboard. I saw also several boats from the Aft Deck away, whether they had been washed off or lowered I cannot say. A couple from the Port Side of the Boat Deck had also got away.

There were few troops or crew at that time on the Port Side. The Captain was still on the Bridge. There was no confusion or commotion at all. At that time I happened to glance over the side and saw what appeared to be the wash of a submarine. It was going away from the sinking ship about 200 or 300 yards off. At that moment the Ship took a great list to Starboard. There was the sound of crashing and breaking of many articles. I was half thrown, hardly being able to keep my balance, to the opposite side of the ship between the foremost funnel, and the end of the Café through a very small passage way, finally coming to a stand still up against the Deck rail. I glanced down the Boat Deck and saw numbers of troops endeavouring to get Boats away, but I don't think they could possibly have done so, as in my opinion many were thrown into the sea when the ship took the great list. The "Royal Edward" soon appeared to right herself and immediately afterwards rose bow upwards.

At that moment I threw myself into the sea and struck out to get away as far as I could from the ship fearing the suction. I soon put a little distance between myself and the ship and then instinctively looked around. I thought it was all up with me. I thought she was coming over on me, but fortunately that did not occur. She just rose high up at the bow, so high that I could see forty or fifty yards of her bottom, and then glided down Stern first. When the Aft funnel was about to go under there was a great hissing noise and steam appeared as though it were a small cloud. There was also a great banging as though explosions were taking place. When the water got as far as the Fore Funnel the whole ship left above the sea appeared to get perpendicular and she immediately went down.

On getting over the chill of the preliminary immersion and having seen what I have already described, I took in the scene around me. There were dozens of soldiers and members of the crew swimming about, some with lifebelts on, others without them, there was a tremendous amount of debris and wreckage floating about. It struck me afterwards that everything that could float from the ship was in the sea. However, in the course of twenty minutes or half an hour I got hold of a wooden grating which appeared to be something substantial, and which eventually proved to be such. During the first hour or so many of the young troops were shouting "Are we downhearted?" and others were singing "Tipperary" or at least trying to. One old soldier quite close to me got hold of what appeared to be half a bottle of whisky and seemed to be enjoying it, being well supported by some substantial wreckage. All this, however, passed off.

The saddening and tragic part was to come and come soon. Another hour passed by, there was a great quiet all around, many had dropped off from portions of wreckage, and too exhausted by weight of clothes and exposure, were drowned. There were some awful cries for aid in their distress. In the course of another half hour I should think, the Hospital Ship "SOUDAN" made its appearance, but from the place where I was clinging to debris

"A Lot of Poor Fellows Drowned"

it seemed a great distance off, say 1½ miles. Land seemed to be about 10 to 12 miles away. It was about this time that I felt the cold and had cramp in my legs and in the muscles of my leg. I was obliged to leave my grating from time to time and swim and get over these conditions. Eventually the "AJAX" made its appearance and lowered boats into one of which I was pulled after being nearly five hours in the water.

At about two in the afternoon the British hospital ship *Soudan* arrived on the scene, bound for Alexandria. Despite the threat of attack, it remained and picked up survivors. What its crew did not know was that UB-14 was in no position to tarry; its compass was damaged, and von Heimburg had decided to head to port for repairs.

About six hundred men were rescued by the *Soudan*, and a few were picked up by other ships. *Soudan* proceeded to Alexandria, where the traumatized survivors were reequipped. Three days later they were sent to Gallipoli. Men who had lost their false teeth were returned to England to have new sets fitted because there were no dentists at Gallipoli.

Of the *Royal Edward*'s crew, 132 men perished. The vessel's master, Peter Wotton, went down with his ship. Married but separated from his wife, he left a six-year-old son to mourn his loss. The animosity between the couple must have been great, for his widow refused to accept his medals when they were offered to her by the government in 1922.

Men from countries not even at war—or not yet at war—lost their lives that day. Fireman Romero (he went by this single name) hailed from Santander, Columbia, and Sailor A. Velasquez was from Peru. Able Seaman O. Benson was a Swede, and Fireman Stanley Mack was from the United States. Like every other civilian-manned vessel of its day, the crew of the *Royal Edward* was truly cosmopolitan.

Among the hundreds of soldiers who died was Pvt. Joe Conway, a thirty-four-year-old chemist from Burnley who lived with his sister before enlisting. One of his friends, a Private Macdonald, wrote about him in a letter home: "Poor Joe Conway is dead. He got picked up, but died about an hour later."[15] McDonald's letter arrived during his sister's wedding party. Another sister, who had traveled from Canada to see their sister wed, had previously dreamed about a ship wrecking at sea and Joe struggling in the water. Pvt. Walter Steward, a twenty-four-year-old fisherman from Gorleston-on-Sea, Norfolk, was a reinforcement for the First Essex. His swimming skills saved his life, and after spending four hours in the water, he was picked up by the *Soudan*. His luck would not hold, however. He was killed at Gallipoli by an "aerial torpedo" while having tea less than two months later.

A number of new medical units were on the *Royal Edward*. One was No. 54 (1/1st East Anglian) Casualty Clearing Station (TF) from Ipswich, Suffolk, which lost two officers and fifty-two other ranks. Among the dead was its commanding officer, Lt. Col. John Dauber, who practiced at the Royal Hospital for Women and Children in London in civil life. The unit's other officer casualty was Maj. James Mowat. A retired staff surgeon in the Royal Navy, he was recalled to duty on August 4, 1914, and appointed to the cruiser HMS *Hermes*. After that vessel was sunk by a German submarine on October 31, 1914, he suffered an "emotional shock" and was invalided out of the navy. When the government issued an appeal for surgeons for the services, he applied to the army and was gazetted major in the RAMC in May 1915.

Sister Alice Kitchen on the hospital ship *Gascon* heard about the sinking that night. She wrote in her diary: "Heard tonight about the *King* [*sic*] *Edward* with 3000 troops sunk by a torpedo. It is so tragic but perhaps a more merciful death than being shot to pieces at the front & getting such fearful injuries as some of them do."

The next transport to fall victim to a submarine was the *Southland*, which was carrying fourteen hundred men of the Australian Twenty-First and Twenty-Third Battalions, along with their brigade staff. On September 2 it was near the island of Strati, en route to Lemnos, when UB-14 launched a single torpedo. It tore a forty-by-twelve-foot hole through the port side. Lifeboats were launched, some in such haste that they overturned, and men dove overboard. Most of the men

"A Lot of Poor Fellows Drowned"

abandoned ship in good order, but thirty-three men lost their lives. The ship's captain, officers, and most of the crew remained onboard. Several soldiers also volunteered to stay on the ship. Together they were able to keep the vessel afloat until the destroyer *Raccoon* arrived to tow it into Mudros Harbor. The men in the water were picked up by the hospital ship *Neuralia*, the seaplane carrier *Ben-My-Chree*, and other vessels. Among the survivors was Pvt. Ivor Williams of the Twenty-First Battalion. On September 2 he wrote in his diary:

> At 9 am I went below and had a shave and at the same time upset a bottle of Iodine over my razer [sic] case, thus making it look as if it was not worth picking out of the gutter. Shortly after I went up on deck and was sitting on a seat with Reg and a couple of others: after a while Reg asked me the time, I looked, it was 9.50 am. Just as I was fastening up my watch the boat gave a lurch, a wiggle, shook violently and then gave a sound of a terrible explosion. On the top of this came a deluge of water and spray. About a minute after this happened the "ABANDON SHIP" Signal was given. This meant every man for himself as we were torpedoed and it looked as if the ship would go under any minute. The boys took it quite calmly as they stopped and lowered all the boats. Every one went down below, got their lifebelt and stood their boat stations as if it was a drill move instead of being in earnest.
>
> We should have been the third boat to leave, but owing to my good luck, I suppose, it was filled before I could get down to it. Anyhow there were four of this party drowned. By about 1 o'clock we had lowered all the boats and they took some lowering too as they were simply painted and stuck on to all the fixed woodwork, a disgrace to the authorities.
>
> During this operation a plank broke and gently tapped me on the head so putting me to sleep for a few seconds. Just as the last boat was lowered, the old ship gave three mighty lurches as if she was settling down or turning over. The decks were at a terrific angle and then began to settle nose first. I fancy we were only 2½ hours off Lemnos.

The sight of all the Torpedo boats coming to our rescue was a sight I shall never forget. There were about five of these and two Hospital ships. After we were hit, all the other transports started off at full speed to get out of the way and just as we got on deck to our boat station another torpedo was fired at us. This missed the stern of our boat by inches. If this had hit us there would not have been anyone to tell the tale. With this the ship's gun was fired, but the barrel split and there we were unarmed there and then. During the process of lowering the boats I had the misfortune to lose the silver pen that Add. gave me, also to break the ring Rita gave me. When all the work was finished we were ordered to go to the gangway where a boat was waiting for us. On our way we saw two of the crew who had been shot for looting.

We were eventually picked up by the Hospital Ship "Neuralia." She is a beautiful boat and when I boarded her I was just done, so collapsed on the deck at the top of the Gangway for about ¼ hour. All I managed to save was my shirt and trousers; but others were not even so lucky as myself. At 2.45 pm the "Neuralia" on which we had a good feed proceeded to Lemnos arriving there at 4 pm. We shall have to sleep on the decks tonight.

Although casualties were light, one of the men who lost his life was Col. Richard Linton, the commanding officer of the Australian Sixth Infantry Brigade. Maj. John Bean, the First Battalion's medical officer, wrote: "Early in 1915 he was given the task of organising one of the new infantry brigades (the 6th) for the 2nd Division of the A.I.F., and in May embarked as its commander. After further training in Egypt, he left with it for Gallipoli at the end of August, travelling in the troopship 'Southland,' which, however, was torpedoed near Lemnos in the morning of Sept. 2. As the boat containing the staff of the 6th Brigade reached the water, it was capsized by some stokers and stewards, who, waiting near the waterline, tried to clamber into it. Colonel Linton was in the water for an hour and a half before he was picked up, exhausted, by one of the boats. He opened his eyes and said: 'Good boys! Good luck,

"A Lot of Poor Fellows Drowned"

boys!' but died two hours later on board the French destroyer 'Massuo.'"[16] His son, Pvt. Robert Linton of the Twenty-First Battalion, survived the sinking and the war. Only one member of the *Southland*'s crew, Trimmer Patrick Courtney, lost his life. This author was not been able to substantiate Private Williams's report of the two seamen shot for looting.

One survivor of the *Southland* who later lost his life on the peninsula was also the second youngest soldier to die during the campaign. Pvt. Jim Martin of the Twenty-First Battalion was only fourteen. He looked older than he was and successfully lied his way into the Australian Imperial Force (AIF) by claiming to be eighteen. When the *Southland* was hit, he dove overboard and spent four hours in the water before being picked up. After arriving at Gallipoli, he developed typhoid, and on October 25 he was evacuated to HM Hospital Ship *Glenart Castle*. He died that night of heart failure. The following morning his lifeless body was deposited back into the sea from which he had been rescued less than two months earlier.

The last transport to be sunk was the SS *Ramazan*, which was carrying Indian reinforcements to Lemnos. On September 19, fifty-five miles southwest of the Greek island of Cerigo, it was shelled on the surface by the German submarine U-35. Only one crewman lost his life; Second Mate Reinis Jauget was a native of Russia who had a British wife. Among the injured crewmen was marine engineer Gerald Braris, a Greek sailor who had lived in England: "During the Dardanelles expedition while effecting a disembarcation of troops at the Golf of Saros, a shell burster [*sic*] in my Cabin I was in at the time, and was only saved by a miracle. I suffered since through the effects of the gunpowder fumes, of a bronchial catargh as well as the damaging of my finger of the right hand, and dispite all medical aid rendered to me, still remains in same condition, thus inabling me to follow my trade ever since."[17]

Turkish Losses

Turkish naval losses during the campaign were dwarfed by those of the British and French. One reason was that they had so few to lose. Another was that most ship-to-ship combat involving Turkish surface craft involved Allied submarines. These submarines carried a limited number of often-fallible torpedoes.

Because there were so few Ottoman warships in the Sea of Marmara and none operating off the Gallipoli Peninsula, submarines were often forced to use their precious supply of "fish" on the civilian vessels that moved troops and supplies down the straits to Maidos, where they would be disgorged and moved overland to the front. One of them was the transport *Nagara*. American newspaper reporter Arthur Ruhl witnessed the sinking. He wrote that *Nagara* "disintegrated in a cloud of yellow smoke and sank, and with her the heavy siege-gun she was taking to the Dardanelles."[18] Allied submarines were so successful that the Turks were forced to move men and material overland via oxen and camel trains. There were no railroads in the area and few proper roads, so the going was slow and arduous.

All of the Turkish warships lost during the campaign were sunk by the British submarine E11 under Lt. Cdr. Martin Nasmith. The sub began the first of three patrols into the Dardanelles on May 19, 1915, and, in common with the other boats of its type, carried a single twelve-pounder deck gun and five torpedoes. Among the vessels it sent to the bottom were the *Nagara* and the ammunition ship *Stambul*, which Nasmith had the audacity to sink while it was moored next to the arsenal in Constantinople.

Nasmith was well aware that torpedoes were a rare commodity and that he could not risk losing them if they malfunctioned. Thus, his crew trimmed them so that they would float to the surface if they missed their targets and could be recovered for later use. To do this he waited until his intended victim was out of sight, then would sail up to the floating projectile. Crewmen would then jump into the sea, pull the torpedo back to the sub, and push it back into the bow tube. Following his orders to "go and run amuck in the Marmara," E11 sank one gunboat, a naval auxiliary vessel, and four steamships on its first voyage. For his exploits Nasmith was awarded the Victoria Cross, and the members of his crew were awarded Distinguished Service Medals.

"A Lot of Poor Fellows Drowned"

Nasmith's second patrol was also successful. On August 8, 1915, he sent the Turkish battleship *Hayreddin Barbarossa* to the bottom off the Narrows with a single torpedo. Fifteen minutes after being hit, the stricken vessel capsized and sank with a loss of 250 men. On August 14 E11 struck again, sinking the destroyer *Samsun* in the Sea of Marmara.

E11 sank the last Turkish warship to go down during the Gallipoli campaign on its third and final voyage into the Marmara. It was the destroyer *Yarhisar*, commanded by Binbaşi Ahmet Hulusi Hasan. At the time, on December 3, 1915, *Yarhisar* was searching for E11. Out of a crew of seventy, thirty-six Turkish crewmen and fifteen Germans were lost. Binbaşi Hasan was among the survivors. Lieutenant Commander Nasmith was the campaign's most successful submarine commander. During E11's three patrols, he and his crew sent eighty-six Turkish vessels to the bottom.

The Gallipoli campaign's two most famous naval casualties were not combat fatalities. On May 15, 1915, Lord Fisher, who felt he was being badgered by Churchill and was unhappy about ships from the Grand Fleet being sent to Gallipoli, resigned his post as first sea lord. He could no longer work with a man who had no naval experience. Fisher also felt that the career politician had no compassion for the men and ships he was throwing away in his futile effort to conquer the unconquerable Dardanelles. That month Churchill was demoted from first lord of the Admiralty to chancellor of the Duchy of Lancaster. On May 20 his friend Hamilton recorded: "Rumours that Winston is leaving the Admiralty. This would be an awful blow to us out here; would be a sign that Providence had some grudge against the Dardanelles. Private feelings do not count in war, but alas, how grievous is this setback to one who has it in him to revive the part of Pitt, had he but Pitt's place . . . If this turns out to be true about Winston, there will be a colder spirit (let them appoint whom they will) at the back of our battleships here."[19]

With his demotion Churchill lost all influence in the course of the war. Frustrated and embarrassed by the demotion, he resigned his chancellorship and secured an appointment as lieutenant colonel and commanding officer of the Sixth (Service) Battalion, the Royal Scots Fusiliers. He served with that battalion in France from December 1915 to May 1916. In July 1917 he rejoined the government as minister of munitions. For the rest of his life veterans of the campaign, and the families of the maimed and fallen, would blame him for his part in initiating it. Some termed him the "Butcher of Gallipoli."

Thousands died at sea on both sides through mines, gunfire, torpedoes, and the usual accidents that befall sailors. A German civilian maritime officer, with whom Arthur Ruhl spoke in May 1915, summoned up the toll:

> He talked of the news—great news for his side—of the *Triumph*, and, opening his navy list, made a pencil mark.
>
> "She's off!" he said. The book was full of marks. In methodical sailor fashion he had been crossing them off since the war began: British and German—*Blücher, Scharnhorst, Irresistible, Goliath*, and the rest—millions of dollars and hundreds of men at a stroke.
>
> "Where's it all going to end?" he demanded. "There's seven hundred good men gone, maybe—how many did the *Triumph* carry? And we think it's good news! If a man should invent something that would kill a hundred thousand men at once, he'd be a great man . . . Now what is that?[20]

The perfect epitaph for those who lost their lives at sea as well as on land.

9

"We Had the Great Experience to Have a Glimpse of Hell"

The June Battles

The Second Battle of Krithia was a failure. With the exception of a few hundred yards gained by the Allies, the main result was thousands of casualties. Nevertheless, the Allies still coveted Krithia and Achi Baba. They were also having a problem finding room for all of the troops, animals, and stores they needed to continue the campaign. They knew that the longer they waited to continue their offensives, the stronger the Turkish defenses would become. Further, they knew that the withdrawal of their warships to Lemnos had given the Turks a morale boost of epic proportions. Hamilton summed up the situation in his diary on May 31:

> One month's hard, close hammering we had at last made the tough morale of the Turks more pliant, when lo and behold, in broad daylight, thousands of their common soldiery see with their own eyes two great battleships sink beneath the waves and all the others make an exit more dramatic than dignified. Most of the Armada of store ships had already cleared out and now the last of the battleships has offed it over the offing; a move which the whole of the German Grand Fleet could not have forced them to make! What better pick-me-up could Providence have provided for the badly-shaken Turks? No more inquisitive cruisers ready

to let fly a salvo at anything that stirs. No more searchlights by night; no more big explosives flying from the Aegean into the Dardanelles![1]

Kitchener ordered Hamilton to try again, and the date for the next assault was fixed for June 4, 1915.

On May 24 Hunter-Weston was promoted to lieutenant general and given command of the newly formed Eighth Corps. This unit included the Twenty-Ninth, Forty-Second (East Lancashire), and Royal Naval Divisions (RND). Despite the loss of so many men in the First and Second Battles of Krithia, he felt it would still be possible to capture Achi Baba with a head-on assault. One wonders what the general's impression would have been had he actually participated in any of the assaults that he and his staff ordered. But he never did. Thus, it is perhaps not so unusual that Hunter-Weston retained his sense of optimism about achieving what so many of his men knew was impossible. They knew that the Turks were every bit as good as they were, especially when it came to defense. And despite stories about the Turks also being short of artillery ammunition, the troops on the ground knew better. They could be hit from the front and rear by enemy guns any time of the day or night, and they were. If the Turks were short of ammunition, it was not at all apparent to the average soldier.

Two factors lulled Hunter-Weston and the French, under Gen. Henri Gouraud,[2] into believing that a third attempt on Krithia might be successful. First, the French and Twenty-Ninth Divisions had finally received reinforcements, and men slightly wounded in earlier actions were returning in greater numbers. Also, the final two battalions of the Royal Naval Division—Collingwood and Benbow—had arrived to complete the division's composition. Another factor was that since the Second Battle of Krithia, the Turks in the Helles sector had limited themselves to raids and small-scale attacks. This gave the Allies the impression that they were too weak to carry out larger assaults. In fact, they were receiving regular reinforcements and had more men than the Allies did.

"A Glimpse of Hell"

Hamilton believed that any further assault on Krithia or Achi Baba should be postponed until more reinforcements—in particular the Fifty-Second (Lowland) Division—arrived and his stocks of artillery ammunition were increased. Nevertheless, commonsense failed him again. As before, he chose to devolve to the recommendations of Hunter-Weston and Gouraud and not to assert himself.

Plans for the coming attack were formulated by Hamilton's staff on the *Arcadian* on May 31, and reparations were carried out over the coming days. On June 1 Hamilton established his headquarters on Imbros, twenty miles away from Helles. The next day he recorded in his diary: "Everything is fixed up for our big attack on the 4th. From aeroplane photographs it would appear that the front line Turkish trenches are meant more as traps for rash forlorn hopes than as strongholds. In fact, the true tug only begins when we try to carry the second line and the flanking machine guns. Gouraud has generously lent us two groups of 75s with H.E. [high-explosive] shell, and I am cabling the fact to the War Office as it means a great deal to us. When I say they are lent to us, I do not mean that they put the guns at our disposal. They are only ours for defensive purposes; that is to say, they remain in their own gun positions in the French lines and are to help by thickening the barrage in front of the Royal Naval Division."[3] The following day Maj. N. O. Burge, of the Royal Marines Cyclist Company, wrote in his diary: "The attack is to be tomorrow, an advance by the whole line after artillery preparation which ought to be finer than the last one as of course both we & the French have now got lots more ashore. The R.N.D. sector is not too strong. Battns. are very weak in spite of the Marine reinforcements & the Hawke, Collingwood & Benbow Batts."

The plan of attack called for the British and French to attack the Turks in full daylight, in two waves. The first wave would capture the first line of Turkish trenches, and the second wave would charge through it to capture the two lines behind. The assault would be preceded by an artillery barrage of land- and ship-based guns. The French 75's, with their ample supply of high-explosive shells, would pummel the Turkish barbed wire on the right of the line. When the barrage lifted, the troops would raise their rifles, bayonets mounted and gleaming in the sunlight, above their parapets. This would lure the Turks—who would have retreated to their reserve trenches during the barrage—back into the front line. The Allied artillery would then shell them again. Then, when the enemy was blown to oblivion, the infantry would attack. Hamilton suggested that the attack begin at 6:00 p.m., when the infantry would have the benefit of the dying sun to aid in the element of surprise. But once again, he devolved to Hunter-Weston's choice to begin the attack at noon, when the defenders would be most alert. The second wave would attack fifteen minutes later, at 12:15 p.m. In an effort to minimize officer casualties, all were to wear other ranks' or "Tommies' tunics" into action. To ensure that nobody was poisoned, orders were issued against eating or drinking anything found in the captured trenches.

Unlike the previous Battles of Krithia, the attacking troops were meant to move forward no more than eight hundred yards. With the help of the Royal Engineers, they would then stop and consolidate their gains and use the new line as a jumping-off point for a later attack. Altogether the British and French could only muster thirty thousand men for the assaults—twenty thousand for the first wave and ten thousand for the second. On paper this amounted to five men for every four yards.

Thirty thousand is a formidable number. But the accepted doctrine of the time was that three attackers were required for every defender, and the Turks were known to have twenty-eight thousand men defending their lines in the Helles sector. The Allies *should* have been wary of succeeding. They were not. Instead, they were enthusiastic about their chances. For the first time since landing, they knew what they were supposed to do and how they were supposed to do it. In the past the infantry had only been told to move as far forward as they could, then dig in.

The Allies had eighteen battalions in reserve. This was hardly enough to support a breakthrough if they were successful or stave off a disaster if they were not. For the first time artillery support seemed to be adequate. But as usual, the British had only a small number of high-explosive shells with which to break through the thick Turkish wire. There would be no land-based artillery to support the Indians and Lancashire Fusiliers attacking on the left because it was believed that the Turkish positions in front of the Forty-Second (East Lancashire) Division—attacking in the center—were stronger and needed extra attention. Instead, the destroyers *Wolverine* and *Scorpion* would provide fire support on the left. The battleships *Swiftsure* and *Exmouth* would provide support off W Beach, but they had to keep moving and zigzagging in an effort to avoid submarines. But doing so, of course, would minimize their effectiveness. The French were also supported by their navy on the right, off V Beach. A cruiser, two destroyers, and two minesweepers would also fire on enemy positions, the minesweepers using their machine guns.

The British also chose to use four Rolls Royce armored cars of the Royal Naval Air Service (RNAS) Armoured Car Detachment. They were manned by the crews that had provided machine gun support from the *River Clyde* during the V Beach landing and had been protecting frontline trenches ever since. Eight of the cars were landed after April 25 (the rest remained on their transports), but so far they had been kept in specially excavated shelters between Pink Farm and the beach. There were simply no roads over which they could safely travel.

The choice to use the cars was an inspired one and was made at the suggestion of the crews. Two would travel on either side of the Krithia Road, one behind the other, over ground and bridges specially prepared for them by the Royal Engineers. Because the British guns only had shrapnel rounds to fire—which were incapable of destroying barbed wire—the backs of the cars were fitted with grapnels attached to long poles. The cars were to back into the Turkish lines, grab the wire with the hooks, and then drive forward, toward the rear.

The Third Battle of Krithia was the first to be fought like those on the western front, where both sides were fully entrenched. The attackers were to climb out of their trenches, into a withering fire, and charge toward the Turkish trenches. It was also the first battle in which systematic planning was carried out and the attacking troops knew what their actual objectives were.[4] The staff even issued trench diagrams of the enemy positions to the officers who would be leading their troops into action. On June 3 explicit orders were issued to each battalion and the supporting units (artillery, medical, and engineers). The British, whose uniforms resembled those of the Turks in color, would employ a novel identification system so they could be identified by friendly artillery observers. Each man would attach a tin disc, roughly cut from an old bully beef or jam tin, to his pack. The discs would catch the sun, and the observers would thus be able to tell how far the attacking infantry had advanced. They also carried cloth screens to erect in front of the captured enemy trenches (what had formerly been the rear of the trench), so the artillery would be able to guide their rounds toward the Turkish trenches beyond. The screens were red with a diagonal white line on the side facing the artillery and khaki on the other so the Turks would presumably be unable to see them. In principle it seemed a sound system. In practice it would be devastating for the attackers.

Rev. Henry Clapham Foster was a Royal Navy chaplain attached to the Second Naval Brigade. The day before the battle the men of his brigade received a shipment of mail, which for many would be their last: "On June 3rd, two young officers, who had been wounded early in May, returned to us, and no sooner had they greeted us than there was a loud cry of 'Mails!' They arrived at an opportune moment, because many were destined to read their last letters from home. How often I have lived over again those last hours! The feeling of uncertainty and unrest was more marked on this occasion than at any previous time, and every officer and man felt that he was, as it were, standing on the edge of the precipice of fate. And yet everyone tried to be light-hearted and happy, but somehow it was a happiness that was unreal."[5]

June 4, 1915, dawned bright and warm, with a slight breeze blowing from the northwest. Capt. John Gillam optimistically noted in his diary that morning: "I awake and rise early. To-day is the battle, and to-night we shall be probably feeding our troops in or beyond Krithia." The troops—those who could sleep—were awoken early and breakfasted on their usual monotonous rations: chapattis for the Indians; greasy tea, fatty bacon, and hard biscuits for the British; and mutton, red wine (*vin ordinaire*), and biscuits for the French. The hour of the coming assault would preclude any chance of lunch. Breakfast would be the last meal for many of the attackers, and they knew it. Many took the opportunity to write their final letters home, and some who had been optimistic about their chances until then took a minute or two to fill out the page at the back of their paybooks entitled "Will." Most were tired after a sleepless night. Those who had spent the night in the trenches had not been able to lie down because the trenches were full of men trekking through them to the positions from which they were to attack.

At precisely 8:00 a.m. the Allied guns opened up on the Turkish trenches and their outlying strongpoints. It was the largest bombardment by land-based artillery since the start of the campaign. The British could muster seventy-eight field guns and howitzers, the French more than forty. Some of the British troops manning the front lines were so amazed by the barrage that they cheered the falling shells. Others were not: "There was nothing impressive about the first three hours of the bombardment, but during the final hour it hotted up a lot and became fierce enough to produce a continuous line of dust and smoke across the whole Peninsula, the first real barrage I had seen. As usual the smoke of the high-explosive shells was dark green, and the usual flying sandbags, pieces of wood, and Turks could be seen by anyone with glasses [binoculars]. The steady whine of shells going overhead, the sharp blasts of the discharge, and the sullen and more distant boom of the burst all mingled into one continuous and exciting noise; with the distinctive hollow roar the guns of a French 75 battery close behind us fired so fast and so incessantly that they sounded like a monster machine gun."[6]

The Turks were not to be outdone and responded by firing on both the forward trenches and the offending guns: "Tremendous shelling now going on, and it seems to grow more and more intense—hundreds of shells bursting along the Turkish positions. Turkish artillery replies furiously, mostly with shrapnel, all along our trenches. No shells come on to the beaches. Hundreds of white puffs of shrapnel all along the line, and fountain-like spurts of black and yellow smoke, followed by columns of earth, are thrown into the air, ending in a fog of drifting smoke and dust."[7] One of the Turkish rounds landed within the lines of B Battery, Royal Horse Artillery, killing eight horses and blowing the right leg off one man. Another shell landed on the Ninety-Seventh Battery, Royal Field Artillery. It killed Sgt. Benjamin Jones instantly. He was not the only member of his battery to fall that day. Four men were wounded while bringing ammunition up to the battery's guns, and two others were wounded while taking messages to the battery. One of the messengers, Gunner Alfred Smith, lingered for ten days before dying at East Mudros. Out of 1,450 rounds fired by that battery on June 4, one gun fired 558.

As planned, the artillery stopped firing at 11:20 a.m., and the infantrymen raised their bayonets, fixed under the muzzles of their rifles, above their parapets. This was supposed to draw the Turks back into their frontline trenches so the Allied artillery could once again bombard them. But instead, Turkish machine guns and artillery opened up on the British and French trenches, taking a heavy toll on the would-be attackers. One machine gun targeted the position of Capt. Thomas Cunliffe, commanding officer of the Machine Gun Section of the First Lancashire Fusiliers. It wounded the twenty-nine-year-old officer four times before killing him with a round in the forehead. All of the gun's crew were either killed or wounded.

At eleven thirty the Allied artillery opened fire again, but the observers could not tell whether or not their shells were having any effect. The wind was blowing the smoke back into the gunners' lines, obscuring their view. Nevertheless, they continued firing, hoping that their rounds were having the desired effect. They were not. Despite the heavy bombardment, the British shrapnel was doing almost no damage to the Turkish positions. What they did not know was that the enemy trenches had been built with loop-holes. These were holes in the parapets, constructed with sandbags, through which a man could fire with virtual impunity unless targeted by a skilled sniper. They were vulnerable to high-explosive shells, but a shrapnel round would have to score a direct hit or send its lethal ball bearings through the tiny apertures.

As the attackers stood in their trenches, waiting for their officers to blow their trench whistles, some men joked to mask the nervousness they felt. Some, too nervous to appreciate the humor or out of earshot, trembled as they waited for the signal to be given. Some vomited. None was criticized. Everyone was frightened, including those who had been in action before. They wondered if their luck would hold. Some knew it would not. Able Seaman Joseph Murray of the Hood Battalion went into action with his battalion that morning. Months later, on November 15, he described the feelings one had while waiting to go over the top:

> The firing line was quite crowded. I cannot say the men were anxious, but the atmosphere was extremely tense. I know the feeling but it is difficult to describe. Each man is totally unaware of those around him; he is in a world of his own and aware only of himself.
>
> He is a little afraid, not of going into action, but of himself, wondering if he will be able to control himself. Would he be able to continue to go forward when those whom he had come to know so well were falling at his side and crying out for help? Would he, after a short rush and having buried his head in the prickly scrub, have the courage to rise again and face those singing bullets that crowded the air just above him? Would he be able to keep up with the few that were left? Would he have enough courage—or madness—to still go blindly forward through the rain and red-hot lead when almost all around him had fallen? Would he survive?[8]

At noon the artillery increased its range in an effort to hit any Turkish reinforcements that might be moving up and, it was hoped, to hit some of their guns. It was also the infantry's turn to attack.

All along the lines officers blew their whistles. English, Indian, French, and French Colonial troops climbed out of their trenches and were met with a withering fire from rifles, machine guns, and artillery. Some were struck by the sledgehammer blows of Turkish bullets as they exposed themselves over the parapets. Men fell back into their trenches, some dead, some writhing in agony under the hot noonday sun. Capt. John Gillam watched the spectacle from his vantage point in a trench above W Beach and wrote about in his diary: "Our shells burst thickly, smothering the Turkish first and second lines and all the way up the slopes of Achi Baba. I see our men in the centre leap from the trenches, and the sun glistens on their bayonets. I see them run on in wave after wave, some falling, and remaining lying on the grass like sacks of potatoes. I can see nothing on the left. Now I see the French on the hill on the right of our line, and the hill is covered with dark figures rushing forward."

On the far left the first wave of the Twenty-Ninth Indian Brigade attacked the Turkish trench J10, the trench in front of their target, without artillery support. They failed. The First Lancashire Fusiliers attacking along Gully Spur were also unsuccessful, most of the men being hit as they climbed out of their trench. Maj. Harold Shaw, the commanding officer of A Company, was among those killed: "When he was killed he was walking about wounded under ghastly fire by the Turkish trenches, encouraging the remnants of his Company."[9]

The men of the second wave, which attacked at twelve fifteen, were no more fortunate, though Capt. Harold Clayton, commanding D Company, did make it as far as J10. His body was found two months later, still tangled in the Turkish barbed wire in which he met his death.

The Turks employed landmines in the area in the Fusiliers' sector. When they detonated, they ignited the dry scrub, which in turn set the uniforms of some of the wounded alight. It is not known how many were burned to death, but some were. As the survivors retreated from the deadly rain of lead, the sun glinted off the tin discs on their backs, making it easier for the Turks to target them. By

"A Glimpse of Hell"

the end of the day the Fusiliers were right back where they started. The results were the same up and down the line.

On the Fusiliers' left the 1st/6th Gurkha Rifles advanced under cover of the cliffs of Gully Spur that overlook the Aegean. They reached the end portion of J10 in relative safety but were fired on as soon as they came into view. The Nepalese riflemen fell in swathes as Turkish bullets tore through their ranks. Their white and native officers, leading the charge with revolvers in hand, were among the first to be cut down. Just as the French Colonials were wont to do when their white officers fell, the Gurkhas beat a hasty retreat. And just like what happened with the Lancashire Fusiliers, the tin discs on their backs reflected the sunlight, making them perfect targets for the Turks. They, too, ended the day back in the trenches from which they had leaped out at noon.

The loss in officers was heavy. It was particularly devastating because most of them had developed a relationship with their men after years among them, learning their ways, their customs, and to some extent their language. Later drafts of officers posted to Indian units were lacking in these qualities, and it told on their ability to lead the brave mountain men.

The Fourteenth King George's Own Ferozepore Sikhs attacked on the Fusiliers' right. Unlike the Gurkhas, who were short men from the mountains of Nepal, the Sikhs were tall, bearded men who hailed from India's Punjab region. Rev. Oswin Creighton wrote of them: "I love the Sikhs. They are so clean and handsome, and have such good teeth. They seem to wash themselves, their hair and beards and cooking-pots in the water in the gully all day. I had some talk with them and their officers, who seem very nice."[10]

While the Gurkhas wore hats that resembled a bush hat (brim down), the Sikhs wore khaki turbans with their regimental badge attached to the front. Their white officers also wore turbans. Enlisted men wore long cotton khaki tunics that reached midway to the knee and were better suited to the warm weather at Gallipoli than the woolen uniforms worn by their officers and the other Dominion forces. The Sikhs suffered horribly in the assault, though a handful reached their goal, the trench J12. One of the officers leading their assault was 2nd Lt. Reginald Savory of D Company. After the war he would write:

Fowle and I took up our positions. He was with the right half of the company, so as the better to liaise with the battalion on our right; and I was in the centre of the left half. Those last few minutes before zero-hour made no deep impression on me, except possibly the familiar feeling of waiting for the pistol before a sprint with a void in the pit of one's stomach and anxiety as to the result. And, then . . . twelve noon . . . off you go. I waited a second to see the men up, looked for Fowle, but could not see him, and then popped over myself. From that moment, I lost all control of the fighting. The roar of musketry was so intense as to drown all other sound, except for that of the guns. To try to give an order was useless. The nearest man to me was a yard away, and even then I could not see him. Soon I found myself running on alone, except for my little bugler, a young handsome boy, just out of his teens, who came padding along behind me and whose duty it was to act as runner and carry messages. Poor little chap. I was fighting a lone battle. The sooner I could get across no-man's-land and reach the cover of the enemy's trenches the better. And then, before I could realize it, I found myself standing on the parapet of a Turkish trench and looking down at the Turk inside it. He seemed an ordinary person. There was none of the "Terrible Turk" about him. He was not even firing, but was leaning against the back of his trench. Yet, if I had given him time, he would have shot me; and there were others on either side of him. I jumped in and skewered him to the back of his trench with my bayonet. Poor devil! I can see his grimace to this day.[11]

The regiment lost so many men that Brig. Gen. William Marshall, commanding officer of the Eighty-Seventh Infantry Brigade, later reflected, "The 14th Sikhs, as a fighting unit, had ceased to exist."

Among those lost on June 4 was Lt. Horace Vaughan, who had joined the Second Royal Fusiliers as a reinforcement less than a month

"A Glimpse of Hell"

earlier. June 4 was his first day in action. On June 17, 1915, Sgt. William Wright wrote to Vaughan's sister from his hospital bed in Egypt:

I am sorry to inform you that he was mortally wounded in action at the Dardanelles on Friday the 4th inst. I was present at the time and nursed him until he died. We were in a general advance to attempt the taking of a hill, known as Achi Baba. We commenced at noon, and before we had advanced more than 50 yards, Lieut. Vaughan received a terrible wound between the legs just above the knees, caused by an explosive bullet. He suffered considerably from loss of blood. Although wounded myself at the same time below the left eye, I managed to get him back into our trench under a murderous fire from rifles and machine guns, also shrapnel. I made him as comfortable as circumstances permitted. He did not seem to feel any pain, and remained conscious to the end, which came peacefully at 5.30 p.m. . . . Although Lieut. Vaughan had been with us only a few days, he had made himself very popular with the men under his command, who were ready to follow him anywhere. We shall all miss him very much.

Lieutenant Vaughan, who would have celebrated his sixteenth wedding anniversary three days later, left two sons behind. The youngest, nine-year-old Justin, would later recall of his father:

It was towards the end of 1914, my father then approaching the age of 38 was spending his evenings after work helping to cope with the influx of Belgian refugees who were flooding into the country. Their tales of hardship and of German brutality were so horrific that, after consultation with my mother, he decided to leave his job and join up before he was too old (38 was the maximum age for enlisting at that time) and he was duly commissioned as 2nd Lieutenant.

Both my father and my Uncle Lionel were drafted to Kingsbridge to complete their training. So Easter 1915 saw my mother, my brother Winston and me, together with our Aunt Bea, holidaying in Kingsbridge.

How fine my father and uncle looked riding on their chestnut horses towards us across the sands of Devon in their smart uniforms—so different in build and looks. Both tall, my father heavily built with round face and slightly ginger hair and with military mustache (he had trimmed off the waxed pointed ends of which he had been so proud); my uncle tall and thin, dark haired, clean shaven and with deep set dark brown eyes.

June 4 was a hard day for the family. Lieutenant Vaughan's brother-in-law, Capt. Walter Paine, was attached to the First Lancashire Fusiliers at the same time as Walter joined the Second Royal Fusiliers. Paine, who was called by his middle name, Lionel, was killed on the other side of Gully Ravine the same day.

The battalions of the Forty-Second (East Lancashire) Division achieved the most success on June 4 and could have turned the tide of the campaign in the Allies' favor. In that sector the 127th Brigade led the assault. It was the first time these Territorial Force soldiers, consisting of four battalions of the Manchester Regiment, were in a major battle. They were supported by the 1/5th Lancashire Fusiliers. They lost a large number of men in the process. Nevertheless, they pushed on well beyond their intended targets, through all of the Turkish trenches and onto the lower slopes of Achi Baba.

It was an amazing feat, one that was not duplicated anywhere else along the line. But there the men stayed, halted by intense fire from the heavily fortified hill. Hamilton, watching the attack from a safe distance onshore, wrote: "The boldest and most brilliant exploit of the lot was the charge made by the Manchester Brigade in the centre who wrested two lines of trenches from the Turks; and then, carrying right on; on to the lower slopes of Achi Baba, and nothing between them and its summit but the clear, untrenched hillside. They lay there—the line of our brave lads, plainly visible to a pair of good glasses—there they actually lay! We wanted, so it seemed, but a reserve to advance in their support and carry them up to the top. We said—and yet could hardly believe our own words—'We are through!'"[12] In fact, they had moved as far as the fourth Turkish trench.

What Hamilton did not realize was that most of the troops he saw were dead or wounded, and though he could not see any Turkish trenches through his binoculars, they were there. So were the machine guns, not just in front of the Mancunians but to their left and right as well. Brave though they were, the Manchesters and Lancashire Fusiliers who made it to Achi Baba did not have a chance.

On the far right, separated from the Forty-Second Division by the Royal Naval Division, the French went into the assault. They attacked their geographical arch nemesis, the Haricot Redoubt. As usual, they were so badly shot up that the Senegalese turned and ran. They were hit so hard right out of the gate that those who survived turned back after advancing only twenty yards. The British who witnessed the spectacle thought they were cowards. Their own troops were pushing on through the rain of lead, so why not the French? In fact, the fire in that area was so heavily concentrated that they had no choice. The Turkish trenches were roughly one hundred yards away, so the French gunners could not fire for fear of hitting their own men. The Turkish defenses were completely untouched during the preparatory bombardments and could fire with impunity on their attackers. Within just a few minutes the survivors were back in their own lines.

The result was that the Royal Naval Division, attacking on the left of the French, were completely vulnerable on their right, and the Turks at Haricot were also firing on them. A domino effect thus occurred, and the naval infantrymen were doomed from the start.

That morning the three battalions of the division's Second Brigade led the assault—Howe on the left, Hood in the center, and Anson on the right. The Collingwood Battalion formed the second wave, and the entire First Brigade was the divisional reserve. With a front of eight hundred yards, the RND's sector was the narrowest of any during the battle.

Early that morning the men of the first wave left their rest camps and moved to the trenches from which they would attack. Reverend Foster watched with a kind of knowing sadness as his flock, tired but anxious, walked silently in the darkness: "On Friday, June 4th, about 2–30 a.m., the Anson Battalion moved off to battle. In many a reverie since then I have seen the picture and heard the tramp of feet. The light was dim, but I could make out the various officers as they waved farewell."[13] He was seeing many of them alive for the last time.

The brigade's officers were ordered to synchronize their watches at 8:15 a.m., and as the minutes ticked away, they stood ready to climb out of their trenches, whistle in one hand and revolver in the other. Each was alone with his thoughts, trying to put on a brave face for his men. It would be the first attack for the Collingwoods. They had no idea what to expect and, not having seen the result of the pitiful bombardments of the earlier battles, were astounded at the intensity of this one.

At noon the officers blew their whistles, and the Turks opened fire. Even as the sailors were climbing out of their trenches, only five feet deep as compared to eight for the Turks, they were being felled. Many men were hit before they were able to climb completely out of their trench. Among the first to fall was Lt. Cdr. Raymond Parsons, the commanding officer of C Company of the Hood Battalion:

> Commander Parsons was standing on one of the short ladders that were provided to enable us to get over the parapet, looking at his watch and then glancing at us beside him, with a comforting smile on his face.
>
> "Five minutes to go, men."
>
> Then another glance at us.—"Four minutes . . . three minutes . . . two minutes . . . one minute, men. Are you all ready? Come on then, men, follow me."
>
> Over we went into the withering machine-gun fire. Poor old Lieutenant-Commander Parsons was killed in the first second and many fell back into the trench.[14]

The sailors continued on until they reached the Turkish trenches. There they found only dead and wounded. The survivors had retreated through their communication trenches.

At twelve fifteen the Collingwoods went over the top and were promptly mowed down. Their goal was to push on through the first-

"A Glimpse of Hell"

wave battalions and on to the Turkish trench behind. Within minutes the battalion virtually ceased to exist. Nevertheless, a few men did make it to the enemy trench and, joined by men of the first wave, advanced to the second trench. They tried to hold out, but in less than an hour they were driven back to their original starting point.

Had the French managed to take the Haricot Redoubt, the tale of the Second Naval Brigade would likely have been different. As it was, the Turks there were free to fire into the sailors. Among the dead in the first wave was Sub-Lt. Frank Baker of the Hood Battalion: "Sub-Lieut. Baker was killed in action on June 4th whilst attacking the Turkish trenches. He had only received his commission a few days previous to the engagement. He was attached to 'C' Company, where he early won the admiration of his platoon by his tact and straightforwardness. On the day he was killed he was leading his platoon, and had almost reached his goal when he was shot through the arm. He was bandaged by one of his men, and advised to go back, to get it properly dressed. He said: 'No, I am needed. I am not going to leave my men.' He again rallied his men, and charged right up to the Turk's trenches, where he was wounded a second time, and did not recover."[15]

Because of a shortage of cotton web equipment, with which infantrymen were normally equipped, the men of the RND went into action wearing leather cavalry bandoleers and cartridge pouches on their belts. Crossing from the right shoulder to the left hip, these belts had five pouches on the front and four on the back, each carrying ten rounds of ammunition in two five-round stripper clips. While practical for mounted troops, they were terribly impractical for infantry. They made it difficult for the men to lie down to fire their weapons, and the men had to prop themselves up to get at their ammunition. A Turkish bullet hit the bandoleer worn by Able Seaman Joseph Murray of the Hood Battalion that day, and it saved his life. But some men were not so lucky: "On 4th June I saw Bell after he had been hit, & his clothes were on fire. It appeared as though the bullet had struck his ammunition, which, by exploding, had caused the fire. He was lying on the ground when we passed,

& seemed to be almost dead."[16] Leading Seaman Harry Bell, must have suffered a terrible death as a result of his bandoleer. Others suffered a similar fate that day.

Able Seaman John Strasenburgh was shot in the right lung and was then put out of his misery by a Turk: "He was shot in the left breast and was left on the parapet of the Turkish trenches. When we got back to our trench, five or six Turks were seen to be bayoneting our wounded. We fired at them and they disappeared."[17] The Collingwood Battalion suffered the worst on June 4. At the end of the day only one of its officers was left standing, and the battalion was virtually destroyed.

The four armored cars that went into action were an absolute failure. Captain Gillam saw them moving up the Krithia Road at noon: "I can see three armoured cars on the right of our centre, which before I had not noticed, one behind the other, each one a short distance to the right of the one in front, moving slowing along the flat ground on either side of the Sedd-el-Bahr [sic] road, and they actually pass over our front line and creep up to the Turkish front, driving backwards. They halt, and I see spurts of flame coming from their armoured turrets as their machine-guns open fire. After about ten minutes I see the car furthest behind move back to our line, now driving forwards, and after a while the remaining two follow."[18]

Chief Sharkey was in the Rolls Royce armored car *Fox* that day. He had landed at Anzac on April 25 and was showing signs of emotional distress over the horrors he had witnessed. By way of a good-bye message, he wrote in his diary on June 3: "For the present, ta-ta all in case I should stop a bullet because as old George Glendinning used to say 'for never knows does one.' I don't suppose I can always escape but in any case I am going to have a good sleep tonight as goodness knows where some of us will be this time tomorrow." He survived the day, but not all of the motor machine gunners were so fortunate. At five in the afternoon on June 4 he took a few moments to record the day's adventures:

Well I am back safe & sound & what a time! Heavens! It was terrible. We drew the fire from all quarters & God only knows how a man or a car ever came back. What a cheer we got from the troops as we dashed along the Krithia Road passing one line of trench after the other. The boys inside the cars were shouting their old war cry "Belt it in" & the Tommies were shouting "Come on the Navy," etc. etc. . . . .

Our poor fellows were going down like sheep. It was an awful slaughter. The cars got a certain distance & then got stuck between the two firing lines. The noise inside the cars caused by the bullets hitting against the armored plate was deafening & then after a bit they started pitching H.E.'s [high-explosive artillery shells] at us, but lucky for us the Turks' shooting was bad & not a car got seriously damaged.

About 12–30 I sent a car to base with its gun damaged & completely out of action.

Lt. Holden's car was sent back with its turret off, Holden himself being badly wounded inside, also was poor Rumming.

Lt. Holden is covered with blood & looks a horrible sight.

Rumming had half his head blown off so they told us & the driver of this car (Scott) practically went mad inside.

Nobody was hurt in "Fox." We had the best of luck. Our tyres were blown to pieces also our wheels but we managed to return to port [their "garage" behind Pink Farm].

It was fair Hell let loose with a vengeance & I don't much care if I ever see another day like it, although I should not have missed it for the world now that I got back safe & sound.[19]

Five men were killed in action that day, and one died of wounds the following day. Chief Petty Officer Geoffrey Rumming suffered paralysis down the right side of his body as a result of his head wound and died two years later. For his gallantry on June 4 he was awarded the Distinguished Service Medal and the French Croix de Guerre.

June 4 was the first and only time the cars were used at Gallipoli, but their crews served with their machine guns in the trenches.

Their vehicles were designed to operate over flat, wide-open spaces, such as existed across the Middle East, and that would be their next destination.

Over the next several days fighting continued as the Turks tried to regain lost territory and the British tried to keep the little bit they had won. For some of the survivors the hell of June 4 would continue as they were forced to bury the dead whose bodies could be recovered. Those left out in no-man's-land and in the enemy trenches were lost, most of them forever. But many had been killed in the trenches or just as they were climbing the trench ladders. Their bodies had to be dealt with quickly. The threat of the living joining the ranks of the dead while carrying them to the rear for burial meant that many of the fallen were buried in the front lines.

The British recorded a loss of forty-five hundred men for the Third Battle of Krithia and the French two thousand. The Turks noted figures ranging from three to nine thousand men, but the British official historian settled on the higher figure. The actual number will likely never be known. There would be no more assaults on such a grand scale in the Helles sector.

With the debacle of this battle, the Allies realized that sector-wide attacks were doomed to failure. During that action the ineffectiveness of the forces on the left and right flanks led to the loss of the entire battle. Hunter-Weston and Gouraud learned that if they were going to captured Krithia and Achi Baba, they would first have to eliminate the Turkish threat at Gully Spur on the left—between the Aegean and Gully Ravine—and on Kereves Spur, the strip of ground to the left of Kereves Dere on the right. As long as these strongpoints remained, the Allies at Helles would be at a distinct disadvantage.

Because of the shortage of British artillery, Hunter-Weston and Gouraud realized that they needed to mass their guns and hit just one area at a time if these two points were going to be captured. Because the French had the largest supply of high-explosive ammunition, they decided that the positions on the Kereves Spur would be assaulted first. Their targets would be the Haricot and Quadrilateral Redoubts on Hill 83, the crest of the Kereves Dere. The date of the attack was fixed for June 21, and it would be supported by gunfire from the French warships.

The French referred to this action as the "Third Battle of Kereves Dere." It was carried out on a front of only 650 yards and supported by seven batteries of their rapid-firing 75's, two batteries of 155 mm howitzers, sixteen trench mortars, and seven howitzers of the British army's Twenty-Ninth Division. The First Australian Field Artillery Brigade, attached to the Twenty-Ninth Division, also joined in. This amounted to one gun for every ten yards of front being attacked. Two batteries, along with the French battleship *Saint-Louis*, were detailed to fire on the Turkish guns on the Asiatic side, to prevent them from firing into the backs of the attackers. Facing the French in that part of the line was the Turkish Twelfth Division.

On the morning of the attack the French and French Colonial infantrymen were given a filling breakfast of soup, coffee, and fresh bread. They were also given an extra ration of army-issue brandy, and some was added to the water in each man's canteen for good measure. The artillery opened its bombardment at 5:15 a.m.: "There is a fearful bombardment going on; every battery on shore is concentrating its gunfire on a Turkish redoubt on the Turkish left, called the Haricot Redoubt, and also on the trenches. The Turkish batteries are replying furiously, but without effect, though 'Asiatic Annie' is rather nasty, her shells falling around the French batteries. One cannot see the effect, because of the dust that the shells are kicking up, which is blowing right down to the beach. The 60-pounders on our right, twenty-five yards away, are joining in with a deafening report; only one is in this action. The echo of her voice plays ducks and drakes around the coast and the few transports about, getting fainter as the sound dies away. French battleship at mouth of Straits firing heavily. Destroyers continually patrolling around her."[20]

At six in the morning the infantry attacked. The French 176th Infantry Regiment was on the left. Their goal was the Quadrilateral Redoubt and a portion of the Haricot Redoubt. The Sixth Mixed Colonial Regiment was to attack Haricot and link up with the troops on its left. The Second Régiment de Marche Afrique was in reserve. The artillery preparation was so thorough that within minutes Haricot was captured.

The Quadrilateral was a much harder nut to crack, and the French were forced to retreat from that position. Unlike previous actions, when they had been unable to make another assault after a failed attack earlier the same day, Gouraud ordered his troops back into action. He was on the verge of success, and he knew it. At 6:45 p.m. the Second Régiment de Marche Afrique charged forward. Its men could not take the whole position, but they did gain a valuable foothold: "We have won an appreciable bit of ground. New enemy trenches are ours. There have been advances all along the line. The guns have performed a very successful task. The prisoners say their trenches are a pulp of corpses. But, also, in our own lines and between the first lines there are heaps of corpses."[21]

Despite strong Turkish counterattacks over the coming days, the French held the ground they had captured and on June 30 were able to complete their conquest of the Quadrilateral. Yet the day held both good and bad for the French. Gouraud was wounded by shrapnel while walking along V Beach to visit his men in the field hospital there, and one of his arms had to be amputated: "The General was blown over a wall of ashlar about two metres high and over a fig tree almost into the interior of the field hospital of the 2nd Division. The ashlar wall was lined by a wall of empty wooden shell cases. The General had his elbow bruised, his thigh broken, his leg broken. They picked him up fainting in the court of the field hospital. The fig tree had broken his fall."[22] Gouraud was evacuated to a hospital ship and did not return to the peninsula until the dedication of the French cemetery there, after the war.

June 21 was a successful day for the French. They not only removed (for the most part) two very painful thorns from their side; they also affirmed to the British that they were capable fighters. For the first time since taking over the sector from the British, they had a reason to be proud of themselves.

One unusual casualty that occurred during the attack was that of a spectator, Lt. Col. Henry Hannan, TD,[23] commanding officer of the 1/8th Battalion (TF), the Cameronians (Scottish Rifles): "Our Colonel was killed that morning by a sniper. He seemingly had been watching the French advance, from our trench, when he was shot through the neck by a sniper. We buried him that morning in Death's Gully. One of the K.O.S.B.'s [King's Own Scottish Borderers] made us a cross for his grave."[24]

With the success of the French assaults, it was now possible for an effort to be made along Gully Spur. In order for that attack to succeed, the British and French knew that they also had to mass their artillery there. Because the British had only a few hundred high-explosive shells at their disposal and too few howitzers from which to fire them, the French sent two 155 mm howitzers and two trench mortars. These mighty weapons could not be moved and emplaced in the British sector until June 27, so the attack was scheduled for the day after that.

Hunter-Weston was promoted to command the Eighth Corps earlier in the month, so Maj. Gen. Sir Henry de Lisle replaced him as commanding officer of the Twenty-Ninth Division. When war was declared in August 1914, he was in command of the Fifth Cavalry Brigade. Later he commanded the First Cavalry Division in France. He arrived at Gallipoli on the night of June 4, 1915, amid exploding shells and the immediate aftermath of the Third Battle of Krithia. He was known more for his exploits on the polo ground than for his command abilities. Never a popular commander, Birdwood referred to him as the "Brute."

That criticism aside, de Lisle took the needs of his troops into consideration for what became known as the Battle of Gully Ravine. The detailed orders he prepared make it clear that he had not only his men's success but also their best interests at heart—the men of the Twenty-Ninth Division, that is, who would attack on the left side of Gully Ravine, but not so for the Scots of the 156th Brigade, who would attack on the right. This formation, newly arrived from Scotland, had been attached to the Fifty-Second (Lowland) Division and was in action for the first time.

The infantry assault was scheduled to begin at midmorning, following a series of artillery and naval barrages. This action would amount to the largest expenditure of shells since the beginning of the campaign. Twelve thousand were allotted; more than sixteen thousand would ultimately be fired along that particular portion of the line. During the Third Battle of Krithia on June 4, only eleven thousand had been fired along the entire British front at Helles.

The bombardment was to begin at nine o'clock in the morning. That particular hour was chosen because the gunners had learned that weather conditions were clearest then. After that, they could expect a thick mist to blow in from the sea. At 10:20 a.m. the field artillery would begin, targeting the thick barbed wire that fronted the Turkish positions. Unlike the Allies, who had metal stanchions from which to string the barbed strands, the Turks only had wooden stakes, which not only made the wire sag but made it more suscepti-ble to shrapnel. In addition to artillery, the British had twenty-two machine guns at their disposal. Between the bursts of artillery fire, they were to enfilade the Turkish trenches to prevent the defenders from escaping the devastating barrage.

The attack would consist of three separate assaults. The first would occur at ten forty-five, in the center of the attack area, against a redoubt called the "Boomerang" (because of its shape) on the eastern side of Gully Ravine, and nearby Turkey Trench. The First Battalion, the Border Regiment, was allotted those targets. It was crucial that these strongpoints be put out of action before the main attacks were launched; otherwise, they could stop the attackers on both sides of the gully. They had on June 4, and attempts to cap-ture them since then had failed. If the Borders were unsuccessful, it might prove necessary to postpone the main attacks. Once those positions were secured, the battalion was to attack through the gully itself, as far north as the junction with trench J11.

At 10:45 a.m. the artillery would lift its fire, and A Company of the First Borders would assault and capture Turkey Trench. B Company would move against the Boomerang; C and D Compa-nies would be in support. At eleven the artillery would shift its fire to targets farther inland, and the main attack would begin.

On the left the Eighty-Seventh Brigade was to attack at eleven o'clock and capture the trenches J9, J10, J11, and J11a. The last was a communication trench that ran parallel to the cliffs above the Aegean and ran from J11 back to J13. At the same time, the Twenty-Ninth Indian Brigade, so badly beaten up on June 4, was to charge along the cliffs to the left of J11a. After the Englishmen of the Eighty-Seventh Brigade had captured J11a, the Indians would occupy the trench to a distance halfway between J11 and J12.

At eleven thirty the second wave (Eighty-Sixth Brigade) was to leave its trenches, jump the three lines captured by the first wave, and capture J12 and J13. A portion of the Twenty-Ninth Indian Brigade was to cover its left, moving along the cliffs and through J11a and up into J13. The last two trenches, J12 and J13, had not been completed by the Turks, so it was thought that they might be lightly fortified. But because of a shortage of shells—the British limited their guns to two shells per gun per day unless an attack was under way—the Turks had been able to dig them in relative safety.

On the other side of Gully Ravine the four Lowland Scottish battalions of the 156th Brigade would also go over the top at eleven o'clock. Their goal was the capture of trenches H11, H12a, and H12. The 1/4th Royal Scots, on the left of their line, were to capture the communication trenches running from H12 into Gully Ravine. If the Scots needed help, the Eighty-Eighth Brigade was in reserve behind them. The same trenches had been taken and lost by the Eighty-Eighth on June 4.

Unlike the assault on the left (west) side of Gully Ravine, which would have a great deal of artillery and naval support, the one on the right would have almost none. The reasons were that the trenches on the left were thought to be stronger and there were more of them. That, and there were simply not enough guns or ammunition to support attacks on both sides. The French had no more guns to spare (though they were asked). This lack of support doomed the Scots to failure from the outset. Experience had shown that a great deal of artillery would be needed for an attack to succeed, and the ravine would have to be hit on both sides simultaneously. The British had no choice in the matter, if they were going to attack at all. They had to attack while the Turks on the other side of the sector were recovering from their losses to the French the week before.

During the Third Battle of Krithia the assaulting troops carried colored screens forward to mark the new front line for the artillery. This simple innovation failed. Either the men carrying the screens were killed, or the Turks ran over them when they retook their trenches. Still, something was needed to help the gunners see how far the friendly troops had advanced. It was thus decided to use a system of tin triangles and rectangles, cut from old biscuit tins, which would catch the sunlight and remain with the attacking troops. As trenches were captured, officers would order a proportion of their men to erect them behind the captured trench so the artillerymen would know how far friendly troops had advanced.

June was excruciatingly hot at Gallipoli. All of the Allied troops wore woolen uniforms with collarless gray cotton shirts underneath. The Anzacs would cut their trouser down to make shorts. Most went about without their tunics and wore either their shirts, sometimes with the sleeves cut off, or no shirts at all. The British wore the full uniform, sometimes without the tunic, out of a sense of discipline and because overzealous quartermasters would dock their pay for any intentional damage. They had the physical discomfort of their clothing to contend with on top of everything else. Just before the Battle of Gully Ravine, they were issued sun helmets (the Fifty-Second (Lowland) Division had them when they landed). While the helmets seemed like a good idea to quartermasters in England, the yellow tint of the new khaki drill fabric coverings made them stand out like mushrooms to the Turks. After being in the sun for awhile, they turned a dirty white. Because of this, many men chose to wear either their service caps or woolen balaclava helmets. But the balaclavas, which were khaki stocking caps, made them look like Turks from a distance, and many of those wearing them were killed by their own men as a result.

In an effort to reduce the discomfort of the attacking infantry, they were ordered to leave their packs behind. Instead, each wore his piece of tin on his back, attached by two string loops worn over each shoulder. The Eighty-Seventh Brigade wore triangles, each side measuring one foot, and the 156th wore rectangles, measuring one foot at top and bottom.

The instructions for the attack specifically noted what each man would carry. In addition to his web gear,[25] each man would carry two empty sandbags tucked into his web belt, two hundred rounds of ammunition, a full water bottle, and one day's iron rations. The heaviest part of the load was the ammunition, carried in pouches on the belt and cloth bandoleers slung across the chest.

June 28, 1915, dawned beautifully, but the day was hot, and only a hint of a breeze was evident. Daylight saw the assaulting troops in their trenches, ready to attack. By seven in the morning they had been fed their usual monotonous breakfast—greasy tea with sugar, hard biscuits, and jam. The meal filled those able to eat, but it also increased their thirst. A few found the tension too much to bear and had to be escorted out of the line: "The men were lying about in the trench, smoking and reading or laughing and chatting. They were in great spirits, but as time wore on and the din became greater, the strain became greater also. Occasionally a man would be led past with his nerves shattered; his hands manacled—a raving maniac for the time being."[26] The presence of such men was bad for morale, and they were capable of disrupting the hoped-for smooth operation about to take place. The same thing happened before every attack.

At nine that morning the Allied artillery opened up with a tremendous crescendo. The results of the explosions were both beautiful and terrible to behold. Before the main barrage began, the French gunners began firing on the Boomerang and Turkey Trench. The Turks responded to the bombardment with one of their own, firing at both the offending Allied artillery and the men massed in the frontline trenches. At eleven o'clock the guns shifted to the trenches farther back in an effort to keep the Turks from moving troops forward to meet the coming infantry attack. RNAS machine gunner Chief Sharkey observed:

At 11.15 an order came down the line for "All troops to show their bayonets above the trench" & machine guns to open "rapid fire."

This lasted 3 or 4 minutes & then came a fresh order for "All troops to get into their equipment & to wait for the order to advance." This was a thrilling moment; no man spoke to another, but climbed into his webbing gear & gulped the remnants of his rum.

Men who had assisted to bury an unfortunate pal perhaps a day or two ago wondered whether they themselves would require burying tomorrow.

The artillery re-opened for a few minutes & from the French side a sweeping cross fire of 75's assisted in the complete demolition of the enemy earthworks.[27]

Sharkey's watch seems to have been running fast, and the troops he was describing belonged to the First Borders. At ten forty-five the officers of A and B Companies yelled, "Attack!"[28] and the riflemen climbed out of their trenches into no-man's-land. From the beginning success was with B Company, which hit the Boomerang: "The first party reached The Boomerang with practically no loss, advancing unseen through the dust raised by the bombardment & set to work at once to clear out the enemy with bayonet and bombs."[29] *Nearly* unseen. According to Sgt. Sydney Evans of B Company: "At the shout of 'Over!' we are up the ladders and racing like the wind for the redoubt, about 200 yards distance. No sooner are we over, than a tremendous burst of rifle and machine-gun fire meets us. Here and there a man stumbles and falls by the way, but we race on and are soon in the trench. The trench has been terribly battered and debris and bodies are lying all about. Poor Ginger McClellan [*sic*] of my platoon is lying dead, having been shot through the head, just as he leapt into the trench."[30]

When Evans's company reached the enemy position, the bombers lit the fuses of their primitive jam tin bombs, waited a second or two, then lobbed them over. Evans continued: "Hastily we set to work to reconstruct the shattered parapet of the trench as far as possible in anticipation of a counter-attack. Sandbags are hastily filled and thrown up, and even some of the dead bodies are initialized for this purpose. We have been here scarcely five minutes before the Turkish batteries opened up a heavy shellfire on us. The air is full of screaming shells and as they burst near the trench, give off little white puff balls of smoke."[31]

As the Borders swarmed over the strongpoint, the surviving Turks tried to escape, and the RNAS machine gunners, lying in wait for just such an exodus, opened fire: "I gave orders for Johnston's gun to be trained on the main 'Boomerang' sap of 'Suicide Street' (& 'Deaths Corner') & he soon found a target—dozens upon dozens of Turks in their endeavour to get away rushed from the redoubt to the Cliffside [of Gully Ravine] & were simply mown down. Then the khaki of our men was seen, showing that the great 'Boomerang' redoubt was at last in our hands."[32]

When the Turks were caught running from the Boomerang, the rest of B Company went over the top. They were not as fortunate as the assaulting platoons and were hit almost as soon as they left their trench: "Down our trench came the order 'Advance.' Man & officer scrambled over the side to meet a perfect hail of lead from the enemy. As they advanced for the trench ahead, huge gaps soon showed in the line & every yard or so could be seen, the withering or twisted bodies of a South Wales Borderer [sic]."[33]

Despite the heavy fire, the Borders made it to the Boomerang. After taking a short break to recover their breath, they went in: "The South Wales Borderers lay under the protection of the Turkish sand bags for a few seconds & then, quietly dropped into the trench. God! what a sight, but what men these soldiers of the 'Old Army.'"[34] The Boomerang was well and truly in British hands.

Unfortunately, A Company's experience at Turkey trench was just the opposite: "Meanwhile A Coy. were experiencing considerable difficulty with TURKEY TRENCH. It was found that about 40 yards of the trench in rear of the enemy's barricade had been filled in & this left the assaulting party exposed to a murderous fire from a previously unlocated trench running from TURKEY TRENCH to

H.12 . . . All the assaulting party were either killed or wounded in crossing the filled in portion & CAPT. HODGSON who was leading the assault was bayonetted."[35]

At eleven o'clock the main attacks commenced. On the left side of Gully Ravine the Second South Wales Borderers (SWB) leaped out of their trenches. They were tasked with capturing trenches J9 and J10, which they did in short order. The artillery and ships' guns had been so effective that the trenches were practically destroyed and their occupants either killed or wounded. Before the attack, the Welshmen had practiced their assault so that for the first time in the campaign each man knew exactly what he was supposed to do. That, combined with the devastating effectiveness of the guns, had made this portion of the operation nearly perfect. But the Borderers were not unscathed. A Company, attacking parallel to Gully Ravine, was hit by fire from positions that had not yet been captured adjoining the Boomerang. From his location on the other side of the ravine, Sharkey watched the Welshmen as they moved from J9 to J10: "Ahead I saw the South Wales Borderers leave the newly captured trench & move forward. The distance of 150 yds. was soon covered & they leapt with a yell into J10. Many unarmed Turks were seen coming in our direction, others fleeing to the rear, a target for all machine guns."[36]

Following on the heels of the Welshmen were the other two battalions of the first wave, which left their trenches at 11:10 a.m. It was their job to leapfrog the SWB in J10 and capture J11 behind it. The First King's Own Scottish Borderers attacked on the right, parallel to the ravine, and the First Royal Inniskilling Fusiliers attacked on their right. The Fusiliers were fortunate. The trenches in front had been largely destroyed along with their occupants, and they suffered few casualties: "They met with little resistance and found in the trenches the enemy's breakfasts—biscuits and hard-boiled eggs—prepared, and some stores of cigars and of German ammunition. A more gruesome find was the bodies of some Royal Dublin Fusiliers killed on April 27 and still unburied."[37]

The KOSB fared much worse, for it was on them that the Boomerang's satellites directed their fire. In addition the Turks had covered that end of their trench with logs, so the Borderers were left standing in no-man's-land, trying frantically to find a way inside. They did find a way in but not before suffering the loss of 8 officers and 223 other ranks. Of that number more than 60 were killed.

At 11:30 a.m. the second wave attacked. The 1/6th Gurkhas charged along the cliffs, cleared the remainder of J11a, and occupied a spur that ran down to the sea, just past J13 (later called "Fusilier Bluff"). To their right the First Lancashire Fusiliers, followed by the First Royal Munster Fusiliers, moved out, leaped over J9, J10, and J11, and captured J12 and J13. On their right the Lancashiremen moved to the right and down into Gully Ravine. They were to connect the right of the Second Royal Fusiliers with the left of the 156th Brigade at trench H12 on the east side of the ravine. The First Royal Dublin Fusiliers were in reserve for the Eighty-Sixth Brigade, and the 1/5th Gurkhas were supporting the 1/6th.

Even though the Turks occupying the J trenches were largely eliminated, their artillery was not, and it fired shrapnel at the attackers. All of the attacking battalions suffered casualties, but all managed to reach and hold their objectives—all, that is, except the Lancashire Fusiliers in Gully Ravine. The battalion suffered its first casualties when Turkish artillery answered the British bombardment with shrapnel. At that time the Fusiliers were not visible to the Turks, but their rounds found them anyway. Those brave men of Lancashire were undeterred, however, and continued to move to their jumping-off point. When they went over the top at 11:30 a.m., stragglers from battalions that had attacked before them were moving back through their ranks.

It was not long before Turks on both flanks fired on the leading companies. As a result, D Company became separated from C, an event that led to the destruction of D Company. C Company thus reached the ravine at the wrong spot—farther south than it should have—and it thus lost contact with the Royal Fusiliers on its left.

Down in Gully Ravine, A Company overran a Turkish position and captured sixty-two Turks. It then established a position between the left end of H12 and the edge of the ravine and from there beat off repeated Turkish attacks. In the meantime C had become dispersed and sent out patrols in search of D Company, which it failed to find. All the while casualties continued to mount as Turks tried in vain to recover lost territory and the Fusiliers probed farther north in the hornets' nest that was Gully Ravine. It was not until after dark that a patrol managed to find the few survivors of D who had taken refuge in J12 and J13.

While the men of the Eighty-Sixth Brigade were fighting and dying, one of their chaplains, Rev. Oswin Creighton, waited for the wounded to arrive at the Eighty-Ninth Field Ambulance near W Beach. It was a terribly emotional day for him, as more of his flock lost their lives or were carried, broken and bleeding, into the white hospital tents:

> At 11 a.m. the infantry went out and the wounded started to pour in. First the slight cases able to walk, in crowds. Everything seemed to be going well. The Turks were on the run and we had got a line or two of trenches. Then later on in came the stretcher cases, and kept coming all night and next day till about 2 p.m. We had five doctors fortunately, and five wagons working the whole time clearing the wounded down to Gully Beach. In twenty-four hours we had had 500 wounded through, and the 88th [Field Ambulance] who are next door, about the same number. We were about as full as possible all the time. Eight died here, but were unconscious. The heat was terrific and the flies were simply awful. It was impossible to keep them off. I was not feeling well and was pretty limp. There is little I can do. The men are just longing for the wagons to take them away. We had men from all regiments. The majority seemed to have shrapnel wounds . . . I went over to "Y" beach in the afternoon to see how they were getting on there, and found them full of wounded, about 400 cases altogether. An artillery officer was lying there with his leg blown off. He died afterwards. I was there, so I did not stop. The L.F.'s [Lancashire Fusiliers] and R.F.'s [Royal Fusiliers] had made the last advance, and I gathered had lost practically all their newly collected offi-

"A Glimpse of Hell"

cers. I was so tired that I slept part of the night, but was up at dawn. They had been evacuating all night.[38]

The 156th Brigade attacked on the right of Gully Ravine, simultaneous with the attack of the Eighty-Seventh Brigade. Consisting of four battalions—the 1/4th and 1/7th Battalions (TF), the Royal Scots, and the 1/7th and 1/8th Battalions (TF), the Cameronians— the brigade had only been on the peninsula for two weeks. Although Gully Ravine was the brigade's first major action, it had already suffered casualties. On the first leg of their trip to Gallipoli, at Quintinshill Station near Gretna Green in Scotland, a fatal signaling error had resulted in the deaths and injury of more than four hundred men of the 1/7th Royal Scots. The loss was so great that only two of the battalion's four companies made it to Gallipoli. Its headquarters staff was also decimated.

For the assault on June 28, the 1/4th Royal Scots were on the right, the 1/7th Royal Scots were in the center, and the 1/8th Cameronians were on the left. The 1/7th Cameronians were in reserve. According to the regimental history of the Royal Scots: "Our cannonade commenced punctually at 9 A.M., but no shells fell on the trenches to be attacked by the 4th and 7th Royal Scots. The only effective covering fire was that provided by the machine-guns of the two battalions, but bullets cannot do more than force the enemy to keep his head down till the moment of assault; they can neither smash trenches nor bemuse a garrison."[39]

When the British bombardment began and the Turks responded in kind, the waiting infantry took the full brunt of the fire. The men suffered their first casualties before they even left the trench. Among those killed at that stage was Capt. and (temporary) Maj. James Henderson, commanding officer of A Company, 1/4th Royal Scots. He was wounded by the explosion of one shell and, as he lay in the bottom of the trench, was killed by the explosion of another.

At eleven o'clock the Scots attacked. They were promptly hit by rifle and machine gun fire from enemy positions that had barely been touched by the British artillery: "At last the hour came and at the word, 'Over you go, lads,' the troops gave vent to one resounding cheer and, filled with the turbulence of battle, swarmed over the parapets into the perils of the open ground. Then the storm beat upon them; a rain of missiles smote their ranks, but slanting their bodies to the blast the survivors dashed on without flinching through the smoke and flame."[40]

In fact, the "storm of missiles" tore great holes in the ranks of the Scots, especially the 1/8th Cameronians. The assault came in part from a nest of six machine guns emplaced around the Turkish trench H13, which the British did not know existed. The part of the line attacked by the Royal Scots had to a small extent been hit by the artillery supporting the Borders' assault on the Boomerang. It had not touched the end of the field being attacked by the Cameronians. Men went down like a row of dominoes. The two Biggs brothers, William and John, fell near one another. Only William's body was recovered for burial. Brothers Alexander and James King were also hit. James was killed instantly, but Alexander lingered until July 3, when he died on a hospital ship bound for Egypt. Capt. William Church, commanding officer of D Company, was also lost: "On 28th June 1915, about a quarter to eleven A.M. I advanced with No. 14 Platoon, No. 4 [D] Company, under 2nd Lieutenant W. N. Sloan, over the parapet. An order was given by a sergeant to lie down, and I saw Captain Church come over the parapet and come up to us. He shouted 'For God's sake men get up and advance.' Almost immediately a bullet went through his chest and he fell. I stood and looked at him for two or three minutes and saw no movement, and was certain he was dead. I was shot through the leg on the parapet of the third trench."[41] In all the battalion reported the loss of 334 other ranks killed and missing and 114 wounded. Within just five minutes the 1/8th Cameronians effectively ceased to exist.

The two Royal Scots battalions were more fortunate than the Cameronians, but their success came at a price. They began taking casualties as soon as the Turkish bombardment began. By 10:50 a.m. they had suffered so many casualties in their densely packed trench that a platoon of the 1/7th Cameronians had to be brought up from the support line to fill in a gap on the left of the 1/7th Royal Scots.

As the First Borders attacked the Boomerang on its left, the men of the 1/4th Royal Scots became increasingly anxious. At 11:02 a.m. the word to attack was given. As soon as the Scots climbed out of their trenches, Turkish bullets began dropping on them. Many were hit by machine guns located in a trench less than a hundred yards to their left, which the British had completely missed. But the attackers continued on, taking H12 and H12a. As the survivors leaped into H12a, shooting and bayoneting the defenders, the remaining Turks bolted.

Even though the Royal Scots had taken their objectives, the 1/8th Cameronians had not, and this was unacceptable to de Lisle. Those occupying the uncaptured portions of H12a and H12 could harass his men by throwing bombs over the sandbagged walls that the Scots had built as barricades. So, de Lisle sent the message: "H12 is to be taken at all costs. If necessary you will send forward your reserve battalion."[42]

The recipient of this order was Brig. Gen. William Scott-Moncrieff, commanding officer of the 156th Brigade. A brave man who was well liked by his men, he had first seen action in the Zulu War of 1879. He was hit by four bullets at the massacre of British troops at Spion Kop during the Boer War—the last one in the leg, resulting in a permanent limp. In 1915 he had two sons, both officers, serving at the front.

That morning Scott-Moncrieff visited his troops in H10 before they went over the top, and he knew what had happened to the 1/8th Cameronians. He also knew what awaited his single reserve battalion, the 1/7th Cameronians, if he followed de Lisle's order. Unfortunately, he had no choice. He had to send his reserve troops into what he knew was a meat grinder, and he knew that the gesture would be a futile one. He received the fateful order at 11:47 a.m. and immediately ordered two of the battalion's companies to attack.

It took nearly an hour for the Scots to get to their jumping-off point, and it was packed with the dead and dying from the previous attack. But at 12:30 p.m. they were ready to go, and go they did. At their head was their gallant general. He knew that he was sending his precious men to their deaths and felt it was wrong to ask them to do something that he would not. When the order to attack was given, the two companies climbed out into a withering fire of shot and shell. Almost immediately, the brave brigadier was hit in the head by a bullet and instantly killed. The attack failed almost immediately.

When Major General Egerton got word that his friend had been killed, he wrote in his diary: "5 p.m. Wounded are beginning to trickle in and I fear the Brigade has suffered heavily. A wounded man says the Brigadier, Scott-Moncrieff, is killed. I hope not, I have no one to replace him with."

As a result of this failure, the remnants of the 1/8th Battalion who had joined the 1/7th Royal Scots in H12a built a sandbag barricade that would later be called "Southern Barricade." A similar wall was thrown up in front, in H12, which came to be known as "Northern Barricade."

The Battle of Gully Ravine was costly for both sides, but the attackers were largely successful in their endeavors. Even though the eastern ends of J12 and J13 and H12a and H12 were still in the hands of the Turks, the British had won a foothold farther inland, and that gave them some much-needed breathing space. More men could be brought in, and artillery could be emplaced closer to the enemy. The Boomerang was also eliminated as a threat to movement on both sides of the ravine. After the main fighting ended, Chief Sharkey observed of that hellhole:

> You stand aside to allow a party of Red Cross men to pass. Each of these men are dragging a corpse—either one of our own men or a Turk & the coolness [with which] they go about their work almost makes you shudder. You pass under an elaborate Construction of overhead cover, stout beams, doors & planks, upon which lie a forward sap. In this sap which faces across the "Nullah" one sees a horrifying & ghastly sight, such as dozens & doz-

ens of bodies smashed & blown to pulp, men's faces as flat as pancakes, blood, skin, bones & rags everywhere.

You then go into a torn & shattered earthwork which would be the most forward part of the "Boomerang" & here was evidence of those deadly aero-torpedoes [fired by the French trench mortars]. Huge gaping holes a dozen feet deep, destroyed parapets, wrecked entanglements & heap after heap of bodies, some half buried beneath the debris of the trench; many were still alive & uttering horrible and terrifying groans & so on through a tunnel into another traverse. There again the same scenes—the same groans, the same story of war.

Such was the toll of the Battle of Gully Ravine.

10

"There Was No One Left to Fire"

Battles of August and the Final Offensives

The failure of the Third Battle of Krithia revealed that an Allied breakout was not possible in the Helles sector, at least not with the resources available. The fighting there had resulted in a stalemate. The British and French were strong enough that the Turks could not to drive them out, and the Turks were experts at defense and were too well supplied with men and munitions. There was no point, however, in the Allies staying where they were. Plans were soon developed for a three-pronged offensive that would, it was hoped, allow them to break out of their positions.

The plans for the coming "push" were complex and demonstrated the kind of innovation that the Allies should have employed all along. As usual, none of the planners considered the possibility of failure and were too far removed from reality to understand the limitations of human endurance. The generals and their staffs felt that this offensive, if successful, would end the campaign once and for all.

The plan called for a breakout from Anzac, supported by a new landing in the Suvla sector, which bordered Anzac to the north. A two-part diversionary attack would take place at Helles, where the British were far too depleted to attempt anything on a grand scale.

The plan was clever yet complex. On the afternoons of August 6 and 7 portions of the Twenty-Ninth and Forty-Second Divisions at

Helles would carry out attacks that were intended to take full advantage of their meager artillery. The Eighty-Eighth Brigade (Twenty-Ninth Division) would attack on the Sixth, and the 126th and 127th Brigades (Forty-Second Division) would attack the following day. This two-day battle would come to be called the "Battle of Krithia Vineyard" and was intended to make the Turks think that a major offensive was taking place there. It was meant to draw reinforcements to Helles and keep the Turkish reserves there from being sent to Anzac. What the planners failed to realize was that by breaking up the attack and allowing *their* full complement of artillery to concentrate on a particular area, it would allow the Turks to do the same.

On the afternoon of the sixth, the First Australian Division would also launch a diversionary attack against the log-covered Turkish trenches at Lone Pine. Named after a single stunted pine tree that once stood there, it was located on 400 Plateau, in the southern portion (far right) of the Anzac sector. The intention was to capture this heavily fortified position and to prevent Turkish reinforcements from moving north to Sari Bair. It was also supposed to allow the main attacking parties to travel north, unmolested, to the two gullies up which they were to move that night. The First Brigade would lead the way. The Second Brigade would then assault German Officers' Trench opposite Steele's Post and, if all went according to plan, Johnston's Jolly, on the northern half of 400 Plateau. If these positions were taken, the right flank of the Third Light Horse Brigade would be protected when it attacked the Nek the following morning.

The main attacking troops—referred to as the "Right and Left Assaulting Columns"—were to move up the Sazli Beit and Chailak Deres. There were two additional groups, the Right and Left Covering Forces, that would precede the assaulting columns. They would depart at 9 p.m., and the assaulting columns would follow at ten thirty. The initial goals of the covering forces were to capture the Turkish outposts that prevented movement up the gullies, which would allow the assaulting columns to carry out their attacks without having to fight their way to their jumping-off points. The covering forces were to use their bayonets so they would not alert the Turks manning positions nearby. It was imperative that noise be kept to a minimum, so rifles were not to be loaded. The Gurkhas would use their heavy-bladed *kukris* instead of bayonets, with which they were supposedly capable of severing a human head. The ultimate goal of the Right Assaulting Force was the capture of Hill Q and Chunuk Bair, and the goal of the Left Assaulting Force was Hill 971. At four thirty the following morning the groups were to carry out a series of joint assaults that were meant to capture the entire range. One of them was to move south from Chunuk Bair, and the other was to push toward that force, from Russell's Top, over the Nek and onto the ever-troublesome Baby 700. This attack, immortalized in Peter Weir's movie *Gallipoli* (1981), would involve the Eighth and Tenth Light Horse Regiments (LHR), with the Ninth Light Horse in reserve. The four groups were placed under the command of Maj. Gen. Sir Alexander Godley, commanding officer of the New Zealand and Australian Division. Because the attacks would take place at night and there would be little natural light, the attacking troops would wear white calico patches on their sleeves and backs so they could be identified by their comrades.

In order to facilitate the breakout from Anzac, a new landing was planned for the night of August 6 at Suvla Bay. Once ashore, the untested British troops who made up the new force were supposed to provide support for the troops on their right attacking at Anzac. Here again, innovation would play a part in the form of armored landing craft called "beetles." Yet incompetence at the planning level, carried out by a general and staff officers far removed from the fighting and who had little or no combat experience, would result in failure and stalemate that would ultimately help to lose the campaign.

The first of the diversionary attacks to take place around Krithia Vineyard at Helles was a failure. So was the one the following day. While a small amount of territory was captured—including the vineyard—the already diminished British battalions were further decimated. Their efforts did nothing to draw Turkish attention away from the Anzac sector. From the start von Sanders knew that the pitiful effort was nothing more than a diversion.

One of those who participated in the vineyard's capture was Lance Cpl. James Morris of the 1/7th Lancashire Fusiliers. Known to his friends as Harry, he survived the day but was killed by a Turkish bomb the following night. Rev. Frederick Welbon wrote to the boy's sweetheart:

By the time you get this you will have known some time of the death of Harry. He was killed in the trench which he had helped to capture from the Turks in the famous charge they made last Saturday morning. I saw him just before they went into the open. The day after they had captured the trench I again saw him, and it was a joyous meeting, for I was afraid he had gone under. The day following Willie Bentley came in and broke down as he tried to tell me that he had seen a lad who had just left Harry lying dead. I saw his officer, who told me twice during that awful night when the Turks were counterattacking, Harry had gone to see if he was all right, and then went back to his post, when a bomb caught him and killed him. He suffered no pain and died doing his duty magnificently. You have a proud memory to cherish. I feel I have lost a friend in him. I often saw him and he was such a perfect gentleman, and so fine a character. I shall miss my little talks with him in the trench. He always talked of you and his joy was that he had been spared in the charge for your sake.[1]

The Twenty-Ninth Division reported losing 54 officers and 1,851 other ranks killed, wounded, and missing on August 6. The Forty-Second Division reported losing 80 officers and 1,484 other ranks during the two-day battle. As usual, men would continue fighting and dying to hold onto their little bit of real estate long after the actual battle had ended.

On August 16 Capt. John Gillam ventured forward to see where more of his precious friends had lost their lives:

I am taken up a sap by one of the officers on duty in the front line, a cheery young man named Moore, who has recently won the V.C. [Victoria Cross]. At the sap-head, looking through a periscope,

I see not fifty yards away in front a sap-head jutting out from a Turkish trench. Turning the periscope round left to right, I see a sight which fills me with sorrow. I see lying in all postures—some alone, some in groups of three to six—the dead bodies of brave British Tommies, who a fortnight ago were alive and well, merry and bright, enjoying bathing off Gully Beach. They had lost their lives in the battle of August 6th, and had never even had the satisfaction of reaching Turkish territory. After the battle our positions in the "H" trenches . . . remained unchanged from what they were before; but hundreds of brave men have gone forth from there never to return, and I am afraid few became prisoners.

The Royal Naval Division was not involved in the battle, but Douglas Jerrold, who served with the Hawke Battalion, would later write: "The frontal attack had become the order of the day and was to continue at Cape Helles right up to the day of the Suvla landing in August, when the 42nd Division was ordered to attack on the left of our line and walked out to their death to show the Turks that they were still alive. None of them, I fancy, reached the enemy's front line. When we took over this part of the line, later in August, we could see, not fifty yards from our own trenches, two rows of dead, lying as they had fallen, a sombre tribute to the triumph of discipline over common sense."[2]

The most successful effort of the offensive was the other major diversion: the attack on Lone Pine. Beginning in May, men of the Second Field Company, Australian Engineers, began digging a series of tunnels under no-man's-land from the Pimple on the right side of the Anzac line. Referred to as the "B Series" on maps, five of these tunnels ran out to a secret firing line opposite Lone Pine. This line was completely underground and was located thirty yards in front of the main Australian line. It ran at right angles to the tunnels and parallel to the Turkish frontline. The engineers constructed these tunnels with the aid of men from the Second Battalion and the Sixth Light Horse Regiment, who removed the soil at a rate of approximately eleven feet per day.

"No One Left to Fire"

The goals of the Lone Pine diversion were simple. After three days of small artillery barrages, a final barrage would take place at 4:30 p.m. on August 6. An hour later the infantry would go over the top. The Third Battalion would attack the center of the line, where it dipped inward; the Fourth Battalion would assault the stronger frontline trench to the north, and the Second would attack the trench to the south. The First Battalion would be in reserve. The main attack would proceed in three waves, each one company strong. The first wave, having filed through the tunnels and into the hidden firing line, would attack from there. The second and third waves would depart from the main Australian line thirty yards behind. The first waves of the Second and Fourth Battalions would have to charge a distance of forty yards, while the Third Battalion would have to cover sixty yards. The third wave of each battalion would be equipped with picks and shovels as well as rifles, so the men could turn the parapets of the captured trenches and dig communication trenches back from Lone Pine to the Pimple. The plan was very well thought out, for a change, and the attacking officers had done their best to understand what they would be up against. They also communicated the plan to their men so that everyone would know his job. For three days before the assault, the attackers were allowed to have as much water as they wanted. The last thing Birdwood wanted was for his riflemen to be stopped by dehydration.

The Turks knew that the Australians were tunneling toward them. Those above ground could see fresh soil piling up behind the lines, and those working underground could hear them. Tunneling, or "mining," was a common practice for both sides. The goal was to dig under the enemy's front line, plant explosives, and blow those manning the trench into the next life. Then both sides would charge the resulting crater, the aggressor hoping to extend his line to that point. Thousands would die on both sides as a result of mining during the war. Most would never be found, their torn and broken bodies forever buried under tons of earth.

Hoping to beat the Australians to the punch, the Turks blew a mine between two of the tunnels on June 29. Nevertheless, the digging continued, and the Turks had no idea that they terminated at a hidden firing line opposite their trenches. Unlike the attacks at Helles, this diversion was a complete success, though a great many men were lost in achieving it. Eric Wren, the Third Battalion's biographer, described what happened after the mines were blown on August 6:

> Everywhere whistles were blowing. The covering artillery-fire had ceased. We were scrambling, hands and knees, up the trench side—we were kneeling—we were walking—we were running . . . The Lone Pine was out there—in front.
>
> As we scrambled over the parapet or emerged from the underground line there came immediately from the Turkish lines opposite the roar of continuous, rapid rifle-fire and the just-distinguishable staccato note of angry machine-guns, tap-tap-tapping, it seemed, in furious rage. Here—there—men staggered, crumpled, pitched forward, sagged sideways. Men shouted, men laughed. Men groaned.
>
> Shells came shrieking. One came to decapitate a bugler—the headless body ran on for several yards before it stopped and dropped. In front khaki-clad figures struggling on the parapet of the first Turkish trench. The glint of steel. Red flashes from a thousand rifle barrels. Khaki figures that were not moving. Men lying huddled together as if awaiting another signal to move forward.
>
> Yes, some were moving—twitching. Others—crawling away—or trying to—maimed—dying. All were perfectly still—a spent wave of dead men.[3]

The headless "bugler" was Pvt. Norman Murray, one of the battalion's signalers. A sheepshearer from Warren, New South Wales, he was originally turned down for enlistment as being medically unfit but was later able to join the Fifth Reinforcements. His friend Pvt. Arthur Mayer told one of the British Red Cross Society's (BRCS) investigators: "Witness saw Murray in the advance from the trenches at Lone Pine on 6th Aug. He was missing after the advance. Witness made enquiries but could not find out anything definite about him and believed he was killed. Murray was a tall man. He came

"No One Left to Fire"

from the N.W. coast, N.S.W. He was an R.C. [Roman Catholic], very argumentative and 'would not be gainsaid.' He was called the bush lawyer."[4]

Another who was killed in the dash forward was 2nd Lt. Jack Merivale. He landed at Gallipoli as a lance corporal in the Sixth Light Horse Regiment. After being promoted to sergeant, he was commissioned in the field and transferred to the Fourth Battalion. His friend Lt. Jim Osborne wrote to the man's sister:

On Friday, August 6th. about 4 o'clock the battalion formed to move up to the attacking point, and Jack was attached to my platoon. On the way there we halted for about ten minutes, and Jack, a man named Hutton and myself had a smoke and a chat together. He was in splendid spirits, and all of us were looking confidently forward to the attack. Later on during the half hour bombardment (from 5 to 5.30 p.m.) I saw him again, and he was supervising arrangements, and setting a first class example to the men by his cheerfulness. The next time I saw him was two or three minutes after he was hit. As far as I can gather he had been hit by a rifle or machine gun bullet whilst making the dash across, and had managed to struggle into the advanced Turkish trench we had just taken. I asked him where he was hit and whether I could give him any morphia. He said "I am done for" and that he had morphia, so I didn't give him any, but helped him with his bandage, and told him he would be alright. We then shook hands, and then I had to pass on. When I returned about half an hour later he was dead.

The charge across to Lone Pine was costly, and when the survivors arrived at the enemy trenches, they were astonished to find that they were covered in thick logs. But they were not to be stopped and eventually found their way into the covered depressions. What ensued was a three-day struggle in the hellish, stinking darkness of the Turkish trenches in which men fought like cornered animals. Among those who died there was Pvt. Alexander Dean of the Third Battalion. His death was so traumatic that four of his mates recalled his passing to the BRCS investigators in 1916 and 1917. He died in the arms of Sgt. Arthur Hine: "On August 7th 1915, in the night time Dean was struck in the neck by a bomb and bled to death. He was in my platoon and I knew him well. We could not take him away as we had no conveniences. This happened in the Lone Pine Trench, Gallipoli. I remember that we buried him some time after."[5]

The Australians were victorious, and their sacrifices are memorialized to this day. Lone Pine, however, was the only successful diversion. The failure of the others would prove catastrophic for their comrades, who were counting on the Turkish resistance—in particular their machine guns—being eliminated.

To the north the two Covering Forces were successful in eliminating the resistance in their sectors. This meant that the Right and Left Assaulting Columns would be able to approach their jumping-off points relatively unscathed. For the most part they did. Ultimately, however, the two forces were unable to achieve their goal of capturing the Sari Bair Ridge. At Chunuk Bair on the right—which was reached after New Zealand, British, and Indian troops drove off the Turkish defenders—shells fired by a British warship landed on the attackers and turned the tide in favor of the Turks. On the left the Australian Fourth Brigade was torn to pieces before it reached its goal, Hill 971. The failures were due in part to the stronger-than-expected Turkish defenses. Yet the lack of support from the British troops who had landed at Suvla on their left was also a key factor.

The most infamous of the failed assaults was the charge of the Australian Third Light Horse Brigade from Walker's Ridge against the Turkish trenches at the Nek. The movie *Gallipoli* leads one to believe that an emotionless British staff officer sent those poor men to their deaths. In fact, it was an Australian officer. He was under the impression that a signal flag, carried by one of the troopers and intended to tell the artillery observers that the attackers were in the enemy trench, had been erected. But he never bothered to see for himself.

Several factors contributed to the failure. The Australian Sixth Battalion, which attacked German Officers' Trench before one o'clock that morning, failed to eliminate the machine guns that would fire

"No One Left to Fire"

into the light horsemen's right flank. Also, the artillery was too weak to make an impact on the defenders. The attack began at 4:00 a.m. and was supposed to last until the light horsemen went over the top a half-hour later. In fact, it ended at four twenty-three. As usual, the Turks manning the frontline trenches retired to the rear to wait out the bombardment and returned when it ended. The apparent failure of the artillerymen to coordinate their watches with those of the light horse officers allowed the Turks time to return and prepare for the coming assault. Added to that, the New Zealanders who should have been attacking from Chunuk Bair on the other side were still trying to fight their way onto the hill. The defending Turks were thus able to devote their full attention to the hapless Australians.

The area over which the light horsemen charged was only wide enough for 150 men to attack in line at one time. Therefore, the force consisted of four waves of 150 men each, or two squadrons per wave (a regiment consisted of four squadrons). The Eighth Light Horse Regiment formed the first two waves, while the Tenth Light Horse formed the third and fourth. At the same time, the Eighth (Service) Battalion, the Cheshire Regiment, would attack in conjunction with two companies of the Eighth (Service) Battalion, the Royal Welsh Fusiliers, to the Australians' right.

The light horsemen were eager for a fight. They had been at Gallipoli since May, but this would be their first big attack. Their enthusiasm changed to anguish when they realized that the Turks were still in German Officers' Trench. When they heard the artillery end seven minutes too soon and their officers, observing through their wooden trench periscopes, could see Turks returning to their trench, they realized that the attack would be futile. Men who only a short time earlier had expected to be celebrating in the enemy trenches that night, instead said their last good-byes and penned good-bye letters to their loved ones. Few expected to see another sunrise. Few would.

From the moment it began, the attack was a complete failure. The Australians began falling even before they made it out of their trench. Although the Tenth LHR, attacking after the Eighth, could have been prevented from attacking, it was not. Those in command of the operation felt it was better to keep up the pressure on the Turks than to end the slaughter. Doing so, they believed, would allow the attack on Chunuk Bair to succeed. They were wrong. In the end hundreds of lives were lost or broken in a futile attempt to secure a victory.

The movie *Gallipoli* portrays two young troopers in the Tenth Light Horse who participated in that attack. One lost his life; the other lost his friend. These characters were loosely based on two brothers, Troopers Wilfred and Gresley Harper. Historian and war correspondent C. E. W. Bean wrote of them: "With that regiment went the flower of the youth of Western Australia, sons of the old pioneering families, youngsters—in some cases two and three from the same home—who had flocked to Perth at the outbreak of war with their own horses and saddlery to secure enlistment in a mounted regiment of the A.I.F. Men known and popular, the best loved leaders in sport and work in the West, then rushed straight to their death. Gresley Harper, and Wilfred, his younger brother . . . last seen running forward like a schoolboy in a foot race, with all the speed he could compass."[6] Like most of the men who went into that fight, their bodies were left laying in no-man's-land because Turkish snipers made it too dangerous for them to be collected. They lay there still, in a mass grave under the battlefield.

Many of the light horsemen were related. Among them were the two Cumming cousins. Driver Alexander Cumming served with A Squadron, Eighth LHR. His cousin, Trooper Richard Cumming, served with A Squadron, 10th LHR. Alexander was killed in the first wave; Richard fell in the third. Alexander was listed as missing. When the Anzacs returned to Gallipoli to establish their cemeteries after the armistice in 1918, his identity disc was found amid the bones and sent to his grieving parents. Richard was shot and killed as soon as he climbed out of his trench and was buried later that night.

At Suvla the plan called for the Eleventh (Northern) Division to land on two beaches, B and C, on the night of August 6. After capturing a small hill called Lala Baba that overlooks C Beach, the troops were to move quickly inland under cover of darkness. Some

"No One Left to Fire"

were to capture a barren ridge called Kiretch Tepe Sirt, which is bounded by the Aegean on its northern side. A sheer drop prevented a landing from taking place there. Other battalions would move to the east, where they were supposed to capture the W Hills and Chocolate Hill. Intelligence, provided in large part by New Zealand scouts who had carried out small raids in the sector over the previous months, had shown that it was lightly held with only a few defensive positions. The area was ripe for the taking.

In order to prevent the same kinds of problems encountered on April 25, the British developed armored landing craft called "beetles," which would be used for the first time to land the troops detailed for the assault. Capable of carrying five hundred men each, these boats could approach the beach in near silence and deliver their human cargo dry. Once ashore, the riflemen, who also wore white patches so they could be identified in the dark, would battle the Turks using only their bayonets. The use of firearms was banned until daylight, to prevent muzzle flashes from giving away their positions. There would be no preparatory bombardment.

The campaign at Suvla was destined to fail from the moment its commander was chosen by Kitchener. Hamilton had asked for either Lt. Gen. Sir Julian Bing or Lt. Gen. Sir Henry Rawlinson, both of whom had proven their mettle in France. Kitchener felt that they were needed more on the western front and instead chose sixty-one-year-old Lt. Gen. Sir Frederick Stopford. He chose Stopford solely on the basis of seniority and could not have made a worse decision. Not only was Stopford retired from the army and in poor health; he was also devoid of any combat experience. As was the case so often at Gallipoli, foolishness prevailed, and the aged general was placed in command of the newly formed Ninth Corps.

The goal of this assault was ambitious in the extreme. Oddly, when Stopford issued his orders to the assaulting troops, he did not stress the importance of capturing the objectives before daylight. Nor did he stress the importance of taking the W Hills, which would have assisted the Anzacs in their attempt to capture Hill 971. Another factor was the secrecy surrounding the operation. The men of the

Eleventh Division did not know where they would be landing or what their objectives would be, and they were not told until the day of the invasion that they were going into action.

The men of the Eleventh Division began training for the landing on Imbros in July 1915. They were all members of the New Army who had enlisted after the outbreak of war in 1914. A few were veterans of the early battles on the western front who had been invalided back to England due to wounds, illness, or frostbite. These new troops were poorly trained and generally in poor physical condition before joining the army. Many had not had the luxury of regular, nourishing meals before enlisting. These inadequacies did not apply to all of the men of "Kitchener's Army," as the New Army battalions were termed, but it applied to a fair number.[7] From the time they arrived on Imbros, they were badly affected by the heat and monotonous diet, and many were hit by dysentery before leaving the island.

The majority of the officers had been commissioned since the outbreak of war, and most of the noncommissioned officers (NCOs) had never seen action either. Due to a shortage of qualified NCOs, some were appointed solely on the basis of their experience as Boy Scouts. Still, they were every bit as enthusiastic as the men who landed on April 25, and they had more training than the Anzacs had before they landed in April. The Australians had nothing but complaints about these citizen soldiers, but they were not well founded. The fact that they were there at all spoke to their courage, and their shortcomings as soldiers were not their fault. The later Australian reinforcements, for example, had only ever fired a few rounds on a rifle range, and many could barely shoot. They had to be trained once they got to Gallipoli.

By July von Sanders knew that an attack was coming. Reports had reached him that fifty to sixty thousand British troops had massed at Lemnos, and more than one hundred troop and supply vessels were nestled safely behind the antisubmarine nets that guarded Mudros Harbor. He knew that another landing was going to take place; he just did not know when or where. With a limited number of troops to guard against the coming invasion, he had to be creative in their placement. Not only did he have to maintain his defenses at Helles and Anzac, he also had to protect the coasts on both sides of the straits. Von Sanders knew that Suvla was an option, but he did not seriously consider it to be a possibility. He thought there was a better chance of a new landing south of Anzac.

On August 6 Turkish forces at Suvla amounted to only one infantry and two *gendarme* (local defense) battalions. Another infantry battalion was diverted to Anzac when the attacks began there on the afternoon of the sixth. The infantry battalion already in place was supplemented by two local *gendarme* units, nineteen artillery pieces, a company of pioneers, and thirty dismounted cavalrymen. Designated the "Anafarta Detachment," it was under the command of Bavarian cavalry officer Maj. Wilhelm Willmer. The force totaled about fifteen hundred men, compared to Stopford's two full divisions (approximately thirty-six thousand men). The detachment did not have a single machine gun at its disposal, nor did it possess any barbed wire, so it was imperative that Willmer keep the size of his force secret. In order to hide his assets from the probing eyes of British reconnaissance aircraft, his men camouflaged their guns and only moved at night.

Willmer knew that his small force would be unable to oppose a landing and could only defend his sector until reinforcements arrived. He broke the detachment up and placed the various pieces inland, on Lala Baba and the Kiretch Tepe Sirt, positioning them so that they could cover one another in true German defensive style.

Two brigades of the Eleventh Division began landing at Suvla at nine thirty on the night of the August 6. One of those who landed with the first wave was Lt. Hugh Campbell of the Eleventh (Service) Battalion, the Manchester Regiment, who detailed the landing and the chaos that followed in a letter to his parents:

We reached here [Suvla] just a week ago tonight and I have been in my boots ever since. At the moment it looks as if there will be no rest for a while. Well, we have done very well indeed, just as we expected, but our losses have been heavy, terrible in fact. Of course you will have seen from the lists the officers' losses we have had the first day. The 11th Manchesters affected the landing and it was stern bayonet work until dawn, 6 hours later. Not a shot was fired on our side as a series of landings was being affected during the night. We waded ashore, I should rather say swam for the water was 5 ft. deep, when the lighter struck a sand bank. A fair number of casualties were sustained on the boat for the night was too light for our purpose and the blighters spotted us before we could disembark. Bradley (Hugh's orderly) was wounded in the shoulder on the boat. We got away and formed up and went for the first trench and they ran like hares, and then we made for a long line of hills, about 4½ miles long, which was the Manchesters special job. Poor Jones [Evanson-Jones] was shot through the heart I should say, for we found the bullet in his ruck sack next day. Marsland got an explosive bullet in his abdomen. Poor old Nosey took a wrong turning and was ambushed and clubbed. We advanced, until weakened by casualties we could go no further and had lost 13 officers in the meantime, but we won about 3½ miles and were relieved by another lot next night. We went into bivouac on a bullet swept slope where Hartley was hit by one of his own men and we returned next day to the beach. Marched out at reveille next morning dog tired and went into another scrap. Allen hit in the shoulder and stern, Painter in legs, Sillery in shoulder, Ellershaw (Adjutant) in arm, badly, and so on, the full yard I will tell you some day. Colonel's wound got worse and he went into hospital—Stevens commands Battalion. I am Second in Command, Adjutant and O.C. [Officer in Command] "P" Company all in one, consequently work day and night, so excuse the frighteningly disjointed letter. Brain out of gear, really nerves, however very steady, bodily health good, fittest man in the regiment probably, but tired. Oh, how tired we are.

Campbell was killed in action nine days later. The "Nosey" he referred to was the battalion's medical officer, Lt. Jeffrey Parker: "It was in the landing on the evening of 6–7 Aug. There was a heavy

"No One Left to Fire"

fire, rifle and shrapnel, and many were wounded before they left the lighter. The remainder had to swim or flounder the few yards to the shore. The doctor was kept busy for a short time with those wounded on board, and then he came ashore like the rest. The last time any of us saw him, he was walking about as if he were just holding his ordinary sick parade, and seemingly quite indifferent to the terrible hail of lead. In his endeavour to get at the wounded, he seems to have walked right into the Turks, and his end was instantaneous. Need I say how much we missed him, and especially in the dreadful days that followed, and we were without our doctor."[8]

From the beginning confusion reigned supreme. The innovation apparent in the Anzac attacks was totally absent from Stopford's plans. Troops were landed on the wrong beaches, landing craft became stuck on uncharted shoals, and the novice infantry, led by inexperienced and uninformed officers, made little headway in the dark. Willmer's gallant defenders took full advantage, sniping at British muzzle flashes and men silhouetted against the moonlit sky. As the British approached the Turks' positions, the defenders quietly melted away, retreating to their predetermined positions.

Just as the average soldier was unaware of his goals and ignorant of the geography, so was Stopford uninformed about the reality of the situation ashore. While the nightmare was unfolding, he slumbered on his command sloop, the *Jonquil*, the whole night through. Unit commanders did not know exactly where to lead their men, nor could they identify main points of geography. Hill 10, for example, located northeast of Lala Baba and the dry Salt Lake,[9] was a main target for the Thirty-Second and Thirty-Fourth Brigades. Rising to only ten feet above sea level at its highest point, it was difficult for the British infantry to pick out on their maps, and they attacked a sand dune instead. The hill was supposed to have been taken the first night. It would not be captured until after dawn the following day.

Before sunset on August 7, Hill 10 was taken, and the British advanced inland to take Chocolate Hill.[10] The majority of those who landed, however, were wandering around on and behind the beaches, unsure of where to go and desperately seeking water. Their officers had not been given specific orders; some were told only to advance inland, and most had not been issued any maps at all: "Even after landing, the troops did not know where they were till the Brigade Clerk, Q.M.S. Fred Weston, found a case of maps on the beach, broke it open and disclosed the fact that we were at Suvla Bay."[11]

Had the British moved inland quickly, they would have arrived at Chocolate Hill in roughly forty-five minutes and met with little resistance. As it was, the delay allowed von Sanders the opportunity to send more than two divisions of reinforcements from Bulair. Thus, less than twenty-four hours after the British landed at Suvla, their fate in the sector was sealed. Attack farther inland they would; overcome the Turkish defenders they would not. The August offensives in all three sectors were a failure.

Hamilton, who should have used his initiative to turn the situation at Suvla in his favor, remained silent as usual. Yet on August 15, with Kitchener's approval, he fired Stopford and sent him home. A few days later the commanding officers of the Eleventh and Fifty-Third Divisions followed.

There would be one last gasp at Anzac and Suvla, on August 21. Veteran and virgin troops attacked in both sectors. At Suvla the newly arrived yeomanry regiments of the Second Mounted Division attacked for the first time. Like the Australian light horsemen and the New Zealand mounted riflemen, they fought at Gallipoli as infantry.[12] They were to act as a reserve. The Eleventh (Northern) Division was tasked with taking the W Hills. The Twenty-Ninth Division was sent up from Helles to capture 112 Metre Hill and Scimitar Hill. At Anzac a composite group of a thousand men, drawn from different units due to the depleted state of all of the Australian and New Zealand units, was to attack Hill 60. The attacks in both sectors were preceded by bombardment lasting only thirty minutes.

The Eleventh and Twenty-Ninth Divisions attacked at three in the afternoon. Following were the gallant yeoman, who crossed the dry bed of the Salt Lake from Lala Baba under constant shrapnel fire. It was their job to support the two leading divisions in their conquests. Many never made it to the other side of the lake, the

"No One Left to Fire"

airbursts thinning their ranks as they moved with their rifles held at port across their chests: "That day I saw an unforgettable sight. The dismounted Yeomanry attacked the Turks across the salt lakes [*sic*] of Suvla. Shrapnel burst over them continuously; above their heads there was a sea of smoke. Away to the north by Chocolate Hill fires broke out on the plain. The Yeomanry never faltered. On they came through the haze of smoke in two formations, columns and extended. Sometimes they broke into a run, but they always came on. It is difficult to describe the feelings of pride and sorrow with which we watched this advance, in which so many of our friends and relations were playing their part."[13]

Pvt. George Honeybourne of the Warwickshire Yeomanry was one of those who survived the crossing:

We made our first appearance in action on Saturday, August 21st, and they gave us rather a hot time. We had to advance over about a mile and half of open country in the daylight. We made the first half mile without seeming to be noticed, and then they let go at us with shrapnel fire; it seemed as thick as hail, and it is almost miraculous so few of us were hit. We lost a considerable number killed, wounded and missing out of our regiment as it was, but our first line took three rows of otherwise almost impregnable trenches while their fire was directed at us. Poor Wally (Coldicott) stopped one with his leg, but I do not think it is at all serious. Arkell (Coldicott) had a piece of shell go through his pants without touching his skin. Nothing hit me but dirt and dust that the shells were kicking up. We were all pretty well beat when we got into the shelter of a hill where they could not reach us. For one thing we had not had a chance to get used to our infantry equipment, and some of us had picks and shovels to carry besides our little entrenching tools. I had one. We also had our rifles, ammunition, two days' hard [iron] rations, and our water bottles.[14]

Among the fallen was Lt. William Niven of the Berkshire Yeomanry, father of the future actor five-year-old David. A big-game hunter who once accounted for eight lions on a single safari in East Africa, he was among the many listed as missing. Pvt. Jimmy Kearney, a polo pony trainer serving in the Gloucestershire Yeomanry, was the black sheep of his family who "chose an open-air life" after leaving university, instead of going into the family business. He was killed about three hundred yards west of Chocolate Hill.

The most notable casualty was Brig. Gen. Thomas Pakenham, fifth earl of Longford, MP. He was the commanding officer of the Second (South Midland) Mounted Brigade. A veteran of the Boer War, he insisted on advancing at the head of his men instead of watching them through binoculars, as so many of his peers chose to do. Maj. Fred Cripps of the Royal Bucks Hussars, who was wounded in the knee that day, wrote:

On 18 August we landed in the early morning having been transferred from our transport out at sea to suitable landing-craft. We came under shellfire in the landing-craft and had some casualties, but once we had landed, we were fairly well protected by the formation of the terrain. On the following day when we became a little more organized, I was talking to our Brigadier-General, Lord Longford, when a shell came over rather close blowing up a wagon behind us. I ducked down but the General did not turn a hair. He turned to me to ask: "What on earth are you doing? Are you frightened?" I had to admit that I had been somewhat scared. "Please," he said, "even if you are frightened, try not to show it quite so obviously to the men under your command." In expressing contrition I promised to do better in future.

Our division was ordered on 21 August to advance across a flat, open expanse of country, covered with scrub and heath, and then to attack the Turkish line in conjunction with the 29th Division and the Anzacs. Our Brigadier-General held a pow-wow for the officers before the attack. At the end he beckoned to me and said, "I wanted to say good-bye to you, as we shall both inevitably be killed this afternoon."

I didn't like the idea at all, but his forecast proved to be fairly correct, for in this baptism of fire, in our brigade twenty-one officers out of twenty-eight were killed and eighty-six men. Lord Longford and the whole of his staff were riddled with rifle fire at close range and all were killed. He himself advanced, with a map in one hand and a walking-stick in the other, at the head of his troops.[15]

Despite their casualties, the yeomen proceeded across the lakebed in textbook artillery formation, spread out so that a single shell would cause a minimum of casualties. As a result, their losses were not too severe, and the troopers made it the two miles to the base of Chocolate Hill. The same could not be said for the Eleventh or Twenty-Ninth Divisions, which were decimated in their attacks. To make matters worse, Turkish shells ignited the dry scrub on Scimitar Hill. Men who had fallen wounded were burned to death, their cries horrifying those not caught in the inferno:

> Our Bn. [battalion] was the Assaulting one of the Brigade, and we had to take a hill about ½ a mile ahead. I never thought it would come off. Every one was cooked with the heat, and almost too weary to stand, with no sleep for 3 nights. At 3 p.m. the Bn. shoved off 700 strong. The furthest any got was 500 yards and none came back from there. They all got mown down by machine gun fire. We lost 9 officers and nearly 400 men. The Turks shelled us very heavily and the whole country, which is covered with gorse, caught fire. This split up the attack and parties got cut up. Many of our wounded were burnt alive and it was as nasty a sight as I ever want to see. There were many very gallant things done that day. Our doctor and one of the stretcher bearers went out under a murderous fire and brought in one officer and 3 men, who were lying out with broken legs, with the fires creeping up to them. They have been recommended for the V.C. and I hope they get it. Our M.O.'s name is Altee. Finally about 7.30 p.m. the survivors came in under orders from the Division and all night long wounded men came struggling back, all with tales of our men, still lying out there. How any of us escaped, I don't know. Our Head Quarters was very heavily shelled and

then the fire surrounded the place and we all thought we were going to be burned alive. Where the telephone was, the heat was appalling. The roar of the flames drowned the noise of the shrapnel, and we had to lie flat at the bottom of the trench while the flames swept over the top. Luckily both sides didn't catch simultaneously, or I don't know what would have happened. After the gorse was all burnt, the smoke nearly asphyxiated us! All this time our Bn. was being cut up in the open and it really was very unpleasant trying to send down calm messages to the Brigade Headquarters, while you were lying at the bottom of the trench like an oven, expecting to be burnt every minute, and knowing that your Bn. was getting hell a hundred yards away! The telephone wire finally fused from the heat. The whole attack was a ghastly failure. They generally are now.[16]

By five that afternoon the main assaults at Suvla were over. The Eleventh and Twenty-Ninth Divisions had failed in their tasks, and the yeomen were sent into action on Scimitar Hill. They charged into the darkness, the smoke from the burning scrub and the stench of charred bodies attacking their senses. The fires also silhouetted targets for the Turks, as usual sufficiently dug in and defended by an array of machine guns and snipers. By nine o'clock that attack, too, had failed.

At Hill 60 on August 21, at the juncture of the Anzac and Suvla sectors, a composite force of Anzac and British troops went into the attack—units of the Fourth Australian Infantry Brigade, New Zealand Mounted Rifles, Fifth Connaught Rangers, and Tenth Hampshires. The Turkish positions were treated to a barrage of thirty minutes before the infantry went over the top at 3:30 p.m. Three waves attacked, and all three were decimated. The little bit of artillery available did little more than warn the Turks that an attack was coming. It also signaled the Ottoman gunners to open up on the attackers. The guns supporting the Anzacs did almost no damage—many sources say none at all—due to the haze that obscured the observers' view. The Turkish gunners, however, ended a great many lives.

When the Anzac bombardment finished, the riflemen went over the top, supported by their machine gunners. The historian of the Fourteenth Battalion, Australian Imperial Force (AIF), described the charge:

At 3:30 p.m. the bombardment ceased and the first wave, consisting of 150 men of the 13th [Battalion] under Lieut. Ford, charged. Suffering heavy casualties crossing the Dere, they drew up at the foot of the hill just at the top of the other side of the Dere. A few minutes later came the turn of the 14th—the second wave of 150 men under Major Dare. A whistle blew, and down the hill they raced like madmen. The Turks were by this time thoroughly aroused and alert, and the moment the crest was passed by our men, artillery, machine-guns and rifles vomited death in their faces. Forty per cent became casualties in that short, wild, frenzied charge. Lieuts. Crabbe and Duffield were killed. Major Dare, Lieut. D. R. Macdermid, and Sgt. Ernie Hill got through unwounded. A timely and courageous display of leadership in this charge on the part of Sgt. Ernie Hill won the M.M. [Military Medal] for that popular N.C.O. The survivors joined up with the 13th Battalion men who had stopped at the foot of the hill. It was impossible to complete the attack on the trench without artillery support, so Major Dare (who assumed command of the survivors of both waves) ordered the position to be consolidated. Fortunately, though it was impossible either to advance or retreat, the position was immune from the Turkish frontal fire, being tucked away in the front of the hill. It now became the duty of the third wave of 200 men (consisting of 100 men each from the 13th and 14th Battalions) to repeat the attack made by the first two waves. It, however, proved impracticable. The Turkish machine-gun fire had now become so hot as to block all advance, and when the third wave attempted to charge it was brought to a standstill, with the exception of Sgt. Bertram Edmonstone and a handful of men, who charged through and survived the deadly fusillade. Many were hit immediately[;] they appeared on the crest, and fell straight back into the gully. Some got a few yards and were wounded, or had to lie down in the scrub, the machine-gun bullets just grazing them. The fourth wave—consisting of a Hampshire battalion—had a similar experience. Scores were shot down, and it, too, failed to support the two leading waves, now isolated, and with no means of communication with their own lines, except over the fearful bullet-swept slope behind.[17]

Just as it had at Suvla, Turkish artillery fire set the dry scrub alight: "To add to the horrors of the day, an enemy shell set fire to the scrub on the hill just crossed by the attacking waves. As the fire spread it ignited the bombs carried by some of the dead lying scattered in the scrub, which, exploding, increased the area of fire. The plight of the hapless wounded was appalling. Some who tried to escape from the flames were shot down by the enemy's snipers. Little assistance could be rendered in daylight on the bullet-swept hill, though under cover of the smoke several wounded men were dragged away by the stretcher-bearers from near the fire. It was a night of horror; the cries of the wounded could be heard calling to their comrades."[18]

Fighting raged all night. The following morning the Eighteenth Battalion, AIF, which had literally just come ashore, was thrown into the assault. One of those who died was forty-two-year-old Pvt. Tom Varley, who claimed to have been thirty-seven when he enlisted the previous May. He also claimed to have served as a sergeant in the United States Army in Cuba during the Spanish-American War, yet this author could find no record of him having served in any capacity in the American forces or even having entered the country. In fact, he was a bricklayer who worked with his father. Before the battalion departed Egypt for the peninsula, he was found to be medically unfit and was going to be left behind with the battalion transport. But when a fellow soldier sprained his ankle, Varley grabbed his rifle and pack and took his place. He was one of the many declared missing after the attack.

The fighting continued for another week, with more units being thrown into the maelstrom. The final attack did not occur until

August 28. When all was said and done, the attackers held one side of the hill, and the defenders held the other. Both sides had been fought to a standstill, and it was to be the final major Allied offensive of the campaign. The fighting would continue, but it would consist mainly of raids and mining under the enemies' trenches.

The Suvla debacle resulted in a series of individual campaigns by officers, including Stopford, and two senior war correspondents, Ellis Ashmead-Bartlett and Keith Murdoch,[19] to expose the truth about Gallipoli. Earlier in the year the War Cabinet, which had been tasked with overseeing the conduct of the campaign from London, changed its name to the Dardanelles Committee. Meeting for the first time on June 7, this austere body was now considering the future of the campaign and whether or not it should be allowed to continue. After meeting on October 14, 1915, its members decided that Hamilton was chiefly to blame. He was ordered to return to England on October 16. Stunned by this turn of events, he was replaced by Lt. Gen. Sir Charles Monro, who had commanded both a division and a corps on the western front. Hamilton's incompetent chief of staff, Braithwaite, was also replaced. Thus, Hamilton and Braithwaite became the campaigns most famous—or infamous—casualties.

11

"Not *Actually* All the King's Men"
The Battles of July 12 and August 12

In modern times Gallipoli was brought to the attention of much of the English-speaking world when a movie by that title was released in 1981. In 2000 the film *All The King's Men* was released and purported to tell the story of the loss of the Norfolk Regiment's Sandringham Battalion at Suvla on August 12, 1915. Highly inaccurate and fanciful in the extreme, it did reflect one truth about the outcome of this small action. The loss of so many men of the 1/5th Battalion (TF), the Norfolk Regiment, which contained many employees of the Royal Sandringham Estate, did greatly concern King George V and Queen Mary. They were personally acquainted with several of the officers who went missing that day, not to mention the groundskeepers and gamekeepers serving in the ranks. And they wanted to know specifically what had become of their trusted servants.

In the film this incident, and the "mysterious" loss of so many men, was portrayed as a unique occurrence. In fact, it was anything but and had occurred on an even larger scale at Gallipoli once before. In that instance the king knew none of the missing men, and he showed no such concern for the massive casualty list that followed. What a pity, for each of the men who died over the course of that two-day battle was every bit as valuable as the king's servants were.

The Battle of Achi Baba Nullah, July 12–13, 1915

With the success of the Allied advances at Helles in June, Major General Hunter-Weston and General Bailloud knew that they had to advance the center of the line. They knew they had to do so quickly because each day gave the Turks more time to bring up reinforcements and dig more trenches. But the Battle of Gully Ravine and the successful French assaults along the Kereves Dere demonstrated to the British the importance of the French artillery and its invaluable high-explosive shells. The British knew that without them they had no hope for a successful advance. Unfortunately, the supply of French shells would not be replenished until July 11. Thus, July 12 was the day chosen for the British advance along the Achi Baba Nullah and a further advance by the French, again along the Kereves Dere.

As a result of heavy casualties suffered in the June battles, the British only had one division capable of making the assault. It was Major General Egerton's Fifty-Second (Lowland) Division, which hailed from the south of Scotland. One of its brigades, the 156th, had been reduced to a mere shadow of its old self on June 28 and was nothing like complete. It would therefore have to remain in reserve, to support the division's other two brigades.

The plan of attack was simple but was designed in such a way that the men who took part in it were doomed from the start. Egerton did not have many resources to work with, but he wanted to avoid the kind of massacre the 156th Brigade had recently suffered. According to his plan, the 155th Brigade on the right would attack at 7:35 a.m., supported by half of the French artillery (the other half would be supporting the French assault). On its left the 157th Brigade would wait until 4:50 p.m. to attack, after the French guns had shifted to back up its attack. The British front would measure a thousand yards across and that of the French, who would also attack at seven thirty-five, would be seven hundred yards. Egerton's reason for splitting the attack was that he wanted to devote as much artillery as possible to the Turkish positions. At the Battle of Gully Ravine his 156th

Brigade had been starved of artillery support and suffered massive casualties. As a result, the brigade's four battalions had to be combined into two. The French would attack trenches on the western edge of the Kereves Dere with four battalions of approximately five thousand men simultaneous with the attack of the 155th Brigade.

What Egerton seems to have overlooked was that as the troops on the right attacked, they would have no support on their left. The Turkish machine guns on their left could thus concentrate on them alone. He may also have failed to consider that the men of the 157th Brigade, who would have to wait for more than nine hours while the 155th attacked, would be experiencing a terribly high degree of anxiety. Not only had they never been in action before; they would have to suffer through the Turkish shelling that would occur in response to the attack, the screams of the wounded, and the awful thirst. Dressed in wool trousers, collarless cotton shirts, and with their equipment over that, they would be roasting as they crouched in their narrow, crowded trenches under a burning sun, tormented by lice and waiting for the signal to attack. The men of the 157th Brigade, who were Highlanders, wore the same uniform but with kilts instead of trousers (and nothing, according to regulations, underneath). The only water at their disposal was carried in their water bottles, and that was not nearly enough to sustain them. Some men would have difficulty maintaining their sanity; some simply could not. Showing his usual lack of understanding, Hunter-Weston agreed to Egerton's plan without suggesting any alterations.

The goals of the assaults were a series of Turkish trenches designated E10, E11, and E12 (along with the connecting F series), located southeast of Achi Baba Nullah. E10 was the front line, E11 the second, and E12 the reserve line. The two battalions on the flanks were only allotted two main trenches. On the far right the 1/4th Royal Scots Fusiliers were to attack E10 and E11 (E12 did not extend into their area of attack). On the far left the 1/6th Highland Light Infantry was to advance up Achi Baba Nullah. Its goals were the trenches E10 and F12. It was a confusing mass, constructed rapidly over the past month or two and badly laid out. Connected by a series of communication trenches, not all of which had been identified from aerial photographs, it would prove a tough nut to crack for the attacking Scots. The original map, dated July 5, showed only two lines of trenches, E10 and E11, but aerial photos taken days later showed a third line, designated E12. An analysis of the photos showed that E12 was not an actual trench or at least was not complete. Hunter-Weston and his staff knew that important detail but did not convey it to the officers who were to lead the attack.

The first two waves were to charge over E10 and E11 and on to capture E12. The third wave would advance to take the second line, E11, and the fourth would hold E10. Royal Engineers were to follow and turn the parapets. They were also supposed to run telephone lines from the new front line back to the rear and dig communication trenches from the captured Turkish trenches back to the British lines. Some of the attacking infantrymen were to carry picks, spades, and empty sandbags for the engineers, who would be heavily laden with tools and spools of wire. Medics from the division's field ambulances would establish dressing stations as close to the front lines as they could and help the battalion stretcher-bearers bring in the wounded.

In this attack, as in the two previous major assaults at Helles, artillery observers would rely on the sun to help gauge the progress of the infantry. Every third soldier was to wear a tin disc, cut from a Huntley & Palmer's biscuit tin, stitched to his pack. Men would also carry kerosene or petrol tins forward to lay on the edge of the forward captured Turkish trench, in the hopes that the reflective metal would catch the rays of the sun. But once again, this innovation would assist the defenders. They, too, would be able to see the reflections, robbing the Scots of the camouflage afforded by nature.

Bullets fired in the confines of a trench can be disastrous for defender and attacker alike, so the Scots had orders to use only their bayonets. Their magazines would be charged (loaded), but they were not to have "one up the spout." That is, they were not to chamber a round out of fear that rifles might go off accidentally.

In addition to the divided nature of the attack, Egerton had built another problem into the plan. He decreed that none of the officers could carry maps or other documents into the assault, which meant that they would have to do the impossible. He expected them to remember every communication trench connecting the three trench lines. He did not want anything to fall into the enemy hands. To imagine that tired, overstressed, and inexperienced men would be able to memorize the maze of trenches that formed the Turkish lines was ridiculous in its conception and proved to be so in reality. After the assault the diarist for the 155th Brigade quoted a remark by Lt. Col. William Peebles, commanding officer of the 1/7th Royal Scots: "I would like to point out the extreme difficulty of working without a map or sketch of such intricate trenches. It was impossible to give or understand any orders given until a rough sketch from memory was given, usually incorrect in important points."[1]

Despite his shortcomings as a planner, Egerton did care about his troops. He was still reeling from the loss of so many men of his 156th Brigade. So, he decided that each battalion would send 10 percent of its men and all but three officers from each company to the rear. In the case of the 1/4th King's Own Scottish Borderers (KOSB), this would amount to 20 men and 2 officers per company. The number was roughly the same for the other battalions. This arrangement would reduce his division's attacking strength to only 208 officers and 7,540 men against the entire Turkish Seventh Division, but it would also give him an immediate reserve to draw from if needed and one that could carry supplies to the attacking troops. He would need this reserve because none of the other divisions in the sector were anywhere near fighting strength. The only other formation at his disposal was the Royal Marine Brigade, but it was understrength due to battle and illness. There was simply no fresh force from which to draw.

On July 12 the attackers arose at three o'clock in the morning. They breakfasted and cleared their trenches of rubbish and unnecessary kit so that men could move along their narrow confines. The sun began rising at a quarter to four, and everyone knew that they were in for a blazing hot day. Even at that early hour, there was neither a cloud in the sky nor a refreshing breeze.

"Not Actually All the King's Men"

The number of shells available was massive by British standards. Each of the three main bombardments—the two on the French and 155th Brigade's fronts and that of the 157th—was allotted five hundred howitzer shells and four thousand high-explosive shells for the field guns. The French artillery opened its bombardment at four thirty in the morning; its main barrage began at 6:55 a.m. The accurately placed high-explosive rounds killed or wounded most of the Ottoman defenders and caused many of the survivors to flee to the safety of the communication trenches. Their trenches were completely ruined and were turned into a veritable moonscape covered in debris, the dead, and the wounded.

When the French artillery opened fire, Turkish guns responded by firing into the French lines. One of their shells struck a particularly vital target, the dugout occupied by the First Division's staff. Maj. Joseph Vassal wrote: "We had a big fight on the 12th, and I had all the wounded to evacuate. The 1st Division is completely reorganized. Before the advance began at 7.15 [sic] a huge '105' shell fell on Post A of the divisional command. Major Romieux, Chief of Staff, aged 45, was killed outright. General Masnou had his skull pushed in and his knee laid open. There were also wounded Colonel Bulleux, Captain Berge, Captain Boissonas, many non-commissioned officers and soldiers." Commandant Jacques Romieux, the divisional staff major, was killed next to Masnou. He was actually forty-three, not forty-five, at the time of his death and had served in the army since 1891. Masnou did not survive his wounds. Vassal continued: "At first I got on rather badly with him because I held my own, but afterwards he loved our discussions. It is terrible to see a man like that die—a man of prodigious energy and unequalled activity and intelligence."[2] Command of the division temporarily devolved to Lt. Col. Louis Vernhol.

At 7:35 a.m. the French artillery shifted to targets farther inland. At the same time, the Scots climbed out of their trenches and charged, yelling, toward E10. The first waves of the 1/4th Royal Scots Fusiliers and 1/4th KOSB leaped from a trench called "Parsons Road." The second waves, from the same battalions, attacked from the support line behind, called "Trotman Road." Simultaneous with the first two waves, the third and fourth waves leaped out of their trenches. After the four waves went over the top, the 1/5th Royal Scots Fusiliers moved forward and garrisoned Parsons Road. Their job was also to dig communication trenches forward from that trench to E10.

The French artillery was so effective that few of the Scots were hit as they ran the fifty yards to E10. Most of the defenders were dead or wounded when the Scots leaped over them, and only the odd Turk dared to lift his bayonet-tipped rifle in an effort to skewer one of the attackers. This was true for the 1/4th KOSB, but the Fusiliers were hit almost immediately by Turkish machine guns firing from their right flank. Nevertheless, the first waves managed to cross what was left of E10 and make for E11.

As the two waves approached E11, about 250 yards farther on, they were hit by machine guns firing from their right and left. The luck of the KOSB ran out as the Turkish gunners targeted both battalions. Not only that, but exploding artillery rounds set fire to the scrub, making visibility difficult for the attackers trying to find their way through the smoke. The Turks used the opportunity to target the Scots as they tried to get their bearings.

The artillery was so successful at mangling the Turkish trenches and breaking up the barbed wire that the Scots came across a mass of broken ground that was even more confusing than the maps they had seen. Individual Turks and isolated groups fired at the attackers, who had difficulty moving over the broken ground. Orders stated that the Fusiliers were to halt there and consolidate their gains while at the same time establishing contact with the French on their right (which they did). The 1/4th KOSB was supposed to leap across E11 and charge on to E12.

The Fusiliers stopped to deal with the last of the resistance in their portion of E11 and to rebuild the demolished trench. Yet they could not overcome those Turks holding the right of the trench—the portion that ran into the Kereves Dere—and this area would continue to be a thorn in their side. The surviving Borderers charged forward in search of E12. What they found was a scrape in the ground where the trench was supposed to be.

"Not Actually All the King's Men"

Many of the surviving Borderers reported that they thought E12 was a "dummy trench." This is doubtful. It is more likely that it was just the beginning of a trench or even a natural depression resembling a trench from the air. Either way, there was no cover for the attackers, and about twenty of them began digging in. The rest, believing that E12 was actually somewhere ahead, continued on in the direction of Achi Baba. Most were never seen again, but thirteen were captured by the Turks in the shallow trench labeled "ST" on the maps. One of them, Pvt. Alexander Nixon, recalled after the war: "Men fell like corn below the scythe. Major Herberton, lying on his side, was waving his revolver and urging us on. I managed to get to the farthest point, that was the third Turkish trench or dummy trench. It was about one foot deep, and we had to set to fill in sandbags. We were packed together and enfiladed from the left . . . Our fire rapidly diminished, till there was no one left to fire. Then I was knocked out. When I came to, our little trench was occupied by a Turk to every two yards. Four or five of our men were lying across me, and I could not get up. I was bayoneted six times in the back while lying there . . . A Turk officer, at the point of his revolver, ordered the Turks to release me."[3]

Before long the Scots realized that their position was untenable, and the battalion commander, Lt. Col. John McNeile, ordered a retreat to E11. He was one of the many who never made it back from E12. He and his adjutant, Capt. James Lang, were killed. Command of the battalion devolved to Maj. William Cochrane, the second-in-command, who recorded in the battalion's war diary: "After advancing a distance of some 400 to 500 yds. Col. McNeile who commanded and was at the front leading the Battn said to me 'we are too far forward, we must get back.' I replied 'Very well, Sir, I'll stop the men and get them back.' The Third trench was seen during the advance or when going back. Casualties were not very heavy during the advance, but when going back the Battn had to pass through the zone of fire of our own artillery, also the fire from the enemy's artillery, machine guns and rifles, causing heavy losses. We then occupied part of the second trench which we commenced consolidating."[4]

As the Scots ran for the safety of E11, which was being consolidated by the 1/5th KOSB, the Turks spotted the reflections of the tin discs on their packs. It was a bloodbath that was made worse by the French artillerymen, who saw the running khaki figures through the shimmering haze of the sweltering summer heat and assumed they were Turks. Few survived to greet their comrades in the 1/5th Battalion. Among the other ranks to fall was Pvt. Adam Smail. Known as "Addie" to his friends, one of them wrote in a letter home: "I have just heard from the Orderley Room that Addie's identity disc, pay book, and bundle of letters belonging to him, were handed in yesterday by the French authorities. The reason for the French people getting them is that they now occupy the part of the line from which our advance took place, so evidently some patrol of theirs had come upon the bodies. There were several others found at the same time. Whilst this will put an end to your suspense, it does not lessen your grief."[5]

Most of the men killed that day were listed as missing and their remains were never recovered. The officers suffered particularly, leading their men into the battered Turkish trench line with revolvers in hand. Of the thirteen officers in the 1/4th KOSB who died at Gallipoli, twelve died that day. One was Lt. James Innes: "Lieut. J. B. Innes, although mortally wounded and with blood streaming down his face, continued to advance until he was wounded a second time, on this occasion fatally. Pipe-Major Bertram spoke to him as he lay dying, and his last words were—'I'm done for.' Poor Innes got one of his arms blown to bits by a shell, and after getting his cousin, Lieut. W. K. Innes, to cut it off, asked for a cigarette."[6]

The following day Innes was buried in a shallow grave near E10 by men from his battalion. Had he made it to the safety of his battalion's dressing station, he may have been treated by the battalion medical officer, Maj. David Taylor. A physician with twenty-two years of experience behind him, he, too, became a victim that day: "We lost our doctor. Sgt.-Mjr. Murray and I were standing not far away when this shell burst, the shrapnel just got him in the head."[7] The battalion lost 60 percent of its strength that day, the first time it saw action in the Great War.

The 1/5th KOSB had the job of consolidating E10 and E11. Not only were the men caught in the open by Turkish machine gun and artillery fire; they also had to contend with the Turks who had taken shelter in the maze of communication trenches. For them the fighting was hard as they grappled with the defenders in the confined spaces that had once been trenches and as they tried to move over the dead. The Scots were eventually victorious, but they paid a high price for their little bit of real estate.

Pvt. James Beattie of the 1/5th Battalion was wounded in the attack. On July 17, 1915, he wrote a letter to his father from his hospital bed in Cairo:

We have had a terrible cutting up in our battalion. On Sunday morning, 11th July, we got orders to pack up all our belongings. We thought we were going away for a rest to a little island called Embros [Imbros], but soon we found out where we were going when we marched back up to the reserve trenches. At six o'clock at night we were told there was to be a charge made in the early morning. The battalion was quite cheery that evening. We had an early start next morning, and at three o'clock we were standing to arms. Breakfast was to be past by five o'clock, and everything ready for the charge at 7.35. I think every man put up his prayer before that time. It was the day of days. I am sure I will never forget it as long as I live. When the word was passed along fifteen minutes before the time, every man was ready for the fray. It came to ten minutes, five minutes, two minutes, then—"Get ready to charge." The shrapnels were bursting all over us. When we were charging the Turks it was pure slaughter. It was something awful to see your comrades fall at your feet. I got over to the Turkish trench we had to take without a scratch. I thought I was lucky, but not a quarter of an hour had passed when I was struck on the forehead with a shrapnel bullet. I did not know where I was. It was my helmet that saved me from being killed. I was watching a Turk lying on the ground with his face down. I noticed him move, and I was getting my rifle up to shoot him when

I was laid low. I was sent straight away to the hospital boat, and it was filled up that night with 1700 aboard. We sailed next day to Alexandria, but the hospitals there were filled up, so we came to Cairo in the train. A terrible lot of Dumfries lads are down.[8]

The battalion lost more than two hundred men killed and wounded.

Egerton was forced to commit the last of his reserves to the first half of the attack. Having none for the second, he telephoned Eighth Corps Headquarters and asked for more men. He knew that there were none readily available, but Hunter-Weston realized that he had to come up with some if the attack was going to continue. So, rather than chastise his divisional commander for squandering his meager resources, he allowed the Royal Marine Brigade—less the Deal Battalion—to move forward from the corps reserve. Hunter-Weston stated, however, that before Egerton could use them, he must first ask permission. Egerton knew better than to argue. At eight o'clock that night Hunter-Weston ordered the three battalions forming the brigade—Chatham, Portsmouth, and Nelson (filling in for the Deal Battalion)—to move up to the Trotman Road and Parsons Road trenches. The brigade was under the command of Brig. Gen. Charles Trotman, RMLI, who was also acting commander of the Royal Naval Division.

During the assault confusing reports were sent back to Egerton, who did not know what the real situation was. To make matters worse, the staff officers whom he had sent forward to find out had failed to return. All were wounded or temporarily lost in the confusion that pervaded the front line. The only thing he could tell his commanding officer was that his brigade had been badly beaten up, and this made Hunter-Weston question the sense of ordering the 157th Brigade to attack. Egerton argued in favor of the assault, stating that it would take pressure off the 155th Brigade and allow it to strengthen its positions. Hunter-Weston agreed, and more lives were lost. The territory was captured, however, and later turned over to the French. The Royal Marine Brigade attacked the following day but had to do so over open ground because the newly dug

"Not Actually *All the King's Men"*

communication trenches leading to E10 were too crowded. The result was a bit more ground for the British but hardly enough to justify the number of lives lost. Douglas Jerrold of the Hawke Battalion wrote: "The only thing to be said [about the Third Battle of Krithia on June 4] was that the chaos was less than after the relatively successful advance of July 13. On that occasion it was indescribable, just hundreds of men wandering about in the captured trench system in the burning sun, with corpses blackened and stinking lining the old Turkish firing steps, the sinister symmetry of their position being the only sign of any method at all. The redeeming feature of that occasion was A. P. Herbert's instruction to the sentries on his platoon frontage. 'Remember, regard all Turks with the gravest suspicion.'"[9]

The Assault across the Kuchak Anafarta Ova

August 12, 1915

Among the Territorial Force (TF) battalions that fought at Suvla was the 1/5th Battalion (TF), the Norfolk Regiment, which belonged to the 163rd Brigade of the Fifty-Fourth (East Anglian) Division. Today the unit is often termed the "Sandringham Battalion" because one of its prewar companies consisted in part of men employed on the Royal Estate at Sandringham in Norfolk. In fact, this group formed only a small part of the battalion, and the company in which it served, E, ceased to exist in January 1915. At that time British army infantry battalions switched from an eight- to a four-company structure, and the men were dispersed.

E Company was formed in 1908 at the behest of King Edward VII and was known then as the Sandringham Company. A fan of the Territorial Force, the king asked Frank Beck, the estate's agent, to form a company of employees in an effort to show his devotion to the Territorial scheme. Beck, already a captain in the Fifth Norfolks, would be its commander, despite the fact that he had no combat experience. Two of his nephews, Albert (known as Alec) and Arthur Beck, also became officers in the company. The company's strength was the same as every British infantry company, one hundred men. Like every infantry battalion, the 1/5th Norfolks consisted of about a thousand officers and men. The battalion was mobilized for war service on August 5, 1914, and volunteered for Imperial (foreign) service on September 20.

Norfolk, a largely rural county, did not have enough men to support more than one infantry regiment. Two of its Territorial Force battalions, the 1/4th and 1/5th, served together at Gallipoli. In common with other TF units, the companies consisted of men drawn from specific areas, with many family members, friends, and work mates serving together. Sending such a battalion into combat could result in devastating losses for communities.

When war was declared, TF soldiers were not automatically required to serve with their units overseas. They were given the option of volunteering, and those who did were issued a sterling silver Imperial Service Badge to wear over the right breast pockets of their tunics.[10] In nearly every account of the First World War, one reads that all of the men in a given unit volunteered, often "cheerfully," to serve overseas. In fact, this was not always the case. The regimental historian of the Royal Sussex Regiment noted of the men of the 1/5th Battalion: "Shortly after their arrival at Mile End [following the battalion's mobilization] the men were asked to volunteer for service overseas. This came as a surprise to some who had not realized the national character of the war and that the fighting would not be confined to regular armies, nor even to belligerents. However, about three-quarters of the battalion agreed, those unable to respond to the call forming the nucleus of a new battalion, the 2/5th. The 1/5th, by means of recruitment, were soon able to complete their establishment."[11]

Like most of the TF battalions that served at Gallipoli, the 1/5th Norfolks were trained in drill and nineteenth-century-type field exercises but were definitely not prepared for the kind of war being fought in 1915. Many Territorial officers had no active service behind them, and this certainly applied to the Sandringham Battalion. Eager for action they were, but ready for war they were not. What practi-

"Not Actually All the King's Men"

cal training they did have came from old sergeants who had served in the Boer War and on India's Northwest Frontier, but there were not many seasoned officers. Most of the experienced soldiers had been tapped for service on the western front in 1914, and many never lived to hear about Gallipoli.

The 1/5th Norfolks were led by Lt. Col. Sir Horace Proctor-Beauchamp, a religious man who was liked by his men but was not popular with his officers. He had retired from the army in 1904 and was recalled to command the battalion ten years later. He had extensive combat experience with the Twentieth Hussars in India, the Sudan, and the Boer War but absolutely no experience leading infantry. All of his fighting experience was on horseback and in open country against a mobile enemy. He was thus unable to lend practical advice on infantry tactics to his junior officers, and this was especially true of the battalion's adjutant, Capt. Arthur Ward. A regular officer in the First Norfolks, he was attached to the Fifth Battalion in 1912 and was not at all pleased with his new posting. He was constantly at odds with the other officers and had nothing but contempt for what he termed "part time amateurs."

In addition to the Norfolks, the 163rd Brigade consisted of the 1/4th Battalion (TF), the Norfolk Regiment; the 1/5th Battalion (TF), the Suffolk Regiment; and the 1/8th Battalion (Princess Beatrice's Isle of Wight Rifles) (TF), the Hampshire Regiment. One might surmise that because most of the men in the brigade had served in the Territorials for years, they would have been well skilled at arms. In fact, the opposite was true. They knew well enough how to march and polish their boots, but these skills would not impress the Turks. Since the outbreak of war, more time was devoted to marching and digging trenches along the coast to guard against an expected German invasion than was spent in training for modern warfare.

The 163rd Brigade landed at A Beach, Suvla, on August 10. The men were astounded at the confusion they encountered. Casualties were lying all over, awaiting evacuation. Supplies were coming in, stragglers were milling about, and the odd shell fell among the tangled mass of men and transport animals. After gathering themselves together from the array of boats in which they had come ashore, they moved inland to their assigned bivouacs. Apparently, no thought was given to the fact that they required a spell in the trenches with experienced troops, as was the custom. If it was considered, it was not done. The next day the battalions moved two miles inland to help dig trenches and perform other tasks.

On August 12 the staff of the 163rd Brigade was notified that its four battalions were to go into action for the first time. Their task was to clear the Kuchak Anafarta Ova (Little Anafarta Plain) of snipers so that the Fifty-Fourth Division could attack Kavak Tepe at dawn on August 13. None of the men knew anything about the ground over which they were to advance or the ultimate goal of their attack. They were simply told to head for the Turkish lines, the exact whereabouts of which were unknown, and to dig in for the night. The officers received their orders at 3:45 p.m. and were handed their maps. The maps turned out to be various issues, all of the Anzac sector, which were recalled shortly afterward. They were then given a variety of maps of the Suvla sector, and it was immediately apparent that they were both inaccurate and lacked obvious geographical features. Would they be covered by other troops on their flanks, the officers asked? Those who issued the orders did not know. In fact, there would be none. To make matters worse, the battalions were not given time to send scouts out to learn about the area the riflemen would be advancing through, nor was there time for the men to fill their water bottles.

At 4:45 p.m., following a short bombardment, the men began their advance. The 1/5th Suffolks were on the left, the 1/8th Hampshires were in the center, and the 1/5th Norfolks were on the right. The 1/4th Norfolks, who had been unloading stores from supply vessels until shortly before the attack, were in reserve. Each of the attacking battalions was to walk abreast, three of their four companies in front and one behind, in reserve. Each battalion consisted of roughly eight hundred men.

The men moved quickly over the parched, broken field—so fast, in fact, that some of them had to struggle to keep up. But it was not

"Not Actually *All the King's Men"*

long before the heat under their webbing began to build up. Not able to stop for a drink of tepid water, the men began shedding equipment instead. Not long after the advance began, men started to fall. Their sun helmets made them look like so many yellowish mushrooms moving forward in a line. The reflections off of their gleaming bayonets, fixed under the muzzles of rifles carried at port arms, did not help. They were perfect targets for the Turks. None of the attackers could see the enemy, but the enemy could certainly see them. Snipers and shrapnel rounds took their toll, but the advancing riflemen did not stop to return fire or help the injured. Their orders were to leave the wounded where they fell; stretcher-bearers would follow and carry them to safety. The officers, identified by their distinctive uniforms, brown leather Sam Browne belts, and the revolvers they carried, were among the first to be picked off.

Under normal conditions the battalions' machine gun would have been emplaced before the attack, to support to the attacking riflemen. No time was given for them to do so, however, and the inexperienced machine gun officers had no idea how to function under the circumstances. The Machine Gun Officer of the 1/8th Hampshires had to rely on the battalion's bandsmen, who worked as stretcher-bearers in combat, to carry his guns and their tripods forward on their stretchers. For a while the battalions were able to maintain contact via runners. But as the men advanced farther and the field became more broken, contact was lost, and the units acted independently.

At some point, as the firing became heavier and casualties began to mount, the Norfolks veered off to the right. Eventually, they advanced out of site of the Hampshires on their left and into a wooded area, dotted with farmers' stone outbuildings. There many of them were surrounded and either killed or captured. Among them was the battalion's commanding officer, Proctor-Beauchamp: "We got up to some buildings, which I took for a kind of block-house, and I heard the colonel, who was not far from me, order someone to see if there was anyone in this place. There appeared to be nobody there, and we went straight on. I believe he was hit in the arm by a bullet. I saw Lance-Corporal Beales bandaging him up. We were resting between the rushes, and he ordered us to have a drink out of our bottles before we went any further."[12] He was never seen alive again, nor was his nephew, Lt. Montagu Proctor-Beauchamp: "Lieutenant Beauchamp, who had been by my side all the time, turned to me as I fell [wounded] and said to me: 'I am very sorry, Jakeman, but we must go through with it.' And on he went with his men—what there were left."[13]

So many men were lost in the assault and the survivors' were so badly affected by their first experience of combat that few accounts of the loss of the battalions' other members survive. Because of the confusion that day, the accounts that do exist rarely note where a man fell: "The last I saw of Capt. Pattrick, who was in command of our company, was soon after the attack commenced. He was just then behind my section, and was urging the men on. He was not more than 20 yards away from me, and we had not gone more than half a mile. I did not see the captain again."[14]

Cpl. Donald Foster had the misfortune of seeing his friend Pvt. Joseph Bentley die: "You will no doubt have seen by the papers that our battalion has been in action, and unfortunately we have not come out of the ordeal without some casualties, and it is with the greatest regret and sorrow that I have to tell you that Joe was killed last Sunday afternoon. He, at the time, was fighting side by side with Jack, and a piece of shell hit him in the head. I cannot possibly describe my feelings as I give you this sad news, but trust you will find room in your hearts to forgive me breaking the news to you. I feel that I cannot offer sympathy in words, but my heart and prayers are for you all."[15]

As the attackers advanced deeper into Turkish territory, too far away for reinforcements to reach them, they were surrounded in the outbuildings and shot down by Ottoman riflemen. Some were wounded and captured. Some of the wounded were finished off by the Turks. Among them were A Company's commanding officer, Capt. Arthur Pattrick, and Acting Sgt. Ernest Beart. Both were last seen cut off in the group of buildings and being disarmed by their captors.

"Not Actually All the King's Men"

Neither was ever heard from again, and it may safely be assumed that they were summarily executed. Others shared the same fate.

The most notable member of the battalion to fall was Capt. Frank Beck, known to his friends as "Black." Pvt. John Dye described seeing him that fateful day: "When we were advancing I saw Captain Beck walking with his stick just the same as he did at Sandringham, putting it down at the same time as he did his left foot. He might have been seen with his hat off or with his revolver in his hand when we were in the thick of it, but I did not see him that way . . . I saw him last in a sitting position under a tree, with his head leaning over on his right shoulder. He had got a bit ahead of me. I do not know whether he was then alive."[16] Eventually, the survivors who could extricate themselves did so after being ordered to retreat. They left 14 officers and 137 other ranks dead behind them, not to mention several wounded who could not be retrieved and a number who were captured.

Somehow over the years the story of the 1/5th Norfolks's advance has become corrupted. Many historians and some of their contemporaries have related that not one member of the battalion survived the day's action. Moreover, they have managed to turn a common occurrence of war into a mystery. In fact, hundreds did survive, and the battalion would see further action at Gallipoli. The loss of so many members of the battalion, a loss smaller than that suffered by many battalions at Gallipoli, was quite common. In this instance, however, there was a difference. The king had a personal interest. Beck was a friend of King George V. Additionally, the king recognized the faces of many of the men serving on the Sandringham Estate, though it could hardly be said that he knew many of them. It was because of this association that he raised questions about their fate, questions that he did not broach about the loss of men in other battles. Those present at Gallipoli, whether they were in the 163rd Brigade or not, knew exactly what happened. The men had advanced too far, away from reinforcements and artillery, and were either killed or captured. It had happened before, and it would happen again.

In this instance the king wanted answers, and he expected Hamilton to provide them. The general could not. Yet even at the time of the attack, King George was unconcerned about the loss: "The Brigade of the LIVth [Fifty-Fourth Division] sent on to Kuchuk Anafarta Ova made good its point. True, one battalion got separated from its comrades in the forest and was badly cut up by Turkish snipers just as was Braddock's force by the Redskins, but this, though tragic, is but a tiny incident of a great modern battle and the rest of the 163rd Brigade have not suffered and hold the spot whence, it was settled, the attack on Kavak Tepe should jump off. Nothing practical or tactical seems to have occurred to force us to drop our plan."[17]

Most of the Norfolks killed on August 12 were killed so far forward of the British front line that their bodies could not be recovered for burial. They joined the legions of men listed as missing, a word that terrified people back home. So many of the battalion's officers were lost—it was they who were responsible for keeping the unit's records—that August 12th's casualties were officially listed as having gone missing on or after August 28. On July 25, 1916, the War Office determined that "in accordance with the decision of the Army Council [these soldiers are] to be regarded for official purposes as having died on or since August 28, 1915."

Many of the Norfolks who "disappeared" on August 12 were found after the war. Their bodies had been dumped by the farmer who returned home and found them on his land. They were identified by their metal cap badges and shoulder titles. Even during the campaign, however, patrols managed to find evidence of the battalion's casualties. Beck's checkbook and pocketbook were found and returned to his family. Oddly, his remains were not found. His gold Hunter pocket watch was located after the war. The Turkish general Musta Bey, commander of the sector in which Beck and his men fell, had it and agreed to sell it to the British authorities in Constantinople. It was given to Beck's daughter Margaret as a gift on her wedding day.

Whenever a patrol came across the remains of a friendly casualty, it would report the find and, if possible, recover the man's identity disc and paybook. It might also bury him, but there was usually no opportunity. Sgt. John Goulder of the 1/5th Norfolks was an exception. During the assault on August 12 he was among the outbuildings with Maj. Walter Barton and Capt. Anthony Knight, discussing their next move, when he was shot in the head by a Turk who was hiding in a tree. Knight, who survived the attack (as did Barton), grabbed the sergeant's rifle and shot the sniper. But like every other man killed there, Goulder's body was left where it was when the survivors retreated. The following October his remains were found by men of the recently arrived First Battalion, the Newfoundland Regiment:

> The block house we held stood just in the center of the line that the Fifth Norfolks had charged into early in August, and from which not one man had emerged. The second or third day we occupied it, a detachment of engineers was sent in to make loopholes and prepare it for a stubborn defense. In the wall on the left they made a large loophole. The sentry posted there the first morning saw about twenty feet away the body of a British soldier, partly buried. Two volunteers to bury the body were asked for. Half a dozen offered, although it was broad daylight and the place the body lay in offered no protection.
>
> Before any one could be selected, Art Pratt and young Hayes made the decision by jumping up, taking their picks and shovels, and vaulting over the wall of the block house. They walked out to where the body lay. It had been torn in pieces by a shell the previous afternoon. At first a few bullets tore up little spurts of ground near the two men, but as soon as they reached the body, this stopped. The Turks never fired on burial parties . . .
>
> When the enemy saw the object of the little expedition, they allowed Art and Hayes to proceed unmolested. We watched them dig a grave beside the corpse; and when they had finished, with a shovel they turned the body into it. Before doing it, they searched the man for personal papers and took off his identity disk. These bore the name "Sergeant Golder [sic], Fifth Norfolk Regiment."

That was in the last part of October; and since August 10th [*sic*] not a word had been heard of the missing Norfolk regiment. To this day, the whole affair remains a mystery. The regiment disappeared as if the ground had swallowed them up . . .

Two hundred and fifty men were given the order to charge into a wood. The only sign that they ever did so, is the little wooden cross that reads

IN MEMORY OF

SERGEANT J GOLDER

FIFTH NORFOLK REGIMENT

KILLED IN ACTION.[18]

Goulder, one of four brothers serving in the army in 1915, had turned his farm over to a friend to manage when he marched off to war in 1914. Two of his brothers also died in the war.

As one looks back on the actions of July 12 and August 12, one is struck by the sadness of so many lives lost for such a useless cause. The events are much more moving when one considers that many of those lost were lifelong friends, some related, and that their communities were so hard hit on a single day. What seems unforgivable, however, is that their king should have been so unmoved by the loss of one group, while that of the other evoked so much emotion for him. Perhaps if every world leader were as moved as King George V was by the loss of his servants on August 12, 1915, the First World War would truly have been the "War to End All Wars."

12

"And All Suffered Severely"

The Great Storm, November 27–28, 1915

August saw the end of the major battles. It was also the last full month of hellaciously hot weather. Sapper George Davies of the Royal Marine Engineers wrote about the change in a letter home on August 29: "It is getting cooler at nights, and the last 2 days here have been cooler. I shall be mightily glad when it is a good deal colder. It will be terrible, though, if we are here when the rainy season starts. Our dug outs will just be under water & what will become of us goodness knows. All I hope is that we are off the Peninsula by then." The change in temperature was gradual and, like everything else at Gallipoli, could also be harsh: "The weather has broken, and we get a strong wind blowing each day now, frequently developing into a gale. A cold wind is now and again thrown in, and at nights we get a little rain. It is very rough, and difficulty is being experienced in landing stuff."[1]

This downpour was the beginning of a gradual cooling period. Indeed, the Allies knew that winter could bring harsh conditions. They knew that when winter arrived in all its glory, it could have an adverse effect on even the heartiest of men. As it was, none of the troops could be described as hearty. Nearly all were suffering from debility and one form of disease or another, chiefly dysentery, and the change in weather exacerbated their suffering. Even though the rations began improving after the August battles, it was too little too late. The damage was already done. The fighting had diminished considerably, but conditions on both sides of the line were as bad as ever.

One thing did improve for the Turks. With Bulgaria's entry into the war on the side of the Central Powers on September 6, 1915, Turkey's armaments were strengthened considerably. Bulgaria's entry allowed Germany to supply its eastern ally by rail. Guns and shells allowed the Ottoman gunners to strike the Allies even harder with a seemingly endless supply of munitions. For the British the only noteworthy addition to their arsenal was the Mills bomb. This factory-made weapon was Britain's first safe and effective hand grenade, but very few made it to the peninsula. Most of the early stocks were sent to the western front.

The British anticipated a hard winter at Gallipoli. They took pains to begin preparing for it after the failure of the August battles and with the realization that neither side would be going anywhere soon. At a meeting of the Dardanelles Commission in London on August 31, Sir Ernest Wedderburn was appointed to the Mediterranean Expeditionary Force. A noted meteorologist, he had written about the correlation between weather and ballistics and seemed a natural choice for the position. He forecast the really harsh winter weather to hit in January 1916.

While tunnelers worked to undermine Turkish positions in the front lines, engineers added more piers along the coast to accommodate the arrival of winter supplies. Among the specialist units imported for the job was the Royal Australian Naval Bridging Train, which constructed piers at Suvla. Headquartered at Kangaroo Beach, the naval sappers only ever ventured near the front lines to look for souvenirs. But the unit did lose four men during the campaign, two of them to shells and two to disease. Chief Petty Officer Artificer (Farrier) Ted Perkins was one of the two lost in action. He was killed when a shell landed on Kangaroo Beach on September 6, 1915. Three days later his commanding officer, Lt. Cdr. Leighton Bracegirdle, wrote to the man's mother: "He was sitting in his

"And All Suffered Severely"

'dugout' with a mate, on the forenoon of the 6th September, when a Turkish shell entered the corner of his dugout and the poor chap he was killed instantly and his mate (Lonie) was wounded." Able Bodied (AB) Seaman Driver Roy Fell later recounted that he was on duty at Kangaroo that day when it was shelled. He took cover near one of the piers when a piece of meat landed near his foot. He initially wondered who would be throwing food at him, before discovering that it was part of Perkins's brain.

The other casualty was AB Driver Charlie Schwenke. He was erecting a water tank with three other men at Kangaroo when the shells started to fall. His job was to paint the completed structure. Before he got the chance to begin, he was hit in the head with two shrapnel balls. Three days later he died on a hospital ship. On September 12, 1915, his sister Freda recorded in her diary what happened when news of his death arrived: "Captain Perkins, a chaplain, came to see the family. For some reason I was ill and home from work. Mum sang out that the minister was here. The next minute Mum was screaming like mad and I rushed up to the front room to see what was wrong. The minister had told her that Charlie was dead. Everyone had been getting mail from loved ones away fighting, but Mum wondered why she wasn't getting any letters. The minister said that the soldiers had been in dugouts waiting for the bombing to start and everything was quiet so Charlie, who loved to play the mouth-organ, stood up and started to play. Unexpectedly a shell came over and exploded near the dugout and Charlie received head injuries. Poor Charlie was placed on board a ship to be taken to hospital but died and was buried at sea."

During the summer Dominion troops dressed for the season: "The Australians and the New Zealanders have given up wearing clothes. They lie about and bathe and become darker than Indians. The General objects to this. 'I suppose,' he says, 'we shall have our servants waiting on us like that.'"[2] In fact, many Anzacs cut their trousers down to shorts using the only tools available: their jack-knives. With no scissors available, they turned their garments into very rough-looking articles indeed, with short, ragged legs of varying lengths. Because they also had no way to measure their work, the initial cuts were always of unequal length, which meant that continued cuts to even up the two sides resulted in some very short shorts indeed.

With the change in weather, men began changing their cutoff trousers for full-length pairs. Others wrote home to request winter clothing, knowing the army's lack of common sense when it came to issuing uniforms suited to the climate. Sapper George Davies asked his parents for warm clothing in a letter home on October 14, 1915:

> I hope we get served out with sweaters, otherwise we shall freeze. I left my two sweaters in my kit bag, and so may never see them again. The one I had from the Llantwit people was such a ripping one, too. I tell you what you can buy for me, & send immediately, that is a <u>cheap oilskin</u>, say cost 12/- or 15/-[shillings] no more, get a drab coloured one. Please draw from my money for it. I am certainly not going to let you pay for all the things you send. Also send a pair of mittens (Pauline can probably get these things), no fingers, but half a thumb on, & a muffler. I suppose we better ask for these things now, for heaven only knows when we shall have our longed for rest & be re-equipped. In time, more than likely, the authorities will serve us out with things, but an oilskin will be a boon. Get a long one, reaching down almost to one's boots.

By late October the change in weather was pronounced. Davies wrote home on the twenty-eighth: "The Weather: O! it has become very changeable. Last Sat. & Sunday it was cold enough for snow, a very cold North wind blowing, seemed to pierce your bones. Thursday: it rained almost all day; we kept nice & dry in the dug out [*sic*]. Monday there was a huge change, it being a most glorious day, as hot as on an English midsummer's day. Tues. was rather cool, the rest of the days have been warm, not as much sunshine. The nights are warm again. Nov. is supposed to be the nicest month of the year here." Davies's last sentence expressed a common belief, which was exacerbated by the official proclamation, that January would be the

"And All Suffered Severely"

worst month of winter. Fortunately, supplies for the winter dugouts were requested in late August, and the new piers would be there to welcome the shipments of corrugated iron and timber.

The proclamation about the weather was wrong. Terribly wrong. The weather changed in November, and neither side was prepared. On November 26 a torrent occurred that dwarfed the earlier storms. Trenches on both sides were flooded. Men and animals were washed away in the rushing waters and drowned. The terrain at Anzac is one of extremes: flat fields, rocky hills, and gullies. Because many of the ANZAC, British, and Indian troops there were quartered on high ground, they were not hit so hard. Still, it was not easy for them. On November 27 Pvt. William Lycett of the Australian Fourth Field Ambulance noted in his diary: "An awful night last night. Thunderstorm and rained in torrents, got washed out of my dugout and had to sleep in hospital tent . . . The mud is awful and am plastered with it, also very cold and raining off and on all day . . . This afternoon made my dugout little more secure against rain and made my bed up off the ground which is wet. Finished duty at 7.30 p.m. and turned in about 8.30 p.m. Cold again tonight."

Helles was hit harder, the land there being relatively flat and punctuated with gullies. Fortunately, many of the trenches were on sloping ground, so a number of units avoided the awfulness that hit their comrades in positions on flatter ground. That evening Lt. Owen Steele of the First Newfoundland Regiment recorded in his diary:

About 6 o'c. it commenced to rain. For 4 hrs. it thundered, lightninged [sic] & rained the heaviest, by far, that I or anyone else in our Regiment had ever experienced. Tons of water came rushing thro' the Trenches. Men lost blankets, rifles, equipment, etc., etc. Sides of Trenches were washed away, fell in, & became actually mud as soon as they got wet. Parapets fell in, were washed down, trenches were filled with debris of every kind. The rivers of water running thro' the trenches and through the drains we had made were filled with floating blankets, equipment, etc., etc. In fact waters were far beyond description. At 10 o'c. it stopped raining and cleared off; then one could get a more vivid idea of the damage done and being done. I cannot attempt to describe its various details. The floor of my dug-out was a foot and a half above the bottom of the drain, yet the water was a foot & a half or more deep in my dugout. It all came in in a rush and at a time when I was keeping it baled out with a cigarette tin nicely, some water having found its way through the roof and down the sides. Up to this time, I had kept all my things dry, but most of it now got wet.

All our Headquarters were completely washed out, all Officers dug-outs, etc. All Orderly Room papers & books were washed away and everything in fact was demolished.

Suvla, a mixture of flat ground, hills and the rocky Kiretch Tepe Sirt, was by far hit the hardest. There is virtually no natural shelter there. Captain Gillam painted a detailed picture of the weather's ravages at Suvla:

The sea is very rough. A lighter full of sick and a few wounded has been washed ashore. Two cases have been drowned. All further evacuation has stopped . . .

We are in the middle of loading our A.T. carts when heavy spots of rain drop, and looking up, we see the sky getting blacker and blacker with storm clouds. Luckily, issuing is nearly finished. The transport of many of the battalions has moved off, when a flash of forked lightning rushes from the sky to the sea, and almost instantly a deafening crash of thunder bursts overhead. This flash is followed by another and another, and then several in different parts of the sky stab the black clouds at the same moment. The rain gently begins to hiss, the hiss getting louder and louder, developing into a noise like the sound of loudly escaping steam, until, as if the clouds have all burst together, water deluges the earth in a soaking torrent. Black night soon falls upon us, changing at short intervals momentarily into day as the forked flashes of lightning stab the earth, sky, and sea. The beach men, bending double under the downfall of water and the struggle against the wind as they walk, appear in vivid detail and disappear in the

"And All Suffered Severely"

fraction of a second as the lightning plays overhead. Soon a pouring torrent of water a foot deep is raging down the gullies, turning the ravines, large and small, down the slopes of the hill into rushing cascades, washing away dugouts as if they were paper, and filling to the brim every crevice and hollow on the lower land. The new camps of trenches into which men have rushed for shelter are half filled with water, which, in less than an hour, overflows the drains on either side that we had dug to prevent such an event happening. All the weary weeks of Engineer labour lost in a short time. I go back to our new dugout and meet a sorry sight. Our cookhouse, wherein our dinner was being prepared, washed off the face of the earth. The roof and the back part of the messroom had fallen in, covering furniture with mud and debris, and flooding the floor with water 6 inches deep.[3]

The Ottomans, on the high ground, were also hard hit. A flood of dead Turks and animals washed down, contaminating many wells: "After the Flood we were very short of Rations for a while and had to do without some meals, for want of both food and water. It was with the latter that we had the greatest difficulty, for all the wells were spoilt, the water they contained being exactly the same as the Trench water. The Doctor condemned the water for drinking purposes and the first day we had nothing to drink, and the second day one lot of water for making Tea, but the drinking of unboiled water was absolutely forbidden, for there were so many dead bodies and rubbish of all kinds around that an epidemic of some kind would have resulted. Even the water that we then had was really only muddy trench water in which we could not have attempted even to wash our hands under normal conditions."[4]

The following morning the men had to contend with the mud: "We wake up to find a drizzly rain falling, blown by a strong north wind. Mud is everywhere, and the whole of the beaches a quagmire. What were once dugouts are now large puddles full of water. The system of trenches for winter quarters across the various gullies and nullahs has ceased to exist. Many of these are full to the brim with water; all have water and mud covering their floors. Twelve men taking shelter in their trench, which was roofed by corrugated iron, and which is situated in the gully in which we lived up to a week ago, have been drowned by the roof collapsing. We have orders to send up medical comforts. We send them up by A.T. carts. For the first time a convoy of A.T. carts is seen on the Gibraltar road in broad daylight."

In any "normal" climate one would expect either more rain or a spell of dry weather. But nothing about Gallipoli was normal. After a day spent negotiating the mud to deliver rations, Gillam continued: "It takes us about a quarter of the time to get back, for the wind literally blows us along, and it is difficult for us to keep our feet in the sticky mud. Once I slip while negotiating the side of a deep puddle, and fall backwards into it, much to the amusement of some passing gunners. At night it steadily becomes colder and colder, and the driving, misty rain turns to snow, a northerly cold blizzard setting in. I am up late arranging about the carting of the rations and blankets to the sea of mud that was once our trenches. It is freezing cold, but we shiver the more when we think of those men lying out in the open behind our front line."[5]

Snow. During the searing summer months no one imagined that snow fell in this area. But by winter the snow was one more cruel element for the troops to endure. Sgt. Frederick George Garrett of Third Light Horse Regiment recorded in his diary: "This morning when Scottie woke me at 3.00 a.m. to go on duty he invited me to come out and see snow. It was then bitterly cold and had been snowing for about a couple of hours. Daybreak presented a beautiful but unpleasant sight. It's snowed off and on during the day and being off duty I got into my dugout and kept well between the blankets. Blowing bitterly and the terraces are terribly slushy. My dugout lets the cold in and it is impossible to get warm with all my clothes on and with 3 blankets and a canvas sheet and a ground sheet underneath. Spent a horrible night trying to sleep."[6]

Across the peninsula men on both sides were hard hit by the cold and were dying left and right. Thousands developed frostbite or suf-

"And All Suffered Severely"

fered otherwise from exposure: "This morning a few have died. Officers in the line, if they were not on watch, were huddled together all night endeavouring to get warmth from each other's bodies. Ration carts were unable to get to many parts of the line owing to the mud and water in places being over the axles of the wheels. Quantities of rum and rations were lost in the mud. Telephone communications broke down, and many men, cut off from the rest and having to watch the enemy, froze and died at their posts."[7]

Pvt. Henry Chapman of the 2/3rd (City of London) Battalion, the London Regiment, was serving in the Dublin Castle sector at Suvla during this period. On January 13, 1916, he described the weather in a letter to a friend:

Now that we were all thoroughly wet through and worn out and hungry and thirsty, all that was necessary to complete our comfort was a good frost—and we had it. Although it was the worst thing we could do, most of us dozed—and we couldn't help it and of course we woke up frozen nearly stiff.

The next day found us on raised sandbags etc., which caused our heads to bob continually above the parapet, with about 10 rifles fit to use and 3 men fit to use them. The Turks were wandering about on the top of the parapet making themselves comfortable and we were exposed to a similar degree.

A truce was mutually understood until some fool of an officer sent the order along to fire, which they did. Whereupon the Turks sent out a sniper who bagged about 20 of our Company including young Harle with a wound in the side (we were unable to shift him and he died from loss of blood and exposure) SM Wilson & C/Sgt Lawrence (both wounded) . . .

We spent yet another night of frost and snow and when morning came we were ordered to retire to the trench known as Dublin Castle. By this time the Battalion had 2 Officers left—the Colonel and Mr. Crompton. It was during this retirement that we lost a lot of fellows, including Duligall, killed by machine gun fire, which at this time was particularly deadly. Poor old Folkes was light headed and refused to leave the trench. We could not persuade or force him. No doubt he died from exposure . . .

All This time (over 40 hours) we had one piece of bread and cheese.

Pvt. Jim Jackson of the 2/3rd Londons was one of those who died of exposure on November 28. His stepmother placed an advertisement in the local newspaper asking for information about her son's passing. More than ninety years later his nephew Jack Jackson recalled that a soldier, lying in hospital at Hanworth Park in Feltham, Middlesex, had responded. He stated that after the blizzard of November 28, he and Private Jackson had dug themselves into a large hole because they were drenched to the skin and had lost everything. From that time on they were without food or water for three days. On the third day an officer asked if anyone would go and try to find some. Private Jackson, the respondent, and two others (who subsequently dropped out from exhaustion) volunteered. En route they came across others who were dying, and Jackson and the letter's author covered the men up as best they could. Shortly thereafter, they found a box of bully beef and began the trip back to their firing line. That was the last the author saw of Jackson; he was the only member of the group to return. Upon arrival he collapsed and was taken to a dressing station, where it was found that he had been frostbitten to the knees. Jackson's body was never found.

Allied diaries frequently mention Turks who were so cold that they had climbed out of their flooded trenches into no-man's-land. There they jumped about and beat their arms in an effort to stay warm. One might assume that this mutual suffering would promote some sympathy from the two opposing forces. In fact, that was not the case, and snipers had a field day on November 28. Lt. Col. Ian Campbell of the Lovat's Scouts recorded: "In spite of the snow which fell all day on the 28th, we got a lot of sniping, the men taking full advantage of the many targets presented. The Turks must have been in an even worse plight than we were. They were to be seen, all over the place, walking about, trying to keep warm and,

"And All Suffered Severely"

in the early morning, there were a lot sitting, like scaups on a rock, along the top of their parapet. We accounted for about thirty by midday. One of the men told me it was better fun than hind shooting."[8]

There was widespread anger over the authorities' lack of foresight. Able Seaman Thomas MacMillan recorded: "A blizzard which lasted four days swept the Peninsula and took a heavy toll of life, particularly among the French Colonials. Their losses from exposure were so severe that they were hurriedly evacuated and the Naval Division took over their sector. No provision had been made to protect us against Crimean conditions; we stood in the clothing in which we left England and which was considered by the wise-men at home to be the most suitable for a sub-tropical climate. Either the 'Spit and Polish' brigade in Whitehall had not the intelligence to foresee the possibility of a winter campaign, or their benighted representatives on Gallipoli were so hopeless as not to be able to realize the need for warm clothing."[9]

Men who had come from warmer climes had an awful time. Pvt. Tom Carberry of the Australian Fourth Field Ambulance recorded: "The Ghurkas who were on the low ground near Suvla Bay, had many cases of trench feet and were being sent away in large numbers. They were not able to stand the cold like our lads. I have watched these men straggling down to the hospitals, and it was a most pitiful sight." When Capt. Watson Smith of the 1/6th Gurkhas inspected his men's feet on November 29, he found ice growing between their toes. Their normally dark feet were white and completely numb.[10]

One of the saddest stories is that of two brothers serving in the 2/3rd Londons. Their battalion's commanding officer, Lt. Col. Frederick Bendall, wrote: "None was wounded, all had died of cold and exposure. Two brothers of 'C' Company had died together. The arm of one was round the other's neck, the fingers held a piece of biscuit to the frozen mouth. It seemed a strange and inexplicable thing that these men who had come there to fight, and had fought bravely, had been killed by the elements."[11] Pvt. Christopher Harris and Drummer Herbert Harris hailed from Islington, a borough of London. The frozen ground was too solid for graves to be dug.

Bendall continued: "In the ravine we camped under tarpaulins, and slept round a fire. They sent us up brandy and tinned chicken from the medical stores, and dry boots and clothes. On each of the succeeding days we stumbled up to the trenches to collect identity discs and to bury our dead."[12]

Within a few days the weather began to warm, and conditions returned to normal. But the losses in men and animals on both sides were horrific. We will never know how many Turks lost their lives or suffered from exposure. In the Suvla sector alone, however, two hundred British soldiers were reported to have drowned in their flooded trenches, and a further five thousand were treated for frostbite. Despite the varied strengths of defender and invader at Gallipoli, nature demonstrated that it, above all, reigned supreme at Gallipoli.

"And All Suffered Severely"

13

"We Have Lost the Game"

Evacuation

On September 6, 1915, Bulgaria joined the Central Powers. The decision had been a precarious one. Before dropping the veil of neutrality, Tsar Ferdinand I wanted to see who had the best chance of winning. In September 1915 the choice seemed obvious: Germany had battered the Russians in Poland and stayed the Allied invaders at Gallipoli, and every major Allied assault on the western front had failed. Clearly, the Central Powers were going to be the victors in this, the greatest war humanity had ever known. With victory came land, and Bulgaria's goal was to gain territory. That territory was going to be Serbia—or so it hoped.

Serbia had earlier signed a treaty with Greece in which Greece promised to come to the aid of its neighbor in the event that its security was threatened. When Bulgaria mobilized its army, the Serbs asked for the assistance of 150,000 Greek troops. Unfortunately, its Hellenic ally needed all of its resources to protect its eastern borders from the Turks. Greece thus asked for troops from Great Britain and France to help the Serbs, and the request was granted. Russia also contributed men.

The threat from Bulgaria was immediate, and time was of the essence. Troops were needed sooner than they could be dispatched from England or France. Much to Hamilton's chagrin, Kitchener ordered that they be sent from Gallipoli. He was told to send one British and two French divisions, but he successfully argued for sending only one French division and the Tenth (Irish) Division. In October they were sent to Salonica, which runs along the northeastern coast of Greece. The loss of troops, when Hamilton really needed more to replace the hundreds being lost to battle and sickness every week, was the beginning of the end for the invaders. That same month the Second Mounted Division returned to Egypt. Once recovered, refitted, and reinforced, the gallant yeomen would continue their fight against the Ottomans in the deserts of the Middle East.

On October 11, less than a week after the Tenth Division began departing Suvla for Salonica, Kitchener cabled a question to Hamilton. If Suvla were evacuated, how many casualties did he envision during the operation? Fearing the worst and imagining the Turks firing into his retreating soldiers' backs, Hamilton estimated at least 50 percent. It was, however, a risk that might have to be taken. Hamilton was enraged by the question and wrote: "If they do this they make the Dardanelles into the bloodiest tragedy of the world! Even if we were to escape without a scratch, they would stamp our enterprise as the bloodiest of all tragedies!"[1]

This was not the first time Kitchener had relayed the possibility to Hamilton. On September 24 Hamilton had written in his journal: "K. has opened the idea of giving up Suvla, saying, 'it might become necessary in certain eventualities to abandon that area.' In my reply I have said, "I hope there will be no question now of the abandonment of Suvla . . . In the Northern zone [Suvla and Anzac] I have now more troops than at the time of my telegram, my line is stronger, the old troops are resting, the new troops are improving, and preparations are being made for a local advance. At this stage withdrawal will be a great moral victory for the Turks. Moreover, it would relieve a large number of enemy divisions to oppose the Russians in Asia, or for other enterprises."[2]

Hamilton was right, but the campaign had become an open wound, and the bleeding had to be stopped. The western front was the priority for men and resources; the Salonica front was being

"We Have Lost the Game"

opened; and troops were already fighting in the Middle East and Africa. Gallipoli might have to be written off. Britain and France needed men to fight in more important places, where they had some chance of winning.

Hamilton was fired on October 16 and departed the peninsula the next day. He declared the event "a melancholy affair." With his departure Birdwood was left in temporary command. In his reports to Kitchener he noted that all units were understrength, poorly armed, and undernourished. The only hope the Allies had of winning was to push the Turks back so far that their guns could not hit the beaches. But with the limited resources available, there was no chance of that happening. The French had also determined that their resources were better utilized at Salonica and were totally opposed to reinforcing Gallipoli.

On October 28 Lieutenant General Monro arrived to take over command from Birdwood, and two days later he visited all three sectors. He asked the senior officers if they felt that success was still in the cards. All answered that a push lasting no more than twenty-four hours might be possible. They were not sure that they could hold off a Turkish offensive, considering their seemingly limitless supply of shells. On October 31 Monro cabled Kitchener with his recommendation that Gallipoli be evacuated. Churchill, on learning of the suggestion, responded, "He came, he saw, he capitulated"— strong words from a man who had once boasted that it would be impossible to secure the Dardanelles.[3]

The Dardanelles Committee was not so sure. It decided to send Kitchener to Gallipoli to make his own assessment. Kitchener also reappointed Birdwood to command of the Mediterranean Expeditionary Force and sent Monro to take command of the troops at Salonica, in effect shooting the messenger.

Upon arrival Kitchener joined Birdwood for a three-day inspection and was shocked by what he found. On November 15 he cabled the committee that he had reached the same conclusion as Monro. He also put Monro in command of all British troops in the Mediterranean outside Egypt, while Birdwood was left in command of the troops at Gallipoli. Lt. Gen. Sir Bryan Malone, commanding officer of the Tenth (Irish) Division, replaced Monro as commander of the British troops in Salonica.

On December 7 the committee agreed to evacuate the peninsula, but not entirely. Suvla and Anzac would be deserted, but Helles would be held for strategic reasons. Lying at the tip of the peninsula, it was considered necessary to keep for political reasons. The members of the committee felt that if all of the sectors were evacuated, the Allies would really be admitting defeat. Helles might become a lynchpin for another attempt to capture Constantinople. In addition to political considerations, the loss of a large amount of shipping during the recent storms made a simultaneous evacuation of all three sectors impossible. That was, however, the scenario originally envisioned.

Birdwood was cabled with the decision on December 8, and plans for an orderly, secret withdrawal of the two sectors began immediately. The goal was to carry out the evacuations under the noses of the Turks, who would be fooled into thinking that business as usual was occurring. Men and equipment would be evacuated in stages every night—the Royal Navy could take off ten thousand each night—and the final stages would occur on the nights of December 18 and 19.

In order to facilitate the evacuation without giving the game up to the Turks, clever means were employed to simulate the presence of men, guns, and stores where there were none. Devices utilizing water-powered weights were attached to rifles so they would fire on their own. Mules delivered empty ration boxes to trenches occupied by uniformed dummies and only a few men. The New Zealand Engineers placed Mills bombs on one side of a *dere* and attached the ring of the pin to the other side of the gully with a trip wire. In order to stop any approaching Turks in their tracks, or at least slow the expected onslaught, contact mines were placed around the forward areas. On the beach stacks of wooden ration crates were created with the outer framework only, making it appear that the massive piles were solid. It worked, and the Turks were dumbfounded when they realized what had happened. Capt. John Gillam recorded in his diary on December 9:

> Yes; the evacuation of Suvla is now a reality. I hear to-day that we have now begun the intermediate stage of the evacuation. It has been a reality for some days. The storm only delayed it. We have just completed the preliminary stage. We hear that it will be but a few days now when not a British subject will be left alive here unless as a prisoner. The shelling to-day is in fits and starts. High explosive shells are searching the beach, bursting well and with a louder explosion than in past days. But West Beach is well protected, and the steady shipment of vehicles and ordnance goes on all day. At night, empty ration carts go up to the line to bring back men's surplus kits, blankets, surplus ammunition, and the surplus part of the usual accumulation of baggage that a regiment takes with it to the trenches and to dumps just behind.

Many have written that no lives were lost during the withdrawals. While it appears to be true that nobody was killed as he was boarding a boat departing Gallipoli for the last time, some were killed in the events leading up to the pullouts. On December 11 the Twentieth Battalion, Australian Imperial Force (AIF), lost two of its officers, Maj. James Harcus, commanding officer of D Company, and the battalion's second-in-command, Maj. Richard Jenkins. Harcus was a former Scots soldier from Orkney whose primary language was Gaelic. Jenkins was a Boer War veteran whose son, Lt. Godfrey Jenkins, was serving with his father. Maj. Gordon Uther, the battalion's adjutant, was also mortally wounded. The three were killed when a shell fell into the trench they were in on Russell's Top while they were going up to inspect preparations for the departure. After the war their commanding officer, Lt. Col. John Lamrock, wrote:

> Poor Uther met his end on the 11th December. He was a wonderful chap, a keen, lovable soldier. He was with two other good soldiers—Majors Jenkins and Harcus. It happened that when it was decided to evacuate Anzac, the new Brigade was ordered to

go back to Mudros, and the 20th were instructed to take over on the night of 13th December, and on the morning of that date the Headquarters staff . . . started to go to Russell's Top to go over the details. When proceeding up Monash Gully sap, a couple of shells were fired at the party from a "75" at Olive Grove, but, as the trench was deep, no harm was done. When the party reached the top, the sentry there said the gun was shelling the wide sap heavily, and a halt was called. After a wait of a few minutes the party set off again, and had barely gone a dozen yards when a shell burst right among it, killing Uther, Jenkins, and Harcus, and only knocking down Fitzgerald and Howard.[4]

The three men were buried next to one another on Walker's Ridge.

One might assume that those who had spent so long suffering at Gallipoli would be elated to be leaving its stinking, fatal shores. Some were, but many were not. Many felt that if only they could get more help, they would be able to take up the fight in the spring and drive the Turks back. They were ashamed at being forced to retreat when they had not been beaten and felt that too many friends had been sacrificed for naught. At Anzac men spent their free time visiting the graves of friends for what was, they assumed, the last time. C. E. W. Bean wrote: "The consideration which did go straight to every man's heart was the tragedy of confessing failure after so many and well-loved comrades had given their lives to the effort. The men hated to leave their dead mates to the mercy of the Turks. For days after the breaking of the news there were never absent from the cemeteries men by themselves, or in twos and threes, erecting new crosses or tenderly 'tidying-up' the grave of a friend. This was by far the deepest regret of the troops. 'I hope,' said one of them to Birdwood on the final day, pointing to a little cemetery, 'I hope they don't hear us marching down the deres (gullies).'"[5] The evacuation was a somber affair. Many of the Anzacs had lost relatives, and they formed a much more tight-knit group than the British or the French.

In fact, those who seemed to be most pleased about departing

"We Have Lost the Game"

were the British at Suvla and those Anzacs who had arrived late in the game. It had nothing to do with cowardice. They were simply fed up. Many of them were already suffering from dysentery when they arrived at Gallipoli, and they had not experienced any of the successes—minor though they were—that the veterans had. They had also not developed the attachments to the ground that the original invaders had fought so hard to take and hold. The experience of the Sixth (Service) Battalion, the King's Own (Royal Lancaster Regiment), which evacuated Suvla on the nights of December 18 and 19, was typical of these other units:

> On December 7, 1915, the 6th Battalion had to give up the cookers which had stood them in such good stead during the great storm in Gallipoli. This confirmed rumours of an impending evacuation. For some time, although digging and patrolling had gone on as usual and the gunners and ships still held their daily duels with enemy batteries, evacuation of sick and stores had been going on. Within a few days of losing their cookers the King's Own water-carts also were taken away from them. On the 16th a battalion bombing party was commended for knocking out a similar party of the enemy, an operation which turned out to be the last in Gallipoli as the line began to be thinned the next night. Those who remained did what they could to simulate normal activity of double their number as two companies embarked on the 18th and two the next day. A full moon, hidden by light clouds, made movement easy on the last two days.
>
> The sea was smooth as silk and a morning mist veiled the deserted appearance of the beach and back areas. All that day there were barely a thousand men still ashore. The full moon was slightly hazy as the last men embarked that night and a party of the Regiment had to wait on the gangway as the sailors tried to get one of the barges in to take them off. A cheer was scarcely suppressed when it was eventually achieved, but even so the Turk was utterly unaware of the operation. The next morning, December 20, he heavily bombarded the empty trenches.[6]

Midshipman Robert Lowry was one of those who helped to carry men away from Suvla. He wrote:

EVACUATION OF SUVLA, SECOND NIGHT DEC. 19TH–20TH

I left the ship at 2.00 p.m. and we got in tow of the same trawler, arriving at Suvla at about 8.00.

We went into our little bay and the steam boat anchored as close in as possible. The launch and pinnace went in and anchored as close as possible with safety and anchored buoying their anchor with a hemp rope bent on to the buoy. This hemp was connected by means of various lines to a stake driven into the sand where the two cutters were.

We then had a trial trip and everything went all right. We went inshore again and all the crew collected in one of the dugouts and made some cocoa, which they found in a neighbouring dug-out. I spent most of the night talking to Flight-sub Lt. Macleod who was in charge of the W.T. [wireless telegraph] set there . . .

We did nothing all night till 3.00 a.m. when the W.T. set was dismantled and brought down to one of the cutters, who took all the signal ratings etc. off to the steam boats. My cutter remained inshore to bring off the beach party etc. This party was to have been brought off at 6.00 a.m. but as everyone was off by 3.30 they were brought off at 4.20 after lighting the largest bonfire I have ever seen.

About 3 day's [sic] stores and a small amount of rifle ammunition had to be burnt. 70,000 gallons of petrol were put over the stuff to make it burn well. The bonfire was lighted at 4.00 a.m. exactly, and everyone was off the beach by 4.20 when my cutter left. The bonfire was quite close to the beach and extended about 150 yards along the beach and about 100 yards inland. It was an absolutely topping blaze.

After getting rid of the army people I went inshore with the beach-master and layoff in case there were any stragglers, but fortunately there were none. If there were, we were to tell them to put their arms down then proceed inshore and let them wade out to us taking care not to let the boat be rushed. After doing this till about 6.30, hailing the beach every few minutes, we went back to the picket boat and soon afterwards got in tow of the tug *Alice* and proceeded to half speed back to Kephalo. We were waiting for our steam pinnace to come back. She had gone inshore to see if there were any more people but they found none.[7]

Having safely left Suvla, Capt. John Gillam wrote in his diary on December 20: "Suvla is Turkish once more."

As a going-away gesture, the Anzacs blew a mine at the Nek just before dawn on December 20, killing approximately seventy Turkish soldiers. Under normal circumstances both sides would scramble for the resulting crater in an effort to hold it and advance their front line. In this instance only the Turks were left to make the attempt, not realizing that they were now playing a one-handed game. At 4:40 a.m. the commanding officer of the Turkish Nineteenth Division reported to the Fortress Group Command: "The enemy exploded three mines in front of trench No. 18. Part of our front trenches has been destroyed. A company commander on his own initiative occupied the craters with his company and met with no opposition. He therefore sent a patrol forward to the enemy trenches and found them empty."[8]

One of the craters penetrated into an Australian trench, and the wary attackers were surprised that their arrival was not greeted with bullets or bombs. The officer present probed the area with his men. Finding it vacant, he sent word back by runner. At about that time the Turks at Bomba Sirt, opposite Quinn's Post, realized that something was up and moved warily forward. Observers were reporting large fires on the beaches, despite the fact that their gunners had not been firing. At 6:40 a.m. North Group Command ordered all divisions to advance. What they found were empty trenches and the odd contact mine. More important, they found tons of vital supplies not yet touched by the fires—rations, ammunition, uniforms, blankets, wagons, and all manner of luxuries the Turks could only dream of. While cautiously looking out for booby traps, men were taking all they could for themselves. By this stage in the campaign some of the Turks' clothing was in tatters, and many donned partial, even complete, enemy uniforms. Greatcoats were an especial luxury, not to mention bully beef and other edibles. Shortly after the war Turkish army major Binbaşi Zeki Bey, commanding officer of the First Battalion, Fifty-Seventh Infantry Regiment, told C. E. W. Bean:

"Well, it was this explosion that really told us of the Evacuation," he said. "I asked my friends on the staff, 'What gave you the first notion?' 'It was the mine that first made us certain,' they said.

"Immediately, a regiment from reserve was pushed up there to occupy the crater," he said, "and these troops got lost and wandered on into your trenches and found them empty. This was reported. Then the fires occurred at Suvla" (two British engineer officers at 4 a.m. set light to the huge stacks of stores on Suvla Beach) "and this gave the show away really.

"At first it was thought that the mine might have been a signal for some action on your part; and even when your trenches were entered it was not yet certain that all the trenches had been left. I had an officer in your trenches by 4 o'clock, and myself went later. The order was given at once to look after the sick, for we saw that you had left a hospital; but we soon found that there were no sick.[9]

At first only the [forward] companies were ordered to advance; later the troops, some of them, went in without orders. On the first day they were everywhere. Stores abandoned by you were ordered to be collected—sandbags and other material for the trenches were sent to our troops at Helles, but the soldiers at Anzac helped themselves to these very largely. Your booby-traps caught very few men. Some on the right of my regiment were caught by a mine, but none of my regiment. The ships' fire next day did little damage."[10]

On December 20 the men at Helles learned of the evacuation via a Special Order of the Day. In addition to describing the successful withdrawals, it noted that Helles would continue to be held. The rea-

"We Have Lost the Game"

son, it stated, was to "[maintain] the honour of the British Empire against the Turks on the Peninsula and [to continue] such action as shall prevent them, as far as possible, from massing their forces to meet our main operations elsewhere." "Elsewhere" meant Egypt, Palestine, and Mesopotamia. Word of the Anzac and Suvla evacuations led to rumors of a similar occurrence at Helles, despite the order. Before Christmas, Able Seaman Thomas MacMillan of the Drake Battalion recorded: "Evacuation buzzes were now very prevalent. The supercession of Sir Ian Hamilton by Sir C. V. Munro did not affect us very much, for we had lost all faith in people with big reputations and high sounding names, and with good reason. The buzzes would have been dismissed contemptuously had there not appeared in our trenches an Anzac non-commissioned officer who told us that Suvla and Anzac had been evacuated while at the same time, he described the harrowing experiences endured by the infantry before the operation was completed. This information accounted for the increase in shellfire on the Helles area. As can be imagined, we anticipated a none too bright ending to our attempt to get away."

One might assume that word of the evacuations spread like wildfire through the Helles sector, but it apparently did not. Joe Murray of the Eighth Corps Mining Company was one of the campaign's most prolific diarists. Yet he did not mention the event until January 3: "To-day we were told that Anzac and Suvla Bay had been evacuated but we were to hold on to Cape Helles. The news of the evacuation stunned us. Had we really admitted defeat? Had all the suffering been wasted and what of the dead?"[11]

The Senegalese were the first to evacuate the sector. They were gone by December 22, and the rest of the French and French Colonial forces departed on January 2 and 3, 1916. The exception was their artillery, which the British needed if they were to protect their now depleted front from a possible Turkish onslaught. The Gallic infantry was replaced not only by the Twenty-Ninth Division from Suvla but also by the Thirteenth (Western) Division, which had evacuated Anzac. Murray described the sector's changing complexion on January 3:

As we moved along the trench we came upon a small dugout which appeared to have been some sort of headquarters. I observed an official notice pinned to a board which read: *The VIIIth Army Corps will be relieved by the IXth A.C. Inform all concerned.* I did not learn till afterwards that this was a piece of camouflage meaning that we would be evacuated about January 9th.

Until reading this notice I had been wondering if the authorities had forgotten that the VIIIth Army Corps existed—in fact I wondered if it had already gone. The French had gone, I knew, as the Royal Naval Division had vacated their brand new "rest camp" on the high ground above "X" Beach and taken over the French sector on the extreme right of the line.

I have no regrets about the absence of the French; I think we shall be much better off now they have gone.

I have lost sight of the 42nd Division; they, too, must have been relieved. Maybe we will be next. The Royal Naval Division is the only Division that has been here throughout the whole campaign. What was left of my battalion, the Hood, did have a few days on the Island of Imbros, a couple of hours' sail away, after the debacle of June 4th. (I was left behind to look after the stores.)

The 29th Division, with whom we landed, were withdrawn to take part in the Suvla landing in August but they are now with us at Cape Helles. The 52nd Division did not arrive until July. The "new" division is the 13th. I have not heard of them before. They are one of the divisions who landed at Suvla Bay and Anzac for the operations in that area and have been there ever since. A few days ago they took over the extreme left from the 29th Division. They belong to the IXth Army Corps so there is some truth in the notice I read.[12]

The notice that Murray found was a ploy to throw off the Turks should they capture any forward positions. It was meant to explain the reason for the Thirteenth (Western) Division suddenly turning up at Helles. Much to the dismay of the division's members, who thought that they had seen the last of Gallipoli, they were instead

"We Have Lost the Game"

sent to Helles to replace the Forty-Second (East Lancashire) Division. That formation was depleted through illness and was a mere shadow of its old self.

Pvt. Walter Bennett of the East Lancashire Regiment was one of those who evacuated with the Forty-Second Division and was not at all sorry to go:

> The coal barges near the beach took us to the destroyer and then to HMS *Chatham*. I was so exhausted I was unable to climb the ship's side so a burly marine reached down and pulled me up and then carried me like a babe in arms below decks and put a cup of cocoa in my hand and said, "drink that son." Since that time I have always had high regard for the Royal Navy and Royal Marines.
>
> We were taken to Tenedos, and I still remember how cold and windy it was. We had no kit, having had to leave everything on Gallipoli. Our lives had depended on not having anything to impede our progress, the clink of a tea mug could have alerted the Turks and our chances of escape would have gone forever.
>
> It did not bother me below decks that I did not see the coastline of the Dardanelles receding into the distance and being blown up by the Royal Engineers. At least I was going home in one piece, so many had lost limbs or their sight. There were no thoughts of the future, only total disbelief that I was out of that hell. Nothing I had to face in the future could be as bad as that. To me it was incredible that I had survived it, and when I later went to France it was a holiday camp to what we had endured at Gallipoli.[13]

After the northern sectors were evacuated, thousands of Turks were sent to reinforce Helles. They had an almost unlimited supply of artillery ammunition, courtesy of Germany and Austria. Not only was the supply greater; the quality of the shells was better than those produced in the Ottoman factories.

The men at Helles must have been terribly discouraged when they learned that Suvla and Anzac had been abandoned, while they would be left alone to defend against an even greater number of Turks over the winter. But relief, of a sort, would soon be at hand.

On December 23 Lt. Gen. Sir William Robertson replaced Gen. Sir Archibald Murray as chief of the Imperial General Staff. Robertson, who had been serving on the western front, began his career as a private in the Sixteenth (the Queen's) Lancers. He would later rise to the rank of field marshal and become the first—and only—man in the history of the British army to rise to that rank from private.

Robertson was one of many in the army who believed that if the war were going to be won, it would be won on the western front. He concurred with Monro that Gallipoli was doomed to failure, and he was in a position to do something about it. On December 24 he sent a coded cable to Monro ordering him to prepare for the evacuation of Helles.

The remaining French infantry would depart first. This was done to avoid any problem that might arise from having two separate commands, which spoke different languages, carry out such delicate operations simultaneously. The British had already learned that the French were prone to carelessness. With the Turks expecting an evacuation at any time, they were concerned about maintaining complete secrecy about the coming operation.

As in the northern sectors, the British at Helles began evacuating slowly, pulling out units or portions of units each night. As a result, portions of the sector were largely devoid of men, and many trenches were blocked or filled in. It was a scary situation for those left behind, and they feared that the Turks would choose that time to attack. They were also getting lost trying to navigate an already difficult system of trenches when they moved to the rear. Familiar evacuation routes were either blocked by barbed wire or gone altogether.

As they made their evacuation plans, the British did their best to make the Turks think that business as usual was occurring. Because the troops had slipped away unnoticed from Anzac and Suvla, those at Helles had to be extra careful. The Turks were watching for signs of another evacuation, just as the British knew they would. There was a greater distance between the front line and the beach than there was in the northern sectors, but the Turkish vantage point on

"We Have Lost the Game"

Achi Baba gave them a bird's-eye view of the activities at Helles. The Turks also worried that they might miss the chance to hit the invaders first if they tried to leave.

Thus, on January 7 Ottoman infantry attacked between Fusilier Bluff and Gully Ravine, following the usual softening up by artillery. The Thirteenth Division on the extreme right suffered the worst of the bombardment. Fortunately, many shells fell on trenches already evacuated or filled in. Many also landed in Gully Ravine, through which a major part of the evacuation was taking place. When the four-and-a-half-hour-long barrage ended, Turkish riflemen climbed out of their trenches and charged into the massed fire of British rifles and machine guns. But the attackers' efforts were halfhearted, and many refused to leave their trenches. Able Seaman MacMillan recorded:

On the second day of our duty, an alarming situation developed. Away on the left, fierce and sustained rifle fire broke out, while the enemy forces mustered all along our front, displaying the points of their bayonets. The bayonets were so close together as to make it unmistakably clear that we were greatly outnumbered. Every available man was rushed to the fire trench and in defiance we in turn held our bayonets high. A plan of action was agreed on. If they came over, we were to inflict as heavy casualties as possible with rifle fire, thereafter leave our position before they got too close, and engage them with our bayonets in the open. The plan was the soundest we could have pursued, and we waited its execution with bated breath.

As time wore on the din on the left died down as if at a given signal, and following the lead from their right the Turkish bayonets disappeared. We had not long to wait for an explanation of the hostile demonstration. According to information the enemy had attacked in force when the light was good, at a point the shortest distance from the beaches; they had hoped to turn our left flank and press on if possible to Cape Helles, thus cutting off the retreat of our troops in the forward area. Had they succeeded, few, if any of our troops would have escaped. By a stroke of good fortune, the Turks attacked the Lowland Division when battalion reliefs were being effected, so that the Scots were doubly strong, and were able to repulse the onslaught and inflict heavy casualties.

Although British casualties were relatively light, the Ninth Worcesters suffered sixteen dead and seven wounded that day. They were part of the Thirteenth (Western) Division.

This assault was the last gasp of the campaign. The following night, Helles was evacuated. Not a single man is known to have died in the withdrawal. Miraculously, not one man was left behind. Capt. John Gillam observed:

> The ship is now nearly full up with troops, and an officer comes in to say we are off. I go up on deck and find that they are just weighing anchor. It is tricky work getting a ship away from improvised piers. The captain is the same Naval officer who used to command the *Whitby Abbey*, which took me to Lemnos and back in July last. To-morrow night will be his last trip to Gallipoli.
>
> At last, after a lot of maneuvering, he shouts from the bridge "All clear aft?" and a voice answers, "Aye, aye, sir," then "Full steam ahead," and we swing round and head out to sea. I watch the lights on shore gradually disappear. One I notice by VIII Corps H.Q., being at the top of a post, flickers out and on as regularly as the ticking of a clock. What it meant I don't know. I have noticed it before during the past few days. Asia fires to "V" Beach, and Achi sends a couple which burst on the high ground at the back of "W" Beach. The lights and the outskirts of the shore disappear. I still see the starlights [illumination flares] sailing in the darkness of the night. These soon disappear. For me the adventures of Gallipoli are no longer realities, but bad memories, and I turn into the wardroom to sleep.[14]

Among the French gunners left behind when their infantry evacuated was Noel Sergent of Fifty-First Battery, Tenth Artillery Regiment. In a letter dated January 23, 1916, he wrote:

"We Have Lost the Game"

Our evacuation was no doubt a "masterful piece of strategy" and a "great moral victory." . . .

The best "souvenir" I got was a 3-speed 4½ h.p. Triumph motor-bike. I've got it with me now. It costs me nothing to run, and it cost me nothing at the start. They were burning and scrapping motor-bikes and even motor-cars. When I found this out I went to the officer in charge of Ordnance and got leave to take the bike away as my own. When I got it here safely the Commandant wanted to buy it from me, but had no luck . . .

The Turks were very nice about it; they let us go with a few shots from Asia on the pinnaces, doing comparatively little damage compared with what they might have done. Our battery was the last French battery to go off. They fired up to 5 in the evening, then at 7 the Captain, Lieutenant, another, myself and 7 men remained at the guns. We rammed earth sacks down the mouths of the guns, then put 26 dynamite cartridges in each and a Cordon Bickford and more sacks. Then we got our packs and banged about with a sledge-hammer, put the breeches of the guns on the trucks and started off. At the crossroads we met the 52nd division coming down quite noiselessly, in fours. This was the last division and that meant that if the Turks chose to attack they could simply come straight through, as our trenches were empty. When we got to Sedd-ul-Behr we left our packs behind the Chateau d'Europe and went on to the water's edge. Just then, as I was emptying the breech into the water, the horn announcing a flash from Asia sounded. That meant 49 seconds before the shell came along. We all got behind anything and the shot went just over our heads on to the quay by the *River Clyde* and the bottom of the old shell went into the sea. We took hold of the breech again and emptied it into the water this time. I got a "souvenir" from the handle just above the kneecap. When this job was over we went back and got our packs on and formed fours, and the old horn went again. The shot was over again, and this time the bottom of the shell came back with a whizz over our heads. There was one poor fellow on a stretcher next door to me. He wasn't moving and looked dead, but they came and carried him off, I daresay to a Hospital ship, just when I wasn't looking. But I don't think he went far. He wasn't one of our men; I think he was a "conducteur." I know one shot knocked out four or five of them all in a bunch, so did nearly every shot, and the papers say we had "no casualties."

We were the last Frenchmen to leave and we got safely to the *Ville de Bordeaux* after running full spit into a schooner, I think a Hospital ship for the occasion. Nothing was hurt except perhaps the flank of the schooner. However we didn't wait to see the damage, but shifted a little further up and dodged about a bit in the dark and got to the *Ville de Bordeaux* in time. From there we came straight here, landing about 10.30 a.m. The rest is uneventful.[15]

There was one phenomenon in common with each of the evacuations. Creature comforts that the men desired but could not get—in some cases that they did not even know were on the peninsula—became available to anybody who could carry them. The inventory of the supply depots was being abandoned because the transports had no room for it. On December 15 Lance Cpl. Edgar Worrall of the Twenty-Fourth Battalion, AIF, recorded in his diary: "Managed to get down to the Rest Gully after a very long spell in the trenches. Things are being given away wholesale. Uniforms, tobacco and food of every description. Feasted on strawberries and cream (canned), fruit salad and stewed fruit, fish, tomatoes, jams of the choicest brands, butter and well—it would take a cook to mention all. I scarcely remember ever feeding so well in my life. All stores given away, ready for evacuation."

The most coveted item was alcohol, and hundreds of jars of rum were to be left behind. Field hospitals abandoned their stores of medicinal brandy, which was used as a nerve tonic and to calm stomach ailments. As one might imagine, men tried to take advantage of the situation: "All the rum has been spilt. That was the greatest blessing of all. The place stinks of rum, and when going along the

"We Have Lost the Game"

beach the water close in had a red tinge. Men actually got down on knees in some places and lapped up the rum. But altogether, there were not many drunks."[16]

All of the evacuations were carried out successfully. Yet the fact that more than forty-two thousand British and Dominion servicemen—as well as twenty thousand Frenchmen and sixty-five thousand Turks—lost their lives in a fruitless campaign overshadows this accomplishment. Long after the war Frederick Knight, who served with the Australian Army Service Corps, wrote a fitting summary:

> Cape Helles was not evacuated until early morning of 9 January. It would be hard to say now what was the general feeling of troops about the Evacuation except that, although they did not like being beaten, they were not ashamed of themselves. It is easier to record remarks which can be recalled.
>
> The first of these was made by a private in the 7th Battalion before we left Anzac. He said, "I don't know. I'll have to leave two of my brothers here, and I would just as soon stay with them."
>
> The second was from Harold Clampett, the son of the Adelaide archdeacon, "Up to now, this has been mostly our own little show, but in future, we shall only be a small part of a very large army."
>
> The third did not come from an Australian but from an ex-enemy. In 1925, a Turkish major told my sister, "If you had not pulled out, we would have done so ourselves."
>
> I think I understood what he meant. They would have retired to more hospitable country, and left Allah, the elements and disease to destroy us.[17]

NOTES

————

Pat's research on Gallipoli was twenty-six years long, and he worked on it almost every day of those twenty-six years. It started out with collecting documents and writing articles asking for information and over time evolved into getting information from the Internet and e-mails.

In our study there are two large filing cabinets stuffed with various documents, such as honor rolls, attestation papers, war diaries, lists of names on war memorials, and letters and diaries from the families of the men who fought at Gallipoli. There are also hundreds of documents that Pat was able to scan or find on the Internet as part of his research. Pat was scrupulous in his scholarship and meticulous about keeping track of his sources. It is, however, a nearly impossible task to trace every scrap of paper back to its origin without Pat's guidance. One example is the moving statements that make up the chapter titles. Many of these are quotes from men at Gallipoli, and not all are directly credited in this work. To have to let a few quotations remain unattributed is deeply disappointing. But I am confident that every one is legitimate and belongs in this book.

Karlann Greenwood Gariepy

1. "A Day Which I Shall Not Forget"

1. Hickey, *Gallipoli*, 46.
2. Young diary, February 25, 1915.
3. Denham diary, February 26, 1915.
4. William-Powlett diary, February 26, 1915.
5. Young diary, March 2, 1915.
6. [Missing source.]

2. "The Results Were Disastrous"

1. In addition to its civilian crew, each trawler had a petty officer, a signal-man, and a naval officer, who was in overall command, as well as the civilian skipper.
2. National Archive ref ADM 179/19.
3. *Challenge of War*, 3:338–39.
4. E. Weaver, HMS *Amethyst*, quoted in Liddle, *Men of Gallipoli*, 47.
5. Vice Adm. J. P. Lucas, French navy, retired, *Souvenirs of Contre-Amiral L. Lucas, Gallipolian* (Winter 1993): 30–31.
6. Midshipman H. M. Denham, HMS *Agamemnon*.
7. Midshipman Peverill William-Powlett, HMS *Vengeance*.
8. Lance Corporal Powell, a Royal Marine artillery gunner serving on the HMS *Irresistible*.
9. Pvt. H. Wilcox, Royal Marine Light Infantry, HMS *Ocean*.

3. "Death on the Eve of Battle"

1. Lucas, *Souvenirs of Contre-Amiral L. Lucas*, 29.
2. One report said that a white ensign, which a British warship would have flown, was hanging over the side; another reported that the ship was flying a French flag.
3. Account of Trumpeter Dudley Lissenburg, 147th Brigade, Royal Field Artillery, Liddle Collection.
4. Diary of Capt. F. J. Thompson, *Sea Breezes* (May 1961).

4. "My God It's All Horrible"

1. Memoir of Capt. Dixon Hearder, AWM 3DRL3959.
2. Ashmead-Bartlett diary, April 25, 1915.
3. Lt. Cdr. John Waterlow claimed to have commanded Tow 1, and in his diary he wrote of his efforts to steer Metcalf back on course when the young midshipman steered off course, to port. Two sources note, however, that Waterlow had been moved to Tow 4 and that Making had replaced him. One of the sources was one of the other midshipman, and the other was an Admiralty document. It must therefore be assumed that Making was in command of Tow 1.
4. Bean, *Story of Anzac*, 253.
5. Bean, *Story of Anzac*, 254.

6. Pvt. Leslie Walker of A Company, 9th Battalion, in a statement to the Australian branch of the British Red Cross Society.

7. Capt. Raymond Leane of C Company, 11th Battalion.

8. Bean, *Story of Anzac*, 260.

9. Hearder memoir.

10. Report to the Australian branch of the British Red Cross on the disappearance of Pvt. Edward James Thrum, No. 234, B Company, 9th Battalion, AIF.

11. Bean, *Story of Anzac*, 327–28.

12. Statement of Cpl. Joseph Carlile of the Seventh Battalion.

13. Diary of Sgt. Walter Leadley, 2nd (South Canterbury) Company, NZEF, April 26, 1915.

14. Account of Cpl. (later Capt.) George Mitchell, MC, DCM, of C Company, 10th Battalion, AIF, from his article "The Anzac Landing" in the April 1, 1935, edition of *Reveille*.

15. [Missing source.]

16. Letter of Pvt. W. H. Rhodes, 16th (Waikato) Company, Auckland Battalion, NZEF, in the June 24, 1915, issue of the *Auckland Weekly News*.

17. Letter to his grandmother from Pvt. Reginald Stevens, No. 6/553, 2nd (South Canterbury) Company, Canterbury Battalion, NZEF.

18. Statement of Pvt. E. S. Fisher of D Company, 7th Battalion, stated from Sarpi Rest Camp at Mudros on the Greek island of Lemnos on November 6, 1915.

19. Diary of Pvt. Harry Cicognani, 4th Australian Field Ambulance.

20. Cicognani diary, May 4, 1915.

5. "Littered with Dead"

1. Diary of Pvt. John Vickers, Plymouth Battalion, RMLI.

2. Vickers diary [likely source].

3. Hamilton, *Gallipoli Diary*, 1:129.

4. Hamilton, *Gallipoli Diary*, 132–33.

5. Vickers diary, April 25, 1915.

6. Vickers diary, April 25, 1915 [likely source].

7. Lamplaugh diary, April 25, 1915.

8. Vickers diary.

9. [Missing source.]

10. Hamilton, *Gallipoli Diary*, 1:146.

11. Walter Parnham, Plymouth Battalion, RMLI, orderly to Lt. Col. Matthews.

12. Hamilton, *Gallipoli Diary*, 1:156.

13. Diary of Cpl. T. Rees, B Company, 2nd Battalion, South Wales Borderers.

14. Vassal, *Uncensored Letters*, 193.

15. Report of Capt. Guy Geddes, 1st Battalion, Royal Munster Fusiliers, PRO Ref. WO 95/4310.

16. Many important topographical features were also missing from British maps. This was a common problem during the campaign and was not alleviated until new maps were created months later.

17. A pom-pom was a highly destructive, 37-mm belt-fed gun, so-called because of the sound it made when fired.

18. Diary of 2nd Lt. Norman Dewhurst, Machine Gun Section, 1st Battalion, Royal Munster Fusiliers, April 25, 1915.

19. Report of Lt. Col. Henry Tizard, commanding officer, 1st Battalion, Royal Munster. Fusiliers, PRO Ref WO 95/4310.

20. Creighton, *With the Twenty-Ninth Division*, 67.

21. Capt. G. W. Geddes's report.

22. Lieutenant Colonel Tizard's report.

23. Capt. G. W. Geddes's report.

24. Account of Chief Petty Officer William Perring, Anson Battalion, RND, in Foster, *At Antwerp and the Dardanelles*, 85–86.

25. Stacke, *Worcestershire Regiment in the Great War*, 79.

26. Lt. Guy Nightingale, 1st Battalion, Royal Munster Fusiliers, in a letter to his mother on May 18, 1915.

27. Gillam diary, April 26, 1915.

28. Account of Chief Petty Officer William Perring, No. 13 Platoon, Anson Battalion, RND, in Foster, *At Antwerp and the Dardanelles*, 85–86.

29. Gillam diary, April 27, 1915.

30. Stewart and Peshall, *Immortal Gamble*, 128.

31. Letter of Lt. Ainslie Talbot, 1st Battalion, Lancashire Fusiliers, to his wife dated May 5, 1915.

32. Capt. Harold Clayton, 1st Battalion, Lancashire Fusiliers.

33. Letter from Lieutenant Talbot to his wife dated May 5, 1915.

34. Diary of Capt. Clement Milward, Indian army attached to the 29th Division as General Staff Officer 3.

35. Creighton, *With the Twenty-Ninth Division*, 72.

36. Diary of Sgt. Harry Staff, 1st Battalion, Essex Regiment.

37. [Missing source.]

38. Creighton, *With the Twenty-Ninth Division*, 81 [likely source].

39. Turning the parapet means to prepare a captured trench for an attack from the rear, the direction the defending British would be facing.

40. Letter from Sgt. Maj. E. Nelson, A Company, 1st Battalion, Lancashire Fusiliers, quoted in de Ruvigny, *Roll of Honour*, vol. 1, pt. 2, 10.

41. [Missing source.]

42. Vassal, *Uncensored Letters*, 46.

43. Vassal, *Uncensored Letters*, 47.

44. Vassal, *Uncensored Letters*, 51–52.

45. Vassal, *Uncensored Letters*, 70 [likely source].

46. Vassal, *Uncensored Letters* [likely source].

6. "Had We Gone Forward"

1. Dewhurst diary, April 30, 1915.

2. Sharkey diary.

3. Pvt. W. Flynn, 1st Battalion, Royal Munster Fusiliers.

4. The published history of the Royal Naval Division does not mention the Drakes retiring during the battle.

5. Gillon, *K.O.S.B. in the Great War*, 147.

6. Hamilton, *Gallipoli Diary*, 1:167–68.

7. Gillon, *K.O.S.B. in the Great War*, 147.

8. Diary of Bandsman Herbert Brown, 1st Battalion, Lancashire Fusiliers.

9. Letter from Lt. Col. R. H. Owen, CMG, commanding officer of the 3rd Battalion, AIF, to Lieutenant Owen's parents.

10. Bean, *Story of Anzac*, 1:493.

11. Diary of Trooper H.F.W. Taylor, 6th Australian Light Horse Regiment, June 8, 1915.

12. Letter from the adjutant of the 2nd Battalion Capt. R. Harrison dated June 29, 1915.

13. Diary of Pvt. Edward Baigent, 12th (Nelson) Company, Canterbury Battalion, NZEF, April 27, 1915.

7. "They Died like Officers and Gentlemen"

1. Von Sanders, *Five Years in Turkey*, 71.

2. Statement to the British Red Cross Society (BRCS) by Pvt. H. O. Solomon, 13th Battalion, March 20, 1916.

3. Report to the BRCS by Sgt. J. A. McRae of D Company, 16th Battalion, March 9, 1916.

4. Statement to the BRCS concerning the death of Pvt. Mervyn William Gray of B Company, 16th Battalion.

5. Murray, *Gallipoli as I Saw It*, 59.

6. Diary of Sgt. Dennis Moriarty, 1st Battalion, Royal Munster Fusiliers, May 6, 1915.

7. Vassal, *Uncensored Letters*, 83.

8. Malthus, *Anzac*, 74.

9. Diary of Sgt. Walter Leadley, 2nd (South Canterbury) Company, Canterbury Battalion, NZEF, on May 8, 1915.

10. Letter from Capt. A. J. Cross of the Wellington Battalion to the principal of Wellington College, quoted in the *Oamaru Mail*, August 20, 1915.

11. Report by Capt. Tom Hastie, staff captain, 2nd Australian Infantry Brigade.

12. Statement to the BRCS by Driver F. Holland, Second BAC, March 30, 1916.

13. Statement made to the BRCS by Private Fox (No. 1540), B Company, 6th Battalion, April 8, 1916.

14. Vassal, *Uncensored Letters*, 110.

15. Diary of Pvt. Henry Cicognani, 4th Field Ambulance, Australian Army Medical Corps, May 18, 1915.

16. Herbert diary, May 19, 1915.

17. Cicognani diary.

18. Diary of Trooper William Dawbin, 6th (Manawatu) Squadron, Wellington Mounted Rifles, May 19, 1915.

19. Letter from Maj. Robert Rankine of the 14th Battalion, quoted in the *Ballarat Courier*, July 12, 1915.

20. Von Sanders, *Five Years in Turkey*, 76.

8. "A Lot of Poor Fellows Drowned"

1. Diary of Midshipman Peveril William-Powlett, HMS *Vengeance*.

2. *From Dartmouth to the Dardanelles: A Midshipman's Log*, 152–54.

3. *From Dartmouth to the Dardanelles: A Midshipman's Log*, 162 [likely source].

4. Letter from Sub-Lt. Charles Philip Voltelyn Van der Byl of the *Goliath*, quoted in Gunn, *Book of Remembrance for Tweeddale*, vol. 3: *The Village and Parish of West Linton (Linton Roderick)*, 11.

5. Denham diary, May 25, 1915.

6. [Missing source.]

7. Cicognani diary, May 25, 1915.

8. Hamilton, *Gallipoli Diary*, 1:247.

9. Murray, *Gallipoli as I Saw It*, 77.

10. Murray, *Gallipoli as I Saw It*, 97.

11. Murray, *Gallipoli as I Saw It*, 78.

12. Carberry memoir.

13. Submarines used oil-burning engines while surfaced. These in turn charged the electrical batteries required for operating under water.

14. Kitchen diary, October 15, 1915.

15. [Missing source.]

16. *Medico's War Reminiscences*, *Reveille*, December 1, 1934.

17. Application for pension to the Admiralty, PRO ref. FO286/749. Spelling errors are those of Mr. Jauget.

18. Ruhl, *Antwerp to Gallipoli*, 200.

19. Hamilton, *Gallipoli Diary*, 1:240.

20. Ruhl, *Antwerp to Gallipoli*, 203.

9. "A Glimpse of Hell"

1. Hamilton, *Gallipoli Diary*, 1:260.

2. Gouraud replaced d'Amade as commanding officer of the Corps Expéditionnaire d'Orient on May 15.

3. Hamilton, *Gallipoli Diary*, 1:261–62.

4. The exceptions were the eighteen battalions held in reserve, widely scattered over the sector. They had no idea if, when, or where they might be needed.

5. Foster, *At Antwerp and the Dardanelles*, 126.

6. Behrend, *Make Me a Soldier*, 141.

7. Gillam diary, June 4, 1915.

8. Murray, *Gallipoli as I Saw It*, 150.

9. Extract from a letter from his battalion commander published in the *Times* of London on October 21, 1915.

10. Creighton, *With the Twenty-Ninth Division*, 103.

11. Savory, *Some Gallipoli Memories*, *Gallipolian* (Christmas 1972).

12. Hamilton, *Gallipoli Diary*, 1:272.

13. Foster, *At Antwerp and the Dardanelles*, 126.

14. Murray, *Gallipoli as I Saw It*, 81.

15. Letter from Petty Officer J. Caldwell of C Company, Hood Battalion, to Sub-Lieutenant Baker's father.

16. Report of Able Seaman Harold Petty, D Company, Anson Battalion.

17. Report by Able Seaman John Buckingham and James Parkinson, Anson Battalion.

18. Gillam diary, noon, June 4, 1915.

19. Sharkey diary.

20. Gillam diary, 6:00 a.m. on June 21, 1915.

21. Vassal, *Uncensored Letters*, 139.

22. Vassal, *Uncensored Letters*, 149 [likely source].

23. TD stands for "Territorial Decoration," a long service medal given to officers of the Territorial Force.

24. Diary of Bandsman John Whitelaw, 1/8th Cameronians, June 21, 1915.

25. Belt, ammunition pouches, suspender straps, water bottle and carrier, bayonet and frog, and either a pick or a shovel tied to the back. Entrenching tools, which were virtually useless anyway, were not to be carried. Reserve and support troops would follow with more picks and shovels.

26. Diary of Capt. Robert Rutherford, 1/4th Royal Scots, June 28, 1915.

27. Sharkey diary, June 28, 1915.

28. De Lisle's orders for the battle specifically stated that the officers were to yell "Attack!" though some apparently yelled "Over!"

29. War diary of the 1st Borders, June 28, 1915.

30. Evans memoir. The man Evans thought was McClellan was actually Pvt. Daniel McLennon.

31. [Missing source.]

32. Sharkey diary.

33. [Missing source.] Sharkey was mistaken; the men were members of B Company of the First Border Regiment. The Second South Wales Borderers were part of the first wave attacking on the other side of Gully Ravine.

34. [Missing source.]

35. First Borders war diary.

36. Sharkey diary.

37. Fox, *Royal Inniskilling Fusiliers in the World War*, 188.

38. Creighton, *With the Twenty-Ninth Division*, 145–46.

39. Fox, *Royal Inniskilling Fusiliers in the World War*, 188.

40. Ewing, *Royal Scots*, 154.

41. Statement from Pvt. Robert Seggie, 1/8th Cameronians, to BRCS.

42. *Official History*, 2:92.

10. "No One Left to Fire"

1. Letter quoted in the *Bury Times*, September 4, 1915.

2. Jerrold, *Georgian Adventure*, 144.

3. Wren, *From Randwick to Hargicourt*, 101.

4. [Missing source.]

5. Statement of Lance Cpl. Alexander Reid, October 24, 1916.

6. Bean, *Story of Anzac*, 2:617–18.

7. The infantry battalions, created after the outbreak of the war, were termed "Service battalions" and were only intended to exist until the end of the conflict. The men who enlisted in them did so either for three years or for the duration of the war.

8. Letter from the commanding officer of the 11th Manchesters, quoted in de Ruvigny, *Roll of Honour*, vol. 2, pt. 2, 244.

9. The Salt Lake, located behind Lala Baba, is dry enough to walk on in summer. It is connected to the sea by a short, narrow waterway called the Cut. After the August landings, the British struck potable water nearby only a meter from the surface, and a number of wells were sunk.

10. Also known as Hill 53, it was given the official designation Chocolate Hill in early September 1915 and was one of the major goals of the Suvla campaign. It was captured on the evening of August 7 and was held by the British for the remainder of the campaign. It is located approximately two thousand yards southeast of the Salt Lake and is often mistakenly referred to as Yilghin Burnu. The hill was so named by the Australians in the adjacent Anzac sector in May 1915 because of its sandy reddish soil and dried brush.

11. Crookenden, *History of the Cheshire Regiment in the Great War*.

12. The yeomanry regiments formed the cavalry branch of the Territorial Force. Raised in large part from rural communities, members had to demonstrate their ability to ride before they were accepted for enlistment. Men from urban areas tended to be from a higher social class, as the average worker could neither afford nor ride a horse. Unlike their Anzac counterparts, they were armed with sabers when mounted but not bayonets. Bayonets were issued in Egypt before the men were sent to Gallipoli.

13. Herbert, *Mons, Anzac & Kut.*

14. Letter quoted in the *Evesham Journal and Four Shires Advertiser*, September 18, 1915.

15. Cripps, *Life's a Gamble*, 100.

16. Letter from Capt. Guy Nightingale, 1st Royal Munster Fusiliers, to his mother dated August 25, 1915.

17. Wanliss, *History of the Fourteenth Battalion*, 69–70.

18. Wanliss, *History of the Fourteenth Battalion*, 70–71.

19. Father of media mogul Rupert Murdoch.

11. "Not *Actually* All the King's Men"

1. NA ref. WO95/4320.

2. Vassal, *Uncensored Letters*, 154.

3. Quoted in Elliot, *War History*, 33n.

4. NA Ref. WO95/4320.

5. Quoted in Gunn, *Book of Remembrance for Tweeddale*, bks. 4–5, p. 18.

6. Brown, *War Record of the 4th Battalion*, 34.

7. Statement by Pvt. Alexander Ruddiman, quoted in Richardson, *For King and Country*, 52.

8. Letter quoted in the *Dumfries and Galloway Standard & Advertiser*, July 31, 1915.

9. Jerrold, *Georgian Adventure*, 140–41.

10. Men who enlisted in Territorial Force units *after* the declaration of war were required to sign an agreement to serve overseas and did not receive the badge.

11. Martineau, *History of the Royal Sussex Regiment*, 101.

12. Interview in the *Lynn Advertiser* with Pvt. Harry Pooley of the 1/5th Norfolks (n.d.; cutting contained in a scrapbook compiled by Colin Coxon, the son of Capt. A.C.M. Coxon, 1/5th Battalion, Norfolk Regiment).

13. Interview with St. Thomas Jakeman of the 1/5th Norfolks, in Captain Coxon's scrapbook.

14. Pvt. Harry Pooley, 1/5th Norfolks, in Captain Coxon's scrapbook.

15. Cpl. Donald Foster, 1/5th Norfolks, in Captain Coxon's scrapbook.

16. Undated article from the *Daily Mail* in Captain Coxon's scrapbook.

17. Hamilton, *Gallipoli Diary*, 2:99.

18. Gallishaw, *Trenching at Gallipoli*, chap. 6.

12. "And All Suffered Severely"

1. Gillam diary, September 14, 1915.

2. Herbert diary, June 11, 1915.

3. Gillam diary, afternoon of November 26, 1915.

4. Steele diary, December 4, 1915.

5. Gillam diary, November 27, 1915.

6. Diary of Sergeant Garrett, 3rd Light Horse Regiment, AIF, November 28, 1915.

7. Garrett diary, November 28, 1915.

8. *Gallipolian* (Spring 1994): 30–31.

9. [Missing source.]

10. Farwell, *Gurkhas*, 102.

11. Quoted in Purdom, *Everyman at War*.

12. Purdom, *Everyman at War*.

13. "We Have Lost the Game"

1. Hamilton, *Gallipoli Diary*, 2:n.p.

2. Hamilton, *Gallipoli Diary*, 2:207n.

3. Churchill, *World Crisis*, 2:908.

4. Lamrock, *Surprised: But the Turks Were There*, March 31, 1930, edition of *Reveille*.

5. Bean, *Story of Anzac*, 2:882.

6. Regimental history [no additional source information], 70–71.

7. Quoted in *Gallipolian* (Christmas 1991): 11–13.

8. Quoted in Bean, *Gallipoli Mission*, 364.

9. In the event that the Turks attacked before the sector was completely evacuated, some medical tents and personnel of No. 1 Australian Casualty Clearing Station were left in place. This scheme was also meant to deceive the Turks, should all go as planned. All personnel, along with their one remaining casualty, were safely evacuated before daylight.

10. Bean, *Gallipoli Mission*, 251.

11. Murray, *Gallipoli as I Saw It*, 183.

12. Murray, *Gallipoli as I Saw It*, 184.

13. Bennett, *Memories of Private Walter Albert Bennett Serving with the 42nd East Lancashire Fusiliers on Gallipoli*, *Gallipolian* (Christmas 1992): 15.

14. Gillam diary, 2:00 a.m., January 8, 1916.

15. Letter quoted in *Gallipolian* (Christmas 1991): 23–25.

16. Diary of Capt. Rev. Walter Dexter, Church of England chaplain to the Second Infantry Brigade, AIF, December 16–17, 1915.

17. Knight, *These Things Happened*, 180.

BIBLIOGRAPHY

Regimental Histories

Alexander, Maj. Heber Maitland, DSO, S. & T. Corps, Indian army. *On Two Fronts, Being the Adventures of an Indian Mule Corps in France and Gallipoli.* London: William Heinemann, 1917. (9th Mule Corps, Indian Army.)

Annabell, Maj. N., NZE. *Official History of the New Zealand Engineers during the Great War, 1914–1919.* Wanganui, 1927.

Anonymous. *From Dartmouth to the Dardanelles: A Midshipman's Log, Edited by His Mother* (HMS *Goliath*). London: William Heinemann, 1916.

Atkinson, Christopher Thomas. *The History of the South Wales Borderers.* London, 1931.

Australian War Memorial (AWM). *The Australian Army Medical Services in the War of 1914–1918.* Melbourne, 1938.

Barrett, Lt. Col. James W., CMG, MD. *The Australian Army Medical Corps in Egypt.* London: H. K. Lewis & Co., 1918.

———. *The War Work of the Y.M.C.A. in Egypt.* London: H. K. Lewis and Co., 1919.

Bastin, Jeremy. *The Norfolk Yeomanry in Peace and War.* Fakenham UK: Iceni Press, 1986.

Belford, Walter C. *Legs Eleven.* Perth: Imperial Printing Co., 1940.

Blackwell, Frank M. *The Story of the 3rd Australian Light Horse Regiment.* Privately published, n.d.

Blenkinshop, Maj. Gen. Sir L. J., KCB, DSO, and Lt. Col. J. W. Rainey, CBE, eds. *History of the Great War Based on Official Documents: Veterinary Services.* London: HMSO, 1925.

Blumberg, Gen. Sir H. E., KCB, RM. *Britain's Sea Soldiers: A Record of the Royal Marines during the War 1914–19*. Devonport: Swiss & Co., 1927.

Bourne, Lt. Col. George H., DSO. *History of the 2nd Light Horse Regiment, A.I.F., 1914–1919*. Reprint edition by John Burridge Military Antiques, Swanbourne WA, 1994.

Brereton, Cyprian Bridge. *Tales of Three Campaigns*. London: Selwyn & Blount, 1926. (Canterbury Battalion, NZEF.)

Brown, W. Sorley, ed. *War Record of the 4th Bn. King's Own Scottish Borderers and Lothians and Border Horse*. Galashiels, 1920.

Buchan, John. *The History of the Royal Scots Fusiliers (1678–1918)*. London, n.d.

Burton, 2nd Lt. O. E., MM. *The Auckland Regiment: Being an Account of the Doings on Active Duty of the First, Second and Third Battalions of the Auckland Regiment*. Auckland: Whitcombe & Tombs, 1922.

Byrne, Lt. A. E., MC. *Official History of the Otago Regiment, N.Z.E.F., in the Great War, 1914–1918*. Dunedin, n.d.

Byrne, Lt. J. R., NZFA. *New Zealand Artillery in the Field, 1914–18*. Auckland, 1922.

C. *The Yeomanry Cavalry of Worcestershire, 1914–1922*. Stourbridge: Mark & Moody, 1926.

Carbery, Lt. Col. A. D. *The New Zealand Medical Services in the Great War, 1914–1918*, Auckland: Whitcombe & Tombs, 1924.

Chataway, Lt. T. P. *History of the 15th Battalion, Australian Imperial Forces, 1914–1918*. Brisbane: William Brooks & Co., 1948.

Collett, H. B. *The 28th: A Record of War Service with the Australian Imperial Force, 1915–1919*. Perth: Trustees, Public Library, 1922.

Cooper, Maj. Bryan. *The Tenth (Irish) Division in Gallipoli*. London: Irish Academic Press, 1917.

Cowan, James. *The Maoris in the Great War*. Auckland, 1926.

Cramm, Richard. *The First Five Hundred*. New York, n.d. (Royal Newfoundland Regt.)

Crookenden, Arthur. *The History of the Cheshire Regiment in the Great War*. Chester: W. H. Evans, Sons, 1938.

Cull, Capt. W. A. *At All Costs* (23rd Battalion, AIF). Personal note from John Meyers of Bribie Island, Queensland.

Cunningham, W. H., C.A.L. Treadwell, and J. S. Hanna. *The Wellington Regiment, N.Z.E.F., 1914–1919*. Wellington, 1928.

Darley, Maj. T. H. *With the 9th Light Horse in the Great War*. Adelaide: Hassell Press, 1924.

Davies, Harry. *Allanson of the 6th*. Lowesmoor, Worcester: Square One Publications, 1990. (6th Gurkha Rifles.)

Dean, Arthur, and Eric W. Gutteridge. *The Seventh Battalion, A.I.F.: Resume of Activities of the Seventh Battalion in the Great War, 1914–1918*. Melbourne: W. & K. Purbrick Pty., 1933.

Eaton, Maj. M. J., RGA. *Memoirs of the 42 Siege Battery, R.G.A.* London, n.d.

Edington, Col. G. H., MD, DSC, AMS (TF). *With the 1/1st Lowland Field Ambulance in Gallipoli.* Glasgow: Alex. Macdougall, 1920.

Elliot, Scott. *War History of the 5th Battalion King's Own Scottish Borderers.* Dumfries, 1928.

Ewing, Maj. John, MC. *The Royal Scots, 1914–1919.* Edinburgh, 1925.

Fallon, Brian T. *Gone but Not Forgotten: A Tribute to the War Dead of "H" Company, 10th Battalion, Australian Imperial Force.* Privately published, 2006.

Ferguson, Capt. David. *The History of the Canterbury Regiment, New Zealand Expeditionary Force, 1914–1919.* Auckland: Whitcombe & Tombs, 1921.

Fox, Frank. *The History of the Royal Gloucestershire Hussars Yeomanry, 1898–1922.* London, 1923.

Fox, Sir Frank, OBE. *The Royal Inniskilling Fusiliers in the World War.* London: Constable, 1928.

Geary, Lt. Stanley, RM. *The Collingwood Battalion: Royal Naval Division a Short History of the Collingwood Battalion in the Dardanelles Together with Biographical Notes of All the Officers and a List of the Men.* Hastings UK: F. J. Parsons, 1919[?].

Gibbon, Frederick P. *The 42nd (East Lancashire) Division, 1914–1918.* London: Offices of "Country Life," 1920.

Gill, Ian. *Fremantle to France: 11th Battalion, A.I.F., 1914–1919.* Myaree W.A.: Advance Press, 2003.

Gillon, Capt. Stair. *The K.O.S.B. in the Great War.* London, 1930.

———. *The Story of the 29th Division: A Record of Gallant Deeds,* London: Thomas Nelson & Sons, 1925.

Grimwade, Capt. F. Clive. *The War History of the 4th Battalion The London Regiment (Royal Fusiliers), 1914–1919.* London: Headquarters of the 4th London Regiment, 1922.

Hanna, Henry, K. C. *The Pals at Suvla Bay, Being the Record of "D" Company of the 7th Royal Dublin Fusiliers.* Dublin, 1916.

Harvey, Norman K. *From Anzac to the Hindenburg Line: The History of the 9th Battalion A.I.F.* Brisbane: William Brooks, 1941.

A History of the East Lancashire Royal Engineers, Compiled by Members of the Corps. Country Life, 1921. (1/1st and 1/2nd East Lancashire Field Companies.)

History of the 5th Royal Gurkha Rifles (Frontier Force), 1858 to 1928. Aldershot UK: Gale & Polden, n.d.

The History of the Old 2/4th (City of London) Battalion: The London Regiment (Royal Fusiliers). London, 1919.

Hurst, Gerald B. *With Manchesters in the East.* Manchester: University of Manchester Press, 1918. (1/7th Battalion [TF], Manchester Regiment.)

Jerrold, Douglas. *The Royal Naval Division,* London, 1923.

Johnson, Lt. Col. R. M., CMG, DSO. *The 29th Divisional Artillery, War Record and Honours Book, 1915–1918*. Woolwich UK, 1921.

Jose, A. W. *Official History of Australia in the Great War of 1914–18*. Vol. 9: *The Royal Australian Navy*. Sydney: Angus and Robertson, 1935.

Keown, A. W. *Forward with the Fifth*. Melbourne: Specialty Press, 1921.

Lancashire Fusiliers' Annual, 1915–1916.

Lock, Cecil B. L. *The Fighting 10th*. Adelaide: Webb & Son, 1936.

Longmore, Cyril. *The Old Sixteenth*. History Committee, 16th Battalion [AIF] Assoc., Perth, 1929.

McCance, Capt. S. *History of the Royal Munster Fusiliers*. Vol. 2. Aldershot UK: Gale & Polden, 1927.

McCrery, Nigel. *The Vanished Battalion*. London, 1992. (1/5th Battalion, Norfolk Regiment.)

MacKenzie, Colin S. *The Last Warrior Band: The Gallipoli Expedition Seen from a Lewis Perspective. Transactions of the Gaelic Society of Inverness*, no. 59 (1994–96): 275–313. (Ross [Mountain] Battery, 1/4th Highland Mountain Brigade, Royal Garrison Artillery.)

McKenzie, K. W. *The Story of the Seventeenth Battalion, A.I.F., in the Great War, 1914–1918*. Sydney: Shipping Newspapers, 1946.

MacNeil, A. R. *The Story of the 21st, Being the Official History of the 21st Bn., A.I.F.* Melbourne: 21st Battalion Assoc., 1920.

McNicoll, R. *The Royal Australian Engineers, 1902 to 1919: Making and Breaking*. Canberra: Royal Australian Engineers, 1979.

Macpherson, Maj. Gen. Sir W. G., KCMG, CB, LL.D. *History of the Great War: Medical Services, General History*. Vols. 1, 3, and 4. London, 1921.

Martineau, G. D. *A History of the Royal Sussex Regiment*. Chichester, n.d.

May, Ralph. *Glory Is No Compensation: The Border Regiment at Gallipoli, 1915*. Great Addington, Kettering, Northamptonshire: Silver Link Publishing, 2003.

Midwinter, Charles. *1914–1919: Memoirs of the 32nd Field Ambulance, 10th (Irish) Division*. [N.p.p.], 1933.

Mitchinson, K. W. *Amateur Soldiers: A History of Oldham's Volunteers and Territorials 1859–1938*. Jade, 1999.

Moody, Col. R.S.H., CB, PSC. *Historical Records of the Buffs (East Kent Regiment), 3rd Foot*. London, 1922.

Moore, James G. Harle. *With the Fourth New Zealand Rough Riders*. Dunedin, 1906.

Morrison, F. L. *The Fifth Battalion Highland Light Infantry in the War 1914–1918*. Glasgow: MacLehose, Jackson & Co., 1921.

Mullaly, Col. B. R. *Bugle and Kukri: The Story of the 10th Prince Mary's Own Gurkha Rifles*. Edinburgh: William Blackwood & Sons, 1957.

Murphy, Charles Cecil Howe. *The History of the Suffolk Regiment, 1914–1927*. London, 1928.

Newton, L. M. *The Story of the Twelfth.* Hobart, 1925.

Nicholson, Col. G.W.L., CD. *The Fighting Newfoundlander: A History of the Royal Newfoundland Regiment.* Government of Newfoundland, 1964.

Nicol, Sgt. C. G. *The Story of Two Campaigns.* Auckland, 1921. (Auckland Mounted Rifles, NZEF.)

Notts. and Derby's Annual. 1922 (Sherwood Foresters.)

Ogilvie, Maj. D. D. *The Fife and Forfar Yeomanry and 14th (F. & F. Yeo.) Battn. R.H., 1914–1919.* London, 1921.

Olden, A.C.N. *Westralian Cavalry in the War: The Story of the 10th Light Horse Regiment in the Great War 1914–18.* Melbourne, 1921.

O'Neill, H. C. *The Royal Fusiliers in the Great War.* London, 1922.

Owen, Bryn. *Owen Roscomyl and the Welsh Horse.* Caernarfon, 1990.

Patterson, Lt. Col. J. H., DSO. *With the Zionists at Gallipoli.* New York, 1916. (Zion Mule Corps.)

Powell-Edwards, Lt. Col. H. I., DSO. *The Sussex Yeomanry and 16th (Sussex Yeomanry) Battalion Royal Sussex Regiment, 1914–1919.* London, n.d.

Powles, Col. C. G., CMG, DSO., ADC, ed. *The History of the Canterbury Mounted Rifles.* Auckland, 1928.

Record of the 5th (Service) Battalion, the Connaught Rangers from 19th August, 1914, to 17th January, 1916.

Regimental History Committee. *The Dorsetshire Regiment: History of the Dorsetshire Regiment.* Pt. 3: *Service Battalions.* Dorchester, 1932.

Reilly, Maj. John (retired). *Biographical and Photographic Sources for Officers of the Highland Light Infantry Who Died during the Great War, 1914–1919.* Unpublished.

Richardson, Gavin. *For King and Country and the Scottish Borderers.* Hawick, 1987.

Rimmer, Edmund. *The Story of the Fifth-Fifth Bedfords.* Manchester Cooperative Wholesale Society's Printing Works, 1917.

Rowe, John. *The North Devon Yeomanry, 1794–1924.* N.d.

Royal Anglian History Committee. *The Story of the Bedfordshire and Hertfordshire Regiment.* Vol. 2: *1914–1958.* Regiment, 1988.

Ryan, Maj. D.G.J., DSO. *Historical Record of the 6th Gurkha Rifles.* Privately published, 1925.

Sellers, Leonard. *The Hood Battalion.* London: Leo Cooper, 1995.

Sherwood Foresters. *The Sherwood Foresters Regimental Annual, 1922.*

A Short Account of the Formation of the 1st Field Coy. Engineers (1914–18) and Its Movements from Embarkation on the "Afric" and the "Clan Macquardale" from Sydney on October 18th, 1914. N.d. (1st Field Company, Australian Engineers, AIF.)

Simpson, Maj. Gen. C. R. *The History of the Lincolnshire Regiment, 1914–1918,* London, 1931.

Smith, S. J. *The Samoan (N.Z.) Expeditionary Force, 1914–1915.* Wellington: Ferguson & Osborn, 1924.

Speed, F. W., ed. *Esprit de Corps: The History of the Victorian Scottish Regiment and the 5th Infantry Battalion.* Sydney: Allen & Unwin, 1988.

Stacke, Capt. H. FitzM., MC. *The Worcestershire Regiment in the Great War.* Kidderminster, 1928.

Starr, Joan. *From the Saddlebags at War.* Hamilton: Australian Light Horse Assoc., 2000. (2nd Light Horse Regiment, AIF.)

Stevens, Frank. *Southborough Sappers of the Kent (Fortress) Royal Engineers.* Tonbridge, Kent: FAST, 2000. (1/3rd Kent Field Company, Royal Engineers.)

Strutt, Lt. Col. G. A., ed. *The Derbyshire Yeomanry War History, 1914–1919.* 1929. Reprint. East Sussex UK: Naval and Military Press, 2005.

Taylor, F. W., and T. A. Cusack. *Nulli Secundus: A History of the Second Battalion, A.I.F., 1914–1919.* Reprint. Swanbourne W.A.: John Burridge Military Antiques, 1992.

Thompson, Maj. Gen. C. W., CB, DSO. *Records of the Dorset Yeomanry (Queen's Own), 1914–1919.*

Tizard, Lt. Col. H. E., Commanding Officer, 1st Battalion, Royal Munster Fusiliers. *Report on the Landing from the Collier River Clyde at V Beach on April 25th 1915.* PRO ref. WO 95/4310.

Twentieth Battalion Manuscript History, 1915. AWM.

Verey, Anthony, Stuart Sampson, Andrew Friend, and Simon Frost. *The Berkshire Yeomanry: 200 Years of Yeoman Service.* Reading, 1994.

Wanliss, Newton. *The History of the Fourteenth Battalion, A.I.F.* Melbourne, 1929.

The War Service Record of the First Australian Field Artillery Brigade, 1914–1919.

Webster, Capt. F.A.M., *The History of the Fifth Battalion Bedfordshire and Hertfordshire Regiment (T.A.).* London: Frederick Warne & Co., 1930.

White, T. A. *The Fighting Thirteenth.* Sydney: Tyrells, 1924.

Wilkie, Maj. A. H. *Official War History of the Wellington Mounted Rifles Regiment.* Auckland, 1924.

Williamson, Sgt. T. *The Disappearance of the King's Company (Sandringham) in Gallipoli: The Day the Hills Caught Fire.* Ilfracombe, Devon: Arthur H. Stockwell, 1979.

Wilson, L. C., and H. Wetherell. *History of the Fifth Light Horse Regiment, 1914–1919.* Sydney: Motor Press, 1926.

Wren, Eric. *From Randwick to Hargicourt: History of the 3rd Battalion, A.I.F.* Sydney: Ronald G. McDonald, 1935.

Wrench, C. M., MC. *Campaigning with the Fighting 9th.* Brisbane, 1985.

Wylly, Col. H. C. *The Border Regiment in the Great War.* Aldershot UK, 1924.

———. *History of the Manchester Regiment.* Vol. 2: *1883–1922.* London: Forster Groom, 1925.

————. *History of the Queen's Royal Regiment*. Vol. 7: Aldershot UK, 1925.

————. *The Loyal North Lancashire Regiment*. Vol. 2: *1914–1919*. London, 1933.

Ships' Histories

Blackburn, C. J. *How the Manx Fleet Helped in the Great War: The Story of the Isle of Man Steam Packet Boats on Service*. Douglas, Isle of Man: Louis G. Meyer, 1923.

Brenchley, Fred, and Elizabeth Brenchley. *Stoker's Submarine*. Sydney: HarperCollins, 2001. (AE2.)

Hersing, Otto. *U 21 rettet die Dardanellen*. Leipzig: v. Hase & Koehler Verlag, 1932.

Stewart, Cdr. A. T., RN, and Rev. C.J.E. Peshall, BA, RN. *The Immortal Gamble*. London, 1917. (HMS *Cornwallis*.)

General References

Adam-Smith, Patsy. *The Anzacs*. Melbourne: Sphere Books, 1978.

————. *Prisoners of War from Gallipoli to Korea*. Ringwood, Victoria: Penguin Books Australia, 1992.

Aspinall-Oglander, Brig. Gen. C. F. *History of the Great War: Military Operations Gallipoli*. 12 vols. 1932. Reprint. London: Imperial War Museum, 1992.

Austin, Ron. *The White Gurkhas: The Australians at the Second Battle of Krithia*. McRae, Melbourne: R. J. and S. P. Austin, 1989.

Bagnall, W. G. *70 Years of My Life*. [Missing source information.]

Bailey, Keith. *Copper City Chronicle: A History of Kadina*. [Missing source information.]

Bean, C. E. W., ed. *The* ANZAC *Book*. London: Cassell, 1916.

————. *Gallipoli Mission*. Nest N.S.W.: Australian Broadcasting Corp., 1990.

Berry, H. *Christ Church Malvern: A Guide to the Church*. Privately published, 2000.

Blyth, Ronald. *Akenfield: Portrait of an English Village*. New York: Pantheon Books, 1969.

Boorman, Derek. *At the Going Down of the Sun*. York: Sessions, 1988.

Bruce, George, and Thomas Harbottle. *Dictionary of Battles*. New York: Stein & Day, 1975.

Carlyon, Patrick. *The Gallipoli Story*. Camberwell: Penguin Books, 2003.

Carter, Jennifer, and Geoffrey Williams. *Morey Memories*. Whiritoa NZ: Whiritoa Desktop, 1993. (A history of the Morey family.)

Cave, Joy B., and Charlie Byrne, eds. *I Survived, Didn't I?* London: Leo Cooper, 1993.

Chamberlain, Denis J. *History of the Bathurst Contingents, 1868–1987*. Bathurst N.S.W., 1987.

Church of Jesus Christ of Latter Day Saints. *Australian Vital Records Index.* Provo UT, 1998.

Cochrane, Peter. *Simpson and the Donkey: The Making of a Legend.* Melbourne: Melbourne University Press, 1992.

Connell, W. A. *Australian Imperial Forces, 1814–1920: Enlistments, Casualties, Major Battles, Honours.* Canberra: Military Historical Society of Australia, A.C.T. Branch, 1972.

Corbett, Sir Julian S. *Official History of the War: Naval Operations.* Vols. 2–3. London: Longmans, Green, 1921.

Cowell, C. Berkeley, and E. Watts Moses. *Durham County Rugby Union, 1876–1936.* Newcastle-on-Tyne: Andrew Reid & Co., 1936.

Creagh, Gen. Sir O'M., VC, GCB, GCSI, and E. M. Humphris. *The Distinguished Service Order, 1886–1923.* Vols. 1–2. London, 1923.

Creswicke, Louis. *South Africa and the Transvaal War.* Vol. 7. London, 1904.

Croydon Corp. *Croydon and the Great War.* Croydon: Croydon Corp. Libraries Committee, 1920.

De Gaury, Gerald. *Traces of Travel: Brought Home from Abroad.* London: Quartet Books, 1983.

Dening, Greg. *Xavier—A Centenary Portrait.* Armadale, Victoria: Old Xavierians Assoc., 1978.

Denton, Kit. *Gallipoli: One Long Grave.* Sydney: Time-Life Books of Australia, 1986.

Dungan, Myles. *Irish Soldiers and the Great War.* Dublin: Four Courts Press, 1997.

Dyer, Dave. *The Lives and Times of the Dyer Family of Alton.* Privately published, n.d.

Erickson, Edward J. *Ordered to Die: A History of the Ottoman Army in the First World War.* Westport, Conn.: Greenwood Press, 2001.

Farr, Grahame. *West Country Passenger Steamers.* London: Richard Tilling, 1956.

Frame, T. R., and G. J. Swinden. *First In, Last Out: The Navy at Gallipoli.* Kenthurst N.S.W.: Kangaroo Press, 1990.

Gaffney, Angela. *Aftermath: Remembering the Great War in Wales.* Cardiff: University of Wales Press, 1998.

Gilbert, Martin. *Churchill: A Life.* New York: Henry Holt, 1991.

———. *Winston S. Churchill, 1914–1916.* London: C & T Publications, 1971.

Gowing, Margaret. *Britain and Atomic Energy, 1939–45.* New York: St. Martin's Press, 1964.

Gray, Edwyn. *The Killing Time: The German U-Boats, 1914–1918.* London: Pan Books, 1972.

Halpin, John. *Blood in the Mists.* Sydney: Macquarie Head Press, 1934.

Hamilton, John. *Goodbye Cobber, God Bless You: The Fatal Charge of the Light Horse, Gallipoli, August 7th 1915.* Sydney: Macmillan, 2004.

Hickey, Michael. *Gallipoli.* London: John Murray, 1995.

Hill, Anthony. *Soldier Boy: The True Story of Jim Martin, the Youngest Anzac.* Ringwood AU: Penguin Books, 2001.

Holden, Wendy. *Shell Shock: The Psychological Impact of War.* London: Channel 4 Books, 1998.

Holt, Tonie, and Valmai Holt. *Major and Mrs. Holt's Battlefield Guide: Gallipoli.* Barnsley, South Yorkshire UK: Leo Cooper, 2000.

Hook, F. A. *The Merchant Adventurers.* London: A. & C. Black, 1920.

Housman, Laurence, ed. *War Letters of Fallen Englishmen.* London: Victor Gollancz, 1930.

Hurd, Archibald. *Official History of the War: The Merchant Navy.* Vol. 2. New York: Longmans, Green, 1924.

James, Brig. E. A., OBE, TD. *British Regiments, 1914–1918.* London: Samson Books, 1978.

James, Robert Rhodes. *Churchill: A Study in Failure, 1900–1939.* New York: World Publishing, 1970.

Jones, Brian. *St. Joseph's, Aberavon: A Parish and Its People.* Port Talbot, Wales: D. W. Jones, 1987.

Kaurihohore Centennial Committee. *The Story of Kaurihohore, 1856–1956.* Auckland: Clark & Matheson, 1957.

Kerr, Greg. *Lost Anzacs: The Story of Two Brothers.* Melbourne: Oxford University Press, 1997.

———. *Private Wars: Personal Records of Anzacs in the Great War.* Melbourne: Oxford University Press, 2000.

The Knox College Register. Dunedin: Knox College Assoc., 1973.

Layman, R. D. *Naval Aviation in the First World War: Its Impact and Influence.* Annapolis: Naval Institute Press, 1996.

Levine, Stephen, ed. *A Standard for the People: The 150th Anniversary of the Wellington Congregation, 1843–1993.* Wellington: Hazard Press, 1993. (Jewish servicemen.)

Liddle, Peter. *Men of Gallipoli.* London: Allen Lane, 1976.

Lipovetzky, P. *Joseph Trumpeldor: Life and Works.* Jerusalem: Youth and Hechalutz Dept., World Zionist Organization, 1953.

MacDonagh, Michael. *The Irish at the Front, London.* London: Hodder & Stoughton, 1916.

Macdonald, Lyn. *The Roses of No Man's Land.* London: Penguin Books, 1980.

McKernan, Michael. *Padre: Australian Chaplains in Gallipoli and France.* London: Allen & Unwin, 1986.

McQuilton, John. *Rural Australia and the Great War: From Tarrawingee to Tangambalanga.* Melbourne: Melbourne University Press, 2001.

Masefield, John. *Gallipoli.* New York: Macmillan, 1917.

Massey, Graeme. *Gallipoli Heroes: A Tribute to the Men from Western Victoria Who Gave Their Lives for Their Country.* Warracknabeal, Victoria: North West Press, 2004.

Massie, Robert K. *Dreadnought: Britain, Germany, and the Coming of the Great War.* New York: Random House, 1991.

Matthews, John. *St. John's Church, Newport, the First 150 Years, 1837–1987.* Newport, 1988.

Mellor, Clive. *In Memory of Charles Ross of the 7th Battalion Manchester Regiment Who Died at Gallipoli, 25 August 1915.* Privately published, [n.d.].

Middlebrook, Martin. *First Day on the Somme.* New York: Norton, 1972.

Mizzi, John A. *Gallipoli: The Malta Connection.* [Missing source information.]

Moorhouse, Geoffrey. *Hell's Foundations.* New York: Henry Holt, 1992.

Morgenthau, Henry. *Ambassador Morgenthau's Story.* Garden City NY: Doubleday, 1918.

Nye, Edward. *The History of Wesley College, 1865–1919.* Melbourne: McCarron, Bird & Co., 1921.

Oxford University. *Register of Rhodes Scholars.* Oxford, 1950.

Pearce, H. W., ed. *Anzac Memorial.* 3rd ed. Sydney: R.S. and S.I.L.A., N.S.W. Branch, 1919.

Petersen, G. C. *Forest Homes.* Wellington, 1956.

Pugsley, Christopher. *On the Fringe of Hell: New Zealanders and Military Discipline in the First World War.* Auckland: Hodder & Stoughton, 1991.

Purdom, C. B., ed. *Everyman at War.* London: J. M. Dent, 1930.

Putkowski, Julian, and Julian Sykes. *Shot at Dawn: Executions in World War One by Authority of the British Army Act.* Barnsley, South Yorkshire UK: Pen & Sword, 1989.

The Register of the Victoria Cross. Cheltenham: This England Books, 1981.

Reichsarchiv. *Dardanellen 1915.* Oldenburg: Gerhard Stalling, 1927.

Robertson, Derek. *All These Fine Fellows: Hawick and District and the Great War.* Hawick, Scotland: Richardson & Son, 2000.

———. *The Men Who Marched Away: Liddesdale and the Great War.* Langholm UK: Eskdale and Liddesdale Newspapers, 1995.

Robertson, Joan. *Anzac and Empire: The Tragedy and Glory of Gallipoli.* London: Collins, 1990.

Scott, William Herbert. *Leeds in the Great War, 1914–1918.* Leeds, 1923.

Shadbolt, Maurice. *Voices of Gallipoli.* Auckland: Hodder & Stoughton, 1988.

Shovelton & Storey (printers). *The All-Australia Memorial: History, Heroes and Helpers (New South Wales Edition).* Melbourne: British-Australasian Publishing Service, 1919.

A Sketchbook of Palmerston North Boys' High School. [N.p.p.], 1977.

Smith, Lt. Col. Neil C., AM. *The Kiwi Connection: Australians in the New Zealand Expeditionary Forces, 1914–1919.* Melbourne: Mostly Unsung Military History Research, 1997.

———. *Australian Prisoners of the Turks, 1915–1918.* Melbourne: Mostly Unsung Military History Research, n.d.

Snelling, Stephen. *VCs of the First World War: Gallipoli*. Stroud UK: Alan Sutton, 1995.

Steel, Nigel, and Peter Hart. *Defeat at Gallipoli*. London: Macmillan, 1994.

Stowers, Richard. *Bloody Gallipoli*. Auckland: David Bateman, 2005.

Taylor, Phil, and Pam Cupper. *Gallipoli: A Battlefield Guide*. Kenthurst N.S.W.: Kangaroo Press, 1989.

Travers, Tim. *Gallipoli 1915*. Stroud, Gloucestershire: Tempus Publishing, 2001.

Venn, J. A., Litt. D., FSA. *Alumni Cantabrigienses from 1752–1900*. Vols. 1–4. Cambridge: Cambridge University, 1944–52.

Von Sanders, Gen. Liman. *Five Years in Turkey*. Baltimore: Williams & Wilkins, 1920.

Waite, Maj. Frederick, DSO, NZE. *The New Zealanders at Gallipoli*. Auckland: Whitcombe & Tombs, 1921.

Walker, Robert. *Recipients of the Distinguished Conduct Medal, 1914–1920*. Birmingham UK: Midland Medals, 1981.

———. *To What End Did They Die? Officers Died at Gallipoli*. Upton-on-Severn: R. W. Walker, 1985.

Warner, Philip. *Kitchener: The Man behind the Legend*. New York: Atheneum, 1996.

Westlake, Ray. *British Regiments at Gallipoli*. Barnsley, South Yorkshire UK: Leo Cooper, 1996.

———. *The Volunteer Infantry, 1880–1908*. Farnham: Military Historical Society, 1992.

White, Michael W. D. *Australian Submarines: A History*. Canberra: Australian Government Publishing Service, 1992.

Whitehead, Diana, and Wendy Whitehead. *The Whitehead Family on Spring Creek*. N.p.p., 1986.

Willocks, James. *With the Indians in France*. London: Constable and Co., 1920.

Wilson, Trevor. *The Myriad Faces of War: Britain and the Great War, 1914–1918*. Cambridge: Polity Press, 1986.

Winter, Denis. *25 April 1915: The Inevitable Tragedy*. Queensland: University of Queensland Press, 1994.

Young, Wilfred. *Australia's Heroic Deeds on the Field of Battle: Biographical Sketches of North Sydney Heroes*. Sydney: Epworth Printing and Publishing House, 1917.

Rolls of Honor and Related Registries

Aberdeen University Roll of Service in the Great War, 1914–1919. Aberdeen: Aberdeen University Press, 1921.

Adelphi Lad's Club Roll of Honour, 1914–1919. Manchester, n.d.

Adler, Rev. Michael, DSO, SCF, BA, ed. *British Jewry Book of Honour*. London: Caxton Publishing Co., 1922.

Albany School Committee. *The Schools of Albany*. Auckland, 1858–1976.

Aldenham School Register. Hertfordshire UK.

Allardyce, Mabel Desborough. *University of Aberdeen Roll of Service in the Great War, 1914–1919.* Aberdeen, 1921.

The All-Australia Memorial, South Australia Edition. Melbourne: British-Australasian, 1920.

Allerton and Daisy Hill War Memorial Souvenir.

A Memorial Record of Watsonians Who Served in the Great War, 1914–1918. Edinburgh, 1920. (George Watson's College, Edinburgh.)

Australia's Fighting Sons of the Empire. Perth, c. 1919.

Balliol College War Memorial Book, vols. 1–2 (Oxford University.)

Bank of New South Wales Roll of Honour. Sydney, 1921.

Bannister, Victoria. *Southport's Splendid Hearts: A Tribute to the Men of Southport Who Gave Their Lives in the Great War.* Privately published, 2002.

Batchelor, Alf, BA. *Melbourne Cricket Club Roll of Honour, 1914–1918.* Melbourne Cricket Club, n.d.

Beaumont, Frank, BA, ed. *The High School of Glasgow: The Book of Service and Remembrance.* Glasgow, 1921.

Bellahouston Academy War Memorial Volume, August 4th, 1914–June 28th, 1919. Glasgow, n.d.

Birkenhead School. *Memorials of Old Birkonians, 1914–1918.* Privately published, 1920.

Blainey, Geoffrey, James Morrissey, and S.E.K. Hulme. *Wesley College: The First Hundred Years.* Melbourne: Wesley College, 1967.

Boas, Hon. Lt. Harold, comp. *Australian Jewry Book of Honour: The Great War, 1914–1918.* Perth: Lamson Paragon, 1923.

Book of Remembrance and War Record of Mill Hill School.

Book of Remembrance of St. Hilda's Church, Westcliff, Whitby, Yorkshire UK.

Boisseau, H. E. *The Prudential Staff and the Great War.* London, 1938.

Brighton College Register, 1847–1922.

Brownlie, Maj. John, ed. *The Great War: New Kilpatrick's Response to the Call of the King.* Glasgow: Samuel A. C. Todd, 1916.

Burgh of Rothesay and Island of Bute War Memorial, 1914–1919.

Burnell, Tom. *The Offaly War Dead: A History of the Casualties of the First World War.* Dublin: History Press, Ireland, 2010.

Bury Times Roll of Honour.

Christ's College Old Boys' Assoc. *The School List of Christ's College from 1850 to 1950.* Christchurch, 1950.

City of Coventry Roll of the Fallen. Coventry, 1927.

Clark, Len. *Under Silent Stars: Charles Robert Lamont.* Minore: privately published, 1993.

Clarke, P., A. Cook, and J. Bintliff. *Remembered: Marple Men Who Fell in the Great War.* Poole, Dorset UK: Oakdale Printing Co., 1999.

Clayton, John T. *Craven's Part in the Great War.* 1919.

Coffee, Frank. *In Memento of the Late Lieutenant Frank M. Coffee of the 24th Battalion, Australian Imperial Force.* Frank Coffee, Sydney, 1916.

Collett, D. W., BA. *Roll of Honour, St. Dunstans College, 1914–19.* London.

Crockman, C. R., and C.L.R. Thomas, comps. *Roll of Honour and War List, 1914–18, of University College School, Hampstead.* St. Albans: Campfield Press, n.d.

Cumberland Argus. *Parramatta District Soldiers Who Fought in the Great War, 1914–1919.* Parramatta, n.d.

Deal Civic War Memorial.

Downside (Catholic) School Roll of Honour.

Dulwich College War Record, 1914–19.

The Education Department's Record of War Service (Victoria).

Edward Worlledge School. *Souvenir to "Old Worlledgers.* Great Yarmouth, Norfolk UK, 1920.

Elizabeth College Register.

Fettes College Register.

For Empire: Victoria's First Expeditionary Force to the Motherland. Melbourne: Osboldstone & Co., 1914. Reprint. Queensland: John Meyers of Bribie Island, 1998.

Fraser, Mrs. *Records of the Men from Lochbroom.* Glasgow, 1922.

George Heriot's School Roll of Honour, 1914–1919. Edinburgh, 1921.

Great Yarmouth Record of the Great War, 1914–18. Vols. 1–8. Norfolk County UK.

Gunn, Dr. C. B. *The Book of Remembrance for Tweeddale.* Vol. 1: *Burgh and Parish of Peebles.* Peebles, 1920.

———. *The Book of Remembrance for Tweeddale.* Vol. 3: *The Village and Parish of West Linton (Linton Roderick).* Peebles, 1923.

Haileybury School, 1862–1911.

Haileybury School Register, 1882–1961.

Harrogate Roll of Honour, 1915–1916.

Harrow School War Memorial. Vols. 2–3 (1915 and 1916).

Hawick News. *Hawick and the War: A Pictorial Record.*

Hennessy, Thomas F. *The Great War 1914–1918: Bank of Ireland Staff Service Record.* Dublin, 1920.

Her Majesty's Stationery Office. *Officers Died in the Great War.* London: HMSO, 1921.

———. *Soldiers Died in the Great War.* London, 1921.

Holcroft, Fred. *Just like Hell: Local Men at Gallipoli (Wigan, Lancashire).* Wigan, 1994.

Imperial War Museum. *Royal Naval Division: Roll of Honour, Drake Battalion.* N.d.

———. *Royal Naval Division: Roll of Honour, Howe Battalion.* N.d.

————. *Royal Naval Division: Roll of Honour, Nelson Battalion.* N.d.

Jesmond Royal Grammar School Roll of Honour. Newcastle-upon-Tyne: Northumberland Press, 1924.

Johnson, R. H. *Gainsborough Roll of Honour.* Gainsborough, 1985.

Kaurihohore Centennial Committee. *The Story of Kaurihohore, 1856–1956.*

Kempster, Brig. Gen. F., DSO, and Brig. Gen. H.C.E. Westropp. *Manchester City Battalions of the 90th and 91st Infantry Brigades Book of Honour.* Manchester, 1916.

King's College Register. Auckland, 1972.

Laverty, Rev. W. H. *Our Sailors and Soldiers Whom We Lost in the Great War, 1914–1918.* Privately published, 1919. (Headley Parish, Hampshire.)

Lee, John A. *Todmorden and the Great War, 1914–1918: A Local Record.* Todmorden UK: Waddington & Sons, 1922.

Lennox and Addington Society. *The War Work of the County of Lennox and Addington.* Ontario, 1922.

Leonard, P. J. *Till All Our Fight Be Fought: The "Olavian" Fallen and the Great War.* Privately published, 2007. (St. Olave's School, Bermondsey, London.)

The Leys and the War. (Leys School.)

List of British Officers Taken Prisoner in the Various Theatres of War between August, 1914, and November, 1918. London, 1919.

List of Members of the Navy, Army, Air Force, Auxiliary Forces, and Mercantile Marine, Belonging to the County Borough of Tynemouth, Who Gave Their Lives in the Great War, 1914–1919. North Shields UK: Northern Press, 1919.

Liverpool's Scroll of Fame.

Lloyd's War Memorial.

London County Council. *Record of Service in the Great War, 1914–18, by Members of the Council's Staff.* London: P. S. King & Son, 1922.

London Stock Exchange. *The Stock Exchange Memorial to Those Who Fell in the Great War, 1914–1918.* London, 1920.

Loretto Roll of Honour, 1914–1920. [Missing source information.]

Malpass, Robert. *Exeter College, Oxford, Roll of Honour, 1914–1918.* Privately published, 2009.

Malvern College Register, 1865–1924. 1925.

Manchester Grammar School. *A Biographical Register of Old Mancunians, 1888–1951.* Manchester, 1965.

Manchester University Record of War Service. Manchester: University of Manchester Press, 1922.

Mansfield's Souvenir of the War, 1914–1919: Photos of Those Who Went from This District to Fight for Justice and Liberty. Mansfield, Victoria: Mansfield Chronicle, 1920[?].

McKay, J. G., and H. F. Allan. *The Nelson College Old Boys' Register.* 1956.

Melbourne University Church of England Grammar School. *War Services of Old Melburians, 1914–1918.* Melbourne, n.d.

Memorial Volume of the Institution of Civil Engineers: The Great War, 1914–1919.

Memorials of Rugbeians Who Fell in the Great War. Vols. 1–2. Privately published, 1916.

Mitchinson, K. W. *Saddleworth, 1914–1919: The Experience of a Pennine Community.* Manchester: Stretford, 1995.

Moss-Blundell, Edward Whittaker. *The House of Commons Book of Remembrance, 1914–1918.* London, 1931.

National Bank of Australasia. *National Bank of Australasia Record of Service of Bank and Staff, 1914–1919.* Melbourne, 1921.

National Committee of Irish National War Memorial. *Ireland's Memorial Records, 1914–1918.* Dublin, 1923.

National Roll of the Great War, 1914–1918. Pt. 6: *Birmingham.* Pt. 8: *1914–1918, Leeds.* Pt. 11: *1914–1918, London* and *1914–1918, Manchester.* National Publishing Company, n.d.

Newfoundland Book of Remembrance.

New South Wales Lands Department. *Officers of the Lands Department Who Fought and Fell for KING and EMPIRE, 1915.* Sydney, 1915.

New Zealand Expeditionary Force Roll of Honour, 1914–1918. Wellington, 1924.

No More Strangers (a Record of Peterborough, Northants, Men Killed in the First World War).

North Road Wesleyan Church, Darlington: Souvenir of the Greatest War in History, 1914–18. (Darlington, Northumberland.)

Northern Assurance Company Roll of Honour.

Oundle Memorial of the Great War, 1914–1919.

Our Heroes: Containing the Photographs with Biographical Notes of Officers of Irish Regiments and of Irish Officers of British Regiments Who Have Fallen in Action, or Who Have Been Mentioned for Distinguished Conduct from August, 1914 to July 1916. Supplement to *Irish Life.* 1916. Reprint. London: London Stamp Exchange, 198[?].

Oxford University. *Oxford University Roll of Service, 1914–1918.* Oxford, 1920.

Paisley's Fallen in the War, 1914–1918. Paisley, 1920.

Pavasovic, Mike. *Men of Dukinfield: A History of Dukinfield during the Great War.* Dukinfield UK: Neil Richardson, 1997.

Pearce, T. D. *A Register of the Southland Boys' High School.* 1930.

Record of Partners, Staff, and Operatives Who Participated in the Great War, 1914–1919. Edinburgh: William Graham, [n.d.].

Record of Service of Solicitors and Articled Clerks with His Majesty's Forces, 1914–1919. London: Spottiswode, Ballantyne, 1920.

Richardson, Neil, and Sue Richardson. *Fallen in the Fight: Farnworth and Kearsley Men Who Died in the Great War, 1914–1918.* Stoneclough, 1990.

De Ruvigny, Marquis. *The Roll of Honour.* Vols. 1–4. London, 1916–18.

Roll of Honour, Arbroath and District, 1914–1919.

Roll of Honour: Members of the Society of Writers to His Majesty's Signet, and Apprentices, 1914–19.

Roll of Honour: Photographs of Footscray's Fallen Heroes at Gallopoli Peninsula, 1915. Footscray: H. Cropley, 1915.

Rugby Memorials. (Rugby School.)

Rutland and the Great War. Salford, Manchester: J. Parfeld & Co., 1920.

School List of Christ's College from 1850–1950 (NZ).

The Scouts' Book of Heroes: A Record of Scouts' Work in the Great War. London, 1919.

Sewell, E.H.D. *The Rugby Footballs International Roll of Honour.* London, 1919.

Sheldon, C. W. *"Roll of Honour": The Story of the Hundreds of Leek Men Who Fell in the First World War.* Leek UK: Counties Publishing, 2004.

Sherborne School Register, 1550–1937. 3rd ed.

South Canterbury Caledonian Society. *South Canterbury Roll of Honour.* 1916.

St. Luke's Roll of Honour. (Camberwell, London.)

Thompson, Robert, comp. and ed.. *Ballymoney Heroes, 1914–1918.* Coleraine: Coleraine Printing Co., 1999.

———. *Bushmills Heroes, 1914–1918.* Coleraine: Coleraine Printing Co., 1995.

———. *Portstewart Heroes, 1914–1918.* Coleraine: Coleraine Printing Co., 2006.

Thorpe, Barrie. *The Men of Wooburn War Memorial.* Windsor UK, 1993.

Tonbridge School and the Great War of 1914 to 1919. London, 1923.

Townsville Grammar School Magazine.

Trowbridge Roll of Honour, 1914–1918.

United Collieries Limited Roll of Employees on Active Service, 1914–1919.

University of Durham Roll of War Service, 1914–1919. Thomas Caldcleugh, Durham, n.d.

University of Edinburgh Roll of Honour, 1914–1919. London: Oliver & Boyd, 1921.

University of London Officers Training Corps Roll of War Service, 1914–1919. London: Military Education Committee of the University of London, 1921.

University of St. Andrews Roll of Honour and Roll of Service, 1914–1919. Edinburgh: R. & R. Clark, 1920.

University of Toronto Roll of Service, 1914–1918. Toronto: University of Toronto Press, 1921.

Vaughan, Edward Littleton, *List of Etonians Who Fought in the Great War, 1914–1919.* Privately published, 1921.

Wanganui Collegiate School Old Boys' Assoc. *In Memorium, 1914–1918*. Wanganui NZ: Wanganui Chronicle Co., 1919.

War Book of Gray's Inn.

War List of the University of Cambridge, 1914–18. Cambridge, 1921.

War Record of the Northern Assurance Company Limited.

War Service Roll of the Members of the Royal Households and Estates of the King and the Queen.

War Services of Old Melburnians.

Watford Grammar School Book of Remembrance, 1914–1918. East Sussex UK: Naval and Military Press, 2006.

Westlake, Ray. *First World War Graves and Memorials in Gwent*. Vol. 1. Barnsley, South Yorkshire UK: Wharncliffe Books, 2001.

Whitgift Grammar School Book of Remembrance, 1914–1918. Privately published, [n.d.].

Winchester College Registers. 1867–1920, 1884–1934, and 1901–46.

Wykehamist War Service Roll. 6th and final ed. October 1919.

Xaverians on Active Service. Xavier College, Kew, Melbourne.

Yarmouth Mercury. On Active Service. 1914–15.

Yeend, Peter, comp. *The King's School Register, 1831–1990*. Parramatta N.S.W.: King's School, 1990.

Yorkshire Rugby Football Union Roll of Honour. [Missing source information.]

Diaries and Personal Accounts

Adlard, Driver John Evan. 1st Divisional Ammunition Column, Australian Field Artillery. AWM.

Aitken, Alexander. *Gallipoli to the Somme: Recollections of a New Zealand Infantryman*. London: Oxford University Press, 1963. (10th [North Otago] Company, Otago Battalion, NZEF.)

Alexander, Lt. A. E. NZ Engineers, NZEF. Liddle Collection.

Algie, Lt. Colvin S., 6th (Hauraki) and 15th (North Auckland) Companies, Auckland Battalion, NZEF. Liddle Collection.

Allanson, Maj. Cecil, 1st/6th Gurkha Rifles, IA. Harry Davies.

Allen, Bandmaster John, Royal Marine Band, Drake Battalion, Royal Naval Division. Royal Marines Museum, Portsmouth.

Alwyne, Sgt. C., B Company, 2nd Battalion, AIF. Mitchell Library.

Antill, Lt. Col. James Macquarie, CB, 10th Light Horse Regiment, AIF. Mitchell Library.

Armstrong, Harold. *Turkey in Travail: The Birth of a New Nation*. London: John Lane, 1925. (67th Punjabis, Indian army, captured at Kut-al-Amarah on April 29, 1916, and held at Afion Kara Hissar.)

Ashmead-Bartlett, Ellis, British war correspondent.

Atkinson, H., Merchant Navy, HM Transport *Aragon*. Imperial War Museum.

Arblaster, Lt. Charles, Machine Gun Officer, 8th Light Horse Regiment, AIF. Douglas Hunter of Albury, Victoria. Via John Meyers.

Atkinson, Pvt. Robert Edward. 29th Divisional Cyclist Company, Army Cyclist Corps. Imperial War Museum.

Auld, Cpl. Robert Wilson, Wellington Battalion, NZEF.

Baigent, Pvt. Edward John, 1st (Canterbury) Company, Canterbury Battalion, NZEF. Colin Townsend.

Baker, Pvt. John A. H. Plymouth Battalion and 2nd Royal Marine Battalion, RMLI. Ros Horne.

Baker, Pvt. Thomas Henry. Chatham Battalion, RMLI. Imperial War Museum Sound Recording 8721.

Barwick, Sgt. Archie Albert, 1st Battalion, AIF. Mitchell Library.

Barrett, Pvt. (Bandsman) Charlie G. D Company, 1st Battalion, Lancashire Fusiliers. Liddle Collection.

Bedford, Pvt. W., Signalling Section, 2/10th Battalion, Middlesex Regiment. Imperial War Museum.

Beere, Pvt. Roderick William, 11th Battalion, AIF. Via John Meyers.

Beeston, Joseph Lievesley. *5 Months at Anzac.* Sydney: Angus & Robertson, 1916. (4th Field Ambulance, Australian Army Medical Corps.)

Beevor, Maj. M. F. *My Landing on Gallipoli.* Privately published, n.d.

Begbie, Pvt. William, 1/7th Battalion (TF), Royal Scots. Regimental Headquarters, Royal Scots.

Behrend, Arthur. *Make Me a Soldier.* London: Eyre & Spottiswoode, 1961. (1/4th Battalion (TF), East Lancashire Regiment).

Bell, Robert, 1st Royal Marine Battalion, RMLI. John Wood.

Benn, Pvt. J. T., D Company, 2/4th Battalion, Queens. Imperial War Museum.

Berryman, Driver Ralph, No. 6 Battery, 2nd Brigade, Australian Field Artillery, AIF. Ralph Seccombe, Pearce, A.C.T., Australia.

Bertwistle, Pvt. W. H., Machine Gun Section, 27th Battalion, AIF. Liddle Collection.

Bird, Gunner Robert, 147th Brigade, Royal Field Artillery. IWM Sound Recording 10656.

Bleakley, Capt. J. F., 1/10th Battalion (TF), Manchester Regiment. Imperial War Museum.

Bloor, Gunner Frank, L Battery, Royal Horse Artillery. Miss Carol Hill, Carlton, Nottinghamshire.

Bock, Pvt. Charles Heinrich, B Company, 5th Reinforcements, 10th Battalion, AIF. Imperial War Museum.

Bollinger, Cpl. (later Regimental Sgt. Maj.) George Wallace, 9th (Hawke's Bay) Company, Wellington Battalion, NZEF. New Zealand History Online.

Booth, Pvt. John, A Company, 20th Battalion, AIF. Mitchell Library.

Bottle, Pvt. Harry, Canterbury Battalion, NZEF.

Bradbury, Lance Cpl. Charles Stanley, No. 14 Platoon, D Company, 1/7th Battalion (TF), Manchester Regiment. MR3/17/125, Tameside Local Studies and Archives Centre.

Brent, Company Sgt. Maj. Frank Thomas, DCM, 6th Battalion, AIF. Sound recording SR 4037, Imperial War Museum.

Breteton, C. B. *Tales of Three Campaigns*. London: Selwyn & Blount, 1926.

Brewer, Pvt. Hector, 2nd Battalion, AIF. Via Bryn Dolan.

Brown, Bombardier A., 66th Brigade, Royal Field Artillery. Liddle Collection.

Brown, Bandsman Herbert, Headquarters Company, 1st Battalion, Lancashire Fusiliers. Matthew Richardson, Leeds, Yorkshire.

Brown, H. A., HM Australian Submarine *A.E.2*. Mitchell Library.

Budd, Pvt. Herbert George, Canterbury Battalion, NZEF.

Burge, Maj. Norman Ormsby, Royal Marine Cyclist Company. Royal Marines Museum, Portsmouth.

Burgess, Trooper Joseph George, 6th Light Horse Regiment, AIF. Mitchell Library.

Button, Pvt. Jack, Royal East Kent Yeomanry. Bob Stinchcombe, Victoria BC, Canada)

Buxton, Pvt. Denis, 88th Field Ambulance, Royal Army Medical Corps (RAMC). Imperial War Museum.

Campbell, Sgt. James, Z Company, 1st Battalion, Royal Munster Fusiliers Liddle Collection. (Account of the battalion's landing from the *River Clyde*, written in May 1915.)

Carberry, Tom. *"With the Anzacs": Being the Personal Experience at the "FRONT" during the "GREAT WAR" (1914–1918) of Tom Carberry, 4th Field Ambulance Corps, as Related by Himself*. (Australian Army Medical Corps, n.d.)

Carbines, Pvt. Arthur Vivian, 11th (Taranaki) Company, Wellington Battalion, NZEF. Colin Townsend.

Cardno, Pvt. J., New Zealand Medical Corps attached Otago Battalion, NZEF. Liddle Collection.

Carkeek, Rikihana. *Home Little Maori Home: A Memoir of the Maori Contingent, 1914–1916*. Wellington: Tōtika Publications, 2003.

Chamberlain, Capt. T. H., B Squadron, Berkshire Yeomanry. Imperial War Museum.

Chamberlin, Jan. *Shrapnel and Semaphore: My Grandfather's Diary of Gallipoli*. Ponsonby, Auckland: Radio Pacific Publishing, 2001. (Sgt. Walter Leadley, 2nd [South Canterbury] Company, Canterbury Battalion, NZEF.)

Chambers, Maj. Selwyn, 9th (East Coast) Squadron, Wellington Mounted Rifles, NZEF. Liddle Collection.

Cicognani, Pvt. Henry Claude (Harry), 4th Field Ambulance, Australian Army Medical Corps. Mitchell Library, MSS 1238.

Clarke, Pvt. W. M., 10th Battalion, AIF. Liddle Collection.

Comyns, Lance Cpl. C. L., Wellington Battalion, NZEF. Liddle Collection.

Cox, Maj. Edward Percy, commanding officer, 11th (Taranaki) Company (later of the 17th [Ruahine] Company), Wellington Battalion, NZEF. Victoria Electronic Text Centre, www.nzetc.victoria.ac.nz.

Creedon, Pvt. Daniel Bartholomew, 9th Battalion, AIF. AWM file 12/1/86)

Creighton, Rev. Oswin. *With the Twenty-Ninth Division in Gallipoli.* London: Longmans, Green, 1916. (Church of England Chaplain to the Eighty-Sixth Brigade).

Cripps, Col. F. H., DSO. *Life's a Gamble.* London: Odhams Press, 1957. (Royal Bucks Hussars.)

Crooks, Lt. T. R., Thirteenth Battalion, AIF. MS. Mitchell Library.

Cumstie, Pvt. Alex, C Company, 23rd Battalion, AIF (Iain A. Macmillan, Kilmarnock, Ayrshire.)

Dawbin, Trooper William Joseph, 6th (Manawatu) Squadron, Wellington Mounted Rifles, NZEF. Te Manawa Museum.

Day, Pvt. William H., Army Ordnance Corps, attached 86th Brigade. Posted online at the Great War Forum, http://1914-1918.invisionzone.com /forums/index.php.

Denham, Midshipman Henry Mangles. *Dardanelles: A Midshipman's Diary* London: John Murray, 1981. (HMS *Agamemnon.*)

Dent, Midshipman Ronald. HMS *Chelmer.* Reprinted in *Gallipolian*, no. 89.

Dewhurst, 2nd Lt. Norman, Machine Gun Section, 1st Battalion, Royal Munster Fusiliers. Privately published by H. J. Edmonds in Brussels, Belgium, 1968.

Dexter, Capt. and Rev. Walter Ernest, Church of England Chaplain to the 2nd Infantry Brigade, AIF. AWM PR00248.

Dickson, Trooper Roy St. Clair, 3rd Light Horse Regiment, AIF. Via John Meyers.

Dill, Cpl. Frederick, 3rd (Auckland) Squadron, Auckland Mounted Rifles. Internet.

Dinning, Hector. *By-Ways on Service: Notes from an Australian Journal.* London: Constable & Co., 1918. (No. 9 Company, Australian Army Service Corps.)

Donn, Pvt. John Murray, 12th (Nelson) Company, Canterbury Battalion, NZEF. Internet.

Doughty, Bombardier (later Lt.) Ralph Dorschel, 2nd Battery, 1st Field Artillery Brigade, Australian Field Artillery, AIF. Peter Kivell.

Drane, Sapper Thomas Edward, 1st Field Company, Australian Engineers. Internet.

Driver, Pvt. Stanly Vivian, 5th Battalion, AIF.

Eden, Pvt. William Tower, 2/10th Battalion, Middlesex Regiment.

Egerton, Maj. Gen. Granville, CB, Commanding Officer, 52nd (Lowland) Division. Public Record Office, CAB 45/249.

Ewing, Dr. William, M. C., DD, Chaplain to the Forces. *From Gallipoli to Baghdad*. London: Hodder & Stoughton, 1917. (Chaplain, No. 11 Casualty Clearing Station, RAMC.)

Facey, Albert Barnet. *A Fortunate Life (Illustrated)*. Ringwood, Victoria: Viking Press, 1981. (11th Battalion, AIF.)

Facey-Crowther, David R., ed. *Lieutenant Owen William Steele of the Newfoundland Regiment: Diary and Letters*. Montreal: McGill-Queen's University Press, 2002.

Farrer, Sapper Thomas Culling, 1st Field Company, NZ Engineers. Public Record Office CAB 45/251.

Fenwick, Lt. Col. Percival Clennell, NZ Medical Corps, NZEF. Liddle Collection.

Finlayson, Lance Cpl. Murdoch 11th (North Auckland) Squadron, Auckland Mounted Rifles, NZEF. Rod Fletcher, Titiranai NZ.

Fisher, Pioneer Pearson Vincent, 72nd Field Company, RE.

Flynn, Pvt. W., 1st Battalion, Royal Munster Fusiliers. Sound recording SR 4103, Imperial War Museum.

Foster, Rev. Henry Clapham. *At Antwerp and the Dardanelles*. London: Mills & Boon, [1918]. (Chaplain, 2nd Naval Brigade, Royal Naval Division.)

———. 2nd Naval Brigade, Royal Naval Division. National Archives.

Fox, 2nd Lt. Stanley, 20th Battalion, AIF. Mitchell Library.

Frankcombe, Pvt. Vernon Egbert, 15th Battalion, AIF.

Gallishaw, John. *Trenching at Gallipoli: A Personal Narrative of a Newfoundlander with the Ill-Fated Dardanelles Expedition*. New York: Century, 1916.

Garland, Trooper Greville, 4th (Waikato) Squadron, Auckland Mounted Rifles, NZEF. Garland family via the New Zealand Mounted Rifles Assoc.

Garratt, Pvt. Charles Ambrose. *Charley's Tale: The Autobiography of Charles Ambrose Garratt*. Exeter: Papyrus, 1988. (Servant to General Kenna, VC; A Squadron, Dorset Yeomanry.)

Garrett, Sgt. Frederick George, Signal Section, 3rd Light Horse Regiment, AIF. Grant Napier.

Geddes, Capt. G. W., 1st Battalion, Royal Munster Fusiliers. *The Landing from the "River Clyde" at V Beach, April 25th 1915*. MS, PRO ref WO 95/4310.

Giffin, C. B. 6th Light Horse Regiment, AIF. Mitchell Library.

Gillam, Trooper Hubert Evelyn. Ivan Walter, Applecross, Perth.

Gillam, Maj. John, DSO. *Gallipoli Diary*. Stevenage, Herts.: Tom Donovan, 1989. (Army Service Corps attached 88th Brigade, 29th Division.)

Gillam, Trooper Sydney Harry Davenport. Ivan Walter, Applecross, Perth.

Gillison, Capt. and Rev. Andrew, 14th Battalion, AIF. AWM.

Giraudoux, Jean, *Campaigns and Intervals*. New York: Houghton Mifflin, 1918. (French army.)

Godley, A. G. *Life of an Irish Soldier: Reminiscences of General Sir Alexander Godley*. London: John Murray, 1939.

Gordon, Pvt. John, 9th Battalion, AIF. AWM.

Gower, Pvt. George, 15th Battalion, AIF. Mitchell Library, Sydney.

Green, Rev. George, Anglican Chaplain, 1st Light Horse Brigade, AIF. Quoted in the *Brisbane Courier*, July 13, 1915.

Gresson, Maj. K. M., 1st (Canterbury) Company, Canterbury Battalion, NZEF. Imperial War Museum.

Hall, Staff Sgt. James, Y Battery, 15th Brigade, Royal Horse Artillery. Bernadette Tither.

Hall, Sgt. Les, 2nd Field Ambulance, AIF. Quoted in the *Herald Sun*, August 11 and 12, 2000.

Hall, Company Sgt. Maj. Sydney Llewellyn. Beryll Chappel and Anton Bantock.

Hamilton, Gen. Sir Ian. *Gallipoli Diary*. Vols. 1–2. New York: George H. Doran, 1920.

Hammond, Lance Cpl., 1/4th Battalion (TF), Norfolk Regiment. Via Dick Rayner.

Hammond, Sgt. E. H., RAMC. Liddle Collection.

Hancock, Lt. Col. Malcom E., 1/4th Battalion (TF), Northamptonshire Regiment. Liddle Collection.

Hannan, E. F. *Twelve Months with the Anzacs* Brisbane: Watson, Ferguson, 1916. (15th Battalion, AIF.)

Hanney, Pvt. George Leonard, 1st East Anglian Field Ambulance, RAMC. Published in *Clan Hannay Society Members*, no. 6, November 11, 2005.

Hargrave, Sgt. John. *At Suvla Bay*. Boston: Houghton Mifflin, 1917. (32nd Field Ambulance, RAMC.)

Harper, Barbara, ed. *Letters from Gunner 7/516 and Gunner 7/517*. Wellington: Anchor Communications, 1978. (Trooper Gordon Gerald Harper and Cpl. Robert Paul Harper, Machine Gun Section, Canterbury Mounted Rifles, NZEF.).

Hazlewood, Pvt. A., 87th (1st West Lancashires), Field Ambulance (TF). Liddle Collection.

Hearder, Capt. Dixon, 11th Battalion, AIF. AWM 3 DRL 3959.

Herbert, Hon. Aubrey. *Mons, Anzac and Kut*. London: Hutchinson & Co., 1919. (Intelligence and Staff Officer, ANZAC.)

Holgate, Pvt. J. W. 3rd Field Ambulance, Royal Marine Medical Unit. Liddle Collection.

Hood, Rev. C.I.O., 54th Division. Imperial War Museum.

Horridge, 2nd Lt. George, 1/5th Battalion (TF), Lancashire Fusiliers. Imperial War Museum Sound Recording 7498.

House, Francis Albert. *Along the Dover Road: A Military Life*. Edited by Theo. House. Privately published. (Royal Garrison Artillery.)

Hunter, Lance Cpl. Henry George, 1st (Canterbury) Company, Main Body, Canterbury Battalion, NZEF. Liddle Collection.

Hunter, Sgt. Robert Alexander, C Company, 15th Battalion, AIF. Via John Meyers.

Huthinson, Cpl. Thomas Ernest, New Zealand Field Ambulance, NZ Medical Corps. Via Jul Snelders.

Hutton, Signaller Arthur Sydney, Headquarters, 3rd Light Horse Regiment, AIF. State Library of South Australia.

Idriess, Ion L. *The Desert Column.* Sydney: Angus & Robertson, 1938. (5th Australian Light Horse Regiment.)

Irwin, Mike, and Eric Peter Duckworth. *The Oak Tree of Gallipoli: The Life of 2nd Lt. Eric Duckworth, 1/6th Battalion, Lancashire Fusiliers.* Northland, Victoria: Veecross, 2003.

Jerrold, Douglas. *Georgian Adventure.* London: William Collins & Sons, 1937. (Hawke Battalion, RND.)

Jess, Brigade Maj. Sir Carl, 2nd Infantry Brigade, AIF. Imperial War Museum.

Kelly, Lt. George Edward Eccleston, 2nd Battalion, AIF. Privately published, n.d.

Kelly, Pvt. William, 14th Battalion, AIF. Internet.

Kemp, Cpl. William David, 16th (Waikato) Company, Auckland Battalion, NZEF. Internet.

Kennedy, Miss Cynthia. Liddle Collection.

Kitchen, Sister Alice, Australian Army Nursing Service, HM Hospital Ship *Gascon.* State Library of Victoria.

Knaggs, Able Seaman Albert Edward Knaggs, HM Australian Submarine *A.E.2.* Jeff Knaggs.

Knight, Frederick Falkiner. *These Things Happened: Unrecorded Memories, 1895–1946.* Melbourne: Hawthorn Press, 1975. (No. 3 Company, Australian Army Service Corps.)

Kyle, Roy. *An Anzac's Story.* Camberwell: Penguin Books, 2003. (24th Battalion, AIF.)

Lamplaugh, Lt. C.R.W., Plymouth Battalion, Royal Marine Light Infantry. Royal Marines Museum.

Larsen, Pvt. James Isaac, No. 8 Platoon, B Company, 14th Battalion, AIF. John Cousins.

Law, Trooper Joseph, 4th (Waikato) Squadron, Auckland Mounted Rifles, NZEF. Daphne M. Hulse.

Lawrence, Sgt. A. E., 2nd Field Company, Australian Engineers.

Lawson, Capt. Edward Francis (later Maj. Gen. Lord Burnham, MC, DSO), Buckinghamshire Yeomanry. Imperial War Museum, ref. 86/36/1.

Leahy, Pvt. Tom, 10th Battalion, AIF. Mrs. Judy Kelly.

Le Brun, Lance Cpl. Frank, 1/8th Battalion (TF), Hampshire Regiment. Anita Le Brun Roe.

Leslie, William Sutherland, unit unknown. Mitchell Library.

Liddle, J. R., 20th Battalion, AIF. Mitchell Library.

Lindsay, Trooper David, 1st Light Horse Regiment, AIF. Internet.

Lissenburg, Trumpeter Dudley Noel Meneaud, 147th Brigade, Royal Field Artillery. Liddle Collection, ref. GS 0970. (Account of Manitou incident.)

Lister, Chief Petty Officer William G., Royal Navy, HMS *Queen Elizabeth.* Via June Cartledge, Internet.

Long, Pvt. Robert Thomas, 32nd Field Ambulance, RAMC.

Louch, Capt. Thomas Steane, MC, 11th (later 51st) Battalion, AIF. Via John Meyers.

Lushington, Reginald Francis. *A Prisoner with the Turks, 1915–1918.* London: Simpkin, Marshall, Hamilton, Kent & Co., 1923. (16th Battalion, AIF.)

Lyall, Gunner Brian, 6th Battery, 2nd Brigade, Australian Field Artillery.

Lycett, Pvt. William Dalton, Tent Division, 4th Field Ambulance, Australian Army Medical Corps. Via Jul Snelders.

Machin, Pvt. George, Portsmouth Battalion, RMLI. Via Roy Swales.

MacMillan, Able Seaman Thomas, Drake Battalion, RND. Imperial War Museum, ref. PP/MCR/C56.

Magill, Cpl. E. L., 7th Light Horse Regiment, AIF. AWM.

Maguire, Leading Seaman James Bernard, Nelson Battalion, RND. John Morcombe.

Malone, Lt. Col. William George, Commanding Officer, Wellington Battalion, NZEF. Liddle Collection.

Mansfield, Pvt. William Watts, 11th (Taranaki) Company, Wellington Battalion, NZEF.

Marris, Pvt. A., Machine Gun Section, Main Body, NZEF. Liddle Collection.

Marshall, Pvt. Arthur Henry, Royal Marine Cyclist Company. Imperial War Museum.

Mason, Sapper Ernest Leonard, 2nd Field Company, RM Engineers, RND.

McGarvie, Trooper David, 8th Light Horse Regiment, AIF. David Collyer.

McHugh, Cpl. William George, Military Mounted Police, 54th (East Anglian) Division. Printed in *Gallipolian* (Spring 2002).

McIlwain, Company Sgt. Maj. John, 5th (Service) Battalion, Connaught Rangers. Imperial War Museum.

McKenzie, Clutha Nantes. *The Tale of a Trooper.* London: John Lane, 1921. (6th Manawatu Squadron, Wellington Mounted Rifles.)

McKenzie, Pvt. James, 5th Field Ambulance, AIF. Mitchell Library, Sydney.

McNaughton, Sapper Alexander John, M. M., 2nd Field Company, Australian Engineers. Via Jul Snelders.

McRae, Sgt. D., 6th Light Horse Regiment, AIF. Mitchell Library, Sydney.

Meatyard, Sgt. William Henry, Plymouth Battalion, RMLI. Royal Marine Museum.

Merriman, Pvt. Frederick, Worcestershire Yeomanry. Worcestershire Yeomanry Cavalry Museum.

Merrington, Rev. E. N., Chaplain 1st Class, 1st Light Horse Brigade, AIF. AWM.

Merivale, 2nd Lt. John Laidley, 4th Battalion, AIF. AWM. (Scrapbook relating to his service.)

Metcalf, Midshipman John Savile. Royal Naval Reserve, HMS *Triumph*. Liddle Collection.

Mills, Sapper Leonard Francis, Divisional Signal Company, RM Engineers, RND June Mills, Huthwaite, Nottinghamshire.

Milward, Capt. C. A., IA, GSO3, 29th Division. Public Record Office, CAB 45/259.

Mitchell, G. D. Account of Cpl. (later Capt.) George Mitchell, MC, DCM, of C Company, 10th Battalion, AIF, from his article "The Anzac Landing" in the April 1, 1935, edition of *Reveille*. Via Earl Howard.

Morgan, Pvt. Percy, 7th (Service) Battalion, Gloucestershire Regiment. Imperial War Museum.

Moriarty, Sgt. Denis, No. 8308, B Company, 1st Battalion, Royal Munster Fusiliers. Alan Osborne and Carol Cox, England.

Morten, J. C., and Sheila Morten. *I Remain, Your Son Jack: Letters from the First World War*. Wilmslow, Cheshire: Sigma Leisure, 1993. (7th Battalion [TF], Manchester Regiment.)

Mure, Maj. Albert Haye, TD. *With the Incomparable 29th*. London: W. & R. Chambers, 1919. (1/5th Battalion [TF], Royal Scots.)

Murray, Joseph. *Gallipoli as I Saw It*. London: William Kimber, 1965. (Hood Battalion, Royal Naval Division.)

Nash, Capt. C. H. Medical Officer, 9th (Service) Battalion, Manchester Regiment. Reg Moule.

Nicholson, Col. G.W.L. *The Fighting Newfoundlander: A History of the Royal Newfoundland Regiment*. Ottawa: Government of Newfoundland, 1964. Reprint. Quebec: McGill-Queen's University Press, 2007.

Nightingale, Capt. Guy Warnesford, 1st Battalion, Royal Munster Fusiliers. Elisabeth Coleman, Smethwick, West Midlands.

Orr, 2nd Lt. Charles Manning, 2nd Battery, Australian Field Artillery. Via John Meyers.

Palmer, Pvt. Hartley Valentine, 12th (Nelson) Company, Canterbury Battalion, NZEF. Liddle Collection.

Part, Lance Cpl. Thomas Reginald, 24th Battalion, AIF. Pauline Carter.

Partridge, Eric. *Frank Honywood, Private: A Personal Record of the 1914–1918 War*. London: Scholartis Press, 1929. (26th Battalion, AIF.)

Patterson, Trooper Thomas Colin Campbell, 10th (Nelson) Company, Canterbury Mounted Rifles, NZEF. Don Wilson, Rai Valley, Marlborough.

Paull, Bombardier H. 3rd Brigade Ammunition Column, Australian Field Artillery, AIF. Imperial War Museum.

Pelly, Pvt. Rolland. 1/5th Battalion (TF), Norfolk Regiment. Dick Rayner.

Phillips, Jock, et al., eds. *The Great Adventure: New Zealand Soldiers Describe the First World War*. Wellington: Allen & Unwin New Zealand, 1988.

Pidcock, Driver John William. 1st Field Ambulance, Australian Army Medical Corps. Frank Pidcock.

Pilling, E. G. "An Anzac Memory: Extracts from the *Rough Diary of Lieut. E. G. Pilling, N.Z.E.F.*" Dunedin: Stanton Bros., 1933. Otago Battalion, NZEF.

Powell, Lance Cpl. Royal Marine Artillery, HMS *Irresistible*. Royal Marines Museum.

Powell, Sydney Walter. *The Adventures of a Wanderer.* London: Jonathan Cape, 1928. (4th Battalion, AIF.)

Price, William Harold. *With the Fleet in the Dardanelles: Some Impressions of Naval Men and Incidents during the Campaign in the Spring of 1915.* London: Andrew Melrose, n.d. (Chaplain, HMS *Triumph.*)

Probert, Cpl. J. K., 2nd Field Company, Australian Engineers. AWM.

Pulley, Pvt. Thomas, 1/4th Battalion (TF), Northamptonshire Regiment. Liddle Collection.

Purdy, Maj. T., 1/5th Battalion (TF), Norfolk Regiment. Via Dick Rayner.

Rawlings, Pvt. C. R., 12th (Nelson) Company, Canterbury Battalion, NZEF. Liddle Collection.

Redford, Maj. T. H., 8th Light Horse Regiment, AIF. AWM.

Rees, Cpl. T., B Company, 2nd Battalion, South Wales Borderers. Liddle Collection.

Reid, Pvt. William, B Company, 1/4th Battalion (TF), Royal Scots. Liddle Collection.

Reilly, Pvt. John Bernard, C Company, 1st Battalion, AIF. Transcribed on Internet; Laurie Favelle.

Robson, A. B., No. 1 Platoon, B Company, Howe Battalion, RND. Liddle Collection.

Rosenthal, Lt. Col. Charles, Commanding Officer, 3rd Field Artillery Brigade, Australian Field Artillery, AIF. Mitchell Library.

Ross, Pvt. William Gordon, 10th Battalion, AIF. Liddle Collection.

Ross-Douglas, Pvt. R. Machine Gun Section, 1/5th Battalion (TF), Royal Scots. Liddle Collection.

Ruhl, Arthur. *Antwerp to Gallipoli: A Year of War on Many Fronts— and behind Them.* New York: Scribner's, 1916. (American newspaper correspondent.)

Rutherford, Capt. Robert Witton Glendenning, Commanding Officer, C Company, 1/4th Battalion (TF), Royal Scots. Regimental Headquarters, Royal Scots.

Salisbury, Pvt. J. V., Royal Marine Medical Unit attached Hawke Battalion, Royal Naval Division. Liddle Collection.

Sampson, Richard, M. C. *The Burford Sampson Great War Diary.* Richard Sampson, 1997. (Capt. Burford Sampson, 15th Battalion, AIF.)

Samson, Air Commodore Charles Rumney Samson, CMG, DSO, AFC, RAF. *Fights and Flights.* London: Ernest Benn, 1930. (Royal Naval Air Service.)

Sharkey, Chief Petty Officer Gerald Valentine, No. 4 Squadron, Royal Naval Armoured Car Detachment (Dardanelles). Imperial War Museum.

Sharman, Pvt. Clifford Alfred Valentine, 26th Battalion, AIF. Liddle Collection–ANZAC.

Shaw, Sgt. William Johnson, No. 1 Platoon, A Company, Deal Battalion, RMLI. Liddle Collection RNMN/SHAW WJ.

Sheldon, Pvt. Ridley, C Company, 1/6th Battalion (TF), Manchester Regiment. MR3/25/28, Tameside Local Studies and Archives Centre.

Sheldrake, Pvt. W. G., 28th Battalion, AIF. Via John Meyers.

Shewen, Lt. Col. Douglas Gordon, 2nd/10th Gurkha Rifles, Indian Army. Liddle Collection GALL 098.

Silas, E., 16th Battalion, AIF. Mitchell Library.

Skidmore, Pvt. Edward Peter, No. 4 Company, Plymouth Battalion, RMLI. Quoted on Ancestry.com.

Skipper, Pvt. A. W., Deal Battalion, Royal Marine Light Infantry. Imperial War Museum.

Smith, Sgt. Egbert Charles, C Squadron, 9th Light Horse Regiment, AIF. Mrs. Shirley Stone of Eastville, Victoria.

Smith, Pvt. F. H., 2nd Light Horse Field Ambulance, AAMC. Mitchell Library.

Smith, Sister Mary Davison, HM Hospital Ship *Aquitania*. Via Mike Smith.

Smythe, Pvt. Percy Ellesmere, 3rd Battalion, AIF. Internet.

Snape, Able Seaman Driver Harold John, 1st Royal Australian Naval Bridging Train. Liddle Collection.

Sparrow, Surgeon Geoffrey, MC, and Surgeon J. N. Macbean-Ross, MC, RN. *On Four Fronts with the Royal Naval Division*. London: Hodder & Stoughton, 1918.

Staff, Sgt. Harry John, 1st Battalion, Essex Regiment. Transcript of interview made on June 20, 1980; Essex Regiment Museum, Chelmsford.

Starkie, Starkie James, 2nd Field Company, Royal Marine Engineers. Susan Eldridge.

Stevens, Trooper Kenneth McKenzie, Main Body, Auckland Mounted Rifles. Liddle Collection. (Memoir.)

Still, John. *A Prisoner in Turkey*. London: John Lane, 1920. (Lieutenant, D Company, 6th [Service] Battalion, East Yorkshire Regiment.)

Strang, Trooper Alexander Ritchie, Machine Gun Section, Wellington Mounted Rifles. Wanganui Collegiate School Museum.

Sullivan, Pvt. Herbert, Deal Battalion, RMLI. Terry Sullivan, Waltham, Grimsby, Lincolnshire. (Memoir.)

Symonds, Pvt. Frederick Heatley, 5th Battalion, AIF. Posted online at Great War Forum, http://1914-1918.invisionzone.com/forums/index.php.

Taylor, Pvt. Alexander, 1st Battalion, Royal Inniskilling Fusiliers. Mrs. M. Pettigrew.

Taylor, Sgt. Harry, A Company, 1/5th Battalion (TF), Essex Regiment. Essex Regiment Museum, Chelmsford.

Teichman, Capt. Oskar, DSO, MC. *The Diary of a Yeomanry M.O. (Egypt, Gallipoli, Palestine and Italy)*. London: T. Fisher Unwin, 1921. (RAMC, attached 1/1st Worcestershire Yeomanry.)

Thompson, Capt. F. J., OBE, Captain of HM Transport *Royal George*. *Sea Breezes* (May 1961).

Thompson, Pvt. James, Plymouth Battalion, RMLI. Robert Thompson, Dunkerton, Bath, Somerset.

Thompson, Sgt. Joseph Cecil, 9th Battalion, AIF. Internet.

Thompson, Sgt. Roy, 11th Battalion, AIF. Graham Perham.

Thorne, Pvt. Charles, Warwickshire Yeomanry.

Tiegs, Pvt. Albert Henry, 11th Battalion, AIF. Via John Meyers.

Tilsley, Sgt. Robert, DCM, Auckland Battalion, NZEF.

Tomes, Pvt. Sydney H., New Zealand Medical Corps, NZEF. Steve Chambers.

Tomlinson, Trooper F. H., 1st Light Horse Regiment, AIF. Mitchell Library.

Tompson, Pvt. Thomas Edward, 6th Company, Australian Army Service Corps. Internet.

Trumpeldor, Capt. Joseph, Zion Mule Corps. Quoted in *Joseph Trumpeldor: Life and Works*.

Tubby, Lt. Col. A. H., CB, CMG. *A Consulting Surgeon in the Near East*. London: Christopher's, 1920. (Consulting Surgeon to the RAMC.)

Tuck, Cpl. George Albert, 6th (Hauraki) Company, Auckland Battalion, NZEF. Alexander Turnbull Library.

Tucker, Pvt. H.F.W., 6th Light Horse Regiment, AIF. Mitchell Library.

Tunnicliff, Lance Cpl. Norris, 12th (Nelson) Company, Canterbury Battalion, NZEF. Internet.

Twistleton, Capt. Francis Morphet, Otago Mounted Rifles. Liddle Collection.

Vassal, Maj. Joseph Marguerite Jean. *Uncensored Letters from the Dardanelles, Written to His English Wife by a French Medical Officer of Le Corps Expéditionnaire d'Orient (6ème Régiment, Mixte Coloniale)*. London: William Heineman, 1916.

Vaughan, Justin Horace, son of Lt. H.W.V. Vaughan, 10th KORLR attached 2nd Royal Fusiliers. Recollections. Courtesy of his nephew Tony Vaughan.

Vickers, Pvt. John, Plymouth Battalion, RMLI. Royal Marines Museum.

Virgoe, Trooper Percy Ernest, 4th Australian Light Horse Regiment. Mrs. Carmen Johnston, Hamilton, Victoria.

Wainwright, Sgt. John, M. M., Signals Section, NZEFRE, attached New Zealand HQ, Anzac. John Wainwright, Brunei.

Walsh, Pvt. Clifford, Auckland Battalion, NZEF. Liddle Collection.

Watts, Sub-Lt. Arthur Egerton, Collingwood Battalion, RND.

Weingott, Pvt. Alexander, 13th Battalion, AIF. Margaret Kirkman, Miranda N.S.W.

Weingott, Pvt. Samuel, 1st Battalion, AIF. Margaret Kirkman, Miranda, N.S.W.

Whieldon, Sgt. J.H., Worcestershire Yeomanry. Worcestershire Yeomanry Cavalry Museum.

Whitelaw, Bandsman John N., 1/8th Battalion, Cameronians. Stella Whitelaw.

Whittey, Trooper Leonard A., 7th Light Horse Regiment, AIF. Mitchell Library.

Wilcox, Pvt. H. C., RMLI, HMS *Ocean*. Royal Marine Museum.

Wilkinson, Norman. *The Dardanelles: Colour Sketches from Gallipoli*. London: Longmans, Green, 1916.

William-Powlett, Midshipman Peverill, RN, HMS *Vengeance*. Liddle Collection.

Williams, Cpl. Ivor Alexander, 21st Battalion, AIF. Hugh Williams.

Williams, Cpl. William, 13th Base Park Company, RE. Dave Russell.

Williamson, Surgeon David J., RM Medical Unit attached as Medical Officer, Drake Battalion, RND. Williamson family.

Wiltshire, Capt. A.R.L., 22nd Battalion, AIF. Mitchell Library.

Woolley, Cpl. Henry James, C Company, 8th (Service) Battalion (Pioneers), Welsh Regiment.

Worrall, Cpl. Edgar Sydney, 24th Battalion, AIF. Ted Harris.

Worthington, Lt. Col. Claude, DSO, 1/6th Battalion (TF), Manchester Regiment. Published in *Great Gable to Gallipoli*, edited by Robert Bonner. Knutsford: Fleur de Lys Publishing, 2004.

Young, Chief Petty Officer A. W., HMS *Agamemnon*. Royal Naval Museum, Portsmouth.

Unit War Diaries

1st Australian Field Bakery (13th Australian Army Service Corp Company) (WO 95/4358)

1/1st City of London Yeomanry (WO 95/4393)

1/1st County of London Yeomanry (WO 95/4393)

1/1st (East Lancashire) Field Ambulance (TF), RAMC (WO 95/4314)

1/1st Highland Mounted Brigade Field Ambulance (WO 95/4592)

1/1st Highland Mounted Brigade Field Ambulance Workshop Unit (WO 95/4592)

1/1st (Kent) Field Company (TF), Royal Engineers (WO 95/4592)

1/1st (Welsh) Field Ambulance (TF), RAMC

1/2nd County of London Yeomanry (Westminster Dragoons)

1/2nd Lovat Scouts (WO 95/4293)

1/2nd (East Lancashire) Field Ambulance, RAMC (WO 95/4314)

1/2nd South West Mounted Brigade Field Ambulance (TF), RAMC (WO 95/2493)

1/2nd (Welsh) Field Ambulance (TF), RAMC (WO 95/4322)

1/2nd (West Lancashire) Field Company, Royal Engineers (WO 95/4314)

1/3rd County of London Yeomanry (WO 95/4393)

1/3rd (East Anglian) Field Ambulance (TF), RAMC (WO 95/4324)

1/3rd (East Lancashire) Field Ambulance, RAMC (WO 95/4314)

1/3rd (Welsh) Field Ambulance (TF), RAMC

1/4th London Mounted Brigade Field Ambulance (TF), RAMC (WO95/4292)

2nd Mounted Division General Staff (WO 95/4592)

2nd Mounted Division Signal Squadron, Royal Engineers (WO 95/4592)

2/1st (East Anglian) Field Ambulance (TF), RAMC (WO 95/4324)

4th London Mounted Brigade (WO 95/4393)

No. 11 Casualty Clearing Station, RAMC (WO95/4356)

No. 13 Casualty Clearing Station, RAMC (WO 95/4356)

13th Field Bakery, Australian Army Service Corps (WO 95/4358)

No. 14 Casualty Clearing Station, RAMC

No. 16 Casualty Clearing Station, RAMC

16th Sanitary Section, RAMC
16th Veterinary Hospital, Army Veterinary Corps (WO 95/4357)
No. 24 Casualty Clearing Station, RAMC
No. 26 Casualty Clearing Station, RAMC
30th Field Ambulance, RAMC (WO 95/4295)
31st Field Ambulance, RAMC (WO 95/4295)
32nd Field Ambulance, RAMC (WO 95/4295)
39th Field Ambulance, RAMC
40th Field Ambulance, RAMC
41st Field Ambulance, RAMC
53rd (Welsh) Divisional Cyclist Company, Army Cyclist Corps
No. 53 Casualty Clearing Station, RAMC
53rd (Welsh) Divisional Signal Company, Royal Engineers
53rd (Welsh) Divisional Sanitary Section, RAMC
No. 54 (1/1st East Anglian) Casualty Clearing Station (TF), RAMC (WO 95/4356)
86th Field Company, Royal Engineers
89th Field Ambulance, RAMC (WO 95/4309)
155th Brigade (WO 95/4320)
ADMS, 10th (Irish) Division, RAMC
ADMS, 53rd (Welsh) Division, RAMC
Auckland Mounted Rifles, NZEF
Bedfordshire Regiment (1/5th Battalion)
Border Regiment (1st and 6th Battalions)
Canterbury Mounted Rifles, NZEF
Cart Corps (1st–5th), Indian army (WO 95/4358)
Deputy Judge Advocate-General, General Headquarters, MEF (WO 154/116)
Dorset Regiment (5th Battalion)
Duke of Cambridge's Own (Middlesex Regiment) (2/10th Battalion)
East Lancashire Regiment (1/4th and 1/5th Battalions) (WO 95/4315)
Fife and Forfar Yeomanry (WO 95/4393)
General Staff, 2nd Mounted Division (WO 95/4292)
Glasgow Yeomanry (WO 95/2493)
Gloucestershire Regiment (7th Battalion)
Gloucestershire Yeomanry (WO 95/4393)
Hampshire Regiment (2nd Battalion)
Herefordshire Regiment (1/1st Battalion) (WO 95/4323)
Hertfordshire Yeomanry (WO 95/4393)
Highland Light Infantry (1/5th and 1/6th Battalions) (WO 95/4321)
Indian Mule Cart Train, Headquarters (WO 95/5358)
Jacob's Mountain Battery (WO 95/4289)
King's Own Scottish Borderers (1/4th and 1/5th Battalions) (WO 95/4320)
Kohat Mountain Battery (WO 95/4289)
Lanarkshire Yeomanry (WO 95/2493)

Lovat Scouts (WO 95/4393)

Manchester Regiment (1/9th Battalion)

Maori Contingent, NZEF

Newfoundland Regiment

Norfolk Yeomanry (WO 95/4325)

Northumberland Fusiliers (8th Battalion)

Nottinghamshire Yeomanry (Sherwood Rangers) (WO 95/4393)

Otago Mounted Rifles, NZEF

Royal Derbyshire Yeomanry (WO 95/2493)

Royal Marine Brigade

Royal Naval Division

Royal Devon Yeomanry (WO 95/2493)

Royal East Kent Yeomanry (WO 95/4303)

Royal Irish Rifles (WO 95/4296)

Royal North Devon Hussars (WO 95/4303)

Royal Sussex Regiment (1/4th Battalion)

Royal Welsh Fusiliers (1/5th, 1/6th, 1/7th, and 8th Battalions)

Royal Scots (1/7th Battalion)

Royal Scots Fusiliers (1/4th and 1/5th Battalions) (WO 95/4320)

Scottish Horse (1/1st, 2/1st, and 3/1st) (WO 95/4321)

Signals Section, Royal Marine Engineers

South Nottinghamshire Hussars (WO 95/4393)

Suffolk Yeomanry (WO 95/4325)

Warwickshire Yeomanry (WO 95/4393)

Welsh Horse (WO 95/4325)

West Kent Yeomanry (WO 95/4303)

West Somerset Yeomanry (WO 95/2493)

Worcestershire Regiment (4th and 9th Battalions)

Worcestershire Yeomanry (WO 95/4393)

Zion Mule Corps, miscellaneous records (WO32/18541,18543, 18544, 18545)

1st Brigade, Royal Naval Division

1st Field Ambulance, Australian Army Medical Corps, AIF.

1st Field Brigade, Australian Field Artillery, AIF.

2nd Field Ambulance, Australian Army Medical Corps, AIF.

2nd Light Horse Field Ambulance, Australian Army Medical Corps, AIF.

1st Battalion, AIF.

14th Battalion, AIF.

15th Battalion, AIF.

108th Field Ambulance, Indian Medical Service

Unpublished Letters (Contemporary)

Beverland, Capt. John Herd, 32nd Field Ambulance, RAMC Arthur Gratton
    Long, Devonport, New Zealand.

Bradley, Cpl. James, 6th (Hauraki) Company, Auckland Battalion, NZEF.

Brookfield, Lt. George Leonard Purchas, 4th (Waikato) Squadron, Auckland Mounted Rifles, NZEF.

Burnham, Maj. Gen. Lord Frederick, Buckinghamshire Yeomanry. Imperial War Museum.

Bush-King, Rev. Charles J., Canterbury Mounted Rifles, NZEF.

Campbell, Lt. Hugh, 11th Battalion, Manchester Regiment. Dr. Jack Oliver, Lockeridge, NR. Marlborough, Wiltshire.

Carthew, Lt. Charles, C Squadron, 8th Light Horse, AIF.

Carthew, Noel. *Voices from the Trenches: Letters to Home.* Sydney: New Holland, 2002.

Chapman, Pvt. Harry J., 2/3rd Battalion, London Regiment. Mr. G. A. Bird, London.

Chapman, Pvt. Sydney Parnell, Wellington Battalion, NZEF. Mrs. E. Shearer, Remuera, Auckland.

Clarke, Sapper Walter Edwin, Divisional Signal Company, NZ Engineers, ANZAC Division. Debbie Davis, Mt. Albert, Auckland.

Coe, Pvt. Nathan William, Berkshire Yeomanry. Hatty Rickards, Roath, Cardiff, Glamorganshire.

Cole, Pvt. R. M., B Company, 3rd Battalion, AIF. AWM.

Cook, Chief Petty Officer John Charles, RNR, HMS *Sarnia*. Via Frank Stevens.

Cullen, Pvt. Edward Henry, 13th Battalion, AIF. Mrs. Joan P. Washington.

Cullen, Pvt. Hugo James, 13th Battalion, AIF. Mrs. Joan P. Washington.

Davies, Sapper George Faraday, No. 1 Section, 2nd Field Company, Royal Naval Divisional Engineers. Mrs. Jean Wallwork.

Dunn, Able Seaman Daniel. Michael Robson.

Dykes, Lt. H. B., 1st Battalion, King's Own Scottish Borderers. Imperial War Museum.

Eunert (alias of Trooper Frederick Charles Trenue), Auckland Mounted Rifles. Mrs. Ray Harding of Takopuna, Auckland.

Flockhart, Maj. Robert Pearce, 5th Battalion, AIF, AWM.

Follett, Pvt. William Henry, 2nd Battalion, South Wales Borderers. Wendy Doyle, Histon, Cambridge.

Garrett, Capt. Henry Fawsett, 6th (Service) Battalion (Pioneers), East Yorkshire Regiment.

Gilbert, 2nd Cpl. David, Royal Marine Engineers, RND. *Gallipolian*, nos. 39 and 42 (1982).

Gillanders, Lance Cpl. Thomas Alexander, 16th (Waikato) Company, Auckland Battalion, NZEF.

Gordon, Sgt. Francis Leslie, 2nd (South Canterbury) Company, Canterbury Company, NZEF. F. Nevill Wilson, Christchurch.

Grant, Chaplain William, Wellington Mounted Rifles, NZEF.

Hall, Company Sgt. Maj. Sydney Llewellyn, 1st Field Company, Royal Marine Engineers. Beryll Chappel and Anton Bantock.

Hammick, Capt. H. A., MC, 1/6th Battalion, Manchester Regiment. Liddle Collection.

Harris, Lt. E. W., 12th Battalion, AIF. AWM.

Hickson, Driver Alfred Cecil, 8th Corps Transport Depot. Alan Trimmer, Christchurch, Dorset.

Inglis, Lt. Harold, 2nd Battalion, South Wales Borderers. Via Charles Woosnam.

Jolly, Sgt. Francis Leslie Gordon, 2nd (South Canterbury) Company, Canterbury Battalion, NZEF. Via Colin Townsend.

Keen, Pvt. Frederick Joseph, Berkshire Yeomanry. Berkshire Yeomanry Museum.

Keogh, N., 15th Battalion, AIF. AWM.

Kidd, Sgt. J. A., 15th Battalion, AIF. AWM.

Lavender, Mr. W. Liddle Collection.

Lawry, Lt. Raymond Alexander Reid, Main Body, Canterbury Battalion, NZEF.

Longson, Lt. R. R., 1/5th Battalion (TF), Argyll and Sutherland Highlanders. Liddle Collection.

Loss of the Royal Edward. Public Record Office MT 23/455.

Luxford, Rev. J. A., Canterbury Battalion, NZEF.

Macleod, Sgt. Alexander, 4th Battalion, AIF.

McPhee, Rev. John Claude, Chaplain, 2nd Infantry Brigade, AIF. AWM.

McPhee, Sgt. John Edmond, 4th Field Ambulance, AIF. AWM 3 DRL/2610)

Makeham, Rev. Edward, Chaplain, 3rd Light Horse Brigade, AIF.

Malet de Carteret, Midshipman Philip Reginald, RN, HMS *Canopus.* Quoted in *Gallipolian* of August 2006.

Margetts, Capt. Ivor Stephen, 12th Battalion, AIF. AWM.

Marshall, Capt. Herman, 5th Battalion, AIF. AWM.

Miller, 2nd Lt. Randolph, 7th Battalion, AIF.

Milligan, Capt. S. L., 4th Battalion, AIF. AWM.

Mills, Sapper Leonard Francis, Divisional Signal Company, RM Engineers, RND. June Mills, Huthwaite, Nottinghamshire.

Mitchell, Sgt. Gregory McCarthy, Auckland Battalion, NZEF.

Morgan, Maj. G. E., 1st Field Company, Royal Marine Engineers. Beryll Chappel and Anton Bantock.

Mychael, Driver Dennis, 1st Light Horse Regiment. Harry Willey.

Nevinson, 2nd Lt. Humphrey Kay Bonney, D Company, 1/10th Battalion (TF), Manchester Regiment. Liddle Collection, ref. GALL 065.

Nightingale, Capt. Guy Warneford, 1st Battalion, Royal Munster Fusiliers. Liddle Collection.

Norman, Sub-Lt. John, Howe Battalion, Royal Naval Division. Jack Clegg.

O'Malley, Pvt. Jeremiah Thomas, 6th Battalion, AIF. James Flahavin, Essendon, Victoria.

O'Reilley, Pvt. Edmond, 2nd (South Canterbury) Company, Canterbury Battalion, NZEF. Mary Newsome, Richmond, Nelson NZ.

Osborne, Lt. Jim, 4th Battalion, AIF. AWM.

Parker, Lance Cpl. William, 1/10th Battalion, Manchester Regiment. Liddle Collection.

Poulter, Sapper George, 2nd Field Company, Australian Engineers, AIF. Donald Sharwood Spence, Mount Waverley, Victoria.

Prettie, Maj. Hon. H.C.O.'C., DSO, 1/10th (County of London) Battalion (Hackney) (TF). National Archive.

Richards, Pvt. Roy, 19th Battalion, AIF. (Mitchell Library.

Robin, Pvt. Lancelot, 10th Battalion, AIF. State Library of South Australia.

Rose, Cpl. John Haberfield, 4th (Waikato) Squadron, NZEF. Mrs. S. Forster, Papakura NZ.

Rushton, Cpl. George William, 24th Battalion, AIF. Harold Hamer, Southport, Merseyside.

Ryder, Sister A. L., Imtarfa Hospital, Malta. Vivian Edwards, Newport, South Wales.

Sampson, Mary G., of Launceston, Tasmania. AWM.

Shorney, Mrs. Louisa. (Mother of Pvt. Arthur Burton Shorney, 16th Battalion, AIF.)

Skellern, Pvt. Sydney, 6th (Hauraki) Company, Auckland Battalion, NZEF.

Smith, Lt. Col. W. R., Commanding Officer, No. 1 Australian General Hospital, Mudros. AWM.

Spence, Sapper Charles, 2nd Field Company, Australian Engineers, AIF. Donald Sharwood Spence, Mount Waverley, Victoria.

Thyer, 2nd Lt. Walter Hervey, 16th Battalion, AIF. Via John Meyers.

Tilsley, Sgt. Robert, DCM, Auckland Battalion, NZEF.

Tyler, Bandsman Frederick John, D Company, 1/5th Battalion (TF), Essex Regiment. Via Brandon Park.

Urquhart, Capt. Murray, 11th (Taranaki) Company, Wellington Battalion, NZEF.

Walthew, Able Seaman Frederick Silby, Hawke Battalion, Royal Naval Division. Mrs. Sheila Halliwell, Sidmouth, Devonshire.

Watson, Cpl. Frank M., Machine Gun Section, Auckland Battalion, NZEF. Mrs. Diana Flatman of Avondale, Auckland, and the Liddle Collection.

White, Sgt. Sidney, 1st Battalion, Essex Regiment. Essex Regiment Museum, Chelmsford.

Wood, Sgt. Maj. Robert, 11th (Taranaki) Company, Wellington Battalion, NZEF.

Yeo, Lt. F. A., No. 4 Squadron, Royal Naval Air Service Armoured Car Detachment (Dardanelles). Printed in the *Gallipolian*, no. 57.

Miscellaneous

Admission Book, County of Middlesex War Hospital, Napsbury (MH 106/1555).

Admission Books, HM Hospital Ship *Assaye* (MH 106/1953, 1914, 1919).

Admission Books, No. 11 Casualty Clearing Station, RAMC (MH 106/433, 434, 435).

Admission Books, No. 19 General Hospital, RAMC, Alexandria (MH 106/1221–32).

Australian Imperial Force Members Deceased prior to Embarkation.

Australian Imperial Force Members Deceased Subsequent to Return and prior to Discharge.

Australian Imperial Force, Staff and Regimental Gradation Lists of Officers, Revised to 6th December, 1914.

Australian Red Cross Society Wounded and Missing Enquiry Bureau Files, 1914–18 War.

Casualty list of the Royal North Devon Hussars.

Crew List, HM Transport *Royal Edward*, July 1915. Public Record Office BT 99/3152.

Embarkation list of the 1/4th Battalion (TF), Royal Sussex Regiment for the landing at Suvla on August 9, 1915.

Embarkation list of the 1/1st Battalion (TF), Herefordshire Regiment.

Enquiry Lists of the British Red Cross and Order of St. John for 1915.

1st Battalion, the Border Regiment: Nominal Roll on Embarkation for Active Service, March, 1915. Carlisle, 1915.

Gallipolian. Journal of the Gallipoli Assoc.

Headquarters, Royal Flying Corps. *List of British Prisoners of War in Turkey, 1st–22nd February, 1916.* AIR/1/892/204/5/697.

List of members of C Company, 15th Battalion, AIF, garrisoning Quinn's Post, Anzac, on April 30, 1915.

Log of HM Transport *Manitou*. Public Record Office BT 165/1067.

Loss of Minesweeper 285 ("Okino"), Mined 8/3/15: Report of Casualties. Public Record Office, ADM 1/8413/60.

Metropolitan Police Orders.

Metropolitan Police Register.

Metropolitan Police Service Records (MEPO 4/467).

New Zealand Division Courts Martial Register.

New Zealand Electoral Rolls.

Nominal Roll of Deceased Members of the AIF and AN and MEF.

Nominal Roll of the 6th Battalion, Border Regiment.

Nominal Roll of A Squadron, 1/1st Buckinghamshire Hussars Yeomanry.

Order of Battle of the Mediterranean Expeditionary Force, October, 1915. General Staff GHQ, MEF, Oct. 1, 1915.

Ordre de Battaille of the Turkish Army, Corrected to August 16, 1915 5th ed. Cairo: Government Press, 1915.

Parnham, W. J., Plymouth Battalion, RMLI. Liddle Collection.

Pocketbook of Sgt. William Johnson Shaw, No. 1 Platoon, A Company, Deal Battalion, RMLI. Liddle Collection RNMN/SHAW WJ.

Proceedings: Field General Court Martial–DAVIS (Pvt. Thomas Davis, 1st Battalion, Royal Munster Fusiliers), ROBINS (Sgt. John Robins, 5th Battalion, Wiltshire Regiment), SALTER (Pvt. Harry Salter, 6th Battalion, East Lancashire Regiment).

Quigley, Dave J., *Nominal Roll of the Officers, NCOs and Men of the 1/8 Hants Regt., otherwise known at Princess Beatrice's Isle of Wight Rifles, as on 31st July 1915*. Privately published, East Cowes, Isle of Wight, 1997.

Records of Courts Martial in the AIF, 1915–19 (WO71/431).

Registers of the Commonwealth War Graves Commission (Gallipoli, Turkey, Iraq, Europe, Asia, Cyprus, Gibraltar, Greece, Malta, Egypt, Great Britain, Scotland, Ireland, and Wales).

Register of Wills (1915–16) held at Somerset House, Probate Office, London.

Reports of Operations, Royal Naval Division (WO 95-4290).

Royal Naval Division Missing Circulars.

Scrapbook compiled by Colin Coxon, son of Capt. A.C.M. Coxon, 1/5th Battalion (TF), Norfolk Regiment. Courtesy of Peter Dearsley.

Service records of the Australian Imperial Force.

Service records of British Army officers (WO 374).

Service records of British Army other ranks (WO 363).

Service records of the Canadian Expeditionary Force.

Service records of the 1st Newfoundland Regiment.

Service records of the New South Wales Police Force.

Service records of the New Zealand Expeditionary Force.

Service records of the (Canadian) North West Mounted Police.

Service records of the Royal Australian Navy.

Service records of the Royal Marines (ADM 159).

Service records of Royal Marines officers (ADM 196/63).

Service records of the Royal Naval Division.

Service records of the Royal Naval Reserve (BT 377).

Service records of the Royal Navy (ADM 188).

Ships' Medical Logs (ADM 101).

Signals and despatches, HMS *Agamemnon* (Royal Naval Museum, Portsmouth).

Signals, Vice Admiral Eastern Mediterranean Squadron.

Staff and Regimental Lists of the Australian Military Forces, 1st January, 1914.

Various European diplomatic documents.

War Diary, Embarkation Officer, Lines of Communication, Mudros (WO 95/2359).

Widows' pension records, British army.

Periodicals and Newspapers

Aberdare Leader
Aberdeen Daily Journal
Advertiser (Adelaide)

Adelaide Observer
Age (Melbourne)
Aldingbourne Parish Magazine
Alnwick Gazette Almanac
Alyth Guardian
Argus (Melbourne)
Armidale Express
Armidalian (Armidale School, N.S.W.)
Army Journal (AUS)
Ashburton Guardian
Aston News
Ashton Reporter
Atherstone News
Auckland Grammar School Chronicle
Auckland Weekly News
Australasian
Australian Coin Review
Badsey Parish Magazine
Ballarat Courier
Ballarat Star
Ballymena Observer
Barnsley Chronicle
Barnsley Independent
Barrier Miner
Bega Budget
Belvederian (Belvedere College)
Bendigo Advertiser
Berrows Journal
Birmingham Daily Mail
Birmingham Daily Post
Birmingham Gazette
Birmingham Illustrated Weekly Mercury
Birmingham News
Birmingham Weekly Post
Blackburn Times
Blackburn Weekly Telegraph
Blackwood's Magazine
Blairgowrie Advertiser
Blaydon Courier
Bromleian (Ravensbourne School, Bromley, Kent)
Bolton Journal
Bradford Weekly Telegraph
Boston & Spalding Free Press

Brisbane Courier
Brisbane Daily Mail
Brisbane Grammar School Magazine
Brisbane Telegraph
British Medical Journal
Bromley Times
Bucks Standard
Bulletin of the Royal Munster Fusiliers Association
Burnley Express & Advertiser
Bury Times
Bury Free Press
Campbelltown Courier
Canterbury Times (NZ)
Capricornian (Rockhampton, Queensland)
Central Presbyterian Association Magazine (Belfast, Co. Antrim)
Carlisle Journal
Carluke & Lanark Gazette
Chailey Parish Magazine
Cheltenham Chronicle & Gloucestershire Graphic
Cheshire Daily Echo
Cheshire Year Book
Chichester Observer & West Sussex Recorder
Christchurch Press
Christchurch Weekly Press
Christ's College Register
Chronicle (Newtownards, Co. Down)
Chronicles of the NZEF
Claro Times
Coleraine Chronicle
Colne Valley Almanack, 1916 and 1918
Courier (Brisbane)
Corian (Geelong Grammar School)
County Express (Worcestershire)
County Herald (Mold, Flintshire)
Coventry Graphic
Coventry Herald
Craven Herald & Wensleydale Standard
Croydon Advertiser
Croydon Times
Cumberland Argus & Fruitgrowers Advocate
Cumberland News
Daily Examiner (Grafton N.S.W.)
Daily Herald (Adelaide)

Daily Mail (London)
Daily Mail (Brisbane, Queensland)
Daily Malta Chronicle
Daily Record (Rockhampton, Queensland)
Daily Telegraph (Sydney)
Dannevirke High School Magazine
Darwen Advertiser
Darwen News
De Astonian Magazine (De Aston School, Market Rasen, Lincolnshire)
Defense Force Journal
Derby Daily Express
Derby Mercury
Devonian Yearbook, 1916 (London Devonian Assoc.)
Dollar (Academy) Magazine
Dominion (Wellington)
Downsman
Dumfries & Galloway Standard & Advertiser
Dunfermline Journal
Durham County Advertiser
Durham County Chronicle
East Anglian Times
East Suffolk Gazette
Eccles and Patricroft Journal
Edinburgh Evening News
Educational News: Journal of the Educational Institute of Scotland
Epsom Advertiser
Erdington News
Essex County Chronicle
Essex Weekly News
Evening Chronicle (Newcastle-upon-Tyne)
Evening Despatch (Birmingham, Warwickshire)
Evening Post (Wellington)
Evening Star & Daily Herald (Ipswich, Suffolk)
Evesham Journal & Four Shires Advertiser
Express & Advertiser (Burnley, Lancashire)
Flight: Official Organ of the Royal Aero Club of the United Kingdom
Freeman's Journal & National Press (Dublin)
Free Press (Birmingham, Warwickshire)
Gainsborough News
Glasgow Academy Chronicle
Glasgow Herald
Grantham Journal
Graphic

Grimsby Daily Telegraph
Grimsby News
Hampshire Telegraph & Post
Handsworth Herald
Harrogate Herald
Hawkesbury Agricultural College Journal
Hebrew Standard
Herald (Melbourne)
Herald Sun
Hereford Times
Hermes: The Magazine of the University of Sydney
Herts & Essex Observer
Hobart Daily Post
Holmfirth Express
Hucknall Dispatch
Huddersfield Weekly Examiner
Hull, Yorkshire & Lincolnshire Times
Ibis (Journal of the British Ornithologists' Union)
Ilkley Free Press
Illustrated London News
Inglewood Advertiser
Inglewood Record & Waitara Age
Isle of Man Examiner Annual 1916 and *1917*
Isle of Wight County Press
Isle of Wight Mercury
Jewish Chronicle
Jewish World
Journal of the Australian War Memorial
Journal of Strategic Studies
Kalgoorlie Miner
Kalgoorlie Western Argus
Kangaroo-Out of His Element (published by the 1st Battalion, AIF, on the
  troopship *Afric* during the journey to Egypt, October–November 1914)
Kapunda Herald
Kenilworth Advertiser
Kettering Leader
Kildare Observer
Kincardine Observer
King's County Chronicle
King's County Independent
Kircudbrightshire Advertiser
Kirkintilloch Herald
Lancashire Daily Post

Launceston Daily Telegraph
Launceston Weekly Courier
Leighton Buzzard Observer
Leinster Leader
Levin Chronicle
Lincolnshire Chronicle
Lincolnshire Leader
Lismore Northern Star
Liverpool Echo
London Gazette
Luton News
Lynn Advertiser
Lynn News & County Press
Maitland Weekly Mercury
Malago (Journal of the Malago Society)
Malvern News
Manawatu Evening Standard
Manchester Evening News
Manchester Guardian
Mannin (Journal of the Manx Society)
Mansfield Advertiser
Marlborough Express
Melbourne Herald
Melbourne Punch
Meriden Mag
Merthyr Express
Methodist
Mexborough & Swinton Times
Middle Eastern Studies
Middleton & North Manchester Guardian
Midland Daily Telegraph
Mid-Sussex Times
Monmouthshire Free Press
Montgomeryshire Express
Morwell Advertiser
Mossley & Saddleworth Reporter
Mount Morgan Chronicle & Gazette
Murray Pioneer (Renmark S.A.)
Nelsonian
Nelson Leader
Nepean Times (Penrith, N.S.W.)
Newark Advertiser
Newark Herald

Newingtonian Supplement (Newington College, Sydney)
Newmarket Journal
New Ranger: Journal of the Connaught Rangers Association
New York Times
New Zealand Alpine Journal
New Zealander
New Zealand Herald & Daily Southern Cross
New Zealand Gazette
New Zealand Listener
Newton & Earlestown Guardian
Norbury News
Norfolk News
North Bucks Times
North Devon Journal
Northampton Independent
Northern Constitution
Northern Miner
Northern Star
Northern Times (Carnarvon WA)
Notts Free Press
Oamaru Mail
Observer (Adelaide)
Oldham Chronicle (supp.)
Oldham Evening Chronicle
Orange Leader
Otago Daily Times
Otago Witness
Palmerstonian (Palmerston North Boys' High School)
Pegasus (Journal of Geelong College, Victoria)
Pelorus Guardian & Miners' Advocate
Peninsula Independent News
People's Journal (Aberdeen, Aberdeenshire)
Pershore Almanac, 1915
Perth Western Herald
Perth Western Mail
Picture World (Birmingham, Warwickshire)
Police Review & Parade Gossip
Pontefract & Castleford Advertisor
Portsmouth Evening News & Southern Daily Mail
Portmuthian (Magazine of Portsmouth Grammar School)
Poverty Bay Herald
Prescot Parish Magazine
Prescot Reporter

Prince Alfred College Chronicle
Queenslander
RMC Journal (Royal Military College of Australia, Duntroon)
Ranger: A Journal for the Connaught Rangers
Raymond Terrace Examiner
Reading Chronicle
Reading Standard
Register (Adelaide)
Reporter (Salford, Lancashire)
Reveille
Riverine Herald
Robertson Advocate
Rockhampton Daily Journal
Rotherham Advertiser
St. Aidan's Parish Magazine (Billinge, Lancashire)
St. George's Gazette
St. John the Baptist's, Ashfield, Parish Notes
Salford Reporter
Scarborough Mercury
Scotsman
Sea Breezes
Sheffield Daily Independent
Sidcup & District Times
Smethwick Telephone
South Australian Register
Southend Standard
Southland Times
Southport Visitor
South Wales Echo
South Yorkshire Times
Staffordshire Sentinel
Staffordshire Weekly Sentinel
Stockport Advertiser
Stockport Express
Suffolk & Essex Free Press
Sunday Age
Sunday Mail (Perth)
Sunday Sun (Sydney)
Sunday Times (Sydney)
Surrey Comet
Sunday Mail (Perth)
Sunraysia Daily
Surrey Advertiser

Surrey Comet
Surrey Times
Sydney Daily Telegraph
Sydney Mail
Sydney Morning Herald
Tamworth Daily Observer
Taranaki Daily News
Tasmanian Mail
Tenterfield Star
Thames Star
Thetford & Watton Times
Third Battalion Magazine, April 1918 (3rd Battalion, AIF)
Timaru Herald
Times (London)
Times (Rotherham, Yorkshire)
Toodyay Herald
Town & Country Journal (Sydney)
Tunbridge Wells Advertiser
Vigilance (Journal of the Queensland AU Returned Services League)
Waipa Post
Wairarapa Daily Times
Waitakian (Journal of the Waitaki Boys College, Oamaru)
Wallasey News
Wanganui Herald
War Illustrated
Warracknabeal Herald
Waterford News
Wedderburn Express
Weekly News (Invercargill NZ)
Weekly Press (Christchurch NZ)
Wendover Magazine
Werris Creek Record
West Australian
West Australian Mail
West Briton
West Wimmera Mail
Western Gazette (Yeovil)
Western Mail
Whitehaven News
Wigan Examiner
Wigan Observer
Windsor & Richmond Gazette
Windsor, Eton & Slough Express

Wisden's Almanac, 1916
Wishaw Press and Advertiser
Woodville Examiner
Woolwich Polytechnic Magazine
Y Dydd (Dolgellau, Merionethshire, Wales)
Yarmouth Independent
Yarmouth Mercury
Yorkshire Evening Post
Yorkshire Herald
Yorkshire Telegraph & Star
Yorkshire Times
Yorkshire Weekly Press
Young Chronicle (Young N.S.W.)

INDEX

A Beach, 261–62

Achi Baba, 295; battles at, 112, 115, 136–37, 188–89, 199, 200–201; landings at, 26, 59, 60

Achi Baba Nullah, Battle of. *See* Battle of Achi Baba Nullah

Addison, Alfred, 109–10

Adjutant General staffs, 29

AE2, 171–72

Albion, 76–77, 89, 109, 110

Alexander, Archibald, 50

Allen, Harold, 55

Allies, 2

All The King's Men, 248

Amethyst, 20, 62

ammunition shortages, 37, 111–12, 115, 206, 211

Anafarta Detachment, 237

Annear, Dick, 45

Anson Battalion of Royal Naval Division, 10; landings of, 74–76, 84, 86, 88, 92, 97, 99; in Third Battle of Krithia, 201–2

ANZAC. *See* Australian and New Zealand Army Corps (ANZAC)

Anzac Beach, 26, 36–58, 117–30; August offensives at, 224, 226, 240; evacuation of, 284–90, 293, 299;

first wave landings at, 39–46, 47–48, 57–58; inland fighting at, 48, 50–51; line gap at, 119–21; losses at, 50, 55–57, 126–27; main body landings at, 58; May battles at, 132–35, 148–54; November 1915 weather at, 273; planning of landings at, 36–40; second wave landings at, 46–50, 58; securing and evacuating wounded from, 117–19; Turk counterattacks at, 121–30, 132

Anzac Day, 55

Appleton, Edgar, 96

Argyll, 74, 76, 79, 81, 83

Ari Burnu, 44–45

Ark Royal, 155

armored landing craft, 226, 235

Armoured Car Division of Royal Naval Air Service, 75, 191, 204–6

Army Service Corps, 175

artillery shortages, 37, 111–12, 115, 206, 211

Ashmead-Bartlett, Ellis, 40, 247

Asiatic Annie, 60, 207

Askold, 103, 165

Asquith, Herbert, 6, 10

Auckland Battalion of New Zealand Infantry, 54–55, 142, 144

Auckland Mounted Rifles (AMR), 150, 151–52
Ault, Edwin, 57
Australian and New Zealand Army Corps (ANZAC), 10; in August battles, 244–46; evacuation of, 286–87, 289; at Lemnos, 34–35; uniforms of, 212, 271; war at sea and, 163–64. *See also* Anzac Beach
Australian Engineers, 228–29
Australian Imperial Force (AIF), 30–31, 39–40, 121, 285

B6 submarine, 171
B11 submarine, 170, 171
Baby 700, 55, 118, 122, 132, 226
Baddeley, Herman, 55
Baker, Frank, 203
balaclava helmets, 212
bandoleers, 203–4
barbed wire, 88, 90, 94–95, 111
Barnett, Alfred, 16
Barton, Harold, 153
Barton, Walter, 267
Batt, Thomas, 45–46
Battle of Achi Baba Nullah, 249–59; attack of, 252–59; overview and plan of, 249–52
Battle of Gully Ravine, 209–23; attack of, 213–20, 221–23; losses of, 220–21; overview and plan of, 209–13, 249
Battle of Krithia Vineyard, 224–34; first diversion attacks of, 226–28; Light Horse Brigade in, 232–34; Lone Pine diversion and tunneling of, 228–32; plan and overview of, 225–26
battleship confiscation by Britain, Turk, 3
Battleship Hill, 42, 48, 55
battleships, role of, 169
Beagle, 156
Bean, C. E. W., 234, 286, 290
Bean, John, 182
Beart, Ernest, 264–65
Beattie, James, 257–58
Beck, Albert, 259
Beck, Arthur, 259
Beck, Frank, 259, 265, 266

Beckwith, Arthur, 109
Beer, Charles, 18
beetles, 226, 235
Behrens, Robert, 72–73
Bell, Harry, 203–4
Benbow Battalion of the Royal Naval Division, 10, 188, 189
Bendall, Frederick, 279–80
Ben-My-Chree, 181
Bennett, Alfred, 111
Bennett, Walter, 293
Benson, O., 179
Bentley, Joseph, 264
Bey, Musta, 266
Bianco, Désiré, 139–40
Biard, Captain, 22
Biggs, John and William, 220
Bing, Julian, 235
Birdwood, William, 209; evacuation and, 283–84; landings and, 36–34, 51; May battles and, 132, 136, 153
Bloody Angle, 132, 133
Blücher, 186
Bodle, William, 175
Bonavita, Joseph, 104
Boomerang, 210, 213–16, 221, 222–23
Bouvet, 23, 25
Bracegirdle, Leighton, 270–71
Braemar Castle, 16, 62
Braithwaite, Walter, 28–29, 30, 64, 247
Braris, Gerald, 183
Braund, George, 121–25, 128–30
Bridges, William, 119–20
Brigade Coloniale, 139
Brigade Métropolitaine, 139
British Red Cross Society, 56–57, 107
Brodie, Theodore, 170–71
Bulair, 26, 60, 106, 240
Bulgaria, 1, 2, 270, 281–82
Bulldog, 156
Burge, Norman, 168, 189
Burt, Bernard, 48
Butler, Graham, 44
Byrne, Albert, 52–54

Cameronians, 209, 219–21
Campbell, Hugh, 237–38

Campbell, Ian, 278
Canopus, 149–50, 162
Canterbury Battalion of New Zealand
    Infantry, 54, 122, 133–34, 142–44
Carberry, Tom, 169, 279
Carden, Sackville, 6–7, 9, 19
Carlile, Joseph, 50
Carr, H. A., 84
Carrington Smith, Herbert, 83–84
Carthage, 167–68
Casson, Hugh G., 71, 73
casualties. *See* losses
Cayley, Douglas, 95
Central Powers, 1–2, 4, 270, 281
Ceylon, 102
Chailak Deres, 225
Chanak, 20, 21, 156
Chapman, Henry, 277–78
Charlemagne, 22
Chasseurs d'Afrique, 102
Chatham Battalion of the Royal Marine
    Light Infantry, 9, 10, 258
Chelmer, 161, 164
Chocolate Hill, 235, 239–43, 308n10
Chunuk Bair, 120, 226, 232–34
Church, William, 220
Churchill, William, 147
Churchill, Winston, 4–10, 19, 185–
    86, 283
Clacton, 74, 76
Clayton, Harold, 196
cloth screens, 192, 212
Cochrane, Archie, 173
Cochrane, William, 255
Collingwood Battalion of Royal Naval
    Division, 10, 188, 189, 201–3, 204
Collinson, Frederick, 140–41
Colonials, French, 102, 105, 113, 196–
    97, 207, 279, 291
Concanon, George, 122–24
Conway, Joe, 179–80
Corps Expéditionaire d'Orient (CEO),
    10, 28
Cosgrove, Billy, 111
Costeker, John, 83, 86
Costello, Brigade Major, 83–84
Courtney, Patrick, 183

Courtney's Post, 51, 118, 152
Creighton, Oswin, 78–79, 93, 197,
    218–19
Cripps, Fred, 242–43
Croix de Guerre, 205
Crowther, Alfred, 52–53, 54
Cumming, Alexander, 234
Cumming, Richard, 234
Cunliffe, Thomas, 194

Daisy Patch, 141, 143–45
Daniell, William, 99–101
Dardanelles Campaign: decision on,
    4–8; destruction of Outer Forts of,
    12–16; minesweeping of, 17–20;
    Narrows attack of, 20–26
Dardanelles Committee, 247, 270,
    283–84
Dardanelles Straits, 2, 4, 9, 20, 38
Dardanos, Fort, 13
Dauber, John, 180
Davies, George, 269, 272
Dead Man's Ridge, 132–35
Dean, Alexander, 231–32
de Lisle, Henry, 209, 221
Denham, Henry, 13, 160–61
de Robeck, John, 19, 21–22, 24–25, 38
Destroyer, 46
de Tott, Baron, 70
De Tott's Battery, 70, 72, 73
DeVilliers, Louis, 126–27
Dhair Hissar, 31–32
Distinguished Service Medals, 184, 205
Distinguished Service Order, 83, 106
Dix, Charles, 40–41, 42
Doughty-Wylie, Charles, 107–8, 110–11
Dove, Wilfred, 56
Drake Battalion of Royal Naval Divi-
    sion, 146, 291
Drewry, George, 74, 79, 81
Dublin, 14, 22, 65, 67–68
Dublin's Castle, 277
Dubsters, 115, 135, 143
Dye, John, 265

E7 submarine, 173
E11 submarine, 173–74, 184–85

E15 submarine, 170–71
E20 submarine, 174
East Lancashire Division, 37, 136, 188, 191, 200, 293
Edmonstone, Bertram, 245
Edward VII, King, 259
Egerton, Wilfrid, 162–63, 222, 249–52, 258
Eighteenth Labour Company of Army Service Corps, 175
Eighth Corps, 188, 209
Eighty-Eighth Brigade, 59, 113, 138, 139, 211, 225
Eighty-Seventh Brigade: at Battle of Gully Ravine, 210–11, 213, 219; at First Battle of Krithia, 113, 114; landings of, 59, 97; at Second Battle of Krithia, 141, 145, 147
Elliott, Harold, 48
Ellison, Gerald, 28
England, Hugh, 164
Eren Keui Bay, 20, 21, 23
Eski Line, 116
Euryalus, 88, 89, 94, 96, 159
evacuation: background and considerations of, 281–84; effects of on Helles, 290–94; of Helles, 294–99; supplies given away during, 298–99; of Suvla and Anzac Beach, 284–90, 293, 299, 310n9
Evans, Sydney, 214–15
Evans, Thomas, 119
Evening Telegraph, 85
Everett, Jack, 96
Exmouth, 191

Faed, James, 159
Fell, Roy, 271
Fentonian, 20
Ferdinand, Franz, 1
Ferdinand I, Tsar, 281
Ferrero, Henri-Jule, 105
Fetherstonaugh, Edwyn, 77
Fifty-Second (Lowland) Division, 73, 189, 209, 212, 249
Fifty-Seventh Infantry Regiment, Turk, 121–22, 290

Finn, William, 78–79
Firle, Rudolph, 156, 157
First Australian Division, 9, 40, 225
First Australian Field Artillery, 207
First Battle of Krithia, 111–17, 131
First Lancashire Fusiliers. *See* Lancashire Fusiliers
Fir Tree Spur, 138
Fir Tree Wood, 138, 141
Fisher, Lord John, 8, 185
Fitzmaurice, Maurice, 161, 162
food and water shortages, 29, 34, 112, 169
forcing the Dardanelles. *See* Dardanelles Campaign
Forrester, Adrian, 99
Fort No. 1, 12, 75, 95
Fort No. 16, 22
Forty-Second (East Lancashire) Division, 37, 136, 188, 191, 200, 293
Foster, Donald, 264
Foster, Henry Clapham, 192, 201–2
Fourteenth King George's Own Ferozepore Sikhs, 197–98
Fowles, Herbert, 44
Fox, 204–5
Frandi, Ateo, 144
Frankland, Robert, 93
Frankland, Thomas, 91–93
French: in Battle of Achi Baba Nullah, 253–54; evacuation of, 294, 296–98; in First Battle of Krithia, 112–13; at Kum Kale, 101–5; and Salonica front, 283; in Second Battle of Krithia, 138–40, 145, 147; in Third Battle of Krithia, 201, 206–9
French, Sir John, 9
French Colonials, 102, 105, 113, 196–97, 207, 279, 291
French navy, 4, 155
Freyberg, Bernard, 106

Gaba Tepe, 36, 42, 48
Galeka, 48, 50
Gallipoli, 226, 232, 234, 248
Garrett, George, 276
Gaulois, 22–23, 25, 27

Geddes, Captain, 80, 82
George V, King, 248, 265–66, 268
Germany, 1–4, 270, 281, 293
Gillam, John: bad weather and, 274–76; Battle of Krithia Vineyards and, 227–28; evacuation and, 285, 289, 296; landings and, 69, 80–81, 86; Third Battle of Krithia and, 192–93, 196, 204
Glew, Ernest, 175
Godley, Alexander, 132–33, 135, 226
Goulder, John, 267–68
Gouraud, Henri, 188–89, 206, 208, 306n2
Grampus, 171
Greece, 2, 281–82
Gresson, Kenneth, 137
Grimshaw, Cecil, 110
Guépratte, Admiral, 22
Guezji Baba, 92, 94–95, 101
Guildford Castle, 69
Gully Beach, 63, 218
Gully Ravine, 63, 66, 97, 113, 141, 142, 145, 147, 295. *See also* Battle of Gully Ravine
Gully Spur, 196–97, 206, 209
Gurkhas, 197, 217, 226, 279

Hall, James, 116
Hamidieh II, Fort, 22
Hamilton, Ian: about, 29–30, 247; Battle of Krithia Vineyard and, 235, 240; evacuation and, 281–83; landings and, 51, 63–64, 67, 69; planning and receiving orders and, 26, 27–30, 37–38; Second Battle of Krithia and, 136–37, 141, 145, 187–88; Third Battle of Krithia and, 189–90, 200–201; war at sea and, 165
Hamilton, Robert, 46
Hamilton, William, 152–53
Hampshire Regiment of Second Battalion, 75, 83–84, 109
Hampshires, 1/8th Battalion, 261, 262, 263
Hannan, Henry, 208–9
Harcus, James, 285–86

Haricot Redoubt, 201, 203, 206, 207–8
Harper, Wilfred and Gresley, 234
Harpy, 161
Harris, Christopher, 279
Harris, Herbert, 279
Harrison, George, 100
Hasan, Ahmet Hulusi, 185
Hayes-Sadler, Arthur, 24–25
Hayreddin Barbarossa, 185
Hearder, Dixon, 36–37, 46
Helles: evacuation of, 290–99; First Battle of Krithia at, 111–17; Kum Kale in, 101–5; landings at S Beach, 69–73; landings at X Beach, 67, 97–101; landings at Y Beach, 59, 60–68; November 1915 weather at, 273–74; overview of landings at, 26, 38, 59–60, 106; securing V Beach, 107–11; Turk counterattacks at, 135–36. *See also* Battle of Gully Ravine; Battle of Krithia Vineyard; Second Battle of Krithia; Third Battle of Krithia; V Beach
helmets, 113, 212, 263
Henderson, Eric, 80
Henderson, James, 219
Herbert, A. P., 259
Herbert, Aubrey, 150
Hersing, Otto, 160, 161, 164–69
Highland Light Infantry, 250
Hill 10, 239
Hill 53, 235, 239–43, 308n10
Hill 60, 240, 244–46
Hill 114, 87, 88, 92, 94, 98–99, 100–101
Hill 138, 87, 88, 91, 92, 94, 101
Hill 141, 108–9, 110–11
Hill 472, 145
Hill 971, 38, 226, 232, 235
Hill, Ernie, 245
Hill Q, 226
Hine, Arthur, 232
HMS *Arcadian*, 165, 189
HMS *Agamemnon*, 12, 13, 21, 160, 161
HMS *Chatham*, 293
HMS *Cornwallis*, 69–71, 72, 74, 156
HMS *Goliath*, 65, 67–68, 69, 156–60, 186

HMS *Hermes*, 180
HMS *Minerva*, 32
HMS *Pathfinder*, 160
HMS *Triumph*, 40, 161–65, 169, 171, 186
HMS *Vengeance*, 14, 162
Hogben, Richard, 18–19
Holbrook, Norman, 170
Honeybourne, George, 241
Horridge, George, 140–41
hospital ships, 155, 168, 169
howitzers, mobile, 4, 7
Hoyle, Humphrey, 140
Hunt, Charlie, 53
Hunter-Weston, Aylmer: Battle of Achi
    Baba Nullah and, 249, 250–51, 258;
    Battle of Gully Ravine and, 209;
    First Battle of Krithia and, 108, 111–
    12, 115; landings and, 61, 63–64,
    68, 88, 93; Second Battle of Krithia
    and, 141; Third Battle of Kereves
    Spur and, 206; Third Battle of Kri-
    thia and, 188–89, 190
Hussar, 74

identity discs, 47, 136, 280
Imperial Japanese Navy, 155
Imperial Service Badge, 260, 309n10
Implacable, 88, 97–99
Implacable Landing. *See* X Beach
Indian Brigade, 136, 142, 191, 196, 211
Inflexible, 21–22, 23–24, 25
Innes, James, 256
Innes, W. K., 256
Intermediate forts, 17–21
Iron Crosses, 157, 167
Irresistible, 14, 24–25, 186

Jacka, Albert, 152
Jackson, Alfred, 48, 49
Jackson, Jack, 278
Jackson, Jim, 278
James, Cornelius, 152
Jarrett, Charles, 81
Jauget, Reinis, 183
Jed, 32
Jenkins, Godfey, 285
Jenkins, Richard, 124, 285–86

Jerrold, Douglas, 228, 259
Johnston, Francis, 142
Johnston's Jolly, 225
Jones, Alexander, 31
Jones, Benjamin, 194
Jonquil, 239

Kangaroo Beach, 270–71
Kearney, Jimmy, 242
Kelly, John, 22
Kemal, Mustafa, 121–22
Kemp, Edwin, 22
Kennet, 32, 34
Kereves Spur, 113, 206–9, 249–50
Keyes, Roger, 64
Kilid Bahr, Fort, 20, 21
King, Alexander and James, 220
King's Own Scottish Borderers.
    See KOSB (King's Own Scottish
    Borderers)
Kiretch Tepe Sirt, 235, 237, 274–75
Kitchen, Alice, 173–74, 180
Kitchener, Lord Horatio, 5; ANZACs
    and, 9–11; Battle of Krithia Vine-
    yard and, 235; evacuation and, 281–
    83; Helles and, 106, 136; Narrows
    attack preparations and, 28–29, 30;
    Third Battle of Krithia and, 188;
    Turks and, 11–12
Knight, Anthony, 267
Knight, Frederick, 299
Koe, Archibald, 61, 67, 68–69
Koja Chemen Tepe, 26
KOSB (King's Own Scottish Borderers):
    in Battle of Achi Baba Nullah, 252,
    253–57; in Battle of Gully Ravine,
    209, 210, 214–17; in First Battle of
    Krithia, 113–15; landings of, 61–63,
    65–66, 68
Krithia Nullah, 135, 138, 145
Krithia Vineyard, Battle of. *See* Battle
    of Krithia Vineyard
Kuchak Anafarta Ova assault, 260–68
Kum Kale, 4, 12, 14, 15, 26, 60, 101–5

Lala Baba, 234, 237, 240
Lamrock, John, 285–86

Lancashire Fusiliers: in Battle of Gully Ravine, 217–18; in Second Battle of Krithia, 140, 146; in Third Battle of Krithia, 191, 194, 196, 200–201; in W Beach assault, 89–95; W Beach losses of, 95–97; W Beach overview and planning and, 87, 88–89; at X Beach, 97–98

Lang, James, 255

Langlands, Bob, 146–47

La Redoubte Bourchet, 147

Larter, George, 55

Lawry, Ray, 143

Layh, Herbert, 48–49

Leadley, Walter, 133–34, 143–44

Leane, Raymond, 45

Lee, Harry, 31

Lefort, Lieutenant, 105

Lelsie, Frank, 99–100

Lemnos, 10, 29, 30–31, 34–35, 175

Light Horse Regiments (LHR), 225, 226, 232–34

Linton, Richard, 182–83

Linton, Robert, 183

Lissenburg, Dudley, 32–33

Lockyer, Hughes Campbell, 97–98

London, 39

Lone Pine, 225–32

Longford, Lord, 242–43

Longridge, Horace, 16

Lord Nelson, 158

losses: at Anzac, 50, 55–57, 126–27, 130, 152, 153–54; in Battle of Achi Baba Nullah, 256, 258; in Battle of Gully Ravine, 220–21; in Battle of Krithia Vineyard, 227; in Dardanelles campaign, 12, 16, 20, 25, 34; due to weather, 276–77, 280; E15 and, 171; during evacuation, 285–86, 296, 299; in First Battle of Krithia, 116; on *Goliath*, 157–60; at Kuchak Anafarta Ova, 265, 266; during landings at Helles, 55–57, 68–69, 73, 84–87, 96–97, 105–6; on *Majestic*, 166; reporting of, 55–57, 121, 266; on *Royal Edward*, 179–80; at Second Battle of Krithia, 139–

40, 148; on *Southland*, 182–83; at Third Battle of Krithia, 203–4, 206; of Turks at sea, 183–85

Lowry, Robert, 288–89

Lucas, L., 27

Lycett, William, 273

Mack, Stanley, 179

Mackie, Alexander, 132

MacMillan, Thomas, 279, 291, 295–96

Macpherson, Robert, 43

Maidos, 39

Majestic, 165–67, 169, 171

Making, Victor, 40, 42, 302n3

Malone, Bryan, 284

Malone, William, 124, 127–30

Mal Tepe, 26, 38–39, 40, 42

Manchester Brigade, 200–201

Manchester Regiment, 141, 200, 237–38

Manica, 155, 161

Manitou, 31–34, 160

Manx Hero, 19

Margesson, Edward, 71–73

Marrow, Ted, 69

Marshall, William, 99–101, 115, 198

Martin, Jim, 183

Mary, Queen, 248

Masnou, General, 253

Mason, William, 12

Matthews, Godfrey, 61–62, 67, 68–69

Maunsell, Tom, 90

Mayer, Arthur, 230–31

McConnachy, Albert, 53–54

McNeile, John, 255

meals, 145, 193, 207, 213

Medhurst, William, 77–78

Mediterranean Expeditionary Force (MEF), 10, 26, 28, 37, 270, 283

Mercian, 96

Merivale, Jack, 231

Messudieh, 170

Messudieh, Fort, 13

Metcalf, John, 40, 42–43, 162–63

midshipmen, 40

Mills bomb, 270, 284

minesweeping the Dardanelles, 17–20, 21

Minns, Arthur, 16
Minoru, 161
Mockett, Walter, 13
Monash Valley, 118, 132, 149
monitors, 169
Monro, Charles, 247, 283–84, 294
Moriarty, Dennis, 135–36
Morris, James, 227
Mothes, Fritz, 152
Mountain, Arthur, 94–95
Mowat, James, 180
Muavenet-i-Miliet, 156–57
Murdoch, Keith, 247, 309n19
Murray, Archibald, 294
Murray, James Wolfe, 28–29
Murray, Joseph, 166–68, 169, 195,
    203–4, 291–92
Murray, Norman, 230–31

Napier, Henry, 83–84, 86–87
Narrows: attack on by sea, 19–25; first
    wave landings at, 40–46, 47–48, 58;
    inland fighting at, 51–55; main body
    landings at, 45, 50–51, 58; overview
    and planning attacks at, 26, 27–30,
    36–40; recovering the dead at, 50;
    second wave landings at, 46–50, 58;
    troop arrival and training at, 30–35
Nasmith, Martin, 184–85
Naval Brigade, 138–39, 145, 148, 203
navies, role of, 155
Neagle, Richard, 176–79
Nelson, J. O., 94
Neuralia, 181, 182
New Army, 236, 308n7
Newenham, Henry, 92, 98–99, 100
New Zealand Expeditionary Force,
    124–29, 142–44, 153
New Zealand Infantry: Auckland Bat-
    talion, 54–55, 142, 144; Canterbury
    Battalion, 54, 122, 133–34, 142–44;
    Otago Battalion, 54, 133–34, 142;
    Wellington Battalion, 124–29, 142–
    44, 153
Nightingale, Guy, 81
Niven, William, 241–42
Nixon, Alexander, 255

Noguès, Charles, 102, 105
Norfolk Regiment, 248, 259–68
Nousret, 23
November 1915 weather, 273–80

observation balloon, 155, 161
Ocean, 24–25
Okino, 18–19
O'Malley, Martin, 85–86
163rd Brigade of Fifty-Fourth Division,
    259, 261–62, 266
Order of Mejidie, 157
Osborne, Jim, 231
Osiris, 33–34
Otago Battalion of New Zealand Infan-
    try, 54, 133–34, 142
Ottoman Empire, 1–2
Outer Defenses, destruction of, 6, 12–16

Paine, Walter, 200
Pakenham, Thomas, 242
Parker, Jeffrey, 238–39
Parsons, Raymond, 202
Pasha, Essad, 149
Pattrick, Arthur, 264–65
Peebles, William, 252
penalties, civilian, 19
Perkins, Ted, 270–71
Phillimore, Richard, 22
Plugge's Plateau, 44–45, 47, 51–52
Plymouth Battalion of the Royal
    Marine Light Infantry, 9, 10, 15, 61–
    62, 63, 65
Porter, Alwyne, 91
Portsmouth Royal Marine Light Infan-
    try, 10, 258
Pour le Mérite, 167
Powell, William, 164–65
Prince George, 33
Prince of Wales, 39
Proctor-Beauchamp, Horace, 261,
    263–64
Proctor-Beauchamp, Montagu, 264
punishment, civilian, 19

Quadrilateral Redoubt, 206, 207–8
Quartermaster General staff, 29

Queen, 39, 40
Queen Elizabeth, 58, 68, 82, 114
Quinn's Post, 51, 118, 132–33, 135

Raccoon, 181
Ramazan, 183
Randrup, Holger, 142
Rawlinson, Henry, 235
Ray, Archibald, 94
Rhodes, W. H., 55
River Clyde: landings at Helles and, 74–76, 78–84, 87; securing V Beach and, 107–8, 109; Third Battle of Krithia and, 191
RND. See Royal Naval Division (RND)
Robertson, William, 294
Robinson, Eric, 171
Romero, 179
Romieux, Jacques, 253
Rooth, Richard, 77, 78
Royal Army Medical Corps (RAMC), 69, 75, 175
Royal Australian Naval Bridging Train, 270
Royal Dublin Fusiliers: in First Battle of Krithia, 115; in June battles, 216–17; landing at Helles, 74–75, 76–78, 80, 85, 88; securing V Beach, 108, 109, 115
Royal Edward, 175–80
Royal Engineers, 69–70, 75, 175, 191, 251
Royal Fusiliers, 88, 92, 97–98, 101, 217, 218
Royal George, 33
Royal Inniskilling Fusiliers, 97–98, 100–101, 142, 216
Royal Lancaster Regiment, 287
Royal Marine Brigade, 252, 258
Royal Marine Light Infantry, 9, 10, 159, 258; Chatham Battalion, 9, 10, 258; Plymouth Battalion, 9, 10, 15, 61–62, 63, 65; Portsmouth Battalion, 10, 258
Royal Marines, 10–11, 189
Royal Munster Fusiliers: in Battle of Gully Ravine, 217–18; in First Bat-

tle of Krithia, 115; landing at Helles, 75, 79–80, 81, 85; in Second Battle of Krithia, 137; securing V Beach, 108, 109, 111
Royal Naval Air Service, 75, 79, 149–50, 191, 204–6
Royal Naval Division (RND), 9–11; evacuation of, 292; landings of, 74–76, 84, 86, 88, 92, 97, 99, 106; in May battles, 146; Narrows land attack planning and arrival and, 26, 28, 31; in Third Battle of Krithia, 188–89, 201–4
Royal Naval Reserve, 10, 18
Royal Naval Volunteer Reserve, 10
Royal Navy: Outer and Intermediate Defenses and, 12, 13, 17, 19–20; strategy and planning and, 3, 4–5, 6
Royal Scots Fusiliers, 186, 211, 219–22, 250–52, 253–56
Royal Sussex Regiment, 260
Ruhl, Arthur, 184, 186
rum, 150, 298–99
Rumming, Geoffrey, 205
Russell's Top, 118, 121–22, 125, 226, 285–86
Russian navy, 155
Russians, 2, 4, 5, 103–4, 155, 165

Saint-Louis, 207
Saker, Richard, 120
Salonica front, 282–83
Salt Lake, 239, 240, 308n9
Samson, George, 74, 79
Samsun, 185
Sandringham Battalion, 248, 259–68
Sanson, Arthur, 152
Saphir, 170
Sapphire, 62, 67–68
Sari Bair Ridge, 232
Savoie, 102–3, 105
Savory, Reginald, 198
Sazli Beit, 225
S Beach, 59, 61, 69–73, 112–13
Scharnhorst, 186
Schwenke, Charlie, 271
Scimitar Hill, 240, 243–47

Scorpion, 171, 191
Scott, John, 98
Scott-Moncrieff, William, 221–22
Second Australian Infantry Brigade, 118, 119, 136, 145, 147–48
Second Battle of Krithia, 136–48, 187; May 7 fighting of, 140–41; May 8 fighting of, 141–48; plan and May 6 fighting of, 136–40
Second Mounted Division, 240–44, 282
Second Naval Brigade, 139, 148, 203
Second Régiment de Marche Afrique, 207–8
Second Ridge, 50–51, 118, 132
Sedd-el-Bahr: assault on, 4, 12, 14, 15, 16; V and Y Beach landing and securing and, 64, 73, 75, 82, 108–10
Senegalese, 102, 105, 113, 139, 201, 291
Serbia, 281–82
Sergent, Noel, 296–98
Sharkey, Chief, 204–5, 213–14, 216, 222–23
Shaw, Harold, 92, 196
Shelford, Thomas, 158–59
"shot heard 'round the world," 1
Shrapnel Gully, 51, 58
Sikhs, 197–98
Silas, Ellis, 134–35
Sinclair-Maclagan, Ewen, 48
Sixth Mixed Colonial Regiment, 101–5, 139, 207
Sloan, W. N., 220
Smail, Adam, 256
Small, George, 12
Smalls, William, 101
Smith, Alfred, 194
Smith, Watson, 279
SMS *Breslau*, 3
SMS *Goeben*, 3
Smylie, Willie, 30
Somali, 33
Souchon, Wilhelm, 3–4
Soudan, 12, 13, 178–80
Southland, 62, 180–83
South Wales Borderers (SWB): in First Battle of Krithia, 114; landings of,

61–62, 65, 69–70, 71–73, 97, 98, 99–101; in Second Battle of Krithia, 142
Special Ration Depot, 150
Spilsbury, Edgar, 43
Stambul, 184
Star of the Empire, 20
Steele, Owen, 273–74
Steele's Post, 51, 118, 225
Steward, Walter, 180
Stewart, Gordon, 52, 54
Stoker, Henry, 171–72
Stoney, George, 110, 111
Stopford, Frederick, 235, 239, 240, 247
storm of November 1915, 273–80
Strasenburgh, John, 204
submarines: Allied, 155, 170–74, 184, 306n13; German, 160–60, 164–69, 173, 174, 175–76, 180, 183
Suffren, 23, 25
sun helmets, 113, 212, 263
Suvla Bay: Battle of Krithia Vineyard at, 234–44, 247, 248, 259; evacuation of, 282, 284–90, 293, 299, 310n9; landings at, 224, 226, 261; November 1915 weather at, 274–75
SWB. *See* South Wales Borderers (SWB)
Swiftsure, 89, 94, 161, 191

Talbot, Ainslie, 91
Talbot, Fred, 133
Taylor, David, 256
Territorial Forces, 135, 141, 259–61, 309n10
Third Battle of Krithia, 210, 212; armored cars at, 204–6; first wave of, 192–96; losses at, 203–4, 206; overview and planning of, 188–92; second wave of, 196–203
Thompson, Astley Onslow, 120–21
Thompson, F. J., 33–34
Thompson, G. L., 149–50
Thompson, James, 16
Thursby, Cecil, 51
tin discs, 192, 196, 197, 212–13, 251, 256
Tisdall, Arthur, 84
Tizard, Henry, 81

Tommy's Trench, 146
transports, 155, 174–83; *Nagara*, 184; *Royal Edward*, 175–80; *Southland* and *Ramazon*, 180–83
trawlers, 17–20, 62, 70–71, 155
Triple Entente, 1–2
Trotman, Charles, 258
tunneling, 228–30, 270
Turk Army: Allied securing of Anzac Beach and, 117–18; Anzac offensive and, 148–54; evacuation and, 289–90, 295–96, 299; in First Battle of Krithia, 113–14; German control of, 3; Helles counterattacks and, 135–36; Kemal's counterattack at Anzac Beach and, 121–23, 125–26, 131–32, 135; knowledge of Narrows land attack, 35, 37–38; at Kum Kale, 104–5; in Second Battle of Krithia, 136–37, 138; Second Division of, 149; September armaments increase of, 270; at Suvla, 236–37; W Beach defense by, 87–88
Turkey, 1–2
Turkey Trench, 210, 213–15
Turnbull, Ernest, 14–15
Turquoise, 174
Twenty-Ninth Division of Royal Army: in August battles, 240, 243, 244; in Battle of Gully Ravine, 209; in Battle of Krithia Vineyard, 224–25, 227; Dardanelles Campaign planning and, 9, 10, 11, 26, 28, 30; evacuation of, 291; in First Battle of Krithia, 115; landings of, 72, 85, 88, 94, 98, 101, 106; in Third Battle of Krithia, 188, 207
Twenty-Ninth Indian Brigade, 136, 196, 211

U-21 submarine, 160–62, 164, 165–66, 167–68
U-35 submarine, 183
UB-14 submarine, 173, 174, 175–76, 179, 180
uniforms, 45, 192, 197, 212, 250, 271–72

Unwin, Edward, 74, 76, 79, 81
Uther, Gordon, 285–86

Van Der Byl, Charles, 159
Varley, Tom, 246
Vassal, Joseph, 73, 102–3, 148, 253
Vaughan, Charles, 100–101
Vaughan, Horace, 198–200
Vaughan, Justin, 199–200
V Beach, 73–87; first wave landing at, 63–64, 75–82; landing rescue operations and losses at, 84–87; overview and planning of landings at, 73–75; second wave landing at, 72–84; securing, 107–11
Velasquez, A., 179
Vernhol, Louis, 253
Victoria Crosses: ANZACs and, 152; Hamilton and, 29; Helles landings and, 81, 84, 96–97, 106; securing V Beach and, 111; war at sea and, 170, 171, 184
Victorian Decoration, 121–22
Ville de Bordeaux, 298
Vinh Long, 102, 103
von Heimburg, Heino, 173, 174, 176, 179
von Sanders, Otto Liman, 2–3; Anzac offensive and, 148, 149, 154; August battles and, 226, 236–37, 240

Walford, Garth, 108, 109–10, 111
Walker, Harold, 124, 127, 129
Walker's Ridge, 118, 121–30, 286
Wall, Frederick, 159–60
Wallack, Gordon, 153
Walsh, William, 47
war at sea: Allied submarines in, 170–74, 306n13; *Carthage* in, 167–68; German submarines in, 173, 174, 175–76, 180, 183; *Goliath* in, 156–60; *Majestic* in, 165–67; overview of, 155–56; retreat of warships in, 168–69; *Triumph* in, 160–65; Turk losses in, 183–85
Ward, Arthur, 261
Warren, Clyfford, 174

Waterlow, John, 302n3
water shortages, 29, 34, 112, 169
W Beach, 87–97; assault at, 89–95; losses at, 95–97; overview, plan, and Turk defenses of, 80–81, 87–89
Wear, 24, 32
weather: changes in, 269–73; of November 1915, 273–80
web gear, 213, 307n25
Wedderburn, Ernest, 270
Weir, Peter, 226
Welbon, Frederick, 227
Wellington Battalion of New Zealand Expeditionary Force, 124–29, 142–44, 153
Wellington Mounted Rifles, 152
Welsh, A. J., 113
Weston, Fred, 240
W Hills, 235, 240
Williams, Ivor, 181
Williams, Weir, 109
Williams, William, 79, 81
Willis, Richard, 90

Willmer, Wilhelm, 237
Wilson, Edmund, 128
Wolley-Dod, Owen, 94, 95
Wolverine, 191
Worcestershire Regiment, 82–84, 94
World War I, overview of, 1–2
Worrall, Edgar, 298
Worthington, Bertie, 12
Wotton, Peter, 179
Wren, Eric, 230
Wright, Alfred, 18
Wright, William, 199

X Beach, 59, 67, 97–101

Yarhisar, 185
Y Beach, 59, 60–69, 101, 107
yeomanry regiments, 240–44, 308n12
Young, A. W., 12–13, 14–15
Y Ravine, 62

Z Beach. *See* Anzac Beach
Zeki Bey, 290

Index